The Evolution of the Ethiopian Jews

University of Pennsylvania Press
THE ETHNOHISTORY SERIES

Lee V. Cassanelli, Juan A. Villamarin, and Judith E. Villamarin, Editors

A complete listing of the books in this series appears at the back of this volume

The Evolution of the Ethiopian Jews

A History of the Beta Israel (Falasha) to 1920

James Quirin

upp

University of Pennsylvania Press

Philadelphia

Copyright © 1992 by James Quirin
All rights reserved
Printed in the United States of America

Library of Congress Cataloging-in-Publication Data
Quirin, James Arthur, 1943–
The evolution of the Ethiopian Jews: a history of the Beta Israel (Falasha) to 1920 / James Quirin.
p. cm. — (The Ethnohistory series)
Includes bibliographical references and index.
ISBN 0-8122-3116-3
1. Falashas—History. 2. Ethiopia—Ethnic relations. I. Title. II. Series: Ethnohistory series (Philadelphia, Pa.)
DS135.E75Q57 1991
963'.004924—dc20 91-47665
CIP

In Memoriam:

Arthur and Margaret Quirin
Thomas Stephen Quirin

Dedicated to:

Ansha, Elsabet, Dennis, and
all the peoples of Ethiopia

Contents

Illustrations

FIGURES

MAPS

Preface

The "Black Jews," or Beta Israel–Falasha, of Ethiopia have fascinated the world for centuries.[1] Unfortunately, until recently this interest has generated more heat than light on the enigma of their origins and cultural identity, and their historical interaction with the people around them.

Two main external perspectives on the Beta Israel emerged over the years: a "persecuted Jews" view, and an "assimilationist" interpretation. Both were fragmented distortions of a larger reality. And both these external perspectives essentially ignored, even while influencing, the people's own changing internal views of themselves.

The attempts by some to describe the Beta Israel as a persecuted *foreign* minority does violence to their history and to Ethiopian history, though it fits into an analogous outmoded view of Africa. It was not long ago when African historiography involved an inordinate emphasis on external influences, no doubt originally derived from the racist assumption that Africans were incapable of creating either great monuments or sophisticated societies by themselves. Such external historiographical assumptions were often reinforced or seemingly justified by internal traditions which associated a people's history with earlier prestigious and external sources.[2] Every civilization in the world has received external influences, but the key to understanding civilizational development is to see what the people did with these influences to make them their own.

A second misleading view applied to the Beta Israel reflected the dominant tradition in Ethiopian historiography until recently—an "assimilationist" perspective—which stated that "the central theme of Ethiopian history . . . has been the maintenance of a cultural core which has adapted itself to the exigencies of time and place, assimilating diverse peoples."[3] To an extent, this view provided an explanation of Ethiopian history from the commanding heights of the central Aksumite-Abyssinian-Ethiopian government and Ethiopian Orthodox Church as they evolved over the millennia. But I would argue that even the development of the central tradition and institutions cannot be understood without an internal analysis of the assimilated peoples and the outlying regions. Such an understanding can only be reached by traveling the often rocky and obscure path through a people's separate history and culture before, during, and after its incorporation into a larger unit.

Even though, for example, the Beta Israel were conquered and partially incorporated in the Ethiopian system after the 1620s, they still maintained their own identity for 350 years after that conquest. The same is true of other cases of conquest during the last century.[4] Better analytical tools are necessary to explain such phenomena.

Ethnohistory aims analytically to reveal the Ethiopian tapestry in its true patterns. The perspectives of such a history are necessary in order to begin to explain, and not merely assume the processes of, both national integration and the continuation of ethnic and cultural diversity during the past several centuries of Ethiopian history. Such perspectives focus on the history of those peoples and groups who have usually been excluded from historical analyses, or treated merely as passive ciphers in the great sweep of events because of their relative lack of power in the general society which resulted from factors of race, ethnicity, religion, gender, or social position. All peoples have histories no matter how remote they may be from the centers of power, wealth, or influence in particular societies. The task of historians is to reconstruct the ways in which people have been agents of their own history within various institutional, geographic, and chronological contexts.

It is misleading, arrogant, and sometimes dangerous for members of a dominant group in any multi-ethnic, multireligious, or multilingual nation such as Ethiopia to assume that everyone else is, or should be, the same as that group through assimilation. On the other hand, it can also be frustrating, misleading, and equally dangerous for the members of other traditions to ignore or disregard the commonalities of history and culture that have created a larger unit. My aim is not the intellectual balkanization of Ethiopia; rather, I hope to understand and explain its remarkable and fascinating history in a more complete light.[5]

This study employs a framework of caste formation as a technique to illuminate Ethiopian historical processes, while using oral traditions as a major source. Caste formation was a two-way process to which both the dominant society and the caste-in-formation contributed. This framework is ideally suited to analyze the internal dynamics and external forces that shaped the history of the Beta Israel in the pan-Ethiopian context.[6]

Oral and written sources that originate from the people being studied are necessary, but like all sources they cannot be used uncritically. In general, Ethiopian historiography has been characterized by a myopic view concerning oral traditions as historical sources. But in writing histories of the peoples of Ethiopia, a sensitivity to sources is essential. In the case of the Beta Israel, this book would not have been possible without my collection of oral traditions.

Along with other recent works on the Beta Israel,[7] this book seeks to explain their history within the broad context of Ethiopian cultural and historical patterns. As such, it contributes to a more complete understanding of the evolution of Ethiopia and the peoples of Ethiopia over an extended time period. It also provides a dramatic example of cultural persistence, adaptation, and evolution in the face of great hardship as the Ethiopian Jews have created their history over the centuries.

Acknowledgments

It would be impossible to thank adequately all the people and institutions who have assisted my research over the years. My primary thanks are due to the people of Ethiopia who welcomed me to their country many years ago as a teacher, but of whom I became and remain a student.

This study would have been impossible without the cooperation of the informants who are listed individually in the Bibliography. They shared their knowledge and opened their homes to me, for which I remain in their debt. I am especially grateful to Yona Bogale, for many years a leading figure within the Beta Israel community, who welcomed me to his home in Addis Ababa and to his family, and who later introduced me to people in Ambobar. He shared his vast knowledge and human concern unstintingly in many informal conversations and long walks through the countryside.

I would particularly like to thank my friend and colleague over many years, Asrat Seyoum, for his research assistance, as well as all the others who assisted my collection and edition of oral information: Fisseha Seyoum, Getahun Mamo, Asnaku Sendecke, Mengistu Abreha, Ghiorghis Mellessa, Ephraim Haile Giyorgis, Gedamu Dessie, Ferede Yazezew, Afework Gedday, Yusef Dawit, Sendecke Derebie, Aschilew Nega, Baede Maryam Welde Yesus, and more recently, Habte-Ab Zerit. Other people whose assistance at key points during my research and writing was much appreciated include Richard Smith, R. C. Bhatia, A. T. S. Rajan, Henry Rosenberg, Gershon Levy, Alebachew Truneh, Erika Linke, Sue Cave, Carley Albrecht, and Wilma Hall. For linguistic assistance and teaching at various times, I thank Getatchew Haile, Ghiorghis Mellessa, Alemayehu Moges, Bernadette Luciano, Cristina Chabert, Robert Johns, Abebe Zewge, Tamara Kaigalithe, Marlin Heise, and especially Wolf Leslau, who first introduced me to the seductive intricacies of the Amharic/Ge'ez alphabet.

Although I lived in the country for four years in the late 1960s, my fieldwork research between January 1975 and February 1976 was made possible through a generous dissertation fellowship and write-up extension from March to September 1976 by the Social Science Research Council. Other research fellowship assistance is gratefully acknowledged over the past fifteen years by grants from the American Council of Learned Societies, National Endowment for the Humanities, American Philosophical Society, United Negro College Fund, Mellon Foundation, and Bush Foundation funds awarded through Fisk University, and by a sabbatical leave from Fisk University.

The Institute of Ethiopian Studies in Addis Ababa under its then director, Richard Pankhurst, was very cooperative in my original research. Other libraries that have assisted my work include the University of Minnesota, the British Museum library, the School of Oriental and African Studies of the University of London, the Andover-Harvard Theological Library, the New York Public Library, the Library of Congress, the Hebrew Union College library, the Hill Monastic Microfilm Library of St. John's University in Collegeville (Minnesota), Yale University, the University of Wisconsin, the University of Illinois, Vanderbilt University, and Fisk University. I thank all these institutions and their library staffs for being so cooperative.

Many scholars have offered significant suggestions and specific assistance over the years for which I am profoundly grateful, including especially Getatchew Haile, Taddesse Tamrat, Donald Crummey, Richard Caulk, Harold Marcus, Robert Hess, Frederick Gamst, Donald Levine, Allan Hoben, Wolf Leslau, Sergew Hable Sellassie, Merid Wolde Aregay, Alemayehu Moges, Asmarom Legesse, Edward Ullendorff, Simon Messing, Frederick Simoons, Herbert Lewis, Kay Shelemay, Veronika Krempel, Walter Harrelson, Michelle Schoenberger, David Appleyard, M. L. Bender, LaVerle Berry, David Kessler, Steven Kaplan, James McCann, I. Leonard Markovitz, M. Crawford Young, William Foltz, Allen Isaacman, Lansine Kaba, August Nimtz, Lee Cassanelli, and William Piersen. I would also like to thank collectively my students and colleagues at Fisk University over the past ten years for their support and insights in many different contexts. All of this named and unnamed assistance has been invaluable in correcting my errors and misinterpretations; any which remain are my responsibility alone.

Note on Transcription

In the interests of readability, I have dispensed with all diacritical marks in transcribing Ge'ez or Amharic, except in the glossary and index. The following system is used for the seven vowel sounds where diacritical marks are employed:

ETHIOPIC SCRIPT	TRANSCRIPTION	PRONUNCIATION
First order	a	*a*bout
Second order	u	r*u*de
Third order	i	mach*i*ne
Fourth order	ā	f*a*ther
Fifth order	ē	g*a*te
Sixth order	e	s*i*t
Seventh order	o	l*o*rd

The pronunciations are approximate, and the sixth order vowel is often silent.

The three "h" sounds are distinguished as follows:

h
ḥ
h̬

The following are used for the glottalized consonants:

q
ṣ
ṭ
ṗ
c̣h

Plurals are anglicized (*rases* instead of *rasoch*). Double consonants indicate gemination. The palatalized *n* as in "onion" is written as *gn*

(Gra*gn*) or *ny* (Tigri*ny*a). I have not distinguished between a*z*ure and a*g*e, rendering both with *j*. Glottal stops in the middle of words are indicated by the apostrophe (Ge'ez), but are not shown at the beginning of words; nor have I distinguished between the two forms of this stop. Certain widely known words in English are retained (Haile Sellassie, Massawa).

Ethiopian names consist of the given (first) name and the father's first name as the offspring's last name. I have followed this convention both in referring to people (unless otherwise known in the sources), and in alphabetizing my bibliography.

The Evolution of the Ethiopian Jews

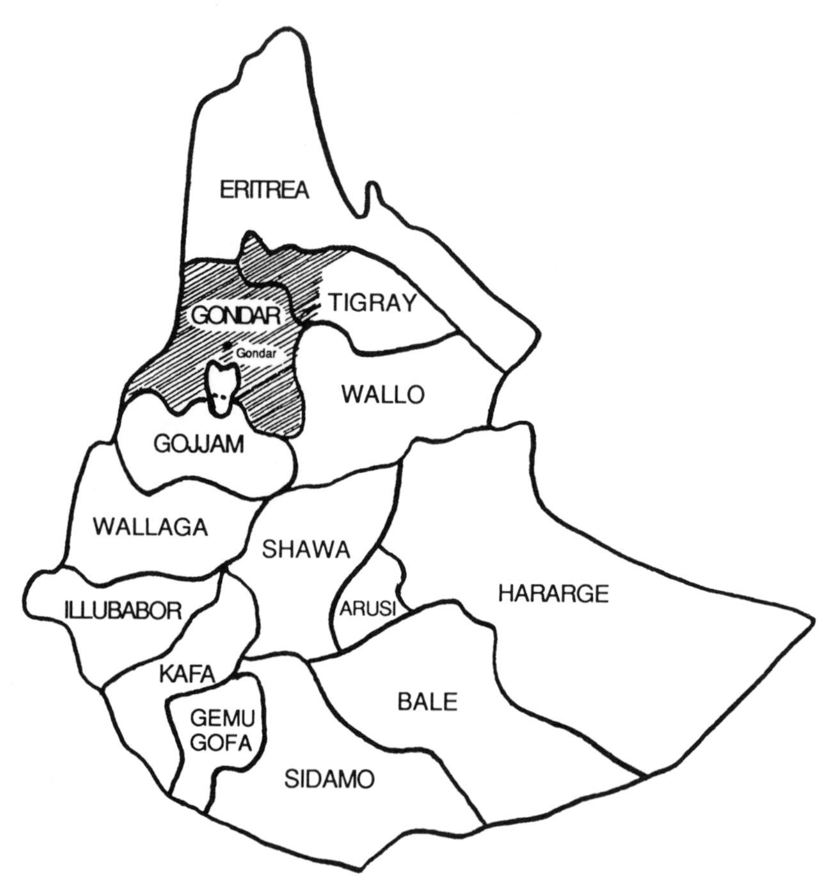

Map 1. Ethiopian administrative regions. The shaded area indicates northwestern Ethiopia. (As this book goes to press, the status of Eritrea is in transition.)

Introduction. The Baseline: Beta Israel Society, 1770–1840

The Beta Israel of Ethiopia captured the imagination of the Western world in the late eighteenth and early nineteenth centuries. European travelers, Christian missionaries, and later, European Jews visited Ethiopia and eventually had direct contact with Beta Israel individuals and communities, leaving extensive information and giving rise to much wild speculation on their identity and history. This interest also led to efforts to change their culture and religion as Europeans attempted either to convert them to Christianity or to save them from conversion.

Before this watershed in Beta Israel history, this group's history and culture had evolved almost entirely within the Ethiopian context, but since then foreign involvement has radically affected their history, culture, and traditions. A snapshot of the people in the early nineteenth century will provide a useful basis from which to discover how they reached this turning point, and what has happened since.[1]

Geography and Demography

This study focuses on northwestern Ethiopia, comprised of the present-day administrative regions of Gondar and southern Tigray (see Map 1). The area is divided geographically, in the Ethiopian terminology common to the rest of the northern highlands, into three main zones: *daga, wayna daga,* and *qolla*. These zones may be correlated approximately with differences in altitude, and therefore climate and vegetation, but they also demarcate somewhat distinct economic and cultural life-styles.[2]

The *daga* is land above about 2,500 meters (8,200 feet) where the climate is cool to freezing. Such areas can grow cereals such as barley and support limited animal husbandry. In northwestern Ethiopia, the primary *daga* lands are in the Samen highlands and Mount Guna near Dabra Tabor.

The *wayna daga* ranges from 1,500 to 2,500 meters (5,000 to 8,200 feet) and is temperate (averaging 60 to 68 degrees Fahrenheit). It is the most densely populated zone, supported by a mixed farming system of animal husbandry and grain cultivation, especially of *tef,* wheat, and barley at higher elevations and maize, sorghum, and millet at lower levels.[3] The soil is of volcanic origin and is relatively fertile and well-watered. In the northwest, the main *wayna daga* districts include the relatively flat and high Wagara plateau; the somewhat more hilly Begamder, Balasa, Saqqalt, and Chelga; and the somewhat lower Dambeya and in Tigray, Shire. The city of Gondar, at the center of this region, is at an altitude of 2,120 meters (6,955 feet), with an average annual rainfall of 1,288 millimeters (51 inches).[4]

The *qolla* lowlands are below 1,500 meters (5,000 feet), and are characterized by average temperatures in the 70 to 90 degree Fahrenheit range, less rainfall, a lower population density, and an economy based on pastoralism or some cultivation of maize, sorghum, and millet. In the northwest, the primary *qolla* areas include Qwara, Qolla Wagara, and parts of Walqayt, Armacheho, Sagade, and Sallamt.

During the baseline period, the Beta Israel were living in separate villages or in enclaves within larger villages dominated by the Christian highland population, particularly in the *wayna daga* zone. But they also lived in either the *qolla* or the *daga,* such as Qwara or Samen, where historically they had important religious centers. In Tigray, they lived mainly in the southwestern region called Shire, but also in other areas such as near Adwa and Antalo.[5]

Although hardly mentioned by travelers and less studied than those in the Gondar area, the Beta Israel in the early nineteenth century also lived in Gojjam province, in several small villages near Agawmeder. They were observed there by the traveler Charles Beke and were also the object of missionary activity in the late nineteenth century.[6] Based on what little is known, these Beta Israel communities were probably comparable to those in the northwest.

Travelers and other visitors have also mentioned communities or enclaves of endogamous artisans in other parts of the country that have sometimes been called “Buda,” “Tabiban,” “Kayla,” or “Falasha” (see Chapter 1 on terminology). In most cases, their identification with the Beta Israel of northwestern Ethiopia that is the focus of this book is dubious, though none of these communities has been systematically studied and their historic origins remain unclear.[7]

Since it is well-known that most of the peoples of Ethiopia and even extending into Somalia have endogamous artisan and/or hunting groups within their societies, the existence of such groups elsewhere in the north, such as in Shawa and Lasta should not be surprising.[8] Any reference to such groups in this book is merely suggestive of the need for further study, and should not be considered an endorsement that they were the same as the Beta Israel of the Gondar-Tigray regions.[9]

Most population estimates are mere guesses, but in the mid-nineteenth century there may have been 80,000 to 250,000 Beta Israel.[10] In the early twentieth century, there were said to be about 50,000.[11] By the 1970s, the estimates made by some actual counting were in the range of 28,000.[12]

Economy and Society

The highland Amhara-Tigrayan ("Abyssinian")[13] economy was based on the mixed farming system of grain cultivation and animal husbandry. Over the millennia, the highland peasants were highly productive, supporting a complex political-religious hierarchy.[14]

Unlike the medieval European peasant under feudalism, the Abyssinian peasantry had direct access to land through their "inherited land-use rights" called *rest*.[15] The *rest* system meant peasant households could make claims to the land-use rights over specific plots and strips of land by virtue of their ambilineal descent ties to an ancestral "first father" of the land.[16]

Since, however, "there are always more legitimate descendants of an ancestral first holder than there are men who hold fields in his land tract," a person's claimed "*rest* rights" were always more extensive than his actual possession of pieces of *rest* land.[17] Therefore, the particular pieces of land a person held depended on his skill in competing for the land with the fellow members of his ambilineal descent group through litigation and political power or influence.

Superimposed on the *rest* system were the *gult* or tribute-collecting rights granted to a political-administrative-religious elite by the king. *Gult*, in other words, was not another piece or kind of land but rather involved the right to collect tribute from the *rest*-holders actually cultivating the land. One individual might hold the *gult* rights over the pieces of land cultivated by scores or hundreds of individual *rest*-holders.[18] Hence, the *gult*-system was the means by which the Abyssinian political economy actualized itself on the local level.

Even in north-central Ethiopia, there were tenant farmers who rented their lands from the owner. In general, tenants in Amhara areas were of two types: those who held some land through *rest* rights but cultivated other pieces as tenants; artisans who were not allowed *rest* rights and, hence, had to cultivate all the land they were allowed to work as tenants. The first type were often ambitious young men trying to advance their social and economic position but who did not yet have much control of land. These young men often worked as tenants temporarily, until they could acquire their own *rest*.[19]

Mixed with these two basic types of land rights in northern Ethiopia called *rest* and *gult* were several variations and combinations which made the overall system highly complex. Churches, for example, were endowed with extensive lands, often held as *rim* land. The term *rim* has been used in various ways, but in the Gondar area it was land held by a church and worked by tenants who paid rent or tribute to the church.[20]

A mixed form of land tenure was called *rest-gult*. In this case, the *gult* rights to tribute collection on certain pieces of land were granted by the king for services rendered, but unlike *gult* in general, in this case the tribute rights could be passed down to one's heirs. In other words, this type of tenure included the best aspects of both *rest* and *gult* forms, and was hence a very prestigious grant to receive.[21]

In the context of this land system in northwestern Ethiopia the Beta Israel worked as tenant farmers and artisans, particularly as blacksmiths, potters, and weavers. In areas near larger towns and cities, they were also carpenters and masons. Though kept in a distinctive and subordinate social position, their economic function as artisans—making plows, pots, and other tools and weapons essential for an agricultural society—made them indispensable.

In most places, they did not control *rest* land-use rights, and hence where they cultivated, they held the land as tenants. In a few enclaves, however, they stated during my research in 1975 that they did hold the land they worked as *rest*. My interpretation of Beta Israel land tenure emphasizes they lost their *rest* land rights as a result of conquest that was finalized in the 1620s (see Chapter 2). But an elite began to acquire land rights during the Gondar era (1632–1755) that were possibly in the form of *rest-gult*.[22]

Culturally, the Beta Israel had many similarities with the local Christian population among whom they lived.[23] Though some still knew an ancient Agaw language, most spoke the language of the dominant society in their region, either Amharic or Tigrinya. They wore the same clothes and ate the same foods as the Christians except the Beta Israel refused raw meat.

Despite their cultural similarities, the two groups held themselves apart socially (see Chapter 4). The Beta Israel kept to themselves or interacted with the dominant Christian society only in a restricted manner. They could not intermarry or even visit one another in their houses. Money the Beta Israel received for their craft goods was paid into a dish of water so no physical contact would take place. The Beta Israel had to purify themselves by washing their bodies and clothes after contact or even conversations with non–Beta Israel.

This social separation was reinforced by the dominant ideologies of each side. Christians considered the Falasha to be evil and dangerous, accusing them of being *buda,* or having the evil eye. This accusation included allegations that the Falasha turned into hyenas at night, devoured cadavers, and caused sickness or even death just by looking at someone. Of course, in highland Ethiopia, not all *buda* accusations were against Beta Israel. Other ethnic minorities and even Christians might be called *buda.* But I argue (in Chapter 4) that in the northwestern region in the early nineteenth century, this term became fixed on the Beta Israel, whatever it may have meant in other regions.

The ideology of separation was also supported by the Beta Israel themselves. They considered the Christians to be impure because of their less rigid eating, religious, marriage, childbirth, and funeral customs. My analysis suggests (in Chapter 2) that, since the fifteenth century, the Beta Israel religious elite began to elaborate an ideology and social practices that aimed to keep them separate from Christian society. This degree of separation continued during the Gondar era (see Chapter 3) and was increased and intensified by the Beta Israel during the mid-nineteenth century (see Chapter 4).

Religious Practices

The Beta Israel were almost always considered by foreign observers to be the Jews of Ethiopia. They followed an exacting schedule of fasts and holy days, including a special veneration of the Sabbath, which began with a ritual washing and the extinguishing of all fires on Friday afternoon, and continued with a prayer-house ceremony on Saturday morning. Their religion seemed to have broad equivalences with practices of the wider Jewish world, except they did not know Hebrew or the Talmud or follow postbiblical practices such as Chanukah.[24]

On the other hand, much of their religion was quite similar to that of

Ethiopian Orthodoxy. Their liturgy and religious books were all in Ge'ez, the ancient religious language of their Christian neighbors. They both had the same religious practitioners and called them by the same terms: monks, priests, and *dabtaras* (unordained but well-educated clergy). Monasticism was a significant institution in each case. They both followed similar religiously sanctioned life-cycle ceremonies involving birth, circumcision, marriage, and death. They had similar Old Testament–sanctioned food restrictions and both practiced offerings and sacrifices. Their religious texts were not only both written in Ge'ez, but in virtually every case, the Beta Israel version of religious books was derived from the Christian version.

These observed similarities, at the same time that each group held itself socially separate from the other and often displayed such negative attitudes toward the other, gave rise to numerous speculations about their origins and historical interactions. This situation also stimulated diverse opinions on Beta Israel identity. Although usually considered to be Jews, controversy flourished as to whether they were normative Jews, lapsed Christians, or some hybrid, and many opinions were expressed on the alleged origins of the group (see Chapter 1). This book seeks to elucidate the fascinating story of Beta Israel identity and historical development in the Ethiopian context, from their earliest but still obscure origins up to the early twentieth century.

1. Ethiopia and the Beta Israel in Historical Perspective

Who Are the Falasha?

Neither Beta Israel origins nor their historical development can be understood outside the context of broader Abyssinian-Ethiopian historical patterns. Neither the "persecuted Jews" perspective, which emphasizes an external Jewish connection, nor the "assimilationist" perspective which sees them as just another of Ethiopia's "museum of peoples" is an adequate framework.[1] Because the topic of Falasha origins has been so controversial, I will summarize previous views before laying out my own perspectives.

Previous Theories on Origins

The question of Falasha origins has long vexed interpreters of Ethiopia. In three broad perspectives, they have been viewed as (1) ethnic Jews descended directly from the ancient Israelites, (2) Agaw converts to Judaism who refused to convert to Christianity when it became Aksum's official religion in the fourth century, or (3) rebels or dissidents against Orthodoxy and the state at various times after the fourth century. I call these the "Lost Tribe," "Convert," and "Rebel" views, respectively. Both the Lost Tribe and Convert views assume there was a separate introduction of Judaism to Ethiopia, independent and prior to the introduction of Christianity. The Rebel view, however, argues against any separate or independent introduction of Judaism and concludes that the "Judaic" or "Hebraic" elements so obvious in Ethiopian society can be explained entirely by the Old Testament ambiance of Ethiopian Orthodox Christianity.[2]

For years, the scholarly consensus was that the Falasha were the descendants of Agaw converts to Judaism. The main debate centered on whether the Jews who converted the Agaw came in through Egypt or through South Arabia. During the last fifteen years, however, pioneering research has raised fundamental questions about that consensus and has moved the debate toward the Rebel view, while, ironically, politics and polemics have been influential in attracting support, including the official view of the Israeli government, for the Lost Tribe hypothesis. While research currently underway in Ethiopia and elsewhere will doubtless push the consensus more toward that of the Rebel perspective, I do not believe the evidence on origins is yet incontrovertible.

The Lost Tribe Perspective

In the most extreme statement of this perspective, the Beta Israel are seen as the direct ethnic and religious descendants of original Jewish immigrants to Ethiopia. Such a view assumes, but does not usually explicitly state, that Judaism was brought by a fairly substantial number of immigrants rather than simply by a handful of "missionaries."[3]

Despite the best efforts of the proponents of this view, there remains no direct evidence of such a large body of immigrants having come into Ethiopia either then or later. It has sometimes even been asserted that such direct ethnic descent is shown by the "light black" skin color and "finely cut features" of the Beta Israel which show them to be a "non-African race."[4] In general, however, it is more accurate to state that their physical features fall within the same range or have similar variations as those of other highland populations of Ethiopia, such as the Amhara, Tigrayan, and Agaw.[5] The only physical anthropological study of the Beta Israel, based on blood type, was inconclusive. All Ethiopian samples studied (Tigrayan, Bilen, Falasha, Amhara, Oromo, and Gurage) showed some congruency with the Arabian population and differences with other East African peoples. But the Falasha blood group patterns were "very different" from those of Persian and other oriental Jewish communities.[6] Although the Lost Tribe perspective emphasizes a direct descent from ancient Israelites, it admits that there was some mixture with the local Agaw population, so it really differs only in degree from the Convert view.[7]

Since 1975, the view that the Beta Israel are ethnic descendants of original Jewish immigrants to Ethiopia—even admitting that some local mixture and conversion also took place—has become the official Israeli position, thereby permitting Beta Israel immigration to Israel under the "law of return." In this view, they have usually been said to be one of the Ten Lost Tribes, especially the Danites, who came to Ethiopia during the original Diaspora, although the specific times and places of provenance have been debated.

In 1973, the chief Sephardic rabbi in Israel recognized the Beta Israel as real Jews, and in 1975 the Ashkenazi agreed. Since that time, and under the disturbances of the Ethiopian revolution since 1974, immigration to Israel steadily increased, climaxing with Operation Moses in 1984, and Operation Solomon as the Ethiopian government was collapsing in 1991. More than 25,000 Ethiopian Jews now live in Israel.[8]

The Convert Perspective

The Convert view of Beta Israel origins assumes that Judaism was brought in prior to, and separately from, Christianity. But there was no large-scale migration, and if a few Jews settled in Ethiopia they quickly lost any separate ethnic identity during the process of intermarriage with the local (Agaw) population. The Falasha are seen as the direct descendants of these early converts. This view thus differs from the Lost Tribe perspective mainly in degree rather than kind. Most of the debate within this perspective has concerned the time and path of diffusion of Jewish influences into Ethiopia and hence has tended to equate all references to Jews as references to Falasha, thereby confusing the two issues. Since no direct evidence exists to support either an early diffusion through South Arabia, or through Egypt and Sudan, both arguments have proceeded by inference.

The case for diffusion through Egypt rests upon the known presence of Jews in Egypt prior to the Exodus, and the existence of a Jewish contingent in the military colony at Elephantine near present-day Aswan in southern Egypt. This Jewish contingent dates to the eighth to sixth centuries B.C.E.[9] The Lost Tribe view—that Jews migrated directly from Israel—also usually assumes that the path of migration was through Egypt. The diffusion from Egypt was variously said to have been at the time of Exodus, when some Jews went south along the Nile instead of toward Israel with Moses, or at the time of the destruction of the First Temple in 586 B.C.E., when some Jews came with Jeremiah into Egypt and then went south, eventually reaching Ethiopia, after the destruction of Elephantine, or after the destruction of the Second Temple in 70 C.E.[10]

The attractiveness of a theory of diffusion of Jews from Egypt is enhanced by the clear early documentation of the existence of a Jewish community at Elephantine. The type of syncretic Judaism practiced by the Aramaic-speaking community at Elephantine may have been comparable to aspects of Beta Israel practices.[11]

Joseph Halévy, the Jewish Semiticist who was the first Jew to visit the Beta Israel villages in Ethiopia in 1867–68, argued for a South Arabian path of Jewish migration to Ethiopia. He noted that there was no reliable evidence of the widespread existence of Jews in Ethiopia before the fourth-century conversion to Christianity, and that the most likely diffusion of Judaism into Ethiopia occurred early in the sixth century C.E., when an Aksumite invasion defeated the Himaryite King, Du Nuwas, and brought back "thousands" of Jewish captives.[12]

Most modern scholars have tended to agree with Halévy's assessment of the significance of the documented historic South Arabian–Aksumite connection.[13] They have argued that since the weight of the evidence clearly documents South Arabian–Ethiopian contacts while the Egypt-Sudan-Ethiopia path is more nebulous, a South Arabian provenance for Jewish influences in Ethiopia is most likely.[14]

But there are problems with this view as well. Despite these well-documented connections between South Arabia and the Ethiopian highlands, there are no specifically documented *Jewish* contacts between the two areas until the Zagwe period (ca. 1137–1270), when a Jewish family migrated to Ethiopia but then converted to Christianity. That was certainly too late to account for a Jewish presence in early Ethiopia.[15]

Even the fourth or the sixth century C.E. is too late to account for Jews in Ethiopia if it is assumed the Jewish introduction was pre-Christian. There has also been a debate on the date of Jewish establishment in South Arabia.[16] Moreover, the Jews of South Arabia knew Hebrew and practiced rabbinical Judaism, including the use of the Talmud, neither of which characterized the Beta Israel–Falasha in Ethiopia.

Of course, these statements illustrate the confusion between the question of Judaic influences on Ethiopian Christian society and the origins of a specific group of people called the Falasha. These are not necessarily the same question.[17]

The Rebel Perspective

The Rebel view emphasizes in different ways the significance of the Christian influences on the development and even postulates a Christian origin of the Beta Israel. The most thorough anthropological study of the Beta Israel, based on fieldwork carried out in the late 1960s, argued that the similarities and parallelisms in Beta Israel and Christian beliefs and customs could most logically be explained as the result of common origins, not acculturation. Veronika Krempel denied there was any historical, religious, or anthropological evidence to justify the conclusions that the Beta Israel were direct ethnic descendants of either Jewish immigrants to Ethiopia or Agaw converts to Judaism. Rather, she concluded that the Beta Israel were

(1) the indirect descendants of those who had not submitted to the political, social, and economic system of Abyssinian feudalism; and (2) those who were expelled or driven off during the process of the establishment of the Ethiopian feudal Christian order.[18] She emphasized that the group had become an occupational caste within the general Christian Amhara society and were without a distinctive religious or ethnographic identity from the dominant Christian society.[19] Though no doubt overstated with regard to a lack of distinctive religious or ethnographic identity, this interpretation puts the analysis firmly within the context of Ethiopian history and society, the only framework within which progress can be made on the overall task of understanding the Beta Israel.

This approach, of course, emphasizes the close connections between the Beta Israel and Christian communities. These connections have already been documented with regard to Beta Israel religious literature which increasingly is seen as deriving directly from Christian sources. Even a book such as the *Te'ezaza Sanbat* ("Commandments of the Sabbath") previously thought to have been independently composed, now seems to have been based directly on Christian models.[20]

Innovative research on the Falasha liturgy, as well as other aspects of the religion, has documented beyond a doubt the Ethiopian Christian origins of the Falasha religious service. The apparent Jewish elements in the Falasha liturgy are not derived from a separate pre-Christian normative Jewish source.[21]

Therefore, ironically, as the Jewish world has been moving closer to an official position on Beta Israel origins congruent with the Lost Tribe or the Convert perspectives, scholarly analysis has created a serious doubt about both these perspectives, at least in an unmodified form.

A Changing Terminology

The historical record indicates their name changed at different times, while different names were used interchangeably at a particular time. The changing terminology reflects an evolving view of who this group was in the context of broader Ethiopian society. I have chosen mainly to employ the term "Beta Israel" [*beta esra'el*] (House of Israel) because it has become the term preferred by the people themselves. The main alternatives, "Falasha" and "Kayla," have both acquired somewhat derogatory connotations in the last 150 years, though "Falasha" is still being used. "Beta Israel" was also a term (along with the simpler "Israel") by which the people called themselves even before the main Western Jewish and missionary impact on them.[22] It seems to me that the use of "Beta Israel" instead of the better-known "Falasha" is analogous to the generally accepted change from "Galla" to "Oromo" for another people, since the word "Galla" similarly originated as an external label and had pejorative connotations.[23]

The origins of the term "Beta Israel" are unclear, though the eighteenth-century Scottish traveler James Bruce explained the term was used by Christians to refer to those who refused to convert to Christianity in the fourth century C.E.[24] A problem in the use of the term "Beta Israel" or "Israel" to refer to the Falasha is, of course, that the dominant Christian ruling dynasty also referred to themselves as the "Israelites" (*esra'elawi*) because of their reputed origin from Solomon and Sheba.[25] Christian society made a clear distinction between "Israelite" and "Jew" (*ayhud*), using the latter term to refer to those who had specifically rejected Christ.[26] By the early nineteenth century, several terms were used to refer to the people, including primarily, "Beta Israel" or "Israel," "Falasha," "Kayla," and some lesser-used terms limited to particular regions.

"Falasha" had become the most common term used by Ethiopian Christians and by foreign observers, and until recently was the primary name by which the group was known to the outside world. The traditional etymology of the word is said to be from the Ge'ez *falasa*, meaning "to separate," "emigrate," or "exile," or from *falasyan* ("foreigner"). Both terms, hence, were taken to imply separation from ancient Israel and migration to Ethiopia.[27]

Some scholars have seen the Ge'ez etymology as just another example of popular etymology with no linguistic basis. They argue the name "Falasha" may simply derive from the province of Qwara, one of the traditional locations of the people. "Qwara" in Agaw is "hwara," and the language of the Agaw people there is called "hwarasa."[28] Robert Hetzron suggested the transference of *hwar* to *fal* is common in other Agaw languages and, therefore, *falasha* may simply be derived from *hwarasa*, the Agaw language of the people of the Qwara region.[29]

The first historical use of the term "Falasha" is still obscure, though recent research has clarified the question somewhat. The term is not known certainly in written sources until the sixteenth century, when it was equated with "Jews" in Ethiopia.[30] Although *falasa* is used in a historical chronicle referring to events in the early fifteenth century,[31] the date the chronicle was composed is unclear, but it was certainly some time after the events described. Oral traditions do not help much. Though some Beta Israel traditions refer in passing to the name "Falasha" as dating to the times of their alleged coming to Ethiopia, this is not the dominant tradition and is probably a later accretion.[32]

In the early nineteenth century, some travelers were told that the term "Kayla" was preferred to "Falasha." The latter was considered an insult because Kayla meant those "who did not cross the sea," referring to the alleged coming to Ethiopia with Menilek I. "Kayla," according to this tradition, meant those who did not cross water and therefore did not travel on Saturday, which was forbidden according to their religion in the early nineteenth century. The implication was that "Kayla" was felt to be the more orthodox term, at least in the Gondar region. But in Qwara the people accepted the term "Falasha" as the correct one.[33] In any case, "Kayla" is clearly of Agaw origin, and since the de-emphasis on any Agaw connection in the people's self-identity following the nineteenth century, the term has fallen into disrepute.

"Kayla" was first used in written records in the seventeenth-century chronicle of Suseneyos (1607–32), which mainly used the term "Falasha" but also referred to the "Falasha who are called Kayla," thus equating the two names.[34] The chronicle of Yohannes I (1667–82) also referred to Kayla and Falasha in the same paragraph, making it clear that the terms referred to the same group of people. Of course, "Kayla Meda" ("field or land of the Kayla") was one of the districts of Greater Gondar inhabited by the Beta Israel.[35]

A variation on these terms was known in the Armacheho region, where the group was called "Kaylasha," combining the two. Further regional variations were reported from the Walqayt and Sagade regions where the people were called *foggara*,[36] apparently suggesting a connection with the area of Fogara just to the east of Lake Tana. Perhaps some of the Beta Israel from that area had migrated north to Walqayt and Sagade.

Other terms have also been applied to the group, such as *tayb* or *tabib*, or *buda* ("evil eye"), as an epithet particularly applied to blacksmiths and potters. The terms *tabib* or *tayb* derive from the Ge'ez *tabba* ("to be wise"—or the noun, *tabib*), which suggests the somewhat ambivalent position of the Beta Israel by the nineteenth century. Though the Beta Israel evidently saw the term in its positive meaning as one with the skill and expertise enough to forge iron and make pots, to the dominant society it was a term of scorn, and also had the connotation of fearing someone with special powers. The term *buda* was more uniformly negative and is analyzed in greater detail below.[37] Of course, both *buda* and *tayb* have been applied as epithets to other endogamous craft groups in the highlands of Ethiopia, without referring necessarily to the Beta Israel–Falasha, thereby complicating the analysis of Beta Israel identity.

A further discussion of terminology must finally consider the connection of the Ge'ez term *ayhud* ("Jews" or "Jewish group") to the Beta Israel–Falasha. In the nineteenth century, this term was "nearly unknown" in referring to this people,[38] but even then it was one term—although not much used—to refer to the people. Of course, the term *ayhud* was also used in different ways historically, sometimes as an epithet to refer to Christian "heretics," or to refer to "pagans" who were clearly neither Jewish nor Christian.[39]

My use of various terms in the course of this book may vary depending on the historical period under consideration, but I employ primarily the term "Beta Israel" (in the interests of readability, I use this spelling instead of the more accurate transcription, *beta esra'el*). The consistency, richness, and continuity of the historical traditions—in both written and oral sources—in most cases constitutes sufficient evidence to justify the association of all these different terms (Ayhud, Falasha, Kayla, Beta Israel, and Israel) with the same group of people, at least since the fourteenth century. Of course, *ayhud* did not always refer to Jews in the chronicle and polemical literature, particularly in the fourteenth and fifteenth centuries, and the term "Israelites," as applied to Christians, referred to the royal dynasty. Even when *ayhud* did refer to those designated as "Jews" by Christian society, we do not know much about the doctrinal content of that name. The analysis below speculates on the pre–fourteenth-century "Judaic" content of Ethiopian society and its possible connections with the Beta Israel–Falasha group later.

Certainly by the sixteenth or seventeenth century, the terms "Falasha," "Kayla," and "Ayhud" were used interchangeably in (Christian) written sources, with the preference eventually becoming "Falasha." A key period was the early seventeenth century, when the last leader of the Beta Israel to be killed was usually called "Gedewon the Falasha," but was sometimes referred to as "Gedewon the Jew (*ayhudawi*)." In addition, "Kayla" was also used to refer to the Falasha at that time.[40]

Hence, the changing terminology reflected the historical context of this group in Ethiopian society. Between the fourteenth and nineteenth centuries, there was a clear evolution from *ayhud* to *falasha,* with the term *kayla* added during the seventeenth century for the Gondar region in particular. By the late eighteenth century, the term *beta esra'el* had emerged in external sources, though we do not know when that term began to be used by the people themselves. Beta Israel has become the dominant internally accepted term in the twentieth century, along with "Ethiopian Jew," now being applied particularly to those who have immigrated to Israel. What is still unclear, and owing to a lack of sources will remain cloudy, is the pre–fourteenth-century identity and terminology. That question can only be addressed from within the framework of the larger Ethiopian context.

Beta Israel–Falasha Origins and Identity

Beta Israel origins were certainly more complex than either the Lost Tribe, Convert, or Rebel perspectives would indicate. Explanations of Beta Israel origins and identity must be congruent with the data concerning their society, religion, and culture, but they must also be related to the development of ancient Ethiopian history from the Aksumite era (ca. 100 B.C.E.–900 C.E.), and continuing with the Zagwe period up to 1270.

The preceding terminological analysis suggests there was a connection between *ayhud* and *falasha* in the fourteenth to seventeenth centuries. Obviously, however, this connection does not mean that all *ayhud* became or were the same as *falasha*, a relationship analyzed further in Chapter 2. What is necessary at present is to investigate what *ayhud* meant in the Aksumite and Zagwe periods which preceded the institution of the new regime in 1270.

The simplistic assumption that the Beta Israel were directly responsible for the "Hebraic-Judaic" features of Ethiopian Orthodoxy is untenable. Any Beta Israel connection to these Judaic features was more complex and indirect.

But linguistic and religious literary analysis strongly suggests that in Aksum there was a pre-Christian "Jewish" element whose origins are obscure. An analysis of references to Jews by foreign travelers and internal traditions are inconclusive but include the possibility there was a separate group in Ethiopia known as Jews before the fourteenth century. But since these latter references do not pre-date the ninth century, they cannot by themselves demonstrate a separate Jewish presence prior to the introduction of Christianity.

The "Judaic" Presence

The "Hebraic-Judaic" features of Ethiopian society are well-documented. Not only the Beta Israel were called Jews. From the eleventh-century Egyptians to the seventeenth-century Jesuits and nineteenth-century Protestants, many foreign Christians have pointed out the "Judaic" aspects of Ethiopian Orthodoxy.

Some elements appear to be of mixed Cushitic-Semitic provenance, including some magical practices of pre-Christian religion, supposedly of "pagan" origin; other elements include magical derivations of apparent Hebraic-Judaic origin, such as magic squares, special designs and secret charms, and the use of magical names and amulets to ward off evil influences.[41]

Other elements are more directly Judaic and associated with the Church, such as the structure of the Church buildings in three concentric circles like the Hebrew temple, musical instruments and notation associated with the Church liturgy, the liturgy itself, the observance of the Sabbath and other feasts and fasts, the practice of circumcision on the eighth day after birth, and food prescriptions derived from Leviticus.[42]

These Jewish practices were first explicitly mentioned in the eleventh century when the Egyptian bishops criticized the Ethiopian Church for observing "customs of the Old Testament," apparently including circumcision, marriage practices, the Saturday Sabbath, and the use of sacrifices.[43]

Studies of the biblical literature translated into Ethiopic show the influence of Hebrew and Aramaic texts, even though the main *Vorlage* was in Greek.[44] A new edition of the Book of Enoch demonstrates both Aramaic and Greek texts were used to make the Ethiopic translation.[45] Analyses of Ge'ez (Ethiopic) vocabulary also suggest the importance of words of Aramaic and Hebrew origin.

There is little debate on the significance and nature of these influences, but there is less agreement on their time and place of origin and manner of influence in Ethiopia. There are two major approaches to explaining how and who introduced Jewish elements to Ethiopia: (1) that there were sufficient numbers of ethnic and religious Jews present in pre-Christian Aksum to account for these elements, or (2) that the "Jewish" elements were brought in by the same people who brought Christianity, a group known as "Jewish-Christians" in the ancient world.

The view that Jewish-Christians introduced Judaic elements along with Christianity was supported by Maxime Rodinson, who argued that the so-called Judaic elements in the Ethiopian Church were not only part of Judaism but also found in the early Coptic and Syrian Christian churches with which Ethiopia had extensive contacts. The Judaic influences in Ethiopia, he argued, were not necessarily from any direct contacts with Jews.[46]

A more recent analysis of Ethiopian Christianity by Ephraim Isaac has emphasized that the Jewish-Christian milieu of that faith reached back to an Aramaic-speaking Jewish-Christian community in Jerusalem. This community went to Syria after the destruction of the Second Temple (70 C.E.), where they acquired Greek influences and adopted the Septuagint as their version of the Bible. Eventually, this "Syrian," Jewish-Christian, Aramaic-speaking but Greek-reading group decisively influenced the origins of Christianity in Ethiopia through Frumentius, the first Bishop of the Ethiopian Church in Aksum, and the Nine Saints, often presumed to have been the main Bible translators.[47]

This rather elaborate theory attempts to explain the documented Syriac and Aramaic influences on Ge'ez and the general "Hebraic-Judaic" influences in Ethiopian Christianity, while simultaneously affirming the accepted fact that the Ge'ez Bible was translated from Greek. This hypothesis, hence, also does not require any separate or prior introduction of Judaism into Ethiopia.

Other explanations emphasize the likelihood that normative Jews in Aksum must have brought the concepts of Aramaic origin expressed in the Ge'ez words *meswat* ("alms" or "charity"), *tabot* ("Noah's Ark" or "Ark of the Covenant"), *ta'ot* ("idol"). H. J. Polotsky suggested that the presence of words of such fundamentally Judaic religious significance in Ge'ez proves that they could not have been brought by Syrian Christians, even if they were Aramaic-speaking, but rather must belong to a distinctive "Judaic leaven in Christianity."[48] In addition, it has recently been shown, for example, that in Ge'ez the word for Friday is "more Jewish than it is in Hebrew." The word "Friday" in Ge'ez means "evening" or "sunset," in the Biblical sense of the "day of preparation" for the Sabbath.[49] In other words, the Ge'ez word for Friday relates to the practice of the Saturday Sabbath.

Furthermore, the alleged role of the Nine Saints of Syrian origin as the Bible translators for Ethiopia has been questioned. Linguistic analysis of the translation suggests that the translators had an adequate knowledge of Ge'ez, but an "inadequate knowledge of Greek,"[50] which is not what one would expect if the Syrian missionaries were primarily responsible for the translations. In contrast, the Aksumite educated class knew at least some Greek as early as the first century but had mostly lost such knowledge by the sixth century.[51] Further historical evidence shows that at least parts of the Bible had already been translated before the Syrians arrived in the sixth or seventh century. For example, a Ge'ez inscription, found in Marib in South Arabia which dates from the early sixth century, refers to passages in the Book of Psalms.[52] One may also ask what books the new Christian community, which dates back to at least the fourth century, used before the Nine Saints arrived two centuries later.[53] It seems at least some of the books of the Old Testament must have been in the country—perhaps brought by early Judaic immigrants before the Syrian missionaries arrived.

Thus, there is persuasive evidence that the "Hebraic-Judaic" elements in Ethiopian Christianity must have been due to a pre-Christian Jewish presence in Aksum. As Getatchew Haile summarized with regard to the Saturday Sabbath:

> Only the Christianity of a nation or community which first practiced Judaism would incorporate Jewish religious practices and make the effort to convince its faithful to observe Sunday like Saturday. In short, the Jewish influence in Ethiopian Christianity seems to originate from those who received Christianity and not from those who introduced it. The Hebraic-Jewish elements were part of the indigenous Aksumite culture adopted into Ethiopian Christianity.[54]

This interpretation does not explain whether such "indigenous" Jewish influences came from South Arabia or through Egypt. But it is in accord with the local traditions that Ethiopia was Jewish before it was Christian, a tradition embodied in the fundamental but controversial legend of Solomon and Sheba as written in the *Kebra Nagast* ("Glory of the Kings").

The *Kebra Nagast* is a "national epic" that describes crucial formative events in the nation's history.[55] These events include the founding of the dynasty through the birth of Menilek I, the son of King Solomon of Israel and the Queen of Sheba; the transfer of the Ark of Zion and hence the legitimizing divine covenant as God's chosen people from Israel to Ethiopia; the introduction and spread of Christianity to Ethiopia; and the development of an imperial ideology in the sense of a justification of conquest to spread the Christian realm.[56] Though it did not receive its final written form until the early fourteenth-century reign of Amda Seyon, it has often been assumed that it was created in at least oral form soon after the Aksumite conversion to Christianity, and in written versions later. If so, it seems as if the traditions must have been created not only to connect the kingdom to an earlier, prestigious kingdom at the center of the Old Testament, but also for the purpose of appealing to a population already familiar with the stories and precepts of the Old Testament.

Hence, the evidence demonstrates a Hebrew-Aramaic linguistic influence on early Ethiopia, but debate continues on whether the influence was due to a normative Jewish presence or can be attributed to Aramaic-speaking Jewish-Christians. Other evidence hints at a Jewish presence between the ninth and thirteenth centuries, but these suggestions are not conclusive.

At least four sources of information from this period have sometimes been taken to refer to Jews in Ethiopia, though none of the references, not even Ethiopian ones, is clear about what they may have meant by the term "Jew." Furthermore, though some have taken these references to Jews to mean Falasha, neither the word "Falasha" nor "Beta Israel" is used at all. The information comes from the description by Eldad the Danite, traditions concerning a tenth-century Ethiopian queen, and the travel accounts of Benjamin of Tudela and Marco Polo.

The "enigmatic" and "obscure" late ninth-century story by Eldad who called himself a Danite has been controversial.[57] Concerned to describe the locations and practices of the Ten Lost Tribes, Eldad said that four of them—Dan, Naphtali, Gad, and Asher—dwelt in "Havilah" in Cush and fought continuous wars against "seven kingdoms with seven languages" who lived "on the other side of the river of Cush."[58] The account also described the ritual for slaughtering animals followed by these people. The passages are too obscure to be of much use, though one scholar hypothesized that because the author seemed to be familiar with the Ethiopic book, *Kebra Nagast,* he must have been referring to Jews in Ethiopia.[59]

The tenth-century queen who in Ethiopian tradition overthrew the last king of the Aksumite dynasty and ruled for forty years is better documented, since the tale is known in more than one Ethiopian version, as well as in Coptic Christian and Arabic sources. But it is no less controversial than the story of Eldad.

Aksumite power was declining by the tenth century.[60] In a letter to King George of Nubia, the Ethiopian king noted that a "queen of Bani al-Hamwiyah" had revolted and had "burned many cities and destroyed churches and drove him (the king) from place to place."[61] The Arabic text giving the supposed place of origin of this queen has been read in various ways to give the interpretation that she was Jewish, Agaw, or from a southern Cushitic kingdom, probably Damot, at that time located just south of the Blue Nile gorge.[62]

Other internal chronicles and king lists, however, not only provided details about the queen but also called her a Jewish queen, variously naming her Gudit (or Yodit, "Judith"), Esato ("fire"), or Aster ("Esther"). Many of these documents said she had burned many churches because both she and her husband were Jewish (*ayhudawi*), and that she ruled for forty years.[63]

At least one group of the traditional king lists in Ethiopia mentions Gudit. Despite the lack of unanimity in the sources, the traditional Ethiopian assumption has usually been that there was such a queen and that she was Jewish.[64]

Based on a historical reconstruction of Aksumite political-economic expansion in earlier centuries, however, the most plausible interpretation of the queen's origin and motives for revolting is that she was not Jewish, but was a "pagan" queen probably of the Kingdom of Damot, well-known in later sources. She was probably counterattacking against an Aksumite king who had sent an expedition to reopen the trade routes to the sources of gold beyond her region. Information from the Arab traveler, Ibn Hawqal, who noted that a woman from southern Abyssinia had revolted and killed the Abyssinian king and had been ruling for thirty years, supports this interpretation.[65]

Rabbi Benjamin of Tudela in northern Spain, a famous Jewish traveler of the late twelfth century, went across Europe as far as India and perhaps China, before returning through South Arabia, taking the Nile valley north to Alexandria and across the Mediterranean to Rome. As in all such accounts, the geographical place names are often difficult to identify. On his way home he was said to have arrived at "Middle India, which is called Ba'dan." Then follows the passage that is sometimes said to refer to the Falasha:

> In it are great mountains and there are Jews who are not subject to the rule of others, and they have towns and fortresses on the tops of mountains. They descend to the land of Ha-Ma'atom which is called Nubia. This is a Christian kingdom, and its people are called Nubians. The Jews wage war with them and loot and plunder, and then return to the mountains. No one is able to defeat them.[66]

Part of the controversy on this story derives from the problem of properly translating and interpreting the place names. Robert Hess argued that Benjamin simply confused the Jews with the Beja of the region north of Abyssinia-Ethiopia and that "Ha-Ma-atom" was really the area of Nubia along the Nile previously inhabited by the Ma'addam Arabs. Hence, the Beja were carrying out raids against the Christian kingdoms of Nubia: Maqurra, Dongola, and Alwa.[67]

The thirteenth-century account by the Venetian traveler, Marco Polo, is more straightforward. He wrote several pages on "the great province of Abyssinia, which is Middle India," including the sentence: "There are also

Jews in this country; and they have two marks, one on either cheek." The reference to the "two marks" is not clear, though it was in the context of Christians having three marks and Muslims one mark on their faces, made by hot irons as signs of their religions.[68]

Thus, except for Marco Polo, none of these early references to Jews in Ethiopia is conclusive either in that they were really referring to Jews, or in the case of the Jewish travelers, even that they meant Ethiopia. Marco Polo's reference is clearer, but even here, we do not know what was meant by "Jew" at that time in Ethiopia, and his mention of branding marks on the cheek has no other corroboration.

New Perspectives

We are thus left with the possibility either that the ancestors of the Beta Israel–Falasha are related to a pre-Christian Jewish presence (the Convert view) or that they only became differentiated later from an original Jewish-Christian group (the Rebel view). In either scenario the mediation of whatever Jewish influences existed through the broader Ethiopian context is critical. Thus, whether the ancestors of the Beta Israel–Falasha were a pre-Christian group who refused to convert or part of the original Jewish-Christian group that split apart, or some combination of the two, they only emerged as a distinctive group through interaction and conflict with the Christian state and society. Aksumite involvement in conquest and evangelization south of the Takkaze can be seen as supporting either perspective on the origins of Judaic influences and on the origins of the Beta Israel–Falasha group. That is, the Christianizing Aksumites may have sent (Judaic) dissidents into exile—such as into the Samen, which was known as a place of exile—and these dissidents then worked among the local (Agaw) population to proselytize a form of Judaism among them. Or the Aksumites may be seen to have introduced a monotheistic Jewish-Christian belief among the Agaw of the whole Tana-Takkaze region as part of their political-economic and religious expansion into the region.[69]

Traditions from both the Beta Israel and Christians demonstrate original close connections between their communities. Beta Israel traditions recorded in 1975 had conflated three versions of origins into one. The traditions have obviously been greatly influenced by Western Judaizing forces operating for the last century, and they frame their responses to questions of origins in terms of when and where they came from. In summary, they state they first came to Ethiopia with the entourage of Menilek I, the first (legendary) king of the Ethiopian dynasty, and later they also came "with Jeremiah" through Egypt and Sudan, entering Ethiopia through Qwara in the sixth century B.C.E. Later, these first two strands were augmented by migrants from South Arabia, as late as the sixth century C.E.[70]

Some of this information is congruent with traditions recorded before there was a Western Jewish influence on the group. In the late eighteenth century, for example, the Scottish traveler James Bruce was told by the people themselves that they came to Ethiopia along with Menilek I and that later, when the descendants of Menilek converted to Christianity, the "Bet Israel," as they were called, chose a prince of the tribe of Judah as their ruler and refused to convert to Christianity.[71]

A half-century later, Antoine d'Abbadie, a French traveler, was told two versions: (1) that they had come with Menilek I and called themselves Levites and (2) that they came after Jeremiah. D'Abbadie argued on this basis that since they called themselves Levites, they could not possibly be the descendants of the Danites or any of the other Ten Lost Tribes who had dispersed after the fall of Judah, since they claimed to have originally come two centuries earlier.[72]

Similar traditions were told to Samuel Gobat, a well-informed Protestant missionary, in the early nineteenth century. The Beta Israel told Gobat they were of the tribes of Levi and Judah and that they originally came with Menilek I.[73]

Such traditions cannot be evaluated except within the overall context of Ethiopian dominant traditions and history. But in some senses these traditions suggest "Falasha origins" in terms of a split from Ethiopian Christianity, despite their explicit statements in favor of the Lost Tribe view stating they had migrated directly from ancient Israel. In other words, these oral traditions show the Beta Israel had the same view of their origins as the Christian dynasty had of its origins. Such congruency could be explained if it is assumed we are speaking of one group which at some point began to diverge into two (or more) groups. The Orthodox Christians may have taken one path, and the ancestors of the Beta Israel another. If this interpretation is valid, the initial divergence must be sought in the obscure period of ancient Aksum when Christianity began to make an impact on the society.

Some little-known Ethiopian traditions support the interpretation of a common origin of the Israelites who later became Christians (à la *Kebra Nagast*) and the Israelites who later became *ayhud* and probably formed part of the background of the Beta Israel–Falasha. These traditions state that when Ebna Hakim (Menilek I) arrived from Israel to take up the Ethiopian kingship, he divided the kingdom among about fifteen governors, the three principal ones of whom were Gedewon, Het, and Adel. These three were said to have had thrones of gold while the other twelve had only silver, iron, or lesser thrones. The specific territories under their governorship were also listed. Adel was granted the central highlands south of Aksum, including Wag, Lasta, Yajju, and Hayq. Het was granted the western borders up to Kassala and Sennar, including Qwara and Achafer west and south of Tana, respectively. Gedewon was said to sit on the right hand of the king and was granted Addi-Abbo, Walqayt, Sagade, Samen, Wagara, Armacheho, Chelga, Saqqalt, Dambeya, and Begamder.[74]

Though one cannot claim this tradition has literal historical validity, it cannot be mere coincidence that the homelands of those called the Beta Israel or Falasha later were nearly identical with the territory granted Gedewon, or that Gedewon was indeed the name (or title?) of several Beta Israel leaders known in the royal chronicles and Beta Israel oral traditions.[75] What this chronicle signifies, at a minimum, is the view of the central Ethiopian tradition that the governors over the people in the traditional Beta Israel homeland had an original close connection with the central dynasty. A phrase near the beginning of one redaction of the *Ser'ata Mangest* ("Laws and Ordinances of Government") which lists the twelve lawmakers who "came forth" with Menilek I suddenly states: "At this point the Falasha were separated."[76] Another version sees the Falasha as among the original judges as well as the keepers of the Ten Commandments and the holy water.[77] The use of the word Falasha here supports the Ethiopian tradition of the intimate Christian connections with the Beta Israel–Falasha who were part of the original Jewish retinue accompanying Menilek I but who later split with the Christians.[78] One version of the life of Takla Haymanot suggests the Ethiopian tradition that Jews entered Ethiopia through Egypt.[79]

Such a view of their original connections is also supported by Beta Israel traditions. The period when the groups began to diverge is not clear, but the logical periods to hypothesize such divergence are the fourth to sixth, ninth to tenth, and fourteenth to sixteenth centuries. The divergences must have occurred in the context of the ebb and flow of centralized political power and Christian proselytization.

A careful interpretation of the scanty documents referring to old Aksum suggests an ideological and religious struggle for control of the people accompanied the expansion of political-economic power and strength.

These periods of struggle between an old and a new religion are also remembered in Beta Israel oral traditions as periods of conflict with the Christianizing state.

According to the Beta Israel tradition collected by Bruce, the fourth century was one such time of struggle and marked the initial split between the old and the new. This was also a time of great political strength and the apparent (first) conversion of the dynasty to Christianity under King Ezana.[80]

The reign of King Kaleb in the early sixth century marked the introduction of a new era. His regnal name, Ella Asbaha, signifies in fact, "introducer of a new era (of enlightenment) (?)."[81] Kaleb engaged in conquests in South Arabia in support of a battle by Christians against a Jewish king and worked to expand Christianity within Ethiopia as well. A new interpretation of the traditional dates suggests Christianity was introduced (i.e., re-introduced) at this time by "Abba Salama" (the new name for Saint Frumentius) after a period in which it had been in decline. The reign of Kaleb is mentioned in Beta Israel oral traditions as a period of conflict, but no details were known.[82]

The next period of Christian zeal was the reign of Gabra Masqal ("Servant of the Cross"), also recalled in his regnal name as Ella Gabaz ("Defender of Zion").[83] The traditional dates for Gabra Masqal saw him as the second son and almost immediate successor of Kaleb in the late sixth century.[84] A new dating for Gabra Masqal has been proposed, putting him near the end of the ninth century.[85]

In any case, his reign was noted for its religious activities on behalf of Christianity. It may also have been a decisive period of political-religious struggle. Traditions link him to the construction or endowment of several churches in Tigray and the Tana-Begamder region. He was also said to have established the religious coronation ceremony, indicating that before him the coronation was purely secular.[86]

If Gabra Masqal's reign was a religious revival, what was it a revival against? An alleged older brother named Beta Israel may hold the key. A power struggle took place between the two brothers for accession to the throne of their father, who had abdicated. Most sources see Beta Israel as the elder son who either seized the throne by force or was attacked by Gabra Masqal after peacefully acceding to it. Beta Israel was defeated and was either killed or, according to another view, went into hiding and became the leader of the *zar* cult.[87]

In the king lists, Beta Israel's reign is usually very short, if mentioned at all. On the other hand, since coins were minted and circulated in his name using either Greek or Ge'ez letters, a process that probably took years, his reign may in reality have been somewhat longer than usually remembered. Hagiographical sources omit his reign altogether.[88]

Perhaps he is ignored in the religious sources not just because his reign was relatively short, but also because he lost a power struggle with Gabra Masqal that had a significant religious component. He may have been challenging the new Christianizing of his brother in favor of an older monotheistic Judaic or Jewish-Christian faith. Though it would be going too far to suggest King Beta Israel in any way founded or established a group who centuries later had the same name, the similarity may perhaps be explained by a congruence of circumstances. The conservatives who disagreed with new proselytization efforts at various times may have used the claim to be the true House of Israel in opposition to the usurpers.[89]

Other scattered pieces of information apply to this question. Whenever Gabra Masqal lived, his reign was contemporaneous with the career of Yared, the traditional author of the Ethiopian hymnary (*degwa*) and composer of church music. In Christian sources, Yared's teacher was an *abba* Gedewon, also said to be his uncle, who taught a church school at Aksum. Yared eventually took over his uncle's position, had a long career in composing music, and retired with several followers to the Samen highlands at the end of his life.[90]

Yared is also remembered, however briefly, in Beta Israel oral traditions. He was said originally to have been a Beta Israel who was a son of a Gedewon. One of Yared's sons was named Israel and other descendants included a line of (Beta Israel) priests in Samen. In these traditions, Yared had been forced to convert to Christianity or be killed at the time of Gabra Masqal's wars against the Beta Israel.[91]

Perhaps the reign of Gabra Masqal was the period when the original redaction of the *Kebra Nagast* was composed, as part of the process of struggle against the old and the new religion of Aksum.[92] Yared may have retired to the Samen to join, or possibly to found, a group of coreligionists that may be called *ayhud,* "Judaized Christians," or perhaps more accurately "Gedewonites," after his teacher and relative.[93] Since Samen was already known as an area to which the king exiled dissidents, Yared would fit into the same pattern by joining such a group.[94]

Perhaps the traditions surrounding an attacking "Jewish" queen called Gudit or Yodit in the tenth century also arose as part of the propaganda campaign against the defeated forces of the Gedewonites. In later centuries,

Yodit was usually the name given to the leading Beta Israel female leader, whether as the sister or wife of Gedewon is not always clear. Jewish and Christian conflicts during the reign of Gabra Masqal may have been conflated in Ethiopian traditions with the tenth-century queen. Such an interpretation would especially make sense if Gabra Masqal's reign really were in the late ninth century. The struggle during his period would have still been very fresh by the tenth century.

This combination of fragmentary Christian and Beta Israel sources, thus, raises several questions that can be used with additional data from later periods to hypothesize on the nature and process of Beta Israel origins and identity. Though the sources do not elucidate the content of their beliefs and practices during this early period, and not to any great extent even later, there seem to have been groups of *ayhud*, or Jewish-Christians or Gedewonites, present in ancient Aksum who for one reason or another rejected the continual efforts to reintroduce and revitalize the Christian content of the ruling dynasty and dominant society. Perhaps the enigmatic references to Jews and Jewish-Christian conflicts by Eldad and Benjamin and Marco Polo referred to these obscure groups in ancient Aksum and Zagwe.

Conclusions on Origins and Identity

These data and traditions concerning ancient Aksum are congruent with theoretical perspectives on the definition and origins of ethnicity, which emphasize the fluidity of ethnic "categories" and the contextual nature of their development. On the basis of present evidence, the Lost Tribe perspective on Beta Israel origins that asserts the present group of that name descends directly from an ancient *ayhud* ("tribe") is untenable because it does not take into account the now well-documented Ethiopian Christian influences on Beta Israel society and religion as constituted by the early nineteenth century, including its liturgy, religious books and language, and the institution of monasticism.

On the other hand, the literary, linguistic, and religious data from Aksum do suggest the presence of a Jewish group of some sort, whether a so-called Lost Tribe or more likely a group of Agaw converts to Judaism or to Jewish-Christianity. At various historical periods of intensive Christian proselytization, some of these Jews or Jewish-Christians refused to go along with the new conversion efforts and reinforced instead the *ayhud* or Gedewonite content of their society. As can be seen in the better documented period beginning in the fourteenth century, this group was also reinforced by dissident or rebelling Christians who joined them, bringing important new religious and literary elements. This dialectical process, whose origins date to ancient Aksum, continued in the new "Solomonic" dynasty after 1270, as the *ayhud-falasha-beta esra'el* identity continued to evolve.

Theoretical and Methodological Perspectives

In its broadest form, I conceive socio-ethnic history to be a focus on those groups—peoples, classes, castes, or women—whose individual histories as well as general contributions to the broader history of a society have usually been ignored. This study from its inception has been an effort to understand better the history of one such group—the Beta Israel–Falasha—within the context of an evolving Abyssinian-Ethiopian entity.[95]

I have found the process of caste formation to be the most useful theme for explaining both these specific and general concerns. But while focusing on caste formation as a process and as the main explanatory variable in Beta Israel history, I have also dealt with ethnicity and class, conceiving both as a dynamic relationship that has evolved over time rather than as primordial or static categories. To a lesser extent, given the general lack of data, the role of gender has also been considered.

Two more general theoretical concerns are the relationship of social and cultural factors in these processes and the relative roles of material and ideological forces. In general, I have found that a similarity or congruence of cultures—as had developed between the Beta Israel and the Amhara-Tigrayan by the early nineteenth century—did not result automatically in the complete social assimilation of these two groups. The continued social separation of the Beta Israel from the dominant Abyssinian society can be explained by the material and ideological factors associated with the caste formation process.

The caste formation process reached a climax in the eighteenth to mid-nineteenth centuries (see Chapters 3 and 4), but its roots lay in the fourteenth and fifteenth centuries (see Chapter 2). Hence, these five hundred years constitute the analytical heart of this book. But the periods both before and after that core period are considered in order to explain the full evolution of Beta Israel history within the Ethiopian context. The question of Beta Israel origins—which has received so much attention—has been considered above, while the first stages of the disintegration of the caste position and the splintering of the Beta Israel are also elucidated (see Chapter 5).

The book ends in the 1920s, when future trends were clear. With the establishment of schools for the Beta Israel by Jacques Faitlovitch in the early twentieth century—which had the purpose of redefining their religion to make it congruent to world Judaic patterns—the basis was laid for the eventual migration to Israel of thousands of Beta Israel, which has occurred in recent years. Though this process was not inevitable and the major results were only achieved after World War II, nevertheless, Beta Israel history since the 1920s more and more loses its internal Ethiopian focus and becomes part of the general stream of world Jewry. That period, hence, deserves a separate study and is not a part of this book.

Ethnicity

The history of the Beta Israel–Falasha demonstrates that neither ethnicity, nor caste and class were unchanging, static verities but rather have themselves been products of that history. Ethnicity, as a marker of "cultural pluralism,"[96] must be seen as "interlocking, overlapping, and multiple."[97] Ethnic identities also emerge and change over time and are not simply "primordial" categories, fixed forever.[98] Groups manipulate forces and factors to utilize diverse aspects of their identities in various circumstances in an "instrumentalist" manner.[99] More fundamentally, a group may be seen to construct its own identity, although always working within diverse and changing contexts and constraints.[100]

In Ethiopia, the fluidity and flexibility of ethnic categories over the centuries is well established, albeit sometimes forgotten or ignored.[101] The key variables explaining both ethnic groups and an ethnic hierarchy are their degrees of cultural and physical distance from the "core" of power and wealth, which since the thirteenth century has centered among the "Amhara."[102] "Amhara," however, may have many meanings including simply "Christian," although this identification is far too simple. There is an important group of Amharic-speaking Abyssinian Muslims throughout the country, and in areas where significant ethnic-religious interaction has occurred, such as in many parts of Wallo province, it is difficult to tell either by religious or kinship criteria who is an Amhara.[103] More generally, the term "Abyssinian" can be used to designate the people and culture associated with the Amhara, Tigrayan, and in some senses, the (Christian) Agaw of Wag and Lasta provinces.[104] In any case, neither "Amhara" nor "Abyssinian" designates a particular descent-based tribe, and people have historically rather easily become Amhara, thereby obtaining land-use rights in the ambilineal descent system.[105]

Beta Israel–Falasha self-identity and their relationship to the larger society have changed over the centuries. From an obscure origin, the Falasha began to emerge as a distinct group by the fifteenth century. Simultaneously with their development into a recognizable people or ethnic group, however, they were also evolving into a caste relationship with the dominant Abyssinian society. Beta Israel experience between the fifteenth and nineteenth centuries demonstrates the salient conjuncture of ethnicity, caste, class, and to some extent gender as factors in explaining their history.

The process of their emergence remains unclear, but it involved both material and ideological elements. An increasing religious and political differentiation between a "Christian" and a "Jewish" element dated back to Aksumite times. As a result of the conquest of peoples in northwestern Ethiopia and the confiscation of their inherited land-use rights between the fourteenth and seventeenth centuries, these people adapted to their lost material basis by becoming tenant farmers and artisans working for Abyssinian society.

Of course, some of the conquered people joined the dominant society and became Amhara, thus retaining their inherited *rest* land-use rights. New Amhara-Tigrayan migrants to the area were awarded *gult* rights to collect tribute from the *rest*-holders, as administrative and ecclesiastical control over the region was acquired by the Ethiopian state. Eventually, by the end of this period in the seventeenth century, the capital of Gondar was established in this area.

But in the meantime, Falasha culture brokers, in the persons of their monks and priests, some of whom were converts from Christianity, began to define what it meant to be Falasha in a fifteenth- or seventeenth-century context. Although using orthodox cultural elements, such as religious books and a liturgy in Ge'ez as well as the institution of monasticism, these culture brokers used such elements to define a Falasha identity that helped them resist Abyssinian conquest.

Although their final defeat in the 1620s resulted in their near disappearance from the written records of the central state and church, they maintained a sense of identity and distinction and were not totally assimilated into Abyssinian society. Indeed, in the mid-nineteenth century a new generation of Falasha intellectuals arose to attempt another revitalization of their religion and society.

Ironically, in the meantime, the historical processes of the seventeenth to nineteenth centuries—particularly their loss of land, their partial incorporation into the Abyssinian social-political structure, and renewed religious threats in the early nineteenth century—meant that this attempted revitalization only reinforced an emerging caste relationship with the dominant society rather than leading to their political or cultural independence.

Caste

Castes, like ethnic groups, are not unchanging categories, but emerge during a dialectical and diachronic process. By the mid-nineteenth century, the Beta Israel had become an occupational caste within the larger Abyssinian society according to the following criteria: birth-ascribed occupational specialization within a ranked social hierarchy, fixed rules of social separation and interaction between the castes and the dominant society, and an ideological justification (expressed in moral or religious terms) of the rigid separation.[106]

These criteria combine the "attributional" and the "interactional" aspects of caste relations. Moral attributes concerning the degree to which various occupations and ways of life are judged to be pure or polluted lie at the heart of caste systems. These attributes provide the ideological justification that supports and makes possible the continuation of the system.[107] But the structure and operation of castes on the local level can only be discerned and explained through an examination of the interactional relationships among them.[108] Since interactional criteria define castes according to a structure of institutions, attitudes, and relationships and are not specific to any one particular culture, they provide a means to analyze caste relations in areas outside of India.[109]

Factors of caste, class, and ethnicity must all be considered as explanatory variables for the social history of "mixed" systems such as Ethiopia. In many societies in southern Ethiopia, the existence of castes within particular ethnic groups has long been recognized, but their histories remain unexplored. Those occupational castes, such as the *fuga* within the Gurage or the *watta* within the Oromo, seem to be divisions within one ethnic group, but their actual origins are unknown.[110]

In the case of the Beta Israel–Falasha caste, its origins must be explained using both the "conflict-conquest" and the "gradualist-integrative" approaches. The former emphasizes the conquest of a separate (ethnic) group which becomes a caste, while the latter focuses on internal processes of socioeconomic differentiation as the key explanatory variable.[111] With regard to the Beta Israel, neither approach is sufficient, but both are necessary to explain caste formation.

Their occupational specialization began to emerge as they were defeated and lost control of *rest* (inherited) land between the fourteenth and seventeenth centuries. In response to the conquest, the men adopted blacksmithing and weaving in addition to working as tenant farmers. Later, they also became carpenters and masons. The women became potters and, during the Gondar era, engaged in other activities associated with church decorating such as making paints.

Over the centuries there emerged clear and rather rigid rules of social separation and the conditions under which limited interaction could occur between the Beta Israel and the dominant society. Both sides formulated these rules. In the fifteenth century, Beta Israel monks and priests were said to have begun the process as a means of maintaining a degree of identity in the face of conquest, land confiscation, and some population dispersal.

In the ensuing Gondar era (1632–1755), the process of urbanization brought people of diverse ethnic origins together. The city was characterized by separate ethnic-religious and occupational enclaves enforced both by custom and royal edict. Hence, urbanization was also a stimulant to occupational specialization and caste formation.

The system of separation and the forms of interaction were fully elaborated by the mid-nineteenth century, which marked the final stage in the process of caste formation. Moral and religious ideologies reinforced the social separation. The ambiguity of a caste relationship was supported by the Abyssinian view that the Falasha were both morally repugnant and feared as *buda* (having the "evil eye"), that is, capable of causing harm and even death just by looking at someone. On the other hand, a Beta Israel religious revival led them to turn increasingly inward and to see themselves as morally purer and superior to Ethiopian Orthodoxy.

Class

The "premodern" Ethiopian polity, in general, "rested upon a moderately developed class structure."[112] It can be called a "class" structure in that there was a clear stratification system comprised of, from bottom to top, "slaves," endogamous artisan groups, landless peasant squatters, *rest* (inherited) land-holding peasants, and "lords." The criteria for this system consisted of both land-use rights and control over dependents.[113] In the broadest sense, the fundamental class division was between cultivators and rulers.[114] In this hierarchy, certainly oppression and exploitation existed as seen in the taxation and labor dues owed,[115] but at least three factors mitigated the degree of exploitation and moderated the emergence of a fully developed class system: the high degree of social mobility (both up and down) between the cultivators and rulers, the lack of horizontal ties among the cultivators and the great significance of dyadic vertical relationships between individuals in each group, and the lack of direct access to the land by the rulers who had to impose tribute rights on a *rest*-holding peasantry that held direct control over the land.[116]

When a consideration of the "endogamous artisan" groups is added to the analysis of northern Ethiopian society, its class nature becomes much clearer than when the focus is only on the differences between the Abyssinian rulers and cultivators, both of whom had access to land and its products. The Beta Israel–Falasha were conquered and thereby lost their inherited land-use rights as part of the northwestern expansion of the Ethiopian state between the fourteenth to seventeenth centuries. They along with other groups, therefore, may be seen as part of an emerging landless "class" in the region. In that position, they fit into the general group of peoples who were characterized by landlessness, as documented in later centuries, such as the Qemant, Wayto, Zalan, Muslims, "Shanqilla" and other "slaves." The *rest*-holding peasantry in northwestern Ethiopia became known as Amhara, while those without became a landless "class."[117]

These various landless peoples, however, never saw themselves as in any way one group or even one category. Hence, the term "class" can be used to refer to them only in a very simplistic way.[118] They continued to relate to each other as separate peoples, while their degree of separation and distinction from the dominant society allows us to describe them all as castes or at least as castes-in-formation. Each group remained essentially endogamous and occupationally differentiated, though some, such as the "Shanqilla," could be gradually assimilated over several generations.[119]

Class analysis may be useful in another sense, especially in analyzing internal stratification criteria within the castes. For the Beta Israel such stratification was related to occupation. Though the Beta Israel claimed to value all artisan work, even for them certain types of craftsmanship were more highly valued than others. Blacksmiths, for example, occupied an ambiguous position in Beta Israel society.[120] While it was claimed their work was highly valued, Beta Israel priests could not also be blacksmiths, though they could be weavers.[121] Despite themselves, the Beta Israel seem to have inherited or acquired some of the same fears of this occupation expressed by the Amhara. Though the Beta Israel, in general, were feared and despised as having the evil eye, blacksmiths seem to have been particularly subject to this superstition.

Class stratification within the Beta Israel caste was stimulated by the emergence of the Gondar urban area during the seventeenth and eighteenth centuries. During the Gondar era, the Beta Israel who became valued artisans—as masons and carpenters—were rewarded with land grants and titles by the Ethiopian state. These land-use rights were most probably of the type called *rest-gult,* which meant the receiver had the right to tribute collection from the land and could also pass it down to his or her descendants.[122] This type of land-use grant was highly prestigious since it was hereditary and could not easily be taken back or transferred to another person by the king like the usual *gult* rights. Such grants, hence, resulted in the partial incorporation of a small Beta Israel elite into the Abyssinian political-military hierarchy and seems to have occurred almost entirely in the greater Gondar urban area. Such incorporation continued on a reduced scale up to the early twentieth century, thereby creating a new, essentially secular elite distinguishable from the traditional Beta Israel religious hierarchy headed by priests and monks.

Gender

Gender, along with race, is one of the two most immediately recognizable markers of group identity. But unlike all the other markers—ethnicity, race, religion, caste, and class—a gender category cannot reproduce itself in the real world and, hence, must always be seen in its relationship to the other categories and identity markers. It is inherently a relational marker, and therefore, its significance must be seen in its impact on ethnic, caste, and class relationships and identities.

Along with class, gender is a means of stratifying other categories such as caste, racial, and ethnic groups. The manipulation of gender—or more prosaically, men's domination of women—has been a characteristic of virtually all human societies. The degree and means of this control have varied from place to place and time to time, and therefore, an analysis of these variations allows us to describe the ethnic and class systems of different societies.[123]

Though not well-documented, in general, the position of Beta Israel women within the Beta Israel group had some commonalities with that of Amhara women in Abyssinian society. Amhara women had the right to own and inherit property, initiate a divorce, and recover from a marriage the property they brought to it and a share of the wealth created during the marriage.[124] Subject to the limitation that Beta Israel did not have much property—especially landed property—to inherit, Beta Israel women seem to have had a similar position. On the other hand, Beta Israel women were clearly subject to severe limitations and restrictions. During their menses, they were kept separate in their "huts of blood," and during childbirth their separation from males was more severe than was the case in Amhara society (see Chapter 4). Furthermore, Beta Israel women potters were as despised and feared by Abyssinians as Beta Israel blacksmiths, and the two collectively were the ones most often accused of having the evil eye.[125]

On the other hand, within the Beta Israel caste, the more rigid treatment of women was seen as an indication of their higher level of moral purity than the Amhara. Thus, even the degree of class and gender stratification within the Beta Israel group worked to reinforce the caste position of the group vis-à-vis Abyssinian society.

Oral Traditions

Oral traditions have provided essential "inside information"[126] as well as the basic interpretative framework for my analysis; hence this book would not have been possible without their collection and utilization. In some cases, the traditions filled in lacunae in the written record. Such was particularly the case for the Gondar era (1632–1755), when the Ethiopian chronicles virtually ignore the Beta Israel after their final conquest in the 1620s and when few foreigners visited the country (see Chapter 3).

In a more general sense, the historical interpretative framework I have developed is based on my analysis of their oral traditions. For example, the fifteenth century—particularly the reigns of Yeshaq (1413–30) and Zar'a Ya'eqob (1434–68)—emerged as a key transitional period from the depth and detail of Beta Israel traditions concerning that era.[127] The traditions emphasized the military defeats, loss of land, and dispersals of the Beta Israel, as well as the creation of Beta Israel monasticism and a sense of self-definition by the Beta Israel monks. Both material and ideological data were crucial to my analysis of this period as the first stage in a process of caste formation.

During the Gondar era, the traditions not only focus on the role of the Beta Israel as masons and carpenters in constructing the royal palaces and churches but also assert their acquisition of land and titles. I was able to use such information to show a process of institutional incorporation as the Beta Israel became a more integral part of the broader Ethiopian structure.

In the mid-nineteenth century, during a period of heightened Beta

Israel persecution, their traditions assert they experienced a religious revival. I use that information as the starting point for an analysis of data from travelers and missionary records to elucidate what the revival meant for the Beta Israel, as well as what it contributed to the consolidation of their caste position.

The limitations of oral traditions, however, also clearly emerge from my data. The information available has often been sketchy, was contained in diverse (if not contradictory) versions, is often overly personalized, and is not as precise chronologically as one would like. Quite often, such as during the Gondar era, only the names of important individuals have been remembered, without any detail about their lives or achievements. Some of the oral data about the key fifteenth-century conflict with Yeshaq is diverse and contradictory in terms of the names and roles of the individuals involved. As is often characteristic of oral traditions, broad historical forces and trends are boiled down to a personal incident or conflict, such as some of the traditions concerning the wars with Sarsa Dengel (1563–97). I see these wars as part of the process of the northwestward movement of royal power during the previous two centuries, although some Beta Israel traditions simply see them as the result of a personal conflict between the king's wife and a Beta Israel at the king's court.

And the chronology—though more exact than is usually possible in purely oral societies—is sometimes vague because of a confusion between different Ethiopian kings, or a confusion between various Beta Israel leaders named "Gedewon" who lived at different times. In general, the greatest weakness of these traditions is their elite character. Though as the traditions of one of the submerged and oppressed peoples of Ethiopia the data are invaluable in a reconstruction of broader Ethiopian patterns, most of the sources and much of the data—as is also the case in Ethiopian written documents—derive from and talk about activities of the political and religious elites among the Beta Israel.

Despite these limitations, careful use of the data has made possible some theoretical and historical reconstructions that would not have been possible otherwise. Only by utilizing data that originate with all the peoples concerned can a true history of Ethiopia eventually be written.

The Relationship of Oral and Written Sources

Ethiopia is especially rich in written sources compared with most African countries. Indigenous written sources include especially the royal chronicles, hagiographies, and a variety of local histories often based on extensive knowledge of local oral traditions. Most of these contain to a greater or lesser degree data passed down orally before being written.

Royal chronicles exist in both long versions of individual kings and short versions of each reign covering several centuries. The chronicles, in fact, comprise a "documentary tradition" and can be evaluated in some respects in a similar manner to oral traditions. Their purpose was to legitimate the origins and authority of the dynasty, just as many "official traditions" do so orally.[128] Some chronicles—such as that of Zar'a Ya'eqob—were written down many years after the king's reign and hence may be somewhat less detailed, but conversely, they may contain a more useful critique of the reign than would have been possible during the king's lifetime.[129] The short chronicles in particular often contain religious and other information passed down orally by monks before their redaction and have less emphasis on political and military matters than the longer court documents.[130]

Similar strictures apply to hagiographies which were written to glorify particular saints and their monasteries, not necessarily to provide an accurate historical record of their achievements.[131] Despite such limitations, hagiographies have been used successfully as historical sources. Even where the "facts" of the saint's life were invented, they may be used to illustrate how people thought and indicate what they considered important.[132]

The strengths and limitations of written sources were taken into account in my analysis. Sources in writing are not necessarily more "accurate" historically than oral sources just because they were written down at some point. I attempted throughout to check the oral and written versions of events against each other when possible. The Beta Israel conflict with Yeshaq (1413–30), for example, is mentioned only briefly in the short chronicle, while the Beta Israel oral traditions concerning it are much more extensive and detailed (see Chapter 2). The conflict during the reign of Sarsa Dengel (1563–97), on the other hand, is treated in great detail in the royal chronicles but much more briefly in the Beta Israel oral traditions. To the Beta Israel, the conflict with Yeshaq appears to have a more fundamental importance than that with Sarsa Dengel. My interpretation of each reign and my overall analytical framework took these variations into account by assigning more weight to Yeshaq's reign and to the fifteenth century in general than to the late sixteenth century, which seems to have been seen primarily as a continuation of previous trends.

Prayers and magical prayers are another type of written source in Ethiopia. In purely oral societies, these might be classified as "formulae."[133]

These writings have been much studied in Ethiopia, but their applicability as historical sources has been underutilized.[134] For this work, their primary usefulness has been to document in writing the well-known attitude in Abyssinian society that has equated Falasha blacksmiths with the *buda* ("evil eye") phenomenon. Some of the manuscripts containing such prayers can be dated to the early nineteenth century, thus documenting one time period when such beliefs were in existence.

Documents that contain data from both oral and written sources include the works of local and amateur historians.[135] My research suggests that most oral data from Amhara informants that had to do with general Amhara-Abyssinian phenomena were really based on such a combination of oral and written sources. Among the Beta Israel, there was generally a clearer division between the two sources. Despite the use of written books (in Ge'ez) by the Beta Israel for religious purposes, I found only one written chronicle which was based on oral traditions written down during the reign of Menilek (1889–1913).[136] One of my informants was a man who had collected data from many sources, including those in writing, and so was really acting as an historian.[137] These histories I found primarily useful in corroborating and helping to interpret what was known from other sources, rather than as independent oral traditions.[138]

Fieldwork Methodology

During eight months of fieldwork in the Gondar area, I sought out the most knowledgeable elders and priests concerning Beta Israel history in general and Beta Israel–Ethiopian relations and others who could talk about the local history of particular regions and villages. I collected oral information from the Beta Israel, the Qemant, and some Amhara in Gondar itself.

My Beta Israel informants were from Gondar and the greater Gondar area, Dambeya, Wagara, and the Shire region of Tigray. These locations were dictated by my thematic focus, the availability of the most knowledgeable informants, and the exigencies of the time. When I arrived in Ethiopia in January 1975, my fieldwork in the Gondar area was delayed by four months because of actual and rumored insecurity in the region due to opposition to the new government. Upon arrival in Gondar, the continued insecurity, shortness of time, and a severe gasoline shortage prevented me from visiting areas such as Samen and Qwara, which might have yielded important information, and limited my stay in other areas such as Chelga and Tigray.

I learned early that due to serious divisions within the Beta Israel community, I had to approach the different individuals through appropriate intermediaries. Fortunately, in most cases, I was able to find younger teachers or others who were from the village or who were personally acquainted and on good terms with the potential informant who could introduce me and act as intermediary and interpreter. I also felt the necessity to avoid all contact, or even the appearance of contact, with missionaries or those associated with the mission to the Falasha. This careful and at times rather slow development and cultivation of contacts with both intermediaries and informants proved essential in eliciting their full cooperation. Using these methods, I was gratified by the extent of the assistance and the quality of information obtained. My experience belied the reputation of the Falasha as suspicious and hostile to outsiders.[139]

My positive experience was made possible by the great cooperation and assistance of my intermediaries, with whom I developed close working relationships and friendships, as well as the cooperation of the informants. The intermediaries came to understand what I was doing and went out of their way to facilitate my work by informing me of potential informants, making contacts, and going with me to their villages.

The interviews themselves were very much joint experiences during which the interaction between the informant and myself, as well as the intermediary, became a part of the process of transmitting the traditions.[140] In most cases, I asked the questions in English and had the intermediary translate them to the most idiomatic Amharic (or in three cases, Tigrinya) phraseology. The intermediary then summarized the informant's answers in English before I asked follow-up questions. My knowledge of Amharic was sufficient to follow the informant's answer and check the intermediary's translation during the course of the interview. In the initial interviews with informants, I began with a general question asking them to tell me what they knew about Beta Israel history. I then asked follow-up questions based on their answers, and based on knowledge I had already gained from other interviews and from written sources. In the spontaneity of the interview process, the intermediary also often asked clarifying questions without a direct prompt from me. After returning to Gondar from a particular village or region, I obtained complete translations of the interviews and returned several times to the most knowledgeable informants for follow-up interviews. When possible, I used research assistants other than the original intermediary to assist me in the complete translation of the interview.

The most useful interviews on history were conducted with individual informants. But group interviews were also useful for local village history. During some of the group meetings, particularly knowledgeable individuals, about whom I had previously not known, came to the fore and provided very useful information.

With two exceptions, these formal interviews were recorded on tape. There were, however, innumerable other conversations with the intermediaries and other people in the villages which added to my knowledge of Beta Israel history and society, but which were not recorded. I drank coffee and other beverages, shared roasted corn and full meals with the people, stayed in their houses, and observed several aspects of their daily and religious life. I witnessed their practice of the Sabbath and the ceremonies of Astasreyo and the Segd, as well as a funeral. I observed and talked with people engaged in the artisan crafts of potting, blacksmithing, and weaving. The people opened up their lives to me, and I will always be grateful for their warm hospitality.

2. The Heroic Age: Conquest, Resistance, and Falasha Identity, 1270–1632

The heroic age marked the beginning of the Falasha (Beta Israel) as an identifiable, named group, formed in response to the impact of a revived Christian state and proselytizing church. Small groups of *ayhud* ("Jews" or "Jewish group") in the northwestern region resisted conversion and sporadically rebelled, while a few of their intellectual leaders joined anti-Trinitarian Christians in theological controversies with Orthodoxy. Some Christian dissidents joined *ayhud* communities, bringing with them or reinforcing important religious elements, such as the Ge'ez liturgy, religious calendar, literature, and the practice of monasticism. Of course, many *ayhud* simply disappeared into Orthodoxy, and many individuals and groups labeled *ayhud* were clearly Christians. Because of the virulent controversies that climaxed during the reign of Zar'a Ya'eqob (1434–68), the word was often used simply as a derogatory term.

Out of this melange of preexisting *ayhud* groups and new influences from Orthodoxy (which was itself very Judaic in background), a community emerged known as the Falasha with a distinct religious, ethnic, and economic identity. Since the state seized *ayhud* inheritable land, the Falasha compensated by becoming skilled artisans while continuing to work the land as tenants. The Falasha community with a political center in Samen successfully resisted Christian conquest until the 1620s, after which a new era began, centered around the imperial capital of Gondar established in the northwestern region.

Imperial Revival, 1270–1478

The imperial revival beginning in 1270 consolidated central control over many regions, including northwestern Ethiopia, the homeland of the Falasha (Beta Israel). Through conquest of the "pagan" and *ayhud* Agaw, the emperors gradually restructured the land system of the region, creating a landless class that included the Beta Israel. The Ethiopian state and church simultaneously refined an imperial ideology that legitimized conquest and rule over non-Christians.

The new so-called Solomonic dynasty arose in Amhara province with strong support from Tigray and Shawa (see Map 2). The dynasty claimed to be Solomonic by overthrowing the Christian Agaw Zagwe dynasty (1137–1270) and "restoring" the Ethiopian kingship to a man claiming descent from the last Aksumite king. The "restoration," hence, was essentially ethnic-linguistic in terms of returning power to a Semitic-speaking dynasty. The new dynasty was also more aggressive in its political-military policies, as Aksum had been, whereas the Zagwe kings had been rather inward-looking, concentrating their resources on building the famous monolithic churches in the central Adafa-Lalibala region.[1]

Tigrayan scribes carried out the final redaction of the *Kebra Nagast* ("Glory of the Kings") about 1320 during the reign of Amda Seyon (1314–44), the greatest military king of this era. As a "national epic,"[2] the *Kebra Nagast* legitimized the transfer of power and the conversion to Christianity, thus establishing a new dynasty of Christian Israelites.[3]

The new dynasty began to Christianize and consolidate its power in Shawa as a step toward controlling the resources, trade routes, and movement of people from the interior to the Gulf of Aden and Red Sea ports of Zeila and Massawa. A peripheral aim was to control the northwestern areas of Gojjam, Agawmeder, Lake Tana, Begamder, Wagara, and the Samen, the areas inhabited by the "pagan" and *ayhud* Agaw.

Since Aksum, the central Christian state had claimed the territory up to the Red Sea–Gulf of Aden littoral. Despite increasing Muslim incursions along the coast, and the decline of Aksumite power, even in the tenth century external Arab sources called the waters along those coasts the "Abyssinian Sea" and considered that Abyssinian rule began at Zeila in the south and the Dahlac islands (Massawa) in the north.[4]

By the time of the Zagwe dynasty, actual Christian rule along the coast had long fallen into desuetude, but with the rise of the new dynasty, such claims were reasserted. The Christian state, therefore, considered the conflicts with Muslims, "pagans," and *ayhud* principalities as rebellions against legitimate Christian rule, as in the case of the Muslim ruler of Ifat, Sabradin, who rose up against "his lord, Amda Seyon."[5] External Arab sources agreed that land claimed by Ethiopia extended to the coast: "Ethiopia is

Map 2. Historic regions, ca. 1200–1850. Regional names are shown in capital letters; towns are marked with a small bullet. The modern capital of Addis Ababa is indicated in brackets.

reached from the Yemen via Aden and the land of az-Zayla where Ethiopia begins."[6]

The first blows to establish actual Christian rule over the surrounding smaller states were against the western "pagan" area of Damot, just to the south of the Blue Nile gorge, which had long dominated the Shawan plateau. But Yekunno Amlak (1270–85) took away the Shawan holdings of Damot,[7] and Amda Seyon (1314–44) made Damot tributary to the Ethiopian state between 1316 and 1317: "And God gave me all the people of Damot into my hands: its king, its princes, its rulers, and its people, men and women without number whom I exiled to another area."[8]

This consolidation of Ethiopian control in Shawa opened up direct conflicts with the Muslim states on its eastern borders. The Ethiopian chronicle of Amda Seyon, as well as the Muslim chronicle of the invasion of Ahmad ibn Ibrahim al-Ghazi "Gragn" ["left-handed"] (1527–43) two hundred years later, makes it clear the major struggles during this period were not simply raids seeking booty but were wars to control the political economy of the whole Horn of Africa region, even when expressed in religious terms, as in the statement put in the mouth of Sabradin who fought against Amda Seyon: "I will become king over all the lands of Ethiopia; I will rule the Christians according to my law and I will destroy churches."[9] Amda Seyon defeated Damot, Ifat, Dawaro, and Hadeyya; his successor, Sayfa Ar'ad (1344–71), "killed many Muslims when they rebelled."[10]

Dawit (1380–1412), Tewodros (1412–13), and Yeshaq (1413–30) all fought against Adal, the new center of Islamic power based on the Harar region. The Christian offensive continued up through the reign of Ba'eda Maryam (1468–78), after which an Islamic revival began that culminated in the Adal-based *jihad* of Ahmad "Gragn," which threatened the continuation of the Ethiopian Christian state. Ahmad intended to take over the Ethiopian state, rather than merely "taking as booty cattle or other things and returning to Muslim territory,"[11] as had often been the case previously.

Ethiopian expansion against the *ayhud* in the northwest was only a tertiary imperial concern at this time. Amda Seyon began imperial moves in that direction. After his campaign against Damot and Hadeyya in 1316 or 1317, he went north to Wagara sometime before 1332, thus claiming direct control over the *ayhud* regions of Begamder, Dambeya, and Wagara.[12] The evolving imperial role there must be seen in the context of Christian evangelism, which reinforced imperial military action even when its origins lay in heightened church-state conflict during the fourteenth century.

Monastic Revival, 1270–1478

An indigenous Ethiopian monastic revival accompanied the secular reassertion of power during the thirteenth to fifteenth centuries, providing the religious context out of which the Falasha emerged from some *ayhud* communities. Two major new monastic houses engaged in evangelization among the *ayhud*. Christian reformers, such as the Estifanosites, had friendly relations with the *ayhud*-Falasha, and several Christian monks joined the *ayhud*.

Amhara-Shawa Monasteries

Two new monastic houses were founded in Amhara and Shawa which began evangelization among non-Christians in their midst, including *ayhud*, "pagans," and Muslims. Before this period, Ethiopian monasticism was derived from the Nine Saints, the missionaries from West Asia who founded monasteries in Tigray and elsewhere in the north, beginning in the sixth century.[13]

The two major monasteries established in the south were Dabra Hayq in Amhara, founded by Iyyasus-Mo'a in 1248, and Dabra Asbo (later called Dabra Libanos) in Shawa, founded by Takla Haymanot in 1284. Their disciples, such as Basalota-Mika'el, founded additional monasteries and churches in the region which became centers of reform and evangelization.[14]

The rise of monasticism was not an unmitigated blessing to either Amda Seyon or Sayfa Ar'ad, who were not much concerned with evangelization and did not appreciate monkish meddling. Like many monarchs in Ethiopian history, they were comparatively tolerant of people's religious beliefs as long as they paid tribute and were peaceful. They saw monastic assertiveness as a threat to imperial hegemony and attempted to bring the new communities under their control as they had always controlled the clergy.

On the other hand, the monastic leaders were often of royal or noble birth themselves and saw no inherent reason why the kings should control them or their communities. Monastic militancy went beyond criticism of abuses to challenge imperial control of the land, the entrance of new monks to monastic training, and the proper date to celebrate religious holidays.[15] The kings attempted some subtle methods of cooptation by plying the monasteries with gifts, but they also responded angrily to monastic criticism by beating, publicly disgracing, and exiling militant leaders to outlying regions or to other provinces.[16] *Abba* Anorewos, for example, excommunicated Amda Seyon for taking his father's concubine and other alleged offenses. The king took his revenge by having Anorewos beaten and by banishing "the men [monks] of Dabra Libanos to the regions of Dambeya and Begamder," and by exiling the *echege* and others.[17]

Ironically, exiling monks often furthered the ecclesiastical goal of evangelization and the royal goal of political control because new Christian communities developed in frontier areas. This was particularly true of the Gojjam–Lake Tana–Begamder triangle in the early fourteenth century where the main subjects of evangelization were the "pagan" and *ayhud* Agaw.

Northern Movements

Two new monastic movements in the northern province of Tigray were relevant to the emergence of the Falasha and their relationship to some *ayhud* groups. These two movements raised important theological issues extending back for centuries concerning the Judaic ambiance of Ethiopian Orthodoxy.[18] They also had direct contact with some *ayhud* groups, either in assisting them or in trying to convert them.

The two new religious movements in Tigray were the Ewostatewosites in the fourteenth century and the Estifanosites ("Stephanites") in the fifteenth century. Ewostatewos (1273–1352) left the country in self-exile for fourteen years; traveled through Egypt, Jerusalem, and Cyprus; and finally died in Armenia. The movement, or house, that he founded was primarily distinctive for advocating the Saturday Sabbath as a true Christian practice that had been followed in Ethiopia for centuries. The Ewostatewosites held that the Egyptian Church's attempt in 1238 to reject the Saturday Sabbath as a Jewish custom was contrary to the practice of the early Church as well as of Ethiopia.

The Ewostatewosites' militant revival of a national custom acquired a strong following, even within the royal courts, despite the tireless opposition of the official Church structure led by the Egyptian bishops and the heads of the Amhara-Shawan monasteries. To the Egyptians and their supporters, the issue was broader than the Sabbath and included attacks on other Old Testament practices of the Ethiopian Church such as circumcision and some marriage customs. The bishops excommunicated the Ewostatewosites, forbidding them to enter churches or to receive Holy Orders, and exiled them to frontier regions. As King Zar'a Ya'eqob recounted later, the bishops "considered all those who observed the Sabbath as Jews."[19]

In truth, the relationship of the *ayhud* to this question of the Saturday

Sabbath was complex. Some *ayhud* who converted to Christianity reinforced the tendency to observe Saturday, but sometimes neglected Sunday: "The Jews refuse to observe Sunday, [that is] the Jews who became Christians in fear of the rulers. But those who were converted on their own will, observe rightfully with [the rest of] the Christians."[20] Christians arguing for the Saturday Sabbath had to distinguish clearly between the "Jewish Sabbath of Saturday" and the "Christian Sabbath of Saturday."[21]

Despite the harsh opposition, the Ewostatewosites flourished. They founded monasteries and engaged in evangelization in Tigray and among the *ayhud* in Begamder, and gradually achieved royal favor. During the fifteenth century, their position gained the support of influential religious scholars such as Giyorgis of Gasecha/Sagla and benefited from an edict of toleration issued by Dawit in 1404.[22] Finally, the issue was resolved by Zar'a Ya'eqob, who "understood the conflict in its true nature as a national movement." The ancient Ethiopian custom of the Saturday Sabbath was restored to legality at the 1450 Council of Dabra Metmaq.[23]

The Tigrayan monk Estifanos (1394–ca. 1450) founded a movement with schismatic religious and political implications, as well as direct relevance for this consideration of the Beta Israel–Falasha. The Estifanosites were essentially moralistic ascetics who had somewhat ambiguous theological positions but were militant in their criticism of "those who claimed to be Christians but did not observe Christian principles."[24] Their interpretation of the Trinity; their refusal to prostrate themselves before Mary, the Cross, and the King; their belief in monastic self-sufficiency and separation from royal control; and their harsh criticism of all secular or religious officials who did not meet their strict moral and ascetic standards caused them to be persecuted, especially by Zar'a Ya'eqob.[25]

Estifanos was flogged and disgraced by Zar'a Ya'eqob and died in exile about 1450. Up to his death, the Estifanosites had apparently refused to prostrate themselves before anything except the Father, Son, and Holy Spirit. After meeting with the bishop, they agreed to bow to Mary but not to the king. Around 1454, the king issued an edict of extermination against them.[26] Though he accused them of refusing to follow the cult of Mary, his main grievance against them was their stubborn refusal to submit to royal authority and to bow down to him personally. The Estifanosites themselves denied the accusations of not bowing before Mary and the Cross, but admitted they would not prostrate themselves before the king.[27]

In Zar'a Ya'eqob's castigation, he called them "enemies of Mary, likening them for the public, with the Jews, because of their refusal to prostrate themselves before the king."[28] They were also called *ayhud* during the reign of Eskender (1478–94).[29] In these cases, *ayhud* was apparently being used as a derogatory epithet for a heretical Christian group. Eventually, however, between the reign of Na'od and the Islamic invasion (1527–43), they were reintegrated into the Church.[30]

Some interesting interaction occurred between the Estifanosites and the Falasha. Refuge and assistance was given to the early sixteenth-century Estifanosite Gabra Masih by a *falasa* ("Falasha") when they met by accident in the wilderness.[31] The *gadl* of Ezra, another Estifanosite, explains that the Estifanosites were accused of not bowing down to Mary and the Cross, for which they were called *falasa*.[32] The label *falasa* may have been used here simply as a derogatory epithet, or perhaps it arose in this case because the two groups regularly cooperated to protect themselves from persecution. Both groups were critical of the Orthodox Church, the Estifanosites from a fundamentalist perspective as a movement "which preached strict observance of Christian virtues by all Christians."[33] The exact identity or position of the Falasha at this time was not yet clear, but the Orthodox Church tended to equate the two and considered both groups as their enemies.[34]

The evidence suggests the Estifanosites "may have attracted minority groups that felt oppressed and underprivileged," such as the Falasha. Linguistic analysis of two important Estifanosite works indicates "the language of their author(s) was not Semitic."[35] Perhaps some (Cushitic) Agaw-speaking Falasha had indeed joined the Estifanosites, probably attracted by their strict morality and ascetic practices and by some of their theological doctrines such as the observance of the Saturday Sabbath and apparent refusal to bow down before Mary and the Cross.

Another view of both the Ewostatewosites and the Estifanosites suggests they were sects of "Jewish-Christians" present in the country since ancient times that were suppressed by Zar'a Ya'eqob.[36] Whether called heretical or schismatic sects of Christians or Jewish-Christians, the views and actions of both groups contributed to the religious ferment of the period. Moreover, their specific interactions with groups of *ayhud* contributed to the emerging self-redefinition of those groups.

Evangelization and Revolts of the *Ayhud*-Falasha, 1332–1508

Political and religious pressures on the *ayhud* resulted in several revolts during this period as the Christian empire extended its direct control over the realm. The dual processes of evangelization and revolt, stimulated also by Christian dissidents, resulted in the formation of the Falasha out of some *ayhud* groups in northwestern Ethiopia between the fourteenth and sixteenth centuries. From the available evidence, these processes occurred principally among the Begamder, Wagara, and Samen *ayhud,* even though other *ayhud* groups in Shawa were among the first to be subjected to Christian Orthodox evangelism in the fourteenth century.[37]

Fourteenth-Century Shawa

One of the most interesting cases of missionary work among the *ayhud* was carried out by the monk Zena Marqos in fourteenth-century Shawa. Zena Marqos was a younger cousin of Takla Haymanot and was said to have been one of his disciples. He was also a nephew of King Yekunno Amlak (1270–85), the founder of the new dynasty. The only source available—the *Gadla Zena Marqos*—does not mention any political activities, conquest, or revolts but only peaceful evangelization among the Shawan *ayhud.*[38]

The *gadl* of Zena Marqos contains the most detailed contemporary account of *ayhud* history and religion, but it is congruent with other sources that see them as a distinctive Old Testament community. They were said to have arrived in Ethiopia in the reign of "Ebna Hakim" (Menilek I). Zena Marqos used prophecies from Isaiah and the Book of Psalms to convince an *ayhudawi* of the truth of Mary and Christ. The man referred to "the words of my ancestors, the Jews." He was said to know already the "books of the prophets" because he had been educated previously in "the laws of the Jews, his forefathers." These *ayhud* knew well the "law of the *Orit,*" but did not believe in the birth of Christ from Mary until convinced by Zena Marqos.

Zena Marqos founded the monastery of Dabra Besrat in Shawa. Churches were built in the area in the fifteenth century specifically for the converted *ayhud.* An *ayhudawi,* renamed Sege Berhan, was appointed chief priest over four of them.[39]

This detailed account of *ayhud* in Shawa in the fourteenth century requires rethinking of the historic location of the *ayhud.* Their center was certainly in the northwestern Begamder-Samen-Tigray area, but apparently small numbers lived elsewhere. The apparent Jewish communities travelers found in nineteenth-century Shawa may have been remnants of these ancient *ayhud,* as well as the result of subsequent dispersals to the region.[40] Likewise, the regions of Lasta and Gojjam may also have been centers of early *ayhud* settlement.[41] On the other hand, we do not know the doctrinal content of the *ayhud* anywhere in very great detail. Since it was used in other contexts to refer to Christian dissidents, heretics, or "pagans," it is clear that not all of those called *ayhud* had a direct relationship to the group that became known as Falasha during this time.

In Shawa, evidence refers only to peaceful acceptance of Christianity rather than to any *ayhud* revolts. In the northwest, however, evangelization stimulated an *ayhud* revolt against Christian incursions, and in this region a direct connection can be made between some of these *ayhud* and the emerging Falasha.

The Northwest: Tana to Takkaze

Between 1316/17 and 1332, Amda Seyon fought battles in Gojjam and Wagara and established royal regiments in Gondar and Saqqalt, thus asserting imperial control over the vast territory between the Blue Nile and Takkaze rivers.[42] Though some churches on Lake Tana's islands were at least as old as the Zagwe period, this area was only partially Christianized. The monastic opponents of Amda Seyon and his successor, Sayfa Ar'ad, whom they exiled to these frontier regions, used Begamder—the traditional area east of Tana—as a fulcrum for evangelization to the north and south.

The first documented example of resistance to the renewed political-religious pressures on those considered *ayhud* occurred in 1332. Amda Seyon used troops from more distant provinces but also some based in the area (Gondar and Saqqalt) who were still loyal and who were commanded by a local governor, the *begamder*, to put down a revolt by the *ayhud* further north:

> He also sent his other troops whom they called Damot, Saqqalt, Gondar, and Hadeyya—men mounted and on foot, strong and skilled (in) warfare, who were peerless in warfare and battle. Their commander was Sagga-Krestos, the *Begamder*. He sent (them) to the land of the traitors to fight those who seem like the Jews, the crucifiers, namely, [the inhabitants of] Samen, Wagara, Sallamt, and Sagade. Formerly, these people were Christians, but now they have denied Christ like Jews, the crucifiers. For this reason, he sent (the troops) to destroy and devastate them, being zealous for Christianity.[43]

This passage expresses the common Ethiopian view that the *ayhud* were essentially renegades from Christianity, a tradition probably due to two factors: some Christians did indeed abandon their religion to join *ayhud* communities during this period; it may also reflect earlier evangelization efforts, as far back as Aksumite and Zagwe times, when some *ayhud* underwent nominal conversion and had since relapsed as royal authority in the area waned. Certainly, the phenomenon of conversions that were only nominal because they had been made under duress is attested to in the literature of the period.[44]

The suppression of the *ayhud* revolt in 1332 by Amda Seyon made their increased evangelization possible during the next fifty years. Several monasteries and churches were established in the Gondar region and south to the eastern shores of Lake Tana.[45]

The most important missionary among the *ayhud* in the area was Gabra-Iyyasus, one of the disciples of Ewostatewos who had accompanied his teacher abroad and was with him when he died in Armenia in 1352. Gabra-Iyyasus then returned to Ethiopia, built a church in Tigray, and soon moved to "the land of Enfraz," a district on hills overlooking Lake Tana from the east.[46]

Though no dates are given, he must have arrived there by the 1360s and soon became involved in missionary work among the *ayhud*, a prosperous group in the area. From their earliest arrival in Ethiopia, they had "increased, multiplied, filled the earth and took possession of the land of Enfraz," as keepers of vineyards who also had cattle.[47] These references imply they were landowners practicing the typical highland Ethiopian mixed farming system that included stockraising and, in this case, vineyard-keeping and grain cultivation.

The conversion of a locally prominent *ayhudawi*, Zana Gabo, and his daughter, renamed Sabala-Ewostatewos, is presented as the result of the saintliness of Gabra-Iyyasus without the use of any force or coercion. Of course, the single source for this story is one-sided, and some vague indications in Beta Israel oral traditions suggest a conflict occurred during the reign of Sayfa Ar'ad (1344–71), which could have been at this time.[48] But, in general, one may hypothesize that the efforts by Gabra-Iyyasus were accepted rather peacefully due to his own moderation as well as the staunch Ewostatewosite emphasis on the Saturday Sabbath.

After Zana Gabo's conversion, "all his relatives, sons of the Jews," came forward and converted. In general, "the children of the Jews believed, received baptism, and entered into his [Gabra-Iyyasus] preaching."[49]

The *gadl* goes on to explain the important role these new converts played in Christianity in the region. The king at the time was said to have been so attracted to the beauty of Sabala-Ewostatewos that he married her. Their children grew up to become priests at the monastery of Dabra San.[50] Other evidence suggests the "Falasha origin of the clergy of Dabra San."

Following the text of the *gadl* was a long prose poem in honor of Saint Gabra-Iyyasus in which the final supplication begins with the stock Falasha formula, "Blessed be God, Lord of Israel," rather than the usual Christian phrase, "In the name of the Father, Son, and Holy Ghost."[51] This formula, in a text dating to a late sixteenth-century redaction of this *gadl*, indicates a Falasha influence on the Christian community of Enfraz two hundred years after the conversion of at least some of the *ayhud* of that region.

Not all *ayhud*-Christian relations were so peaceful, as illustrated by the case of Qozmos during the late fourteenth century. Qozmos was a Tigrayan monk who joined a monastery in the Tana region, probably a short time before the death of Yafqeranna-Egzi in 1372, whose *gadl* contains the story of Qozmos.[52] Soon he quarreled with the head of the monastery on the question of consecrating women as nuns and went to another monastery. This quarrel may be related to the problem of monks and nuns living together that developed in the new Shawan monastic communities in the fourteenth century.[53] Qozmos wanted to solve this problem simply by not allowing women to become nuns.

Qozmos was a rigid ascetic. He asked to live in a separate cell and refused all cooked food, eating only peas soaked in water, and refused even to receive the Eucharist because it was prepared with baked bread.[54]

Finally, Qozmos fled Begamder before an order to chain him up and force him to eat could be carried out. After a three-day trip, he arrived in Samen and Sallamt, where he lived on roots for a while, but was eventually well-received by the people of the area:

> The people of Samen and Sallamt lived in the Jewish faith [*bahaymanota ayhud*] and were exceedingly evil and thoughtless. When those heretical ones saw Qozmos living in the wasteland, they gave him food to eat but he refused to accept it. They asked him, "What do you eat?" He said to them, "If you have honey, give it to me so that I may eat." They said to him, "Can you write?" He said to them, "Yes." They brought him honey and milk, and he wrote [copied] the *Orit* for them.[55]

He also gave them water, over which he had prayed, that helped heal their sick. Eventually, the *ayhud* became convinced that Qozmos was the prophetized son of God.

They helped him gather a great army which then attacked the Christians in Dambeya and Begamder:

> They went out and encamped by the *kantiba* of Dambeya and they fought him and defeated him and he joined with them. Then he [Qozmos] went out and

> burned many churches and arrived in the region of Enfraz and he killed *abba* Ge[r]dlos and *abba* Yohannes Kama and *abba* Tense'a Madhan with their thirty-seven followers. At that time, the words of the prophet St. *abba* Yafqeranna Egzi were fulfilled. The others who died because of this evil one were innumerable throughout Enfraz, monks and nuns. Then he killed many officials and governors.[56]

Eventually, King Dawit (1380–1412) had to send the governor of Tigray with troops to suppress the revolt.

Thus, during the fourteenth century, the Ethiopian kings, Amda Seyon in 1332 and Dawit fifty years later, had to send troops under loyal local leaders to put down revolts. In both periods, the kings' main wars were with Muslim and other states to the south and southeast, and they did not personally lead the troops against the *ayhud,* who were still a peripheral problem.

Up to the uprising led by Qozmos, the available hagiographical sources for evangelization among the *ayhud* of Shawa and Begamder suggest the rather peaceful nature of the proselytization process. Qozmos's revolt, however, provides an inkling of the tensions generated within the *ayhud* communities by evangelization. The *ayhud* were anxious to acquire religious texts from renegade Christians, but some reacted violently against conversion. *Ayhud*-Christian relations, thus, expanded and intensified during the fourteenth century, leading to a conflict in the early fifteenth century that the extant oral and written sources suggest was a turning point in Beta Israel history.

Yeshaq and the Wagara *Ayhud* Falasha

This first major war in a two-hundred-year series of conflicts broke out during the reign of Yeshaq (1413–30),[57] who was forced—at least partly because of the Qozmos uprising during his father's reign—to begin to take the northwest *ayhud* more seriously. The conflict against Yeshaq was due to expanded political-economic as well as religious pressures on *ayhud* society.

Since Amda Seyon, kings had maintained a political-military and clerical presence in Begamder, Dambeya, Saqqalt, and the immediate Gondar region. Various hints indicate this official presence was accompanied by a small degree of migration into the region from both Amhara-Shawa and Tigray. *Kantiba,* for example, which became the title of the governor of Dambeya during this period, originated as a title in Tigray. The use of such a title may suggest an influx of people from Tigray, though the title could have been imported without migration.[58]

The northwest was, thus, gradually being incorporated into the administrative structure of the Ethiopian state. In practical terms, these developments required the transformation of the land tenure system. The king granted *gult,* or tribute-collection rights on peasant lands, to local administrators, monasteries, churches, and garrisons. *Gult* grants were considered "entailed estates or fiefs with large revenues assigned to them."[59] This process is well documented for the early sixteenth century by Portuguese observers who noted that the provincial officials,

> who are like kings, are all tributary to the Prester John [Ethiopian emperor]. . . . The lords who are beneath these, even though they hold their lordships from the hand of the Prester John, pay their tribute to the other lords. . . . The lands are so populous that the revenues cannot but be large; and these lords . . . eat at the cost of the people and the poor.[60]

Although this documentation is from the sixteenth century, we may assume that the process began with the fourteenth-century conquests of Amda Seyon, who instituted the direct royal presence in the region.[61]

The *begamder* (governor of Begamder), the *kantiba* (governor of Dambeya), and the heads of garrisons stationed at Gondar and Saqqalt in the fourteenth century were probably all external appointees, that is, Amhara or Tigrayan administrators. Yeshaq, if not Dawit before him, began to change this policy to attempt the incorporation of local rulers into the Ethiopian administrative structure.

Both oral (Beta Israel) and written (Christian) sources corroborate the view that Yeshaq's reign was a turning point in Beta Israel history. According to written sources, he instituted a divide-and-rule policy by appointing a "renegade Jew (*ayhudawi*), Bet-Ajer," to be governor of Samen and part of Dambeya. He then appointed Badagosh, the nephew of Bet-Ajer, to be a liaison with the king and keep his uncle in line by ensuring the payment of tribute. Yeshaq invaded Wagara, however, when Bet-Ajer refused to submit the tribute.[62]

Beta Israel oral traditions support the view that there were internal splits in the ruling family, some favoring an accommodationist relationship with Yeshaq, and others desiring to maintain their complete independence. The traditions differ among themselves on the precise nature of the splits and on the names of the individuals involved. They are unanimous, however, that the leader of the Beta Israel was named Gedewon and generally remember him as a king, not just as a local chief. Bet-Ajer was a member of the ruling family, usually remembered as a son of Gedewon, but sometimes as his daughter or grandson.[63]

It is quite possible that the oral and written traditions are not in conflict on this question of leadership, but that the oral versions are simply more complete. Gedewon may have been, indeed, the overall Beta Israel leader whose headquarters was east of Wagara, perhaps in the area called Menna, not far from the confluence of the Balaguez and Takkaze rivers that mark the southern reaches of the Samen.[64] An *Amba Gideon* (Mount Gideon) was still known in that region in the nineteenth century.[65] Bet-Ajer may simply have been Gedewon's subordinate in Wagara, further to the west, as he is called in one chronicle the ruler of the "Falasha of Maraba," a district in Wagara. Perhaps Bet-Ajer was originally appointed to his position by Gedewon and was then confirmed by Yeshaq. Or perhaps the name "Bet-Ajer" (with its variant spellings) derived from the apparent title of an Agaw ruler in the time of Amda Seyon, "Abet-Azar."[66] In any case, control of the rich agricultural plain of Wagara was a key to the conquest of the rugged Samen to the north and to the consolidation of control over Gondar and Dambeya to the south.

The war broke out when Gedewon and the senior members of the ruling family in Wagara refused to recognize Yeshaq's claim to the overlordship of the area or to pay him the tribute demanded. The junior relatives, however, were in conflict with the senior rulers over religious and/or political issues and favored an accommodationist policy with Yeshaq. The Beta Israel traditions differ in their emphases on political or religious disputes, as well as in their use of individual names, but are congruent on the main lines. According to a tradition transmitted through the ruling families in Wagara, the main issue was a competition for power between Gedewon and his nephew, whom Gedewon tried to kill because of a prophecy that the nephew would be the next ruler. The nephew and his mother (Gedewon's sister) went to Shawa and sought the aid of Yeshaq, who returned with his army.[67]

A tradition transmitted through the monastic leadership, which I recorded from an informant claiming descent from Gedewon, asserted that the conflict was between Gedewon and his illegitimate son by a Christian prostitute. The Beta Israel priests demanded that he kill the son, but the mother and the child escaped to Shawa and sought the aid of Yeshaq.[68] An oral tradition collected in 1848 also asserted that the junior relative went to Shawa to seek Yeshaq's aid. In so doing, he "showed" the wheat of Wagara to Yeshaq,[69] indicating perhaps that Wagara was rich enough to pay the tribute demanded by the king.

Whatever the specific issues in the dispute, the junior relatives urged Gedewon to pay the tribute and submit to Yeshaq. When he refused to pay,

Yeshaq invaded Wagara and was assisted in his battles by the junior relatives and by others in the area with grievances against the Falasha.[70] In the Christian chronicle, "they made war from dawn to dusk" before the Falasha were defeated.[71] In some Beta Israel traditions, the war lasted seven years and was only concluded when some local Muslims betrayed Gedewon.[72]

After some bitter battles, Gedewon was defeated and killed, and the junior members of the family were rewarded with land and offices in Wagara. Both oral and written traditions agree that a junior relative was appointed the Wagara *shum* ("chief") because of his assistance to Yeshaq.[73]

As a result of their defeat, the Falasha were forced to convert or lose their land, many churches were built, and Christian migration to the area increased significantly. Yeshaq built churches in Wagara and Dambeya, the most famous of which was the still-existing Yeshaq Dabr at Kossoge in Wagara.[74] Church construction was followed not only by the forced conversion of many *ayhud* but also by the migration of Amhara-Tigrayan Christians to the region.[75] The names of most of these migrants are unknown, but there are traditions about a certain *kantiba* Arbuye, who was from Tigray and claimed descent from the Aksumite king, Gabra Masqal. He arrived at Danqaz, just southeast of Gondar, after the defeat of Gedewon and married Gedewon's daughter, whom he converted to Christianity. Their Christian descendants moved to Saqqalt.[76]

For the first time, *ayhud* land was confiscated. Yeshaq proclaimed that:

> "May he who is baptized in the Christian baptism inherit the land of his father; otherwise, let him be uprooted from his father's land and be a stranger (*falasi*)." Since then the [Beta] Israel were called Falashas (*falashoch*).[77]

Beta Israel traditions are congruent with this etymology of Falasha, but some personalize the story. Soon after Gedewon's death, his wife gave birth to his last son, whom she named Falasa, meaning " 'the reign has departed from the Beta Israel.' This is the reason his descendants are now called Falashas."[78] Hence, both traditions support the view of Falasha origins that says they were dispossessed rebels against the Christian kingdom. But in both cases, the references are to people who were clearly *ayhud* (or in the quotation above, "Israel") before their rebellion; the resistance of this group to the Christian state was part of the story of their evolution, but it is not the total explanation of their origins.

Despite the coercion, many Falasha refused to convert and, therefore, were deprived of their rights to inheritable (*rest*) land. Thus, their traditions regarding Yeshaq's proclamation state simply that Yeshaq said: "I have taken all your land."[79] They could continue to be agriculturists in Wagara and in general in the highland plateau regions only as tenant farmers on the land of the new settlers.[80]

Other Falasha dispersed out of the rich plateau regions such as Wagara to low-lying or wilderness regions that did not support as much productivity as Wagara. Some Beta Israel traditions document this movement by tracing the lives of Gedewon's children and their descendants. Some went to the lowland Sudan border area near present-day Matamma. They suffered much there from diseases, and later Yeshaq gave them permission to go to Walqayt. One son of Gedewon, Yeheyyis Tameno, fled to Armacheho, said to be "a densely forested area" at that time. His descendants intermarried with Christians and converted at the time of Galawdewos (1540–59), living in Saqqalt, Chelga, and today in Alafa. The son named Falasha was said to have gone to Sagade and his son to Walqayt, where they were granted the right to live by Ba'eda Maryam (1468–78). Another son, Solomon, went to Saqqalt, and his son Sim'on moved to Qwara to escape intensified Christianization efforts later in Saqqalt. Gedewon's brother Atti fled to Samen but was captured by Yeshaq's army. Later, he escaped and went to the lowlands of Qolla Wagara. Gedewon's sister Hewan was also said to have gone to Samen but later married a Muslim and changed her religion.[81]

Whether these specific details can be corroborated in other sources such as saints' lives or historical notes that may be found in local churches will depend on future research. I have cited some of these details to indicate the fundamental importance given to the conflict with Yeshaq in Beta Israel traditions. The written sources available also indicate the significance of this conflict because it marked the beginning of land confiscation and the beginning of the end of *ayhud* political independence. Yeshaq's defeat of Gedewon consolidated imperial control from Begamder and Dambeya as far north as Wagara. It was to take another two hundred years to get complete control of the peaks of Samen.

Meanwhile, the combination of land expropriation, Falasha dispersal, Christianization, and the migration of new Christian settlers to the region speeded up the process through which the northwest would become a "traditional Amhara area." The brilliant standard history of this period makes suggestions toward developing a land history of Ethiopia that need further investigation. Taddesse Tamrat explained the expansion of *gult* grants as the result of imperial conquests during this period. Furthermore, he suggested that over time, particularly in the new areas of conquest, these originally nonhereditary *gult* grants became fixed and hereditary *rest*-rights among the descendants of the first *gult*-holder:

> In fact it seems that the land holdings known as *Rist,* or hereditary estates, in the more ancient parts of the Christian kingdom, were also in origin *Gults,* and their transformation into *Rist* was only a measure of the degree of religious and ethnic equilibrium long created in these areas since the Aksumite period. . . . Gradually . . . with an increased social contact and intermarriage between the two classes, the difference between them became less, and *Gults* were transformed into hereditary holdings. Wherever this development was impeded by deep religious and ethnic prejudices, the *Gult* system maintained its original character, and the power of the Christian kingdom always remained alien and only skin-deep.[82]

Except for the fact that this reconstruction downplays the role of force in the process, in general, it may explain how the *gult* land granted to the governors, soldiers, and immigrants to the northwest could become hereditary. "Social contact and intermarriage" between the Amhara-Tigrayans and the Falasha and other Agaw peoples of the area certainly occurred, but "ethnic and religious prejudices" also remained, and only the use of forced expropriation could create the physical and social space necessary for the transformation of *gult* to *rest* in the hands of the Christian population.[83]

The evangelization and conquest that reached a climax during the reign of Yeshaq were essential to this transformation of the land system of northwest Ethiopia. The process was not complete until the early seventeenth century, however, mainly because of the fierce resistance carried out by the Falasha of the Samen, which is the site of the highest and most rugged peaks in Ethiopia. Though the main story of that resistance belongs to the reigns of Sarsa Dengel and Suseneyos, 1563–1632, the late fifteenth century was important for the relationship between evangelization, revolts, and power struggles in the central court.

Samen Ayhud and the Royal Court, 1434–1508

The defeat of the Wagara *ayhud* had required for the first time the personal involvement of the Ethiopian emperor. During the next three-quarters of a century, evangelization and conflict with the *ayhud* in the provinces—in the northern redoubts of Samen in particular—were increasingly connected to power struggles in the central court. In this sense, events at the court cannot be understood without reference to local areas.

Despite Yeshaq's decree for all *ayhud* to convert or lose their land, the northern *ayhud* were still independent in the mid-fifteenth century when the monk Takla Hawaryat attempted the first documented evangelization of them. Sometime before 1454, Takla Hawaryat traveled to Sallamt, the border area between Samen and the Takkaze River. In Sallamt, an *ayhudawi* governor commanded a mixed *ayhud* and Christian army which was about to embark upon a campaign against some Christians when Takla Hawaryat arrived. He was able to prevent the war by persuading the governor not to attack, and the Christians in the army greeted him happily. The Jews were not so happy, and one "Jewish prophet" (*nabiya ayhud*) became angry about the monk's activities. Eventually, however, Takla Hawaryat convinced him that Christ was the Messiah whom the ancient prophets had foretold, and the *ayhudawi* was converted to Christianity.[84]

Takla Hawaryat proselytized in Sallamt and Samen, where many *ayhudaweyan* had previously converted to Christianity only out of fear of the "edict of the king." Now, the monk "adjured them in the name of the *Orit* of Moses because they feared the *Orit* as the law of the Jews." Takla Hawaryat finally baptized thousands in the area.[85]

Although the chronology is not clear, it was probably after Takla Hawaryat's evangelization in Sallamt and Samen that a revolt against Zar'a Ya'eqob occurred there:

> The *Gad Yestan* of these princesses[86] ravaged every district. The word of the king was not followed. Rather, those [*Gad Yestan*] became like the word of the king and destroyed the land of Ethiopia. Because of them [the *Gad Yestan*], Amba Nahad, ruler of Sallamt; Saggay, ruler of Samen; and the *kantiba,* ruler [of Dambeya] revolted. All of them revolted and became Jews (*ayhud*), abandoning their Christianity. And they killed many Amhara people. When the king came to fight them, they prevailed over him, expelled him, and burned down all the churches of their districts. This all happened because the *Gad Yestan* ravaged them [the Christians], taking their goods, and pillaging their houses until not one *ma'etab* [remained] on their necks.[87]

The identification of the *Gad Yestan* is problematical, but they were probably local people who had been appointed representatives of the king and, hence, were mainly *ayhud*.[88]

Although Zar'a Ya'eqob was defeated in this attempt to suppress an *ayhud* revolt, his chronicler nevertheless called him the "exterminator of the Jews."[89] That title was probably related to his policies of "religious nationalism," in which he tried to eradicate all dissidents to his own theological views and opposition to his centralized control.[90] He and his immediate successors seem to have viewed the *ayhud* as a serious ideological challenge to royal power. Unlike the Muslim and "pagan" states, the *ayhud* were not a serious military threat in the fifteenth century. But they did pose a challenge to the basic legitimizing ideology of the new dynasty. As long as the *ayhud* existed as a viable community and attracted Christian renegades, heretics, dissidents, and rebels to their ranks, they presented a challenge to the ruling dynasty's claim to embody the smooth and legitimate transfer of the right to rule from ancient Israel to Ethiopia, as expressed in the *Kebra Nagast*. Zar'a Ya'eqob was quite aware of the nature of the threat and responded with polemical anti-Jewish diatribes, as well as with the execution or exile of his enemies.

Several theological controversies provide the context for Zar'a Ya'eqob's policies. Some of the issues go back a long time, but are well-documented beginning in the reign of Dawit (1380–1412). At the court of Dawit, a certain *ayhudawi* ("Jew") who questioned the divinity of Christ was defeated by the arguments of the Christian religious scholar, Giyorgis of Gasecha/Sagla, and was then ordered executed by the king.[91] In a second controversy, Giyorgis had to argue against the view of the Christian Bitu/Betu that at the end of the world, "the son will come along without his father." This issue was never decided on its merits.[92]

The major debate at the court of Zar'a Ya'eqob concerned the Godhead and Trinity where the "anti-Trinitarians" Za-Mika'el, Asqa, and Gamaleyal were declared "heretics" and accused of being *ayhud* because of their views. The dissidents said the Trinity was one being with three attributes, using the analogy of God the Father as the Sun, Christ as the sun's light, and the Holy Spirit as the heat. This view was rejected by the emperor, who argued the Trinity should be understood as three equal and distinct suns, rather than as one sun with three attributes. On the Godhead, they stated on the basis of John 1:18 ("No one has ever seen God . . .") that "God had no *malke'* ('trait,' 'appearance') like the *malke'* of man." That is, God does not look like (have the traits or appearance of) man. Zar'a Ya'eqob, however, argued on the basis of Genesis 1:26–27 ("Let us make man in our image and our likeness . . .") that since man was made in the image of God, this meant the "nature of his invisible Godhead has traits like man's."[93]

The emperor argued that the analogy of the Trinity as one sun implied a limitation of the Trinity to one aspect only: the *sem* ("name") without including *malke'* ("appearance," "stature," "hypostasis," "figure," "form"). Zar'a Ya'eqob sometimes considered these anti-Trinitarians simply as mistaken Christians, but at other times, as in the *Mashafa Berhan* ("Book of Light"), he said the people of Ethiopia considered them Jews (*ayhud*) because of their tendency to emphasize only one aspect of the Trinity.[94]

To refute the anti-Trinitarian teachings of this group, Zar'a Ya'eqob wrote homilies, such as the "Homily in Honor of St. John the Evangelist" and the "Homily in Honor of Saturday."[95] In the latter, for example, he criticized the anti-Trinitarian group, stating: "O you heretic, enemy of truth, friend of the Jews [*ayhud*], why do you deny the personhood of the Trinity, although you have been baptized in the name of the Trinity."[96] In the same work, he stated: "When a serpent kills, it kills the body, but these heretics kill the soul and the body. They make a son of hell one who listens to their teaching because they teach him Judaism [*gabra ayhud*]."[97] Probably all three of these Zamika' elites went into exile—possibly joining *ayhud* communities—or were executed by the king.[98]

An attempted coup d'etat against Zar'a Ya'eqob involved several high officials and their relatives, whom he accused of using magical powers and of becoming *ayhud* in order to destroy him. One of them was Galawdewos, who "became a Jew, abandoning his Christianity and denying Christ."[99] Another involved was the *behet wadada* Isayeyyas and his wife. Isayeyyas was accused of becoming a "magician."[100] In another passage, the king clearly equated magician with Jew:

> But you, Christian, do not listen to the magician but go according to the teaching of this book; the book, whose content is drawn from the eighty-one canonical scriptures, deals with the worship of God in a pure heart free of superstition and with a reproach to the magicians who are called Jews and idolators.[101]

In the view of the editor of the book composed by the king, *Tomara Tesbe't* ("Epistle of Humanity"), the book itself was probably written as a result of this coup, in order to show what would happen to rebels. Speaking against the rebels, the king said: "You deserve death and not kingship, O magician who is called a Jew and an idolator."[102]

Zar'a Ya'eqob also labeled other opponents *ayhud*, such as the Estifanosites. A passage from a chronicle by the Estifanosites describes their persecution at the hands of the king. He justified his harsh actions by calling them Jews: "He [Zar'a Ya'eqob] severely tortured his [Estifanos's] followers too, after him, and called them enemies of Mary, likening them, for the public, with the Jews, because of their refusal to prostrate themselves before the king, and so he executed them."[103]

These theological controversies thus involved the *ayhud* in two senses: those who took positions antithetical to the emperors were sometimes labeled *ayhud* in a derogatory sense, even if they were clearly Christians, and those who were considered really *ayhud* in a religious (and ethnic) sense. The king used *ayhud* as an epithet against his political enemies, whatever their actual religious beliefs. He also condemned those whom we must take to be religious Jews of the period, as for example, in the *Mashafa Milad* ("Book of the Nativity").[104]

In all of these ways, Zar'a Ya'eqob conceived of Judaism, however he interpreted it, as his main religious (ideological) enemy. Despite all his efforts, however, he was not able to eradicate its threat to imperial Orthodox unity. Although the last years of the fifteenth century are not well documented, conflicts with the *ayhud* clearly continued and sometimes played a role in power struggles in the central court.

Zar'a Ya'eqob's son, Ba'eda Maryam (1468–78), was in fact more successful than his father in suppressing actual Jewish revolts. After seven years his army defeated Amba Nahad, the leader of the *ayhud* in Sallamt, who promised not to revolt again, to restore churches, to reestablish Christianity, and to allow new royal regiments in their lands.[105]

During the thirty years after the death of Ba'eda Maryam, the *ayhud* took advantage of and perhaps contributed to power struggles at the central court to try and assert their independence in the Samen. Two such cases may have included the power struggle around 1485 during the regency of the boy-king Eskender (1478–94), and the six months of civil war in 1494 that led to the reign of Na'od (1494–1508). Eskender was said to have "joined the religion of the Franks" by 1484.[106] His pro-Catholic policies concerning the Sabbath and food prohibitions[107]—as was the case with Suseneyos later—may have resulted in actions that attacked not only the Judaic aspects of Orthodoxy, but also the position of the *ayhud* more directly. Fragmentary evidence taken in 1488 in Cairo suggests a revolt in Samen by the "descendants of Israel" had occurred "four years ago" against the Ethiopian king, and a war against the Samen Falasha during the reign of Eskender was mentioned in a later chronicle.[108]

By the reign of Na'od (1494–1508), the *ayhud* were seen as a serious threat to the central government. The hagiographical sources suggest some *ayhud* had only outwardly converted to Christianity and were still influential in court circles preaching their real beliefs, and perhaps plotting against the kings. Such agitation would, of course, have been facilitated by the atmosphere of intrigue during the regency of Eskender, and the six months of civil war in 1494. According to the contemporary *gadl* of Marha Krestos,

Na'od brought these *ayhud*, or wolves in sheep's clothing, before him in the first year of his reign, made them confess they were really Jews, and then executed many of them.[109]

The same events are recorded in a Miracle of Mary, the manuscript of which also contains other miracles that summarize much of the Jewish-Orthodox religious conflict since the reign of Zar'a Ya'eqob:

> Furthermore, listen, our brothers, to what has happened during our days when Satan, in order to fight the saints, raised enemies, many traitors, bitter Jews, small foxes who spoil our vineyard, and a wicked army which appointed them teachers. In order to avenge them, because of her Covenant, Our Lady Mary made a king for them on the throne of their father Na'od our king. She became a helper and a refuge for him. She revealed a mystery to our king Na'od before those Jews when he humiliated them in their courts, when they told him in their very silliness and foolishness, saying, "[God] was not born from Mary," Our Lady. He, on his part, became wrathful against them, like Elijah the zealot, burning by her love. He killed some of them with spears; he made some of them fall by his sword; he burnt some of them with fire; he tortured some of them in prisons, interrogating them and bringing them to the court of litigation, suffering, shame, misery, nakedness, (and) destitution for the sake of her glory and for the sake of the Covenant of Our Holy Lady Mary. In this way, he exterminated those foxes found in the garden of the sheep.[110]

Another source, the *gadl* of Habta Maryam, the father confessor of King Na'od, also views the king as a deliverer from the power of the *ayhud*.[111] Intrigues at the central court that seemed to have involved *ayhud* may have been connected to Falasha revolts in Samen that are documented by Islamic, Jewish, and later Ethiopian sources.[112]

The chronicles, hagiographies, and oral traditions thus document a connection and a process of transformation of the *ayhud* to the *Falasha* from the early fourteenth to the early sixteenth centuries. The transformation occurred in the context of political-religious ferment and struggle among Orthodox Christians, Muslims, *ayhud*, and followers of other religious beliefs for the control of the evolving Ethiopian region. Warfare and bloodshed to control the political economy of the Horn constituted part of the struggle. Another part involved an ideological battle waged within Orthodoxy as well as between Orthodoxy and the *ayhud* in particular. The evidence shows that *ayhud* not only was a derogatory label for whomever was not considered Orthodox at a particular time but also was a specific group or community. During the fifteenth century, this community began to redefine itself, particularly by modifying its economy and religion under the influence of Orthodox Church and state domination.

From *Ayhud* to Falasha: Economy and Religion, 1380–1508

The *ayhud* responded to conquest and evangelization by elaborating the economic and religious institutions and practices which laid the basis for the Beta Israel–Falasha identity that has lasted up to the recent past. Some *ayhud* adopted artisan crafts and others—stimulated by renegade Christians—founded monastic communities in which they developed a literature, liturgy, historical traditions, and a sense of social separation that created and perpetuated a new sense of group identity.

Hence, the fifteenth century was critical for the beginning of caste formation, a process that culminated in the mid-nineteenth century. These significant developments did not mark the beginning of the *ayhud*-Falasha as a people, but the fifteenth century was crucial for the emergence of the institutions and practices that characterized the Beta Israel–Falasha as a group for the next several centuries. Before analyzing the transformation, it will be useful to summarize what was known about *ayhud* society already.

Ayhud Society and Religion

The content of *ayhud* society and religion in various Ethiopian regions in the period before extensive Christian evangelization under the new dynasty is very obscure, and only a few brief indications can be gleaned from the sources. According to the Ethiopic sources already cited above, the *ayhud* were said to have the same origins as the Christian community, that is, to have come with Menilek I, to have had the *Orit* (Old Testament), and to believe that a Messiah would come but had not come yet.[113]

As documented in Ethiopic sources already discussed on the theological controversies, the *ayhud* were known as strict anti-Trinitarian monotheists and as followers of the Saturday Sabbath (*sanbata ayhud*). As they became better known to the outside Jewish world in the fifteenth and sixteenth centuries, their strict observation of the Sabbath that required all fires to be extinguished was especially noted as a Jewish custom.[114]

Two annual religious observances were recorded, at least by inference: the day of supplication known as *mehellanna* or later as *segd*, and the Fast of Esther (*soma aster*). But foreign Jews especially emphasized that they did not celebrate Chanukah and did not have the Talmud or speak Hebrew, although they did speak their own language, presumed to be Agaw.[115]

On the other hand, since these sources are all from the fifteenth or sixteenth century, we do not know when or from where such practices originated. Both *mehellanna* and *soma aster* have comparable observances among Ethiopian Christians, from whom they may derive, either during this period or some centuries earlier.[116]

Ayhud political-economic structure is not known in any detail. Those in fourteenth-century Begamder were prosperous and cultivated their own fields. They were said to have vineyards and herds of cattle in the *Gadla Gabra Iyyasus*. By the sixteenth century, they were still somewhat independent in Samen and Sallamt, and were organized around four or five princes, or kings, though some were said to be shepherds. They even had regalia of kingship, such as horns and crowns. These aspects of their society were changing during the three hundred years of conflict between 1332 and 1632.[117]

Falasha Artisans

Information on the material basis of *ayhud* society before and just after the critical war with Yeshaq is lacking, except to suggest briefly that they were prosperous. Both Christian written and Beta Israel oral sources focus on the political and religious concerns of the elites, rather than the material conditions of the masses. Abyssinian society was primarily agricultural and had practiced mixed farming and herding for several millennia B.C.E. Ironworking for making tools and weapons appears to have developed by the fifth century B.C.E., and numerous iron goods have been found dating to the Aksumite era. The plow was used in pre-Aksumite times and probably began to be iron-tipped as soon as ironworking knowledge developed. Ironworkers, masons, potters, jewelers, and other craftspeople flourished in urban Aksum.[118]

No direct information has been found, however, as to the ethnic or religious background of these artisans, or of the possible role of the *ayhud* in Aksum. Some Beta Israel traditions assert they had been artisans since their alleged origins in ancient Israel. To see all ancient blacksmiths as Falasha distorts the issue. Some Christian traditions assert that the "Jewish" usurper Gudit (Yodit or Esat) in the tenth century was supported by blacksmiths, but it remains unclear whether Gudit was in fact Jewish. In general, artisans before the fifteenth century cannot be identified as necessarily *ayhud*.[119]

In the fifteenth century, it was alleged that Zar'a Ya'eqob had some blacksmiths at his court executed, accusing them of sorcery, and the *Gadla Marha Krestos* in the early sixteenth century refers to the evil eye of a blacksmith—both well-documented accusations against the Beta Israel in later centuries. Lebna Dengel (1508–40) issued a prohibition against giving communion to artisans in a monastery at Ankobar. Possibly these were the *tabib* noticed in that area by later observers (see Chapter 1). None of these references, however, mentions the Falasha as such. The first unequivocal explicit reference to Falasha blacksmiths dates only to the seventeenth century.[120]

It is possible that those later called *ayhud* were already engaged in some craftwork in ancient times, perhaps focusing on smithing. But it is more logical to assume that such artisanry became part of the *ayhud*-Falasha economy only in the fifteenth century as their land began to be confiscated after their defeat by Yeshaq. Yeshaq reportedly gave them two choices: to convert or lose their land. Traditions assert that some, indeed, became Christians but that the main response was to refuse to convert. Henceforth, the Falasha—in provinces directly controlled by the Christian state—could continue to practice agriculture in the *wayna dega* fertile highland areas only as tenant farmers for the new Christian settlers and, therefore, probably had to supplement their income with craftwork.

Yeshaq may have provided an additional incentive for the newly landless to become blacksmiths in the workshops he established in order to improve his armies' weapons. Since the time of Amda Seyon (1314–44), the Muslim armies in conflict with the Christian kings had been better armed, especially for hand-to-hand combat, because they had a more plentiful supply of iron swords and daggers. The Ethiopians relied mainly on bows and arrows and throwing spears. Swords were imported from Muslim countries and used mainly on ceremonial occasions.[121] Dawit and later Yeshaq, in particular, were said to have imported Turkish and Egyptian technical advisors to supervise new workshops making swords and coats of mail.[122] Such workshops could have attracted Falasha workers, who may have already had some metalworking ability. Such a practice would have given rise to the traditions already mentioned that blacksmiths accompanied the kings' peregrinations at the wandering royal capitals.[123]

Falasha Dispersals and Monasticism

As some Falasha were becoming more dependent on craftwork, others who lost land in the productive highlands of Wagara and Dambeya dispersed to economically marginal areas such as Qwara, Armacheho, Qolla Wagara, Sagade, Walqayt, or Samen.[124] By the nineteenth century, the Beta Israel of Walqayt and Sagade were known as *foggara,* suggesting some had dispersed at an unknown time from Fogara, an area just east of Lake Tana.[125] But in most cases, the dispersals probably reinforced preexisting communities since the *ayhudaweyan* were living in Samen and Sagade, for example, at least as early as the fourteenth century.[126] The precise dates of Beta Israel dispersals are unknown, but traditions relate them to their defeats, especially that by Yeshaq (1413–30) in Wagara and continuing throughout this period.[127]

The ecologically marginal and isolated nature of these dispersal lands made them ideal for the new monastic communities the Beta Israel created during this era, in the same way that Christians were establishing monasteries in frontier areas.[128] Beta Israel monasticism, indeed, fits into the general pattern of the revival of Orthodox monasticism in Shawa and Tigray which often developed as a response to the loss of independence to centralizing political authorities.[129]

Monasticism for the Beta Israel was even more fundamentally important as the institution became the main basis for the development of the distinctive Beta Israel–Falasha identity that was to last for the next several centuries. The monks created and passed down the liturgy, literature, the code of social interaction, and the detailed oral historical traditions that defined the meaning of the Beta Israel experience and allowed them to survive as an identifiable group despite conquest and land expropriation.

They must have developed the institution of monasticism as a result of contact with Orthodoxy, probably during the fifteenth or no earlier than the fourteenth century, the period of most intense *ayhud*-Christian contacts. Christian monks tried to convert the *ayhud* but were in turn sometimes sufficiently attracted to the existing *ayhud* religion to abandon Christianity altogether and join *ayhud* communities.

The dominant Beta Israel traditions assert that the origins of their monasticism and much of their religious life were due to a man named *abba* Sabra, who was possibly a Christian from Shawa who came to Dambeya or Wagara and who may have either built a church at Danqaz or joined Yeshaq Dabr in Wagara before renouncing Christianity and adopting "the faith of the Israelites."[130] *Abba* Sabra is usually linked to his disciple, Sagga Amlak, an alleged son of Zar'a Ya'eqob, and hence dates from the mid-fifteenth century.[131]

After joining the *ayhud*, *abba* Sabra established a monastery at Mt. Hohwara in the Armacheho region, west of the Wagara plateau. This location continued to be one of the main centers of Beta Israel monasticism up through the early twentieth century.[132] In addition to seeing him as the founder of Beta Israel monasticism, traditions attribute to him almost all elements of the Beta Israel religious life, including teaching the correct life based on the *Orit* (Pentateuch, or more generally, Old Testament) "in all the regions where he thought that the Falashas applied it incorrectly,"[133] writing a collection of prayers and other religious books[134] and instituting at least part of the religious calendar.[135]

One of his most important accomplishments was the establishment of the Beta Israel laws of purity, called the *attenkun* ("don't touch me") laws, a characteristic aspect of Beta Israel life.[136] As a means of maintaining their societal integrity and structural separation from Christian society, the Beta Israel practice of social isolation based on their laws of purity became an important technique that received its greatest elaboration and is most clearly documented for the early nineteenth century, when it formed an important part of the developing caste relationship with Orthodox society. Its roots lie with *abba* Sabra and the fifteenth century, when greater contact with and influence by Christian society necessitated such laws of separation if group identity were to be maintained.

The origin of Beta Israel monasticism is intertwined with an alleged son of King Zar'a Ya'eqob. According to traditions, this son became attracted to the teachings of *abba* Sabra and decided to convert to the Beta Israel religion. After a testing period during which he had to eat special foods, he was allowed to join them. Then he and *abba* Sabra settled down to live at Hohwara. Zar'a Ya'eqob offered a reward for information concerning the location of his son. One man saw him and led the king's army to the place, but when they got there, God hid the Beta Israel settlement from view. The son thereby acquired the name Sagga Amlak ("Grace of God") among the Beta Israel because God had saved him by his grace from discovery. The king never did find his son.[137]

The phenomenon of Christians joining an *ayhud* community during this period is documented in written Christian sources. The case of the Christian monk, Qozmos, during the late fourteenth century has already been discussed. Another case, which has interesting similarities to the traditions about Sagga Amlak, has been documented from a Christian "Miracle of Mary." A Christian cleric joined an *ayhud* community until one day "the ruler of the Christians" sent an army which captured him despite his attempts to hide on the "mountain of the Jews." He was brought to the Christian ruler, who executed him and scattered his dismembered body to several regions as an example of what happens to apostates.[138] Rather than Sagga Amlak, this may be the story of Zamika'el, one of the "heretics" at the court of Zar'a Ya'eqob.[139]

Given the present state of the documentation, it is impossible to correlate precisely the oral and written sources, but the very existence of such traditions, as well as the existence of clear procedures among the Beta Israel for the acceptance of converts into the community,[140] suggests the significance of such phenomena. Whatever the exact nature of the *ayhud* religious practices before the fifteenth century, about which there is scant documentation, the Beta Israel–Falasha religion as it has come down to us clearly dates mainly to this critical period of *abba* Sabra and Sagga Amlak, probably in the mid-fifteenth century.

There is somewhat sketchier information about several other early Beta Israel religious figures, who may have been involved in the establishment of monasticism in different regions and/or as authors of religious books. These include *abba* Saquyan and *abba* Halen, both from Qwara and both mentioned in Beta Israel prayers.[141] In Beta Israel traditions, Gorgoryos founded an ascetic order in Walqayt and wrote a book, *The Apocalypse of Gorgorios.*[142] But this Gorgoryos was clearly a Christian author, and the *Apocalypse* was most likely originally a Christian work.[143]

Qozmos or Gabra Iyyasus may have introduced monasticism to the Beta Israel,[144] but the documentation is not explicit. Perhaps the ambiguity concerning the origins of Beta Israel monasticism reflects regional variations. *Abba* Sabra went to Hohwara; *abba* Halen and *abba* Saquyan were in Qwara; and Qozmos went to Samen. By the nineteenth century, the main centers of Beta Israel monasticism included Samen, Hohwara, Qwara, Qolla Wagara, and Saqqalt.[145] Perhaps different individuals played a principal role in starting monasteries in these various regions at different times.[146]

Literature, Liturgy, and Oral Traditions

The development of monasticism was a key to the survival of a distinctive Beta Israel religion and was at the heart of the emerging caste relationship with the dominant society that allowed the group to resist total incorporation despite extensive cultural influences. Acculturation was evident: the texts were written in Ge'ez, and the literature and liturgy were essentially derived from Christian sources. But resistance to incorporation was also part of the developing caste relationship as the monks used the texts and liturgy to enhance a separate consciousness and religious praxis while passing down the oral historical traditions that recorded resistance to the Christian state.

Beta Israel literature was mostly derived from Christian Ethiopic (Ge'ez) sources. The most important texts are clearly the *Orit* (Pentateuch/

Old Testament), the apocryphal and pseudepigraphical books such as Jubilees and Enoch, and the special treatise, *Te'ezaza Sanbat* ("Commandments of the Sabbath").

The Christian Ethiopic Bible was probably translated from the Greek during the early classical period of Church expansion in Ethiopia, between the fourth and seventh centuries.[147] The books of Jubilees and Enoch are still considered an essential part of the Ethiopian Bible; indeed, the complete text of Enoch is extant only in Ethiopic.[148] The most complete and accurate manuscript of Jubilees is also the Ethiopic version.[149]

It is not known precisely when the Beta Israel acquired these books, but the *Orit* was "copied" for them by Qozmos during the late fourteenth century.[150] And in the mid-fifteenth century, *abba* Sabra "taught" the *Orit,* suggesting it was already in the possession of the *ayhud* by then.[151]

The *Te'ezaza Sanbat* is, along with the *Orit,* the most important Beta Israel religious text. Although in its complete form, it is known only among the Beta Israel, its parts were compiled from various sources, such as the Christian book, *Dersana Sanbat*. It also draws heavily on the *Orit,* especially the books of Exodus, Jubilees, and Enoch, and was influenced by Arabic texts.[152] Its personification of the Sabbath may seem an original element, but some Christian works also personify Sunday.[153] The supposed originality of the work, hence, comes more from its combination of material from various sources and the uses to which it was put in the society than from its being a work originally written independently by the Beta Israel.[154]

The dating of the compilation is problematical. The Christian-Arabic influences in the work suggest a date not earlier than the fourteenth century when such influences from the Coptic Church in Egypt became significant in Ethiopia.[155] But it is likely that different parts of the *Te'ezaza Sanbat* derive from different times and, therefore, it is indeed possible that the different parts were brought together by *abba* Sabra in the mid-fifteenth century as a central part of the Beta Israel religious redefinition of that century.

Beta Israel prayers are an apparent example of indigenous creations, less directly derived from Christian texts. Some prayers have passages in Qwarenya, an ancient Agaw language.[156] One writing called the *Sanbata Sanbat* has about 20 percent of its text in Agaw.[157] Several of the prayers mention *abba* Sabra and Sagga Amlak, suggesting their composition during or shortly after the lives of these two men, probably in the fifteenth century, and other prayers were said to have been written directly by *abba*

Sabra. But even the Beta Israel prayers often have direct Ethiopian Christian models, including even Beta Israel magical prayers which contain Christian elements.[158]

Several other texts appear to have survived only among the Beta Israel, though they were probably copied from Christian texts no longer extant. These include the *Apocalypse of Gorgorios,* the *Death of Aron,* and *Abba Elijah,* all of which may date to the fourteenth or fifteenth century.[159]

Other Beta Israel writings that were certainly copied and adopted from Christian Ethiopic texts include the *Apocalypse of Baruch* (*Fifth Baruch*); *Testaments of Abraham, Isaac, and Jacob;* the *Death of Moses;* the *Book of Angels;* and *Ezra.*[160] For some of these texts, both versions are still extant, such as the *Apocalypse of Baruch.* In that book, the Christian opening, "In the name of the Father, the Son and the Holy Spirit," was replaced by the Beta Israel formula: "Blessed be God, the Lord of Israel." In general, references to Christ were replaced by "God"; "church" became "sanctuary"; and "Gospel" became "Book." Some less obvious Christological elements were overlooked by the Beta Israel copyists.[161]

Thus, Beta Israel literature is essentially derived from Ethiopic Christian sources, even apparently those works which had seemed least derivative, such as the *Te'ezaza Sanbat* and the prayers.[162] The key to this literature is not their sources, but their uses in the new society. The same is as true for Ethiopian Christianity. Both derived a large portion of their texts from sources outside their societies, but both adapted them and used them for their own ends to maintain a degree of independence. The Beta Israel had a more difficult task in maintaining societal integrity because their source was geographically and culturally contiguous, while Ethiopian Christianity could develop independently because its influences and connections were the more distant Syria, Alexandria, Jerusalem, and later Rome.

In the case of the Beta Israel, the uses to which they put the texts suggest creative attempts to avoid assimilation despite acculturation. In a time of military defeat and economic decline, the new monastic communities led the way as the Beta Israel attempted to manipulate Christian cultural elements to maintain societal integrity and autonomy. Ironically, both groups were drawing on their common ancient Hebraic heritage while interpreting it differently. The Christian state, with an imperial ideology embedded in the *Kebra Nagast,* viewed itself as the legitimate successor of ancient Israel with the right to impose its rule over the peoples of the area, while the Beta Israel used the ancient Hebraic heritage as a means of resisting oppression and maintaining a coherent community[163] in the same way that ancient Israel has served as an inspiration for other oppressed peoples in world history.[164]

To the Beta Israel, the *Te'ezaza Sanbat* was "the Book of Israel, concerning the greatness and the glory of the Sabbath of Israel."[165] On the "last day" in facing God's judgment, the female figure Sabbath would "intercede for those who belong to her" (those who had followed the rigid Sabbath precepts) in order to achieve "eternal rest."[166] In this apocalyptic vision, whatever its sources and origins, the *Te'ezaza Sanbat* may be seen as the Beta Israel national epic comparable to the *Kebra Nagast* for Ethiopian Christians.

Recent research on the Beta Israel liturgy clearly documents its derivation from the Christian liturgy.[167] A comparative analysis of portions of the Beta Israel liturgy and the Ethiopian Christian monastic liturgy demonstrates their intimate connection:

> Contemporary liturgical comparison and an early manuscript source thus closely relate the Falasha prayerhouse liturgy to that of the Ethiopian church and its monastic institutions. They are consistent with Beta Israel oral traditions that monks who joined their community in the fourteenth and fifteenth centuries wrote their prayers and established Beta Israel liturgical tradition. Comparison of contemporary *wazema* ["evening ritual"] texts in the two traditions reveals remarkable parallelism in general formal organization and specific scriptural sources.[168]

Likewise, the Beta Israel religious calendar and liturgical cycle is derived from the Ethiopian calendar and the same sources it is based on: the Alexandrian Jewish calendar, the book of Enoch, and various Arabic-Coptic computus treatises that have been labeled the *Abu Shaker*.[169] As with the Beta Israel liturgy and literature, the Jewish influences were received through the filter of Ethiopian Christianity.

The evidence of Christian–Beta Israel connections from the religious calendar of festivals and fasts, therefore, reinforces the evidence from the literature and liturgy. The connections were close and intimate. Both drew on a common fund of religious belief and practice that is still vague in outline due to a relative paucity of sources concerning pre-Christian Aksum. Certainly during the period of about 1380–1508, the Beta Israel religion was greatly influenced and stimulated by Christian contacts. This was undoubtedly the single most important period for such influences since the murky Aksumite period, of which we may never know very much. The influences were so intense as to have suggested to some scholars that Beta Israel society and religion were *simply* formed by dissident Christians during this period.[170]

On the other hand, we must also use the evidence from the chronicles and oral traditions that document the resistance of the Beta Israel to Christian submersion. Not only did the Beta Israel monks borrow—or even convert—from Christian society, but they also tried to formulate the means by which their people could resist assimilation. Artisanry provided a semi-autonomous means of subsistence despite the loss of land. Social separation provided a means to resist biological assimilation. The monastic communities provided the needed intellectual leadership to formulate the ideological basis for separation and resistance at that time, and the means by which to pass down a legacy of heroic resistance through oral historical traditions that would inspire future generations. The detailed and precise data in these traditions since the conflict of Gedewon with Yeshaq—even if the various versions do not always agree with each other—also reinforce the interpretation that the fifteenth century was a key period in these transformations. It was essentially due to the key role of the Beta Israel monks and monastic communities since the fifteenth century as creators, synthesizers, codifiers, and perpetuators of religion and history that a Beta Israel identity survived and at times even flourished despite conquest and oppression. The next century was one of transition as the Beta Israel political leadership centered in the Samen continued to resist conquest by political-military means, even while the religious leadership of the monastic communities was formulating a new basis of identity.

Conquest and Incorporation of the Samen Beta Israel, 1508–1632

The Ethiopian state completed its expansion into northwestern Ethiopia during the sixteenth century, despite the heroic and well-documented resistance of the Samen Beta Israel. They resisted domination by either the state or by outsiders by assisting a variety of third forces, such as the Muslim invaders against the Ethiopian state, then the Portuguese contingent against the Muslims, and finally, various crown pretenders against the Ethiopian kings, always taking advantage of the rugged terrain of the Samen. Their ultimate defeat ended forever the political autonomy of the Beta Israel, marking the conclusion of a 300-year period of sporadic warfare in Begamder, Dambeya, Wagara, Walqayt, Sagade, and Samen. During this final stage of the conflict, many Beta Israel suffered death, dispersal, enslavement, and land confiscation. Along with the other defeated minorities in this region, the Falasha, or *Kayla,* as they also began to be called, were forcibly incorporated as a part of the landless lower class within the Ethiopian empire.

Simultaneously, however, the state's need for loyal soldiers and skilled artisans as the kings began to build more permanent stone palaces led to the emergence of more peaceful incorporative trends that would characterize Beta Israel–Ethiopian government relations in the ensuing centuries. Some Beta Israel were drafted as Falasha regiments under the king's personal control. Others probably first began to work as stonemasons during this century. A few apparently acquired titles such as *azmach* ("general"). On the other hand, it appears Beta Israel monks continued to assert their authority in opposition to these incorporative forces, thus leading to a secular-religious tension within Beta Israel society that would last into the next, Gondar, era.

International Factors, 1508–1597

During the sixteenth century, the Abyssinian dynasty was shaken out of its relative isolation by international forces that resulted in the birth of a "new age."[171] These forces included the climax of its centuries-old conflict with regional Islamic powers, as the local war with the Adal-based Ahmad ibn Ibrahim al-Ghazi "Gragn" ("left-handed") between 1527 and 1543 involved the two major world powers in the Red Sea area, the Ottoman Turks and the Portuguese. Both brought with them a more deadly military technology; in addition, the Portuguese relationship eventually created deep religious divisiveness that shook the foundations of the Abyssinian state and Orthodox Church alliance.

The Ottoman Turks first moved into the area with the takeover of Egypt in 1517 and then began a gradual expansion down both Red Sea coasts. They assisted the Islamic invasion of Ahmad ibn Ibrahim by providing firearms and skilled riflemen. Later, from their foothold at the port of Massawa they tried to influence Ethiopian politics, until repulsed by Sarsa Dengel (1563–97).[172]

Portugal had had contact with the Abyssinian kings since the late fifteenth century and sent a large expedition to the region at the invitation of the court which stayed between 1520 and 1526. Then in 1541, at the request of Lebna Dengel, a 400-man Portuguese force arrived in the country and helped defeat Ahmad in 1543. Portuguese and other Jesuit efforts for the next half-century eventually converted two kings to Catholicism, Za-Dengel (1605–7) and Suseneyos (1607–32), and nearly undermined the dynasty.[173]

The main regional forces in this period were the *jihad* of Ahmad "Gragn" and the accompanying Oromo migrations. The Islamic invasion facilitated the Oromo migrations, and together these forces redrew the ethnic-linguistic and religious map of what is today central and southern Ethiopia.[174]

An international economic factor that began to have a greater impact on the region was a significant increase in the Red Sea slave trade during this century, a trend which continued and climaxed in the mid-nineteenth century. The slaves were exported mainly through Massawa to the north-east, and through the new Funj kingdom of the Sudan to the northwest, which resulted in expanded relations in that direction.[175]

These international factors resulted in several internal changes that directly affected the dynasty's relationships with the Beta Israel: the gradual northwestern displacement of the Ethiopian capital to the Beta Israel heartland, an increase in slave raiding, and a reorganization of the military regimental system by Sarsa Dengel. The heightened pressure on the Beta Israel in Samen culminated in a series of bitter wars as they resisted imperial incursions; at the same time, however, the Beta Israel were incorporated more closely into the Ethiopian political economy as soldiers and artisans.

The Muslims and the Portuguese, 1508–1559

During the Christian–Islamic wars of 1527–43, the Beta Israel tried to manipulate the new international forces involved to their own advantage. Ahmad ibn Ibrahim burst upon the scene with a force that ultimately resulted in the control of most of the Ethiopian empire and the forced conversion of much of the Christian population to Islam.[176] Ahmad around 1535 reached the northwest, where he defeated an Ethiopian force in Wagara. The general of the king's forces then fled to Samen, where he was pursued by Ahmad.[177]

Some of Ahmad's advisors argued against entering the Samen, which they considered the "most difficult" region in Abyssinia to fight a war because of its rugged terrain that contained numerous natural "strongholds and fortresses." Ahmad replied: "We will not abandon the Samen until we have converted it, for it is the head of all the country; if it believes, all the country will believe."[178]

Lebna Dengel's general, Sa'ul, took refuge at Bahr Amba, a royal stronghold at least since the reign of Zar'a Ya'eqob.[179] As the Muslim chronicler noted:

> The Samen was possessed by the Jews of Abyssinia who call themselves Falasha in their language. . . . The men of Bahr Amba had reduced them to servitude forty years ago, obliging them to serve them and to labor for them. After the victory of the *imam* over the general Sa'ul, they [the Falasha] all came to find him [Ahmad] . . . and told him: "Between us and the men of Bahr Amba there is an enmity that dates from forty years; now we are going to kill those who remain and we will take their fortresses."[180]

Ironically, the Jewish name of the king's general, Sa'ul, suggests he may have been of Beta Israel origin, hence illustrating the incorporation of some Falasha into royal service.[181]

Ahmad's soldiers and the Falasha together took over Bahr Amba. Ahmad appointed a Muslim governor over the area and went on to establish control over the northwest region. Thus, Falasha assistance was valuable in Ahmad's conquest of at least the Bahr Amba area which he used as a launching pad to consolidate his control over the rest of the region.[182]

A second tantalizing but not unambiguous reference to the Beta Israel and Ahmad occurs in the short royal chronicle. In an Ethiopian battle against Ahmad in 1539 or 1540, many Christian leaders were killed and others were captured by Ahmad. As the chronicle states: "Gedewon and Yodit, the mother [?]-in-law of the king [*hamata negus*], and a large number of soldiers were taken as well as considerable booty."[183] This reference suggests that Gedewon and Yodit, the traditional names for Beta Israel leaders, were still on the side of King Lebna Dengel as late as 1539, if this chronology is correct. The editor of one version of this chronicle asserted in his notes that Gedewon "did not hesitate" to switch sides (apparently after he was captured?),[184] though the text itself only says they were captured. Another editor/commentator on the Ethiopian chronicles refers to this same incident as meaning that "Gideon and Judith," the king and queen of the Jews in Samen, "after having suffered much from Gragne, had at last rebelled and joined him."[185]

The assumption that Gedewon and Yodit did join Ahmad after having been captured by him may be justified, but the chronicle does not state that explicitly. Interestingly, only one of the editors commented on the chronicle's assertion that Yodit was the mother [?]-in-law of the king (*hamata negus*), meaning she must have been related by marriage to the royal family.

Other traditions support this view by stating that Ya'eqob, a son of Lebna Dengel who died about 1550, had married a Falasha named Wesenabi. Although no other information seems available about her, she was probably related to Gedewon—perhaps his sister—and hence, a member of the Beta Israel ruling family, and therefore called Yodit in the chronicles.[186] If this reference is accurate, it is not so surprising, as intermarriage was a traditional means by which Ethiopian kings tried to incorporate their subjects into the realm.[187]

So the Falasha of Bahr Amba, at least, had welcomed Ahmad's invasion about 1535 as a means of freeing themselves from Ethiopian rule. The Falasha as a whole, under the leadership of Gedewon, may have come to that strategy in 1539, four years later.

But when the Portuguese force, requested by Lebna Dengel, finally reached the country in 1541 and his son, Galawdewos (1540–59), was the new king, the Beta Israel again switched sides and actively aided the Portuguese force against the Muslims.[188] In one incident, the Beta Israel assisted da Gama in retaking an *amba* from the Muslims, after which the Beta Israel leader was made governor of the area. According to the Portuguese sources, he and twelve other Beta Israel converted to Christianity as well,[189] but the main Beta Israel interest was probably to escape Islamic overlordship.

In any case, between mid-1542 and February 1543, when Ahmad was killed, the Samen became practically the headquarters of Galawdewos and the Portuguese forces, and the *imam* was finally killed just east of Lake Tana.[190] Some Beta Israel traditions put so much emphasis on their positive relationship with the Portuguese as to suggest it was they who "brought" the Portuguese to Ethiopia.[191]

Although the sources are vague, Galawdewos was mainly concerned with Oromo incursions from the South,[192] and probably desired good relations with the Beta Israel in his rear. Beta Israel traditions have a vague but positive view of Galawdewos, saying in general, "he liked them very much."[193] Other traditions refer to him stopping the persecution of the Beta Israel that in some areas dated back to the fifteenth-century wars with Yeshaq.[194] His chronicle praised his policies, characterized by his sense of justice to the poor, strangers, and workers and said he "did not scorn those who performed hard labor but inveighed against those who were lazy."[195]

Galawdewos was also the first king who broke the pattern of the wandering capitals and after 1549 built a "city" in the Waj district of Shawa as a refuge for people dispersed in the upheavals of the Islamic wars. It included a royal palace ornamented by gold and precious stones worked by Syrian and Armenian artists, as well as "Francs" and Egyptian engineers. He restored churches and built new churches and monasteries, the most famous of which was Tadbaba Maryam.[196]

Perhaps the Beta Israel worked as masons on these buildings, in view of their good relations with Galawdewos and their known role in such work a century later in Gondar. But the evidence is only suggestive, as the royal chronicle does not mention the Beta Israel at all and the oral traditions are vague.

Rebellions and Slave Raiding, 1555–1597

The good relations with Galawdewos came to an end near the conclusion of his reign. In 1555 or 1556, a traveler who went through Wagara reported that the Falasha were "restless," and another source stated they rebelled that year.[197] They were probably feeling the imposition of the royal presence in the region and having rebuilt their strength during a decade of peace decided to reassert themselves.

After the death of Galawdewos, his brother Minas (1559–63) was determined to crush the Beta Israel and started a war against their leader Rade'et in the Samen in 1559–60. A Jesuit on the Red Sea coast heard from a merchant from Dambeya that the Falasha had been willing to submit and pay taxes, but that Minas had demanded that they all convert to Christianity as well, and this they had rejected.[198] Minas, therefore, mounted an expedition against them, but it was unsuccessful.[199] Beta Israel traditions asserted that Minas stopped his attack after a prophecy that he would not be successful. He then made a treaty with them and brought 12,000 Falasha troops into his army.[200] Even if the number of men is exaggerated, the tradition illustrates a phenomenon that was to become prominent under later emperors.

After this battle against Minas, there were no wars for twenty years. The situation changed rapidly in the late 1570s as Sarsa Dengel (1563–97) carried out a series of bloody campaigns against the heroic resistance of the Samen Falasha. This sudden change may have been due to the increased importance of the "northern factor" in Ethiopian international relations, which included the defense of the realm against Jesuit and Turkish manipulations and the desire to take advantage of increased trade opportunities with the Funj kingdom in the Sudan and through the Red Sea port of Massawa. In 1578, Sarsa Dengel finally marched against and defeated Yeshaq, the local Red Sea governor who had allied himself with the Turks.[201]

This campaign in Tigray marked a climax in Sarsa Dengel's northward thrust that had begun in 1571, when he established his capital in the Emfraz region, east of Lake Tana.[202] Although, of course, he campaigned in many parts of the empire, sometime before 1586 he had a permanent stone palace erected at Guzara near Emfraz.[203] This first stone palace in the northwest illustrated the gradual transference of the Ethiopian capital to this region that was to culminate in the Gondar dynasty. This new location of the capital in the Begamder-Dambeya-Gondar triangle was rather ideally placed to deal with the Turks to the northeast, the Sudanese Funj kingdom to the northwest, and the Oromo migrations from the south. Of course, the establishment of the capital here increased the pressure on the Beta Israel in Samen as the king sought to achieve full control over the Tana-Takkaze region.

Thus, the king's desire to control this key area led him to carry out several campaigns between 1579 and the 1590s against the Falasha who had been growing ever stronger since their defeat of Minas in 1560. The fact that these battles are the best-documented in the 300-year history of the Beta Israel–Ethiopian wars suggests the king and court took their political importance seriously, even though these conflicts, along with many of the campaigns of Sarsa Dengel, seemed to be merely slave-raiding expeditions. Sarsa Dengel's slave raiding against Gafat, Damot, the Oromo, and others may have helped increase the Red Sea slave trade and led him to open up new trade relations with the Funj kingdom, but his campaigns in Samen against the Beta Israel also had the clear political purpose of consolidating his control of the northwest.[204]

Sarsa Dengel's first battle with the Beta Israel took place between October and December 1579 with the king returning to his capital by March 1580.[205] The two main reasons given for the conflict in the chronicles are that Rade'et, the Beta Israel leader, had refused to pay tribute, and that he had belligerently renamed the peaks of Samen after those of ancient Israel.[206] Beta Israel traditions personalize the conflict by stating that Sarsa Dengel's wife had been insulted by a Beta Israel *azmach* named Surafel who was at Sarsa Dengel's court.[207] Incidentally, such a tradition supports the view that some Beta Israel had been incorporated into the king's army, perhaps during the time of Minas (see above). Surafel, then, could have been the leader or general over this regiment.

The initial phase of this battle began when the king arrived at the Wagara-Samen border and started pillaging Muslims and Jews who lived in Shawada. But upon hearing that these Jews had previously been Christians and had come to the king's camp to submit peacefully and return to Christianity, he returned their cattle.[208]

In the second phase of this battle, Kaleb (or Kalef) carried out a scorched-earth policy to prevent the king from obtaining provisions. When bombarded with canon and attacked, Kaleb's forces fought back by rolling stones down the hill. But they were overcome and many were captured. One woman who was tied to her captor threw herself off a cliff, taking him with her to death. Others followed her example. Even the Ethiopian chronicler, who was an eyewitness, expressed his admiration of Falasha bravery, comparing it with that of the ancient Israelites against the Romans. Although Kaleb escaped death in this conflict, he was said to have gone mad over all the killing.[209]

Sarsa Dengel next moved on to attack Rade'et in his *amba*. Eventually, Rade'et had to send messages to the king appealing for mercy. Rade'et was pardoned but was led away in chains to exile in Waj (in Shawa). The short chronicle noted, significantly, that Rade'et's trumpets and crowns were taken to the island of Daga (in Lake Tana), thereby supposedly ending the Falasha kingship.[210]

Sarsa Dengel remained several months in Samen, holding a mass on Rade'et's *amba*, and later celebrating Christmas and then Easter of 1580 in the region. He also issued a proclamation to the scattered Falasha, telling them not to fear, to return home, and to obey the chiefs he had appointed over them.[211]

A second campaign against the Beta Israel, who were again led by Kaleb, occurred in 1582–83. The long chronicle omits any account of these years and the short chronicle states merely that Kaleb was defeated.[212]

A third major battle took place in 1587–88. Gweshan, the new Beta Israel leader, was said to have raided Wagara, burning harvests and houses. Sarsa Dengel personally attacked one *amba*, cutting off its water supply, and sent other forces against a second *amba*. Two Beta Israel chiefs led a counterattack, saying "it was better to die honorably than to live in shame." Others who had been captured attempted an escape, but were recaptured and then executed. About 200 women and girls, whose husbands and fathers had been killed, were sent as slaves to the king.[213] Gweshan, seeing that he was defeated, jumped off a cliff with fifty or sixty family members and followers, feeling that "rather than going with the king and touching the hand of a Christian, he preferred death."[214] Later, their bodies were recovered and their heads were cut off to be sent to the king. Gweshan's wife and sister were captured to be enslaved, but they also threw themselves off a cliff to their deaths. Gedewon, the brother of Gweshan, escaped by another path with about fifteen men.

It must have been at least by the time of these battles in 1587–88, if not earlier, that Sarsa Dengel took the Beta Israel woman, Harago, as his mistress. She was called *emabet* ("princess") and was probably a sister of Gedewon and hence a member of the Beta Israel ruling family.[215] Sarsa Dengel had no sons by his wife, but he had four by Harago, including Za-Maryam, whose birthdate is not known; Ya'eqob, born in 1590; Kefla Maryam; and Matako.[216]

One version of the chronicles used by Bruce says that after Sarsa Dengel's defeat of Gweshan, he marched to Qwara, "through the country where the Jews had many strongholds, and received everywhere their submission."[217] Certainly, the Beta Israel also lived in Qwara at this time, and this tradition may well be accurate though it is not substantiated elsewhere.

The short chronicle mentions that Sarsa Dengel went again to the Samen in 1593, but does not add details.[218] He spent the rest of his reign mostly in the south, fighting against the Oromo in particular. These wars often took on the characteristics of pillaging and slave-raiding. Even the chronicler noted that after the last Falasha conflict in 1588, the king promised to lead his army to other areas where they could find cattle, slaves, and other riches that had not been available in great quantity in the relatively poor Samen area.[219] Despite the name of "Gold Mountain" given to one of the Beta Israel capitals, the chronicler makes clear they were not a wealthy people.

For the Beta Israel, the consequences of the wars against Sarsa Dengel were mixed. Enslavement, death, and destruction were the results for many. But despite the loss of many battles, the war was not over. They maintained a degree of political autonomy into the reign of Suseneyos under Gedewon, who had escaped during the last battle. Indeed, the Beta Israel played an important role in the power struggles and succession disputes of the next few years.

Indirect evidence also suggests that some Beta Israel were being incorporated more closely into the Ethiopian political economy during the reign of Sarsa Dengel as artisans and soldiers. Since at least the reign of Zar'a Ya'eqob, a corps of artisans—masons called the *aqet zar*—had traveled with the king. During the reign of Sarsa Dengel, they constructed the camp whenever the king moved, and also acted as his advisors.[220] As masons, they must have worked on the stone palace Sarsa Dengel had built at

Guzara/ Guba'e (Emfraz) during the 1570s to 1580s. Since the Beta Israel were the principal masons of the Gondar kings later, and the palace of Guzara is in the Gondar style of architecture, perhaps the *aqet zar* were composed of Beta Israel masons, at least in part.[221]

Sarsa Dengel also instituted a reorganization of the army that may have had an impact on the Beta Israel. He began to dismantle the system of locally based garrisons of soldiers (*chewa*) who derived their income from tribute and often intermarried with the local population, thus becoming provincial powers somewhat removed from direct control by the king. Sarsa Dengel began to call upon the *chewa* to accompany him on campaigns outside of their own regions;[222] simultaneously, he increased the size of the royal bodyguard by recruiting new men directly dependent on him personally. These changes can be seen as a move toward a "national army"[223] and have usually been seen as positive changes to strengthen the empire.[224] On the other hand, such drastic changes probably weakened the local garrisons at any time the king was not personally present, particularly in the south, and hence facilitated the gradual Oromo incursions.[225] For the Beta Israel, these changes probably resulted in the incorporation of some of them—especially after their defeats by the king—into the new royal regiments. Beta Israel oral traditions which recall the important role of *azmach* Surafel at the king's court supports such an interpretation. Surafel may have been the leader of the Beta Israel regiments. As already noted above, Sa'ul, a general under Lebna Dengel and Galawdewos, was possibly a Beta Israel, and Minas was said to have brought some into his army,[226] and as will be seen below, this was a common occurrence during the Gondar dynasty, beginning with Fasiladas.

Thus, the impact of events on the Beta Israel during the last half of the sixteenth century was ambiguous. On the one hand, they suffered a great deal from warfare, pillaging, and enslavement and were almost, but not quite, totally defeated militarily. On the other hand, in this transitional era they apparently began to play more important roles within the larger society as artisans and soldiers, both of which became characteristic during later centuries. In the meantime, the Samen Beta Israel continued to try to manipulate the politics of the time to maintain a degree of political autonomy.

Succession Disputes and Crown Pretenders, 1597–1632

From Sarsa Dengel's death in 1597 to the accession of Fasiladas in 1632, the Beta Israel again became a factor to be reckoned with by the Abyssinian monarchs as they attempted to take advantage of the power struggles and religious uncertainties to improve their position. Although Sarsa Dengel did not have any sons by his wife, the immediate succession struggle was complicated by the four sons he had by Harago, his Beta Israel mistress. The oldest of her four sons by Sarsa Dengel was Za-Maryam, the first to be presented at court as Sarsa Dengel's successor, but he died six months later in 1595. So when the king died in 1597, the nobles proclaimed the seven-year-old Ya'eqob king, hoping to control him through a regency dominated by Sarsa Dengel's sons-in-law. Harago was not made a member of the regency, but her brother Gedewon was confirmed as governor of Samen.[227]

As Ya'eqob grew older, he tried to assert his right to rule without the regency. In 1602 he fought a battle against one of the regents, and the next year he was impeached, put on trial, dethroned, and exiled to another province, one of the few such cases in Ethiopian history. To legitimize this unusual deposition, Ya'eqob was accused of being an impostor (not the son of Sarsa Dengel), of renouncing Orthodoxy and engaging in pagan religious rites with the Oromo, of committing sexual abominations, and of being mentally deficient.[228] There is no evidence of his having done any of those things, or even that he was trying to impose his mother's Beta Israel religion. He was apparently "guilty of nothing other than of having tried to be king,"[229] although that assessment does not consider Ya'eqob's mother's origins. Perhaps the nobles were concerned about that question too, at least secondarily.

Za-Dengel then ruled briefly until Ya'eqob returned to the throne in 1605. Ya'eqob attempted to gain Portuguese support by granting some land to their priests near Maraba in Samen, a Beta Israel stronghold. He was, however, defeated in battle and killed on 10 March 1607 by Suseneyos, who then granted additional land to the Portuguese near Maraba.[230]

The circumstances of Ya'eqob's death were obscure and many rumors circulated during the reign of Suseneyos (1607–32), as many pretenders to the throne arose, claiming to be the real Ya'eqob. One reason for the rumors was the conversion to Catholicism first of Za-Dengel and later of Suseneyos, which aroused great opposition and conflict among the clergy who probably started many of the rumors.[231]

In the context of the disputed successions, the rebellions of crown pretenders, and religious controversy, the Beta Israel under Gedewon attempted to maintain a degree of political autonomy by supporting some of the rebels against the throne. Significantly, in these episodes, they seemed to realize total independence was no longer possible but wanted an Ethiopian king who would let them live in peace, maintain their own religion, and remain semi-autonomous governors of Samen.

One of the first *waranna* ("rebels") against whom Susneyos had to fight was "Kefla Maryam, the son of Harago." The conflict with Kefla Maryam and his brother Matako, both sons of Harago, occurred early in his reign. Both had been appointed to high positions when their brother Ya'eqob became king. When Suseneyos came to power, he accused them of abusing their power and had them executed.[232] Another rebel claiming to be Ya'eqob rose in Tigray in 1608 but was executed by the king.[233]

Though the Tigray rebel did not involve the Beta Israel, the next man claiming to be Ya'eqob, who arose in Sallamt in 1614 or 1615, was supported by Gedewon. While the governor of Sallamt was on campaign elsewhere, a man named Takluy (or Amdo) rose up and proclaimed: "I am king Ya'eqob, son of king Malak Saggad [Sarsa Dengel]." Officials of the governor arrested Takluy with no difficulty, but then "Gedewon the Falasha" sent a force that freed Takluy and brought the rebel to him. Gedewon assisted Takluy in raising an army, drawn especially from the poor and oppressed, hence challenging the king's rule in Samen as well as Sallamt.[234]

The king responded to Gedewon's efforts by ordering the governors of Samen and Sallamt back to their posts and sending an army to Samen. The rebellion continued, however, and Suseneyos sent reinforcements and then joined the battle himself. The forces ravaged the *ambas* of Meseraba, Hoch, and Hankase where they were said to have killed "all the Falasha."[235]

They besieged Gedewon's headquarters at Sagannat for two months, killing many of the troops of Gedewon and Takluy. One of Gedewon's men, Qamatra, "the greatest of all the Falasha" warriors, fought valiantly but was killed by a gunshot. Eventually, Gedewon appealed for mercy and struck a deal with the king, betraying Takluy to save his own life. The king then crucified and decapitated the rebel in the middle of his camp.[236]

The chronicler, as a supporter of King Suseneyos, accused *ras* Yamana, the king's brother and one of his generals, of being less than assiduous and even negligent in fighting Gedewon in this battle in 1616. The chronicler also noted that Yamana had agreed to let his son, Walaye, marry Gedewon's daughter, but Suseneyos was angry at Yamana and vetoed the idea.[237]

The next episode in Abyssinian–Beta Israel relations illustrates the increasingly harsh views of Suseneyos toward them. As he was mourning the deaths of his son and mother in April 1617, he ordered his officials Yolyos, Walda Hawaryat, and Yona'el to "kill all Falasha who lived in Wagara, Jan Faqara, Jan Arwa up to Semen, and Kinfaj, Gala, Zoj, Acheqan, and Jewi." Except for a few who were said to have escaped with one Finehas, "all Falasha" (men) in those areas were killed while the women and children were enslaved. The Falasha in Dambeya and "all the regions of his reign" were made to convert to Christianity. Suseneyos thereby "erased the memory of Judaism from his empire" with this mass baptism. He further ordered the Falasha to plow the fields on Saturday as a "sign of denial of their religion of Judaism."[238]

The anti-Jesuit Bruce asserted without evidence, though not without reason, that this massacre and mass conversion were due to the advice of his new Catholic advisors as the king increasingly turned toward Catholicism.[239] According to the short chronicle, he became a Catholic in 1616, that is, just before the above episodes, though he did not proclaim it publicly until 1622.[240] He also began to take Catholic advice to eradicate all so-called Judaic elements in Ethiopian Christianity, for which the Jesuits had been pushing since the reign of Galawdewos.[241] Later in his reign, for example, Suseneyos ordered his brother Se'ela Krestos, also a convert to Catholicism, to eliminate the "Jewish Sabbath" in his governorship of Damot. In that province it was not a question of the Beta Israel, but of the Ethiopian Christians being ordered to work on Saturday that aroused great opposition.[242]

In 1618, Yolyos, the king's son-in-law; Yamana Krestos, his elder brother; and others organized a revolt against him because of their fear the king was going to impose Catholicism by force.[243] Based on Yamana's earlier agreement to let his son marry Gedewon's daughter, it seems he was less antagonistic toward the Beta Israel and saw their religion as less threatening to the Orthodox Church than Catholicism. Was he trying to form a new alliance that included Gedewon against the Catholic king?

From the Beta Israel perspective, Gedewon was trying to use marriage into the royal family as a strategy for obtaining a favorable position in the Samen. In this, he was pursuing a classic political strategy. But Suseneyos's veto of this marriage offer made the strategy void for the time being.

Sometime after these events, another attack on Gedewon in Samen was carried out by the king's troops. This time Gedewon repulsed the attack just as the king's army was reaching their place of worship, the "*mesgada* Falasha." The army retreated to Wagara, where the king met and rebuked them, sending them back to guard the approaches to Samen to prevent Gedewon from attacking the surrounding districts. Later, there were more skirmishes.[244]

In 1624 or 1625, Gedewon tried one more time to interfere in royal politics by supporting one Za-Manfas-Qeddus, the son of Arzo who was the grandson of the former king Minas. Za-Manfas-Qeddus was brought and Gedewon proclaimed him the legitimate king. Suseneyos sent an army under the new governor of Samen. After heavy fighting in which Gedewon inflicted many casualties due to his use of firearms, the king's army was finally successful in killing "Gedewon the Jew who lived in the time of four kings."[245]

The next year, 1625 or 1626, marked the last campaign against the Beta Israel after more than 300 years of intermittent warfare. Suseneyos went to the Samen with a force that included his son, Fasiladas, "to fight the son of Gedewon and to eradicate the Falasha who remained."[246] His victory ended the political autonomy of the Beta Israel forever.

It was also about this time that Suseneyos expelled from the country a certain Solomon of Vienna, a Jew who had come into Ethiopia some years previously. He apparently had tried to establish contacts with the Beta Israel, but there is little record of what he did except to embroil himself in religious controversies at the king's court.[247] The growing influence of the Jesuits at the court, together with the final defeat of the Beta Israel, sealed his fate.

During the last years of his reign, the Catholic-Orthodox controversy reached a climax. Finally, in June 1632, because of the staunch opposition to his attempts to Catholicize the country and the bloodshed this had caused, Suseneyos decided to issue an edict of toleration allowing people to follow either belief, and he turned over effective power of government to his son, Fasiladas. When he died in September 1632, Fasiladas moved to restore the Orthodox faith.[248]

Significantly, the next mention of the Beta Israel after their final defeat came after Fasiladas had been made governor of the Samen in 1630, and some of his soldiers were Beta Israel. In one campaign, he ordered his "Falasha who are called Kayla" to scale a steep *amba* which none of his other troops could master and kill the guards posted at the top.[249] Hence, during the reign of Suseneyos, but working under Fasiladas, who was soon to succeed his father, the Beta Israel continued to be incorporated into Ethiopian institutions. Their traditions indicate they received titles of *azaj* and *azmach* during the reign of Suseneyos because of their military prowess.[250]

Some Beta Israel possibly also worked as masons during this period. Their traditions record they first received land payments for their construction work during Suseneyos's reign at Azazo and Abba Samuel, two towns near Gondar.[251] Perhaps this was for work on Suseneyos's palace and church at Azazo, built between 1622 and 1625.[252] In general, Suseneyos's reign was a period of increased stone construction, with Portuguese technical assistance. Earlier, the missionary Paez had supervised the construction of a palace at Gorgora,[253] on which the Beta Israel may have worked.

In general, despite the bloody campaigns against the Beta Israel during the reign of Suseneyos recorded in the chronicles, their own traditions as set down in the nineteenth century remember him in a positive light. Their brief indigenous written chronicle stated that during the reign of Suseneyos, "All those who had survived, had rested in the shade [of the trees without a roof over their heads], had lived in the forests and deserted places, entered the country and returned to the religion of their ancestors."[254] The sense of this statement would seem to be that the Beta Israel, along with the Orthodox Christians, benefited by the edict of toleration issued by Suseneyos in 1632, when the failure of his pro-Catholic stance had become evident. As this edict accompanied the effective transfer of the government to Fasiladas, another tradition recorded in the nineteenth century suggested it was Fasiladas who allowed them to return to the religion of their ancestors.[255]

Thus, the heroic age came to an end after 350 years of conflict, resistance, and identity formation. By the early seventeenth century, a Falasha religious identity had emerged from a coalescence of some *ayhud* and Orthodox Christian influences, their political autonomy was ended forever, and further steps had been taken to incorporate them into the overall Ethiopian political economy as an occupational caste. Before I turn to an analysis of these trends and the new tensions of the Gondar era, it will be useful to summarize the pre-Gondarine Ethiopian social formation and the position of the Beta Israel in it by 1632.

Political Economy, Religion, and Society, 1270–1632

By 1632, northwestern Ethiopia had become a "traditional Amhara area."[256] More broadly, the Ethiopian state and Abyssinian social formation had come to dominate the area. The *gult* grants of the Amhara-Tigrayan settlers gradually became *rest* at the expense of the conquered Beta Israel and other local peoples whose land was expropriated.[257] The kings awarded new *gult* grants to the upper echelons of administrative and ecclesiastical officialdom, especially as royal control over the whole area was completed with the gradual transfer of the Ethiopian capital to that region during the sixteenth and seventeenth centuries.

The Beta Israel by 1632 comprised a large part of the new landless class in the Ethiopian tributary social formation in the area. In that social position, they were similar to other peoples such as the Qemant, Wayto, Muslims, Zalan, and slaves of various origins. They were clearly distinguished from the landed *rest*-holding peasantry, even by this time identified as Amhara, though many called Amhara must have been the result of conversion and intermarriage with the *ayhud*-Falasha and other Agaw, such as the Qemant. These *rest*-holders were also distinct from the *gult*-holding upper class, though the boundaries in this case were more flexible and could be crossed by individuals as they rose and fell in the social order, based on their changing access to wealth and power.

The landless can be called a class, however, only in the most rudimentary sense.[258] Each group within this classification maintained such a high degree of separation from others that they can be considered castes or at least castes-in-formation. Each was essentially endogamous, with its own occupational relationship to the dominant society of Abyssinians, either as artisans (Falasha), traders (Muslims), pastoralists (Zalan), hunters (Wayto), or laborers or servants (Qemant, "Shanqilla," and others). Some also worked as farmers, especially as tenant farmers.[259]

Each group held itself apart from the others, to a greater or lesser degree, and of course, these divisions also worked to the advantage of the dominant society which could control each one separately. These groups were both peripheral and essential to Ethiopian society, a relationship typical of castes. They were essential not only for the specific tasks performed, which were despised or low prestige jobs in the Abyssinian value system, but also because their existence provided a ready target for the release of tensions that some analysts have argued were peculiar to the *rest*-holding system.[260]

The position of the *ayhud*/Beta Israel/Falasha/Kayla/caste-in-formation was becoming clear by the early seventeenth century. They had been conquered and affected by evangelization. Many died, some dispersed, a few were enslaved, and some assimilated into Abyssinian society. But many had responded by forging a new identity defined by a specific economic relationship to the dominant society as artisans and tenant farmers, by a social order based on separation, and by a body of religious beliefs and practices that was heavily influenced if not derived mainly from Ethiopian

Orthodoxy, but whose guardian monks defended as distinctive and superior to any other beliefs. Although, since they had been conquered, they nearly disappeared from the Ethiopian written chronicles for the ensuing centuries, Beta Israel oral traditions, passed down for the most part by their monks, attest to their continuing struggle for survival and identity as history passed inexorably into the next phase.

3. The Gondar Era: Urbanization, Imperial Policies, and the Beta Israel, 1632–1755

The establishment of Gondar, the largest permanent urban center in highland Ethiopia since ancient Aksum, had a significant impact on Ethiopian social structure, relations among its peoples and classes, and on the continuing process of Beta Israel caste formation. Although even in a preindustrial context towns must be considered as "electric transformers,"[1] their significance in Ethiopian history has been too long ignored or misunderstood.[2] "A town is a town wherever it is":[3] certainly Gondar and several other locations in the region may be considered as urban centers based on their functional organization and their demographic composition. What is necessary is to make Gondar's role in transforming human relations clearer and more explicit in the Ethiopian context.

Gondar brought people of diverse ethnic and religious backgrounds together. The landless took up jobs as artisans (Beta Israel and Muslims), traders (Muslims), laborers (Qemant), and servants or slaves ("Shanqilla"/"Bareya," Oromo) and, hence, naturally came into more contact with each other than had been the case in rural society. This contact, interaction, and their similar position as forming a lower class did not, however, overcome ultimately the caste differences among the groups. Both the physical division of the city into ethnic-occupational enclaves and imperial policies eventually reinforced the emerging caste relationship of the Beta Israel with the dominant Abyssinian society.

The kings granted the Beta Israel some land and titles in the immediate Gondar area in payment for their work, but at the same time, they were kept—and kept themselves—separate from Christian society. The grants and titles signified the continuing incorporation of the Beta Israel into the Ethiopian political economy and gave some of them a greater stake in the dominant system, thus precluding the likelihood of further armed revolts. But the urban experience did not last long enough, nor were the grants of land and titles extensive enough to transform the position of the Beta Israel, even in the Gondar vicinity, into something beyond the caste relationship.

The Founding of Gondar

The traditions and legends that surround the founding of Gondar illustrate its significance to the three major peoples living in the region at the time: Amhara, Beta Israel, and Qemant. Up to now, only accounts from the dominant Christian, Amhara perspective have been utilized in reconstructing the establishment of the city. Since the city was important to all three of these groups—and to others—a broad spectrum of traditions and legends must be utilized in order to arrive at a better understanding of the actual processes involved as well as how each group has interpreted the processes.

The founding of a permanent capital at Gondar was the historical culmination of imperial expansion in the region. The distant predecessors of Gondar were Aksum and Adafa (Lalibala). Both were characterized by great architectural achievements, were founded as political capitals by the ruling emperor, and continued as significant religious and cultural centers long after their decline in political importance.[4]

The "wandering capitals" of the Shawan kings between the thirteenth and sixteenth centuries were the semi-urban predecessors to Gondar. These mobile tent cities, which were clustered around the emperor and his entourage, exhibited a functional specialization, ethnic-linguistic diversity, and density of population characteristic of urban centers everywhere, despite their mobility.[5] Even the mobility of these tent cities was only partial, as kings developed favorite spots to which they periodically returned.[6] Likewise, the permanence of the stone construction at Gondar did not stop the kings from traveling throughout the empire for parts of most years,[7] though of course, everyone in the city did not leave.

The dominant Christian traditions surround Gondar's founding with an aura of prophetic inevitability. A retrospective "prophecy" explained that since the reign of Lebna Dengel (1508–40), the kings would establish a new capital at a place beginning with the letter *G*.[8] Hence, Sarsa Dengel built a fortress palace at Guzara northeast of Lake Tana.[9] Suseneyos had a palace built at Gorgora and later at Gomnage (Danqaz), and one of his campsites in the Dambeya region was at Guender, or Guendra (i.e., Gondar).[10] Finally, Fasiladas remained at Gomnage four years before settling at Gondar around 1636.[11]

Several versions of Amhara traditions exist concerning the founding of Gondar which emphasize the personal role of Fasiladas in fulfilling this prophecy. In one version, first Suseneyos and later Fasiladas had the vision that his capital should be built at a place beginning with *G*. One day, Fasiladas heard the roar of a lion which he had his soldiers follow until it disappeared at the place where his palace stands now. The soldiers asked people near a church in the region, Arba'ettu Ensesa, what the place where the lion disappeared was called, and they said it was Gondar. Fasiladas then came and had work on his palace started immediately.[12] In other versions of this story, Fasiladas was following a buffalo that disappeared into a pond. An old man then came out of the pond and told him to build the palace there. In a variation, he was following his mule, which had escaped, until it arrived at the place where Gondar is, and the people there told him it was called Gondar.[13]

Traditional Amhara information also recalls two landlords named Weini and Seini who owned the central part of the town where the kings' palaces were to be built at the time that Fasiladas arrived. When Fasiladas decided to construct his palace, he had Weini and Seini moved to land outside the city.[14] In addition to these two landlords, traditional information indicates there were five "*rest*-holders churches" (*ya restegna dabr*) in the region before Fasiladas arrived there in the 1630s: Gondaroch Maryam, Gondaroch Giyorgis, Abwara Giyorgis, Qeha Iyyasus, and Arba'ettu Ensesa.[15] These traditions indicate Weini and Seini and most other landlords in the region were Amhara, Tigrayan, or possibly Christian Agaw from Lasta who had come to the region in the fourteenth and fifteenth centuries. One popular etymology of *Gondar* derives it from a Tigrinya word.[16] The founding of *ya restegna dabr,* thus, must be seen as part of the process of Christian migration to the area during the conquest of the Beta Israel.

Traditions on the founding of Gondar from the perspective of the Beta Israel have not previously been taken into account. One apparently apocryphal etymology of the name Gondar, nevertheless, suggests the significance of the Beta Israel factor in its founding. According to this tradition, during the campaign of *ase* Yeshaq (1413–30) against the Wagara Beta Israel, his soldiers were told to camp and *gon-edar* ("spend the night by his side") on the site of the future Gondar. A traveler was told by Gondarian informants that the word was derived from two words in the Falasha dialect: *gon* meaning "side" and *dar* meaning "government."[17]

In other Beta Israel traditions, Weini and Seini were considered descendants of their leader, Gedewon, who fought Yeshaq in the early fifteenth century. Gondar was said to have been founded by the Beta Israel and then taken over by Fasiladas because he wanted to found his capital near the area, if not at the exact location, where Gedewon had ruled. Other landlords in the area were also said to have been Beta Israel.[18]

This same tradition, however, which asserts that the Beta Israel founded Gondar, also noted that other people already lived in the area when the Beta Israel arrived.[19] Perhaps these other inhabitants of the area were Qemant whose possible role in the establishment of Gondar also has not historically been taken into account. Qemant traditions are ambivalent on this question and, hence, mirror their ambiguous relationship to the Amhara immigrants. Some Qemant traditions assert the original inhabitants' ethnic identity was unknown or that they were Amhara.[20] Other traditions assert the Qemant were among the main inhabitants of the area when Fasiladas arrived.[21] Linguistic analyses and some popular traditions suggest the name Gondar may be of Qemant or Agaw origin.[22]

Thus, a broader view of the founding of Gondar emerges from the use of unofficial and minority traditions to supplement the official versions. Gondar's founding was important to and remembered not only by Amhara traditions, but also by those of other groups in the area, especially the Beta Israel. Those Beta Israel traditions concerning Gondar's establishment recall it as an event to which they contributed as much as the Amhara, since it was their land that was appropriated for the capital. Some Qemant traditions have a similar perspective.

In summary, Gondar's founding culminated the church-state expansion to the northwest that Amda Seyon had begun when he established a regiment by that name there. Continuing Beta Israel opposition required an ever-increasing imperial presence. Ahmad ibn Ibrahim's Islamic invasion was also finally defeated in the region in 1543.[23]

The specific site of Gondar offered practical geographic, climatic, and political-economic advantages. It was the fulcrum from which the rich plains of Dambeya to the southwest and Wagara to the north could be controlled. It was above the malarial shores of Lake Tana while still offering an adequate water supply from the two rivers and numerous springs in the area. The natural fortifications of the northern mountains provided protection from possible Beta Israel revolts from that direction, though these did not materialize after the 1620s. As a local historian noted after having explained the legendary accounts concerning the search for a place beginning with *G:* "I believe that Gondar was selected as capital of Ethiopia not by reason of the predictions of fortune tellers, but because of its natural beauty, its fertile soil, and its excellent climate."[24]

Gondar Social and Physical Structure

Gradually, Gondar emerged from its origins as an administrative center to become established as a permanent urban settlement, thus distinguishing itself from its immediate political predecessors at Guzara, Gorgora, and Gomnage (Danqaz).[25] As an urban center, it remained rooted in the surrounding rural life and social structure, but developed features characteristic of pre-industrial cities elsewhere.[26] In particular, its social structure can be read in the physical structure of its class-ethnic-religious enclaves broadly distributed in concentric circles from the royal compound at the center. The three-tiered division of *gult*-holders, *rest*-holders, and the landless in pre-Gondarine rural society continued but was modified in the urban setting.

Social Structure: Class Divisions

As Gondar evolved from a king's residence and administrative center into a true city, the population grew and became more diverse. It attracted more upper-class administrators, military and religious officials, and the historically landless artisans and laborers as well as many people in between. The divisions between the classes thus became more visible, if not more explicit.

Gondar was probably expanding in population during its entire first century, continuing up to at least the mid-eighteenth century. In the beginning, traditional information notes it was a frontier village inhabited only by "patriots, nobles, and soldiers."[27] Later estimates about its population differ greatly. An eighteenth-century contemporary was told that the king's army by itself stationed in Gondar accounted for 40,000 horsemen and many other troops.[28] About the same time, Bruce said Gondar contained 10,000 households,[29] which must have meant at least 40,000 people. Other traditional estimates range from 80,000 to 280,000.[30] As the city expanded, a larger percentage of both the upper and lower classes would have been found there than in a typical rural area, because of the relative permanence of the king's residence and the large amount of construction of new castles and churches.

The city grew because each king after Fasiladas decided to build his own palace in the same royal compound rather than in some other town, which had occurred in the preceding half-century.[31] They also had built and endowed more than forty stone churches and other construction projects such as bridges in Gondar and the immediate region. The number of *makwannent* ("nobility") and high ecclesiastical figures resident in the city increased as the royal court and church leaders became settled in one place and as more churches were built. Both the top religious officials, the *echege* and the *abun,* lived in the city.

The many new churches built under royal patronage had to be staffed. The middle-level clergy in each church engaged in clerical and educational pursuits, thereby attracting students to the city. Others who worked for the churches in the city included scribes, *dabtara,* and other officials. These people fit into the middle-level classes between the high-ranking *gult*-holders and the historically landless artisans.

As the kings stayed in the city for longer periods of time,[32] the population became more permanent. And even when they left on military campaigns, the permanence and variety of the functions, buildings, and interests in the city meant that not everyone left with the king as had been the case with the "wandering capitals" before.

To build the edifices and serve the officials, the population of the low-ranking artisans, laborers, and servants or slaves also increased, though estimates are difficult to make. Some of the artisans received payment for work through land grants and titles, thereby perhaps beginning to create new class divisions which crosscut religious and ethnic boundaries.[33]

The city also became increasingly a center of regional and international trade. At least eight general and specialized marketplaces are remembered in Gondar's traditions, suggesting an extensive production of local craft goods. The city was thus rooted in the local and regional production and exchange system concerning mainly agrarian commodities, one of the essential characteristics of true urban areas.[34] Though based mainly on the local economy, the city was also on two of the major routes for exports from Ethiopia's south and southwest: west through Matamma to Sennar and beyond, and north through Massawa. The kingdom was not, in fact, isolated from the international economy, and some emperors were actively seeking to expand trade, especially with Islamic areas. The actual amount of international trade in slaves and other goods was probably increasing and was, hence, one of the economic factors illustrating the significance of Gondar,[35] though not the primary reason for its founding and flourishing.

Though most of the traders carrying these goods were Muslims, an increasing number were Christians, probably related to the Christian political dominance at the capital. In general, the lack of access to land by Muslim traders kept them in a lower-class position, though lack of information concerning them prevents a thorough analysis. Perhaps some were granted land along with some of the artisans.

The middle level of traditional Abyssinian class structure was made up of the *rest*-holding peasantry. In the Gondar era, some urban or peri-urban residents in the greater Gondar area certainly continued to practice agriculture in outlying regions.

But recent research indicates the traditional peasantry may not have been the only group in this middle category. From the early eighteenth century, a new class of "gentry," midway between the nobility and the peasantry, may have been emerging. After about 1730, land increasingly became a commodity which was bought and sold. Donald Crummey has found evidence of almost 1,700 land sales between 1730 and 1850. This research is at a preliminary stage and the rather sudden development of land sales cannot yet be explained. As Crummey cautiously noted, "It is tempting to relate the sales to the impact of Gondar's development as an urban center, but such a relationship would be speculative."[36] It is a speculation that should be a stimulant to further research and thought. Such a development would certainly be congruent with the experience of other urban centers, including some in Ethiopia.[37]

Physical Structure: Peoples and Quarters

The physical structure of the city mirrored its class structure, in common with the type of enclave construction that existed in other pre-industrial cities. It was also based on the structure of the pre-Gondarine wandering capitals in which the king lived at the center. In Gondar, the royal compound that evolved gradually was surrounded by a wall with twelve named gates, depending on what enclave was on the other side of the gate or who was supposed to use it.[38] The quarters nearest the wall were mostly inhabited by the nobility and upper clergy. These quarters included (see Map 3): the Echege Bet (R-2) in the Enkoyye Mask area (R-3), where the *echege,* the highest-ranking Ethiopian-born ecclesiastical official, lived; Gera Wambar (R-5), where slightly lower-ranking members of the upper nobility lived; and Debb Anbasa (R-6), where the mayor of the city may have lived, although other sources said he lived at Faras Bet (R-12). Many nobles lived in Qagn Bet (R-4), where many fine houses with a surrounding garden space had been built.[39]

Probably the only high-ranking member of the society who did not live in these central residential areas was the *abun,* the Egyptian-born bishop and head of the Church who lived—at least some of the time during the Gondar dynasty—in Abun Bet or Abun Mask (R-7), a separate area to the northwest of the city center.[40] Despite his high official rank, the physical separation of the *abun* may reflect his somewhat tenuous position as a foreigner in the Ethiopian social system.

In a secondary ring slightly further away from the central locations

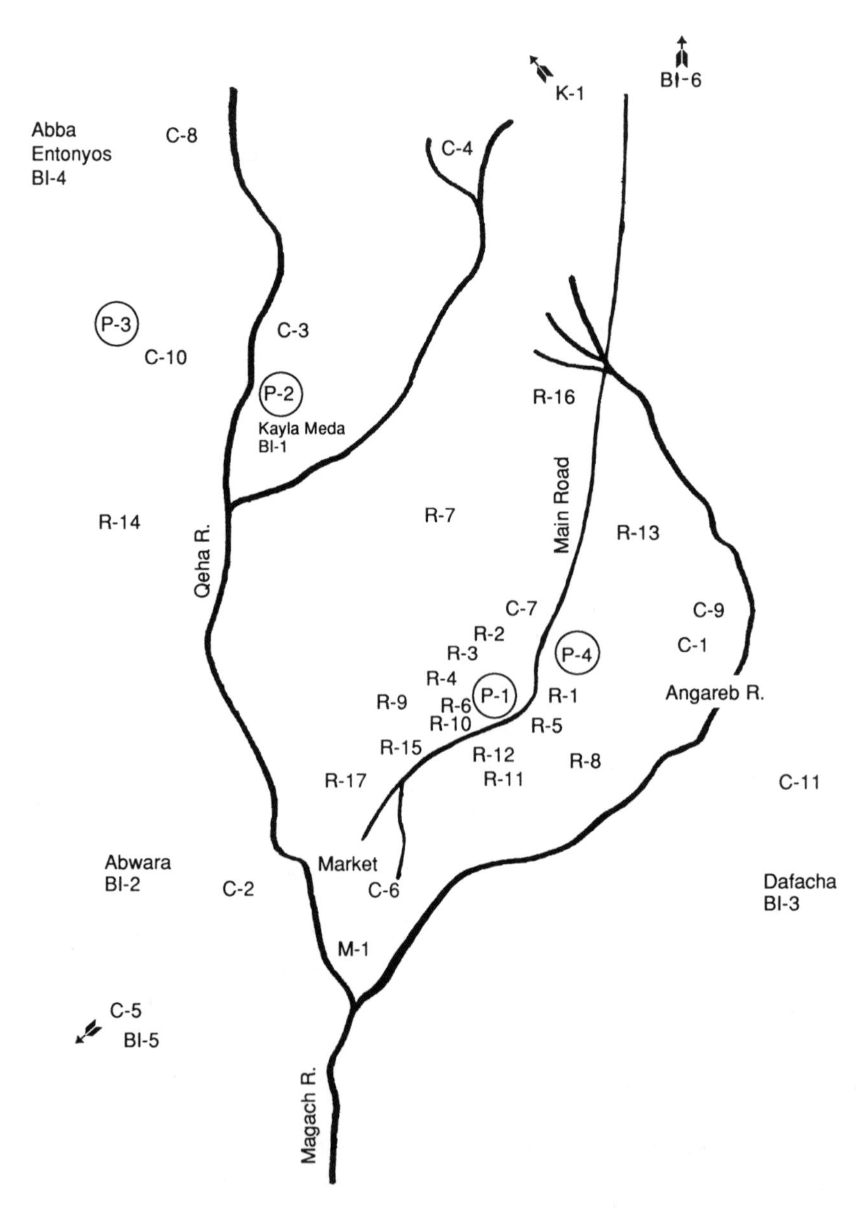

Map 3. Gondar, 1636–1868.

Key:

Christian Churches
C-1 Arba'ettu Ensesa
C-2 Abwara Giyorgis
C-3 Qeha Iyyasus
C-4 Gondaroch Giyorgis
C-5 Gondaroch Maryam
C-6 Fit Abbo
C-7 Madhane Alam
C-8 Abba Entonyos
C-9 Dabra Berhan Sellase
C-10 Dabra Sahay Qwesqwam
C-11 Dafacha Kidana Mehrat

Beta Israel Quarters
BI-1 Kayla Meda
BI-2 Abwara
BI-3 Dafacha
BI-4 Abba Entonyos
BI-5 Gondaroch Maryam
BI-6 Walaka [modern area]

Qemant Area
K-1 Kerkerr

Muslim Area
M-1 Eslam Bet

Royal Palaces
P-1 Royal Compound
("Fasiladas Gemb")
P-2 Fasiladas
("Fasil's Bath")
P-3 Qwesqwam
P-4 Ras Gemb
("Mika'el Sehul Gemb")

Residential & Other Quarters
R-1 Adannagar
R-2 Echege Bet
R-3 Enkoyye Mask
R-4 Qagn Bet
R-5 Gera Wambar
R-6 Debb Anbasa
R-7 Abun Bet
R-8 Erq Bet
R-9 Dengaye
R-10 Ba'ata
R-11 Dabra Metmaq
R-12 Faras Bet
R-13 Alga Meda
R-14 Qera Meda
R-15 Qwadoch/Qwaloch
R-16 Tigray Mechohiya
R-17 Turkoch Mandar

Sources: G. Lejean, *Voyage en Abyssinia* (Paris, 1872), map; G. Lejean, "Notes d'un voyage en Abyssinie," *Le Tour du Monde,* 12 (1865): 250, map; Ghiorghis Mellessa, "Gondar Yesterday and Today," *Ethiopia Observer,* 12/3 (1969): 164–76; interviews with Garima Taffara on 25 August, Jammara Wande on 26 August, Berhan Beruk on 14 August and 20 August 1975; fieldwork observations.

were the principal Christian residential areas. These included Dengaye (R-9), which was densely populated with narrow streets where most of the Christian traders lived. Erq Bet (R-8) and Dabra Metmaq (R-11) were both areas where teachers of religion and the scriptures lived.[41] These people would fit into the middle-ranking classes in the city.

The lowest-ranking classes, which included most artisans and the Muslim traders, lived in outlying enclaves further away from the city center. The Muslim traders or *jabarti* lived in Eslam Bet or Eslamge (M-1) near the main Saturday market area, a location chosen by Muslims near the junction of the two rivers that flow by Gondar, as Bruce noted later, because of "their frequent ablutions."[42] Besides working as traders, Muslims also engaged in craftwork as weavers, tailors, tanners, and leatherworkers. Some of the tailors, who may not have all been Muslim, were known as *qwad serri*. They made decorations for the king's clothes and lived in an area called Qwadoch (R-15). On occasion, Muslims were used as ambassadors by the king to Muslim countries, such as was the case in the embassy sent by Fasiladas to Yemen.[43]

Some of the goldsmiths and silversmiths were foreigners (often called "Turks") and lived in Turkoch Meder (R-17). This is an area where troops from Sennar may have been quartered during the reign of Iyyasu I (1682–1706).[44] Tanners were probably both Christian and Muslim, and tanneries were located near the rivers on the city's outskirts. Most of the leather-workers were Muslims, and tent-makers who lived in Emfraz near Lake Tana were also Muslims.[45]

Blacksmiths were Beta Israel. The Beta Israel also worked as carpenters, masons, potters, and weavers. They lived in four main areas close to Gondar: Kayla Meda (BI-1) Abwara (BI-2), Dafacha (BI-3), and Abba Entonyos (BI-4). They also lived in several villages in the Gondar region: Gondaroch Maryam (BI-5), Abba Samu'el, Azazo, and Tadda.

The Qemant also worked as carpenters and perhaps masons, as well as laborers on the new construction. They lived mainly at Kerkerr (K-1) just to the northwest of the city. They also lived at Chelga, west of Gondar toward Matamma. They were primarily responsible for hauling the heavy timber used in construction work to the city, and some in the nineteenth century brought firewood. Their presence in the city was so well known that reference to them was made to illustrate a point in the Amharic commentaries on Ge'ez texts.[46]

In addition to artisans, laborers, and traders, the other main groups in Gondar's lower classes were the domestic servants and slaves. Very little is known about the servant or slave group, but they did most of the domestic work such as cooking, baking, washing, grinding, and brewing in the royal, noble, and other households throughout the city. An official called the *west azaj* ("inside commander") was in charge of the royal workers. They were treated as inferiors, probably comparable to domestic slaves elsewhere in African societies.[47] Avenues of advancement were marriage into Amhara society and/or joining the army.

The quarter known as Addanager (R-1) was the main area inhabited by the palace slaves and is the only non–upper-class quarter near the gates of the royal compound. Their physical location illustrated their social position of complete dependence. In origin, most were "Shanqilla," Agaw, or Oromo captured in wars on Ethiopia's borders to the south and west. Perhaps the number of slaves held internally increased as the extent of slave-raiding for export apparently increased during this period, but there has not been sufficient research on this question to quantify it.[48]

Some quarters in peripheral areas around the edges of the city were named for their functions rather than their inhabitants. These included Faras Meda or Faras Bet (R-12, "horse field"), where the royal horses were kept, Alga Meda (R-13, "bed field"), where some army units were stationed, and Qera Meda (R-14, "slaughtering field"), where animals were butchered. Other areas included burial grounds and specifically designated garbage dumps. As a center of trade and tribute-collection by the government, other peoples who lived in the vicinity, such as the Wayto along the shores of Lake Tana, or the Agaw from Agawmeder, also contributed to the life of Gondar, even if they did not live there.[49]

The Beta Israel in Gondar

Some Beta Israel in Gondar and its vicinity received grants of land and titles for their work as masons and carpenters building the city's new castles and churches while others became soldiers in the kings' new regiments. Their rewards of land and titles began to create new class divisions in Beta Israel society, with an elite that was upwardly mobile within the overall Ethiopian social structure, while the masses remained landless blacksmiths, potters, weavers, and tenant farmers. This also indicates a rural-urban bifurcation because the land grants were all in the greater Gondar area.

To some extent, the landless Beta Israel continued to be treated as part of a general lower class involving an increased number of laborers, craftsmen, traders, and servants or slaves in the urban environment. Although economically based class divisions may have become more relevant in the city, ethnic and religious distinctions continued to be significant criteria determining the urban social structure. Although they were incorporated to a greater extent into the Ethiopian political economy, the Beta Israel maintained their cultural and religious identity and held themselves aloof socially, thereby reinforcing the continuing process of caste formation.

Occupations: Artisans and Soldiers

The Beta Israel began to redefine their roles in Gondar—and within the Ethiopian social structure in general—by working as builders (masons and carpenters) and soldiers. Other men continued to be blacksmiths and weavers. Women diversified their occupations to become church decorators and paint-makers as well as continuing as potters. According to their own traditions, the Gondar era marked the peak of their artisanal skills, both in terms of level and diversity of abilities.[50]

The emphasis on the occupations of mason and carpenter, as well as soldier, was significant because these jobs were of a higher status in Amhara society than those of blacksmith, potter, or even weaver. To the extent that they adopted these occupations, the view of the dominant society toward the Beta Israel became less negative and their opportunities for upward social mobility were enhanced.[51]

The Beta Israel did, however, also continue in their traditional occupations, the men as blacksmiths and weavers and the women as potters. In the seventeenth century, they were said to be "almost the only persons" to work as weavers.[52] By the end of the Gondar era, however, many of the weavers and the tailors within the city were Muslims.[53] Perhaps the Muslim role in this occupation increased simply as a function of their role as traders who brought the cotton into Gondar from the lowland Sudan border area.

The Beta Israel had also worked as blacksmiths since the fifteenth century. During the Gondar era, they were known as "excellent smiths," making a variety of iron goods, such as plows, sickles, lances, spears, and swords.[54] Their skill as blacksmiths increased as they began to make new items such as the nails and tools used in construction work. Their own traditions also assert they began to repair firearms as early as the reign of Fasiladas.[55]

Their abilities were well-known beyond the boundaries directly controlled by the Gondar kings, according to Amhara traditions. For example, when Iyyasu II (1730–55) sent an expedition to Shawa about 1730 to collect tribute, Abbiye, the king of Shawa, kept behind some of the Beta Israel blacksmiths attached to the expedition to make spades, plowshares, spears, and swords for him.[56]

Historically, blacksmiths had been at least partly under royal patronage, making and repairing weapons for the army, as the documentation concerning the fifteenth and sixteenth centuries suggests. This royal connection probably facilitated their gradual transformation to such jobs as mason and carpenter when possibly the sixteenth- and certainly seventeenth-century kings began to build in stone in the Gondar region. Perhaps some Beta Israel became masons and carpenters as early as the reigns of Galawdewos (1540–59) or Sarsa Dengel (1563–97),[57] though the first written documentation of their work in such occupations is from the seventeenth century.[58] Their own traditions assert they first worked as builders and were rewarded with land grants during the reign of Suseneyos (1607–32).[59] Therefore, they may have been the "new workmen" taught by the Jesuit missionary Paez to work as masons and as "carpenters and joyners" on Suseneyos's palace at Gorgora about 1614.[60]

In general, both written and oral sources from all perspectives—Beta Israel, Amhara, and Qemant—agree that the Beta Israel were the main masons and carpenters who constructed the stone palaces, churches, bridges, and walls during the Gondar era, although they were assisted by some Qemant and Muslim workers. The masons cut and laid the stones and made the mortar. The carpenters built the massive wooden beams, doors, and also thatched the roofs.[61]

The question of the architectural responsibility for the construction is not entirely clear. Fasiladas's architect, according to a contemporary source, was an Indian.[62] Popular Ethiopian traditions often refer vaguely to the Portuguese or other foreigners;[63] in general, these were probably Indians, Levantines, or Portuguese Indians from Goa.[64] But sometimes, Ethiopians were said to have been the architects as well as the construction workers. During the reigns of Yohannes I and Iyyasu I, for example, an Ethiopian architect named Walda Giyorgis was named in the chronicles.[65] It would not be surprising if some of the Beta Israel rose to the level of architect. The title of the royal architect was said to have been *liqa tabiban*.[66] *Tabiban* is a word often used later to refer to the Beta Israel, and one (Amhara) source named a certain *bejrond* Taklu as a Beta Israel architect.[67]

The Beta Israel view of their importance as builders is dramatically illustrated in their version of an Ethiopian tradition concerning the building of the castle. As Fasiladas was having his main castle constructed, the work which was done during the day kept falling apart at night. The Beta Israel assert that when the castle began to fall apart, the foreign architect asked the king to bring other workers to help him. So he brought the Beta Israel, whose skill was much admired, and the castle was completed without further problems.[68] Parenthetically, this tradition also points to the reign of Fasiladas, rather than that of Suseneyos or others, as the key period for the emphasis on Beta Israel occupations as masons.

A significant occupation of the Beta Israel in Gondar was that of soldier. This profession was particularly important because military ability remained the single most important avenue of social mobility for non-Christians. Having fought the Ethiopian kings for three hundred years, they certainly had a good reputation as fighters, and had perhaps been used in that capacity as early as the sixteenth century.[69]

Fasiladas recognized their possible usefulness to him as he attempted to reorganize the government and army in the aftermath of the disruptions of the Suseneyos years. He had been governor of Samen briefly before becoming king. Perhaps because of this experience, he formed several squadrons of Beta Israel soldiers, and during his reign, Beta Israel traditions recall that 150 of their men rose to prominent positions as war leaders and advisors.[70] The squadrons continued under Yohannes I (1667–82), aiding him in his wars against the Oromo.[71] During the reign of Iyyasu I (1682–1706), it was said that "his armies are even composed of Muslim and Jewish soldiers," and that one of the bodies of royal guards was composed of Jews.[72] Though the time reference is unclear, nineteenth-century oral traditions recorded that five hundred Kayla (Beta Israel) served as soldiers under one Gondar king.[73] The numbers are unclear, but the role of Beta Israel as soldiers is well-established during the Gondar era.

Beta Israel women developed some new crafts to supplement their traditional role as potters. One of these, deriving from their knowledge of soils, was paint-making.[74] Such paints were probably those used by the Beta Israel carpenters to paint the split-cane roof they constructed for the palace of Iyyasu II (1730–55).[75]

Beta Israel women were also said to have made the *gulilat,* or seven-pointed cross with ostrich eggs on the ends of the points, the characteristic ornament on top of churches.[76] Other women decorated fancy cloth that was hung on the interior walls of churches and other buildings.[77]

Castles, Churches, and Land

As the main builders of castles and churches during the Gondar dynasty, the Beta Israel were rewarded or paid in goods and land, either in the form of grants or as royal recognition of their rights to live in certain areas. These developments began to reverse the process by which the Beta Israel had been dispossessed of their land since their fifteenth-century defeat by Yeshaq. As a result of their acquisition of land rights, some began to rise in status toward the middle stratum of Ethiopian society. Since the land was on the fringes of the city, there was plenty of room to practice agriculture as independent cultivators as well as to work as artisans in Gondar.[78] On the other hand, the grants were of a limited nature, geographically dispersed, and confined entirely to the greater Gondar area. Hence, they helped create a rural-urban bifurcation in Beta Israel society but did not transform their overall social position as landless artisans within the Abyssinian-dominated social structure. In general, the Beta Israel acquired land "everywhere near churches. . . . They had some plots in between, here and there. They did not have one definite area, but were scattered among others."[79]

The nature of these land grants is somewhat unclear. The Beta Israel informants all said in the mid-1970s that in the scattered areas where they still held their own land, it was *rest* ("inherited") tenure derived from an ancestor who had received it during the Gondar dynasty. But anthropological and historical studies suggest the king cannot grant *rest* rights, rather he grants the *gult* ("tribute") rights over certain pieces of land.[80] Perhaps what occurred during the Gondar era was similar to the process suggested for the pre-Gondar era in which *gult* grants gradually became *rest* rights over the generations. In the 1950s, for example, Falasha in Begamder said they held land as *rest-gult* granted their ancestors by Menilek for service in his armies.[81] Another possibility is that the churches held the land as *rim* land (i.e., ecclesiastical land that could be bought and sold) upon which they settled Beta Israel workers who then were allowed to treat it as *rest* and pass it down to their families.[82] Other artisans, such as the Greeks who arrived during the reign of Iyyasu II, were also granted land as a reward for their service.[83] Whatever the exact nature of the land holdings, the Beta Israel viewed their increased access to land as a step up from being merely tenants.

The earliest Beta Israel settlements in the Gondar area were at Kayla Meda, Abwara, and Gondaroch Maryam. These areas are in the vicinity of three of Gondar's five *restegna dabr* ("landlords' churches"), ancient churches built before Fasiladas founded the capital. The exact dates of their construction cannot be determined, but they were probably all built between the fifteenth and seventeenth centuries and, therefore, are the manifestation of Abyssinian migration to the region during the conquest of the Beta Israel.[84]

Kayla Meda may have been the oldest settlement area, since that is the only one which includes one of the terms used to refer to the Beta Israel ("Kayla") during this period. Probably, they lived there even before the Qeha Iyyasus church was built, or their community in that area would have been called after the church. Their traditions assert only that they lived there sometime before Fasiladas and that he then confirmed their right to remain. The place is mentioned several times in the chronicles.[85] It was also the location of a pottery market,[86] which clearly suggests its connections to the Beta Israel. The residential decrees of Yohannes, which referred to them as Kayla,[87] probably had the effect of ratifying their claims to Kayla Meda. Still in the nineteenth century, the Beta Israel in the Gondar region preferred the name Kayla to Falasha and called their language Kaylinya,[88] again suggesting the longevity of their claims to land at Kayla Meda.

Abwara was also a pre-Fasiladas Beta Israel settlement area.[89] They must have lived there at least since the construction of Abwara Giyorgis, which they probably helped build, perhaps in the sixteenth century.[90] Similarly, Gondaroch Maryam must have been an early Beta Israel area from the time they helped build that church, but its precise date of origin is uncertain.[91]

Other pre-Fasiladas Beta Israel settlements near Gondar included Azazo and Abba Samu'el, located between Gondar and Azazo, and where they had lived at least since the reign of Suseneyos, who built a church at Azazo.[92] In the 1970s there was a community at Azazo, but they did not know when their ancestors began to live there. There was no longer a Beta Israel settlement at Abba Samu'el.[93]

The Gondar era proper began with Fasiladas (1632–67), who built one large castle ("Fasil's Gemb") in what became the royal compound in the city center, perhaps a smaller building near the Qeha River ("Fasil's Bath"), seven churches, and several bridges. He probably used Beta Israel workers from areas in which they had already settled, such as Kayla Meda and Abwara, rather than awarding new grants of land near any one of these buildings.[94]

Beta Israel masons helped construct two small buildings in the royal compound and two churches near Gondar—Abba Entonyos and Tadda Egzi'abher Ab—raised by Yohannes I (1667–82). One of the buildings in the city center known as the Feqr Gemb ("Love House") was popularly associated with Yohannes.[95] In 1679, Yohannes spent a week at Tadda supervising the masons and carpenters building his church there.[96]

The two Beta Israel communities in 1975—at Abba Entonyos across the Qeha River and up the hills to the northwest of the city and at Tadda further south of the city—claimed to still hold *rest* land dating back to the land received from Yohannes by their ancestors as payment for building these two churches.[97] They were said to have received 25 *kelad* of land at Tadda and an unknown amount at Abba Entonyos.[98]

The next king, Iyyasu I (1682–1706), built a large castle in the royal compound and two churches, including the large and famous Dabra Berhan Sellase. The Beta Israel worked on these buildings, but their payment is uncertain. The role of Iyyasu I as the king who measured the land[99] and also his reputation as a grantor of large amounts of land to churches make it likely that his reign marked the stabilization of the land situation for the various peoples in the city, including the Beta Israel and the Qemant whose traditions support this interpretation.[100]

In the decade of political instability following Iyyasu's assassination in 1706, the kings built some churches, but no palaces. Dawit (1716–21) and Bakaffa (1721–30) revived the practice of building castles. Bakaffa built a large palace and two churches and finished the massive wall around the royal compound in the city center.

The Beta Israel probably began to live at Dafacha at that time, where they either received land or had existing land claims legitimized for having worked on Bakaffa's church of Dafacha Kidana Meherat.[101] This area, however, was also in the vicinity of the pre-Fasiladas church, Arba'ettu Ensesa, and the church of Dabra Berhan Sellase built by Iyyasu I. Perhaps they began to live there in the pre-Fasiladas era while the district was renamed because of their work for Bakaffa.

Iyyasu II and his mother Mentewwab were the last rulers to carry out large-scale construction work in Gondar. Iyyasu II had a castle built in the royal compound, and Mentewwab built the church of Dabra Sahay Qwesqwam and nearby castle on the hill to the west of the city.[102] The Beta Israel did most of this work.[103] They were credited in the chronicle with having built the split-cane roof on Iyyasu's castle.[104] Some of those workers were from established communities and did not receive new land grants, but some were said to have received land at Gallagar, some distance from Gondar.[105]

Offices: *Azmach* and *Bejrond*

According to their traditions, the Beta Israel received titles as well as land in recognition of their important roles both as soldiers and artisans. These titles were a significant aspect of the kings' attempts to incorporate the Beta Israel more closely into the dominant institutions. This policy undermined effectively all vestiges of Beta Israel political independence, even in the Samen, and probably even at the local rural village level. From this time on, the principal secular leaders of the Beta Israel were those recognized as such by the dominant society rather than those necessarily related to their own previous ruling family.

However, the Beta Israel monks and priests continued to function independently without being sanctioned by the Ethiopian state. These religious leaders probably exercised their authority mainly in the rural monastic centers outside the greater Gondar region. During the height of construction and growth in Gondar, the secular leaders in Gondar were well-respected and have been remembered in their oral traditions to a greater extent than the religious elite—even in traditions passed down through the monastic tradition! It seems that during the Gondar interregnum, the close and cordial connection of the Beta Israel with the kings led them to emphasize the path of political incorporation to social mobility and advancement of their people, whereas in the ensuing era, the separationist forces became stronger again.

The relative fluidity of Beta Israel roles and social rank in Gondar is illustrated by the types of titles they received. For their work as soldiers and artisans, they received titles such as *azmach* ("general") or *azaj* ("commander") with primarily military and administrative connotations, as well as the title *bejrond*, which meant for the Beta Israel "chief of the workers."[106]

Beta Israel traditions emphasize that they were known mainly as *azmach* or *azaj* rather than *bejrond* during that time.[107] In the Ethiopian Order of Precedence of titles of 1690, *azmach* (in this case *dejazmach*) ranked #11 while the *bejronds* were #22 and #23.[108] Also, according to Beta Israel traditions, *azmach* or *azaj* ranked higher than *bejrond* because the former involved general administrative duties while the *bejrond* was merely the head of artisans: "The *azmach* was a government administrator for many people, but the *bejrond* was only concerned with the Beta Israel."[109] This distinction reinforces the Beta Israel tradition that they had achieved a relatively higher degree of upward mobility during that period than they had either before or afterward, such as in the nineteenth century when they were mainly known as *bejrond*.[110]

On the other hand, just as the Beta Israel remained blacksmiths as well as builders and were granted the relatively lower title of *bejrond* in addition to *azmach*, even the Beta Israel title-holders did not advance to the highest possible ranks within the hierarchy. Unconverted Beta Israel were seldom, if ever, appointed to provincial governorships—which would have required rule over non–Beta Israel. They were not even appointed, for example, to the governorship of Samen, their longest-standing bastion of political power. Rather, in the seventeenth century, the Samen was ruled by the *agafari*, who was often a member of the Ethiopian royal family.[111] By the latter part of the eighteenth century, the Samen was ruled by the ancestors of *dejazmach* Webe, a Beta Israel family that had converted to Christianity.[112]

Beta Israel traditions contain a substantial degree of agreement on a small list of their leaders who were known as *azmach* during and just before the Gondar era, but they are not always clear about during which reigns they lived. During the reign of Sarsa Dengel (1563–97), for example, one Beta Israel *azmach* was named Surafel, and during the reigns of Suseneyos (1607–32) and Fasiladas, another was named Zakaryas. Nothing is remembered about most of these officials, though Zakaryas was said to have been the chief of the carpenters and an important royal advisor during the reigns of both Fasiladas and Suseneyos.[113]

According to their traditions, several other Beta Israel had the title of *azmach* during the reigns of Suseneyos, Fasiladas, or Yohannes I, such as: Ermyas, Solomon, Ya'eqob, and his son Sim'on. In the royal chronicle, Suseneyos had a conflict with "Ermyas the Jew."[114] Perhaps this is the same person remembered in the oral traditions after he reconciled with Suseneyos.[115]

The Beta Israel *azmach* Solomon lived sometime in the seventeenth century.[116] Interestingly, this is the same name but cannot be the same person as the foreign Jew at the court of Suseneyos who caused some commotion before being expelled from the country.[117] The short Beta Israel written chronicle from the nineteenth century also refers to this incident, but records that his name was Abraham.[118]

Azmach Ya'eqob came to Gondar from Samen at the time of Fasiladas and may have settled in the Abwara district.[119] Perhaps this was the same person who later moved to Tadda during the construction of a church there for Yohannes I and became the founder and first *rest*-holder of the Beta Israel community there, although that may have been another person.[120] Ya'eqob's son, Sim'on, also became an *azmach*.[121]

During the first half of the eighteenth century, several Beta Israel were remembered as *azmach,* such as Mored, his son, Hezkeyas, Sebrahin, Mammo, and the three known traditionally as the "last great *azmaches*": Menase, Effrem, and Gondarit.[122] Another Beta Israel leader from the Gondar era was Malka Saddeq.[123] Hezkeyas, Mammo, and Effrem were also all recorded in written chronicles of the period, but as these names are not unique, it is impossible to tell if they are referring to the same people remembered by the Beta Israel. In the chronicles, Hezkeyas was for a time the governor of Samen, but at some point rebelled against the king and claimed to be a descendant of *ase* Ya'eqob, the half–Beta Israel king of the early seventeenth century whose death had given rise to many crown pretenders.[124]

At least two prominent men named Mammo, one of whom was the

brother of Mentewwab, are recorded in the chronicles.[125] Likewise, in the chronicles, an Effrem lived during the reign of Bakaffa and the early part of Iyyasu II's reign.[126]

The case of Gondarit is interesting because so few women are recalled. She was said to have been a potter who lived at Kayla Meda, where there was a potter's market. She was the leader of the Beta Israel there and was the twin of her brother Menase (Effrem was another brother).[127] In Beta Israel traditions, however, she was not unique as at least four other women are said to have been leaders of their communities: Rahel, Milat, Abre Warq, and Roman Warq.[128]

The relatively prominent place of a few Beta Israel women during the Gondar era suggests again the importance of this period as a time of upward social mobility for many individuals in their society. Never again would women be remembered in such high positions, though a few men continued to obtain some titles in later generations. This upward movement is all the more surprising given the relatively low position women seem to have held within Beta Israel institutions, notwithstanding the traditions about Gudit in the tenth century and later queens named Yodit.[129]

In general, Beta Israel traditions assert forty-four or forty-five people were appointed *azmach* during the Gondar era.[130] Another informant stated there were 150 advisors and military Beta Israel during the reign of Fasiladas alone.[131] Whatever the exact number, the period is remembered for the appointment of larger numbers to the office of *azmach* or *azaj* than at any time before or since. Although *azmach* was the highest office received, many also were known as *bejrond*, which for the Beta Israel referred only to the leaders of their artisans.

The Beta Israel title of *bejrond* does not seem to be the same as the royal *bejronds* who were keepers of the treasury, the lions, and the crowns, as noted in the chronicles.[132] Amhara oral information agreed that Beta Israel leaders of the workers were known as *bejrond*, but said they were just chosen as such by their fellow workers and then received royal confirmation.[133] The Amhara traditions also said the *bejrond* collected taxes from the artisans,[134] but some Beta Israel traditions asserted they had nothing to do with tax collection.[135]

An early *bejrond* during the reigns of Suseneyos or Fasiladas was named Debzu. Others during the seventeenth century included *maggabi* Sefenyas, *bejrond* Abraham, and *terabi* Janal.[136] An Amhara informant asserts a *bejrond* Taklu was a Beta Israel architect during the reign of Fasiladas, though he is not remembered in Beta Israel traditions.[137]

In the eighteenth century, the royal chronicle referred to the "chief of the carpenters, *bejrond* Isayyas" who was working on the church of Dabra Sahay Qwesqwam being built by Queen Mentewwab during the reign of Iyyasu II (1730–55).[138] Beta Israel traditions identify this *bejrond* Isayyas as a Beta Israel,[139] thereby providing a near certain correlation between the oral and written documentation.

Thus, during the Gondar period, the Beta Israel were rewarded for their military and artisanal skills with appointments to the titles of *azmach* and *bejrond*. These titles illustrate the process of incorporation and upward mobility that occurred. But in each case, the dominant traditions and the written chronicles do not record the Beta Israel as having received the highest possible positions even within these categories. As *azmaches,* they were advisors to the kings, according to their own traditions, but were not appointed to provincial governorships. As *bejronds,* they were chiefs of the workers but were not guardians of the treasury, lions, or crowns, as were most of those officials remembered as *bejrond* in the chronicles. In both positions, they were closely connected to and thereby obviously dependent upon the kings. The upward limits to these appointments became clear during the next period as the decline in the power of the monarchy adversely affected the Beta Israel.

For the continuation of the process of caste formation, the appointment to offices was important in two senses. It brought the Beta Israel, at least in the Gondar region, more closely into the institutions of the dominant society so that they were no longer seen as an independent political entity but as merely another part of the Ethiopian state. Their increasingly closer connections to the monarchy may also be seen as a manifestation of their emerging caste relationship. The monarchy provided employment opportunities as masons and carpenters in building the new churches and castles, and as soldiers, and thereby acted essentially as the "protector" of the Beta Israel against attacks or persecution by the dominant society. In this case, castes developed in conjunction with a strong central government.

Social Relations and Imperial Policies

Both the type of social relations among the peoples and imperial policies on those relationships contributed to the development of the Beta Israel as an occupational caste. On the one hand, the Beta Israel, along with other ethnic groups during this era, were more completely incorporated into the Abyssinian-dominated political economy than ever before. This phenomenon can be called a process of institutional incorporation, as the Beta Israel increasingly lost their political and economic independence.

On the other hand, the Beta Israel maintained a relatively high degree of separation in cultural and social matters and, therefore, did not become socially incorporated.[140] Their position was somewhat analogous to the Qemant and Muslims but different from the "Shanqilla," Oromo, and probably Agaw in terms of the degree of social incorporation that occurred.

Ethnic Hierarchies

The Abyssinian view of the ethnic hierarchy in pluralistic Gondar is at once self-evident and difficult to document. These views, of course, provided the ideological justification of the actual power relationships in the Ethiopian class system. Oral traditions from two knowledgeable Amhara informants provide a starting point:

> At that time, the Christians were more respected. As for offices and ranks, the other people were also given offices and appointments. In the palace, because the Christians had more education, privileges were given to the Amhara Christians. The others did not have belief in them and they never came close to the king, to the throne or the palace. They lived all alone by themselves.[141]

The Amhara tended to view the high status and the privileges they received as the natural order of things:

> Even if they married to other ethnic groups or religious groups, the Amhara was always proud over other ethnic groups. But the others were not like the Amhara. The other ethnic groups would only respect and be proud of their family. For example, if a Falasha or a Qemant married an Amhara he would be proud of his children and his family, but he would not be proud of his background, where he came from, his ethnic group. But the Amhara would say he was from the *liqawent* ("nobles"), from the main priests, from the *azajoch* and from all these higher positions. He put himself into a higher position. The Amhara was proud and prejudiced.[142]

Thus, in the Amhara view, the non-Christian and landless classes ranked behind themselves in approximately the following order: Muslims, Qemant, Beta Israel, Wayto, and "Shanqilla."[143] Foreign observers, who dealt mainly with members of the Abyssinian upper class, tended to assimilate this ethnic perspective. Hence, one contemporary observer considered the Amhara and, secondly, the Tigrayans as the most "civilized" people in Gondar.[144]

Documentation from the period supports the interpretation that the Amhara populace maintained "proud and prejudiced" views with regard to ethnic minorities. For example, Christians would not eat meat killed by a Muslim or drink from a cup used by a Muslim without purifying it by saying prayers and breathing into it three times: "as it were to drive away the evil spirit." They also greeted Muslims with the left hand as a sign of contempt.[145]

Likewise, in the seventeenth century, the Abyssinian mass of the urban population, who were called "silly vulgar people" by the German scholar, Job Ludolphus, believed the Beta Israel blacksmiths were a "sort of mortals that spit fire, and were bred up in hell," and it was alleged that blacksmiths and goldsmiths were accused of witchcraft and sometimes killed.[146] In the next century, some people believed that hyenas were "Falasha of the mountains, who . . . come down into the town to eat Christian flesh in the night."[147] Some traditions record disputes from the Gondar era when the Beta Israel were accused of being *buda* (having the "evil eye"). The widespread existence of magical prayers against the danger of the *buda* shows this belief was long-standing among the Christian population in the country.[148] The tradition of the evil eye was also manifested in Ethiopian paintings, which always show evil persons in profile so that innocent observers are not harmed by admiring a beautiful painting. For example, two Jewish soldiers in a painting in the church of Abba Entonyos, built and decorated during the reign of Yohannes I, are shown in profile.[149] The evidence suggests this attitude, and negative actions toward the Beta Israel as a result, became much more virulent in the nineteenth century, but it certainly existed as well during this earlier Gondar era.[150]

Institutional Incorporation and Social Mobility

Such ethnic distinctions and negative attitudes, however, were never an absolute barrier to social advancement in the Abyssinian social system, neither in pre-Gondarine rural society, nor certainly in the urban setting. As in any hierarchy, social mobility was possible. The mobility was probably both upward and downward since some members of the upper nobility and clergy might, from time to time, lose control of sufficient *gult* land to maintain their positions because of warfare, politics, or demographic factors.[151] Also, in pre-Gondarine society *rest*-holding peasants could advance through military ability to an officer's rank and then be rewarded by *gult* grants. Such grants would tend to become hereditary after some generations, thus providing the economic basis for a new member of the nobility at least on the local level.[152]

During the Gondar era, opportunities for such advancement expanded since the kings formed new regiments and also probably enlarged their household staffs in the settled environment of the city. In general, present-day informants explained upward mobility as a result of "ability and honesty, not religion or ethnic group." Appointments were said to have been made on the basis of "knowledge and cleverness" as well as "service and ability," not according to religious or economic criteria.[153]

These statements can be accepted as accurate within limitations. "Knowledge" could be more readily acquired by Christians through the church educational system than by non-Christians who might not join such schools. "Ability" might be more readily recognized in an Abyssinian peasant who succeeded in attaching himself to a noble with less difficulty than a non-Christian minority would find.

On the other hand, the significant role of the Gondar kings, who practiced relative ethnic and religious toleration, provided new opportunities for people to advance within the Ethiopian institutions without sacrificing their cultural integrity. The kings encouraged institutional incorporation primarily through the royal regiments and the royal household.[154] In the early sixteenth century, regiments of royal professional soldiers, called *chewa,* were stationed in the provinces under the direct control of the king. During the upheavals of the sixteenth and early seventeenth centuries, the kings lost direct control of these regiments to provincial governors, but responded by forming their own regiments and royal bodyguards under their personal control.[155]

Many of these new military units were the so-called "black horse" composed of "Shanqilla," Funj (Sudanese), and *wellaj* (Amhara-"Shanqilla" mixed offspring), captured in raids along the western Ethiopian lowlands.[156] But other peoples also made up these new royal regiments and bodyguards, including especially the Beta Israel, Muslims, and Oromo, and probably others such as Agaw, Qemant, and Amhara. Kayla regiments, for example, fought for Yohannes I; the armies of Iyyasu I included "Muslim and Jewish soldiers," and one of his royal guard units was composed entirely of Beta Israel; Iyyasu II employed "Muslim riflemen."[157] Other Agaw, "Shanqilla," Oromo, and Qemant were incorporated through work as domestic servants, household guards, pages, and stewards.[158]

The recruitment of the "Shanqilla," Oromo, and Agaw was most likely to occur as a result of capture in warfare. Some of these people, as was the case with Oromo children taken by Iyyasu I in 1689, were forcibly baptized as an incorporative technique.[159] On the other hand, groups such as the

Muslims, Qemant, and Beta Israel were more likely to join the army voluntarily and were not forced to convert.

The differential imperial policies toward the "Shanqilla," Oromo, and Agaw, on the one hand, and the Muslims, Qemant, and Beta Israel, on the other, probably resulted from the higher vulnerability of the former group. The "Shanqilla," Oromo, and Agaw had been transported farther from their homelands but were offered a change to a new life through incorporation. Others, of course, were simply sold into the international slave trade through Matamma or Massawa.[160]

On the other hand, the proximity to Gondar of the Muslims, Qemant, and Beta Israel group and their valuable artisanal and mercantile services to the monarchy led to the use of royal patronage to ensure their loyalty. Each king built his own palace instead of using that of his predecessor as a means of enhancing his claim to legitimacy.[161] In addition to this widespread construction, some kings such as Yohannes I, in particular, may have established workshops within the royal compound.[162] International trade probably increased due to the stabilization of relations with the contemporary Funj kingdom and the continuing demand for Ethiopian trade goods. These particular minorities performed essential services in all such activities.

Once brought into the general Ethiopian institutional framework, they advanced through promotion and rewards. For those in the military, promotion to *azmach* or *azaj* was possible. Royal household servants could become a *west azaj* ("inside commander") in charge of other domestic servants. The title of *nagadras* ("head of the traders") was given to the chief large-scale trader who represented the others to the king. Others known as *nagadras* were simply the heads of particular caravans. The leaders of the Beta Israel artisans became known as *bejrond*.[163]

Land grants, or the confirmation of previous land-use claims, was an essential part of the imperial policy of incorporation. The Beta Israel received new rights or had previous claims recognized at Kayla Meda, Abwara, Dafacha, Tadda, Abba Entonyos, Abba Samu'el, and Azazo.[164] The Qemant had their rights to land at Kerkerr and probably other places confirmed.[165] Muslims were assigned Eslam Bet in Gondar but also had their claims in Samen and perhaps elsewhere recognized. Some, such as a Muslim servant, received a new grant from Fasiladas.[166] Even foreigners, such as the Greeks who came to settle during the reign of Iyyasu II and who possessed essential craft skills, were granted land.[167]

The land grants issued by Iyyasu I (1682–1706) may have been part of a larger overall economic policy designed to rationalize the land tenure system and regulate trade. Iyyasu is traditionally said to have been the king who measured the land and established fixed boundaries.[168] These efforts may have helped to resolve land disputes in a frontier area that for centuries had been characterized by virulent disputes over land. The Qemant, in particular, view Iyyasu's efforts in this light.[169]

Iyyasu I also issued decrees regulating trade duties[170] and establishing official customs posts on the Gondar-Tigray route.[171] The purpose of these decrees was to regain control of a source of royal revenue that had been steadily appropriated by regional authorities during the seventeenth century.[172] To the extent that these decrees were actually enforced, they benefited the Muslim traders who would not have to fear extortionate levies by local governors.

Both the regulation of the land by fixing boundaries among various claimants and the regulation of trade duties and routes facilitated the incorporation and social mobility of ethnic minorities such as the Beta Israel, Qemant, and Muslims. They each benefited economically by the stabilization of such regulation and they, therefore, acquired a greater stake in the Abyssinian institutions into which they were being gradually incorporated.

Imperial Policies of Social Incorporation

The policies of the kings on the question of the social incorporation of diverse peoples were more ambiguous than their policies regarding institutional incorporation. These policies reflected the ambiguity of the urban social situation as well as the nature of Amhara social structure.

Pre-Gondarine Amhara society was organized according to functional specialization in which *gult* grants and titles were awarded primarily on the basis of political-military or religious achievements, rather than on kinship criteria.[173] Similarly, though ethnic intermarriage and sexual relations occurred, neither the state nor the dominant Abyssinian population had a policy of creating political structures and loyalties on the basis of such social relations.[174]

During the Gondar dynasty, the influx of diverse peoples into the city must have resulted in greater degrees of social and sexual interaction among them than previously. The *wellaj*, for example, resulted from Amhara-"Shanqilla" unions.[175] Some Oromo married into the royal dynasty and other Amhara-Oromo relations certainly existed.[176] Agaw from Lasta were said to have intermarried with the Amhara.[177]

Amhara social and sexual relations with the Muslims, Beta Israel, and probably Qemant were less extensive than those with "Shanqilla," Agaw, and Oromo. The former group was probably less willing to abandon its religion and totally assimilate to the Amhara than was the latter. On the other hand, some traditions suggest that such relations did take place. A Beta Israel tradition asserts that "about half of the Amhara [of Gondar] have Falasha ancestors," including many prominent figures of the dynasty.[178] Whether the actual claims in this tradition are historically accurate, the existence of such accounts suggests that social relationships were probably more fluid during the Gondar era than either before or after it, and that the desire by the Gondar Beta Israel for social relationships with other people was certainly greater than in the nineteenth century.

Some Gondar kings wanted to avoid such social incorporation. Yohannes I, for example, issued decrees aimed specifically at the Muslims and Beta Israel. At a royal council in 1668, he proclaimed a policy of "segregation of the Francs, Muslims, Turks, and also of the Falasha, called Kayla, who are of the Jewish religion, so that they do not live with the Christians."[179] The "Francs," actually descendants of the Portuguese, were told they had to leave the country immediately unless they converted and received baptism in the Ethiopian Orthodox Church. Other Catholic missionaries to Gondar later were either killed or forced to leave.[180] The Ethiopian Muslims (*jabarti*) were allowed to remain but had to live in a separate quarter and could not have Christians work for them or marry them. The Beta Israel similarly were ordered to live separately from Christians. The decree's purpose was to prevent further "hatred and disputes" which had occurred among the groups in the past.[181] The first decree may not have been effective as it was renewed ten years later, again specifically segregating the Muslims and Beta Israel.[182]

These decrees did not create the segregated living areas but rather confirmed an already existing situation that may, however, have been in the process of changing under the impact of urbanization and economic change. The Muslims had begun to live in a separate quarter sometime before 1648, when they were observed by a Yemenite envoy.[183] The Beta Israel had also lived in separate areas such as Kayla Meda and Abwara at least since the reign of Fasiladas.[184]

The precise reasons Yohannes felt it necessary to reinforce urban segregation are unclear but are probably related to changes caused by urban growth and political power struggles. With an expanding population stimulated by the tremendous increase in construction and trade during the early seventeenth century—activities carried out largely by the Muslims and Beta Israel—there was probably more ethnic interaction than ever before. Such interaction might have led to increased conflicts and/or sexual relations.[185] The new importance of these non-Christian minorities probably aroused the hostility and suspicions of the Christian priests. Since Yohannes's close association with and subsequent veneration by the priests is well known, they were probably instrumental in influencing him to issue these segregation decrees. He was also no doubt specifically concerned with increasing his political support during the doctrinal infighting that characterized the whole Gondar era.[186]

Traditions suggest other kings followed policies aimed at encouraging social interaction and marriage only within class and ethnic categories. It was said that "an Amhara would only marry an Amhara."[187] Iyyasu I was said to have appointed an official "whose main job was to bring husband and wife together. He would bring a wife from the *liqawent* ['nobles'] and a husband from the *liqawent*. He would match all people according to their rank and dignity. That was his main job."[188] This practice was continued by Bakaffa (1721–30), during whose reign "people from one religious group and ethnic group used to be married, not anybody else."[189] In 1732, a prominent provincial governor argued that the monarchy should follow a policy of rigid separation from the Oromo.[190] Near the end of the century, the king and highest Church officials ordered all Amhara-Tigrayans not "to serve or mingle" with the Oromo.[191]

These decrees and regulations should not be overemphasized. Those of the early eighteenth century are not well-documented and those later in the century concerning the Oromo specifically probably had more to do with the political struggles for power during the early stages of the *zamana masafent* than they had to do with ethnic relations per se. There was a high degree of "ethnic and cultural propaganda" surrounding these power struggles.[192]

As long as the monarchy was confident and secure, it was tolerant of ethnic and religious diversity and tried to utilize the talents of all peoples for the good of the realm while enhancing its own power and wealth. With regard to the social incorporation of minorities, it was more willing to countenance close relations with those who converted to Christianity and assimilated themselves to Abyssinian society, as was the case with some "Shanqilla," Agaw, and Oromo. Peoples who were less likely to convert and assimilate, such as the Muslims and Falasha, were held apart by royal decree whenever natural divisions and antipathies began to erode. Thus, even during a period of relative strength, such as the reign of Yohannes I, the monarchy was willing to manipulate ethnic relations for political reasons. And during a period of weak imperial power, the degree of ethnic propaganda could become quite malicious, as prejudices were exacerbated for political purposes.

In general during the height of the Gondar era, the kings tried to utilize the skills and obtain the loyalties of their diverse subjects while responding to the social changes of the urbanizing period. In this respect, they were somewhat more successful than they were in the maintenance of central control over the provinces, which were becoming increasingly autonomous and whose governors became ever more influential at the royal court. According to evidence from the oral traditions of such diverse groups as the Amhara, Beta Israel, and Qemant, the Gondar dynasty's socio-ethnic policies were respected and relatively successful. A fitting epitaph for these policies was expressed by the chronicler's statement on the death of Iyyasu II in 1755 that Muslims, Christians, Qemant, Falasha, soldiers, monks, and merchants all mourned and wept.[193]

Summary: Gondar's Role in Beta Israel Caste Formation

Royal patronage following the Beta Israel conquest in the 1620s began to incorporate them into Gondarine political-economic institutions. Titles and land grants or recognition of previous claims gave them a stake in the Abyssinian-dominated political-economic structure. They were increasingly defined by their roles within the larger society rather than as an independent people. This institutional incorporation into the Abyssinian political economy during the Gondar era thus marked one of the stages in the process of caste formation.

A different form of institutional incorporation was used in Samen, the site of the last Beta Israel military conflict in the 1620s, to undermine all vestiges of Beta Israel independence. In Samen the monarchy had a conscious policy of asserting direct control. The governor of Samen, whose title was *agafari*,[194] was usually the eldest and favored son of the king, thus ensuring direct royal control.[195] For example, both Fasiladas and Iyyasu I were governors of Samen before they became emperors.[196] At times, Samen was used as a royal prison.[197] The tolls from the Samen customs post at Lamalmon, the main pass between Gondar and the Red Sea, went directly to the king rather than to the local rulers, as was often the case elsewhere.[198] The tradition that the Beta Israel royal family survived in Samen until 1800[199] may be accurate, but they obviously had no national power, or even local autonomy, after Gedewon's last defeat in the 1620s. Only by the end of the eighteenth and early nineteenth century did the governorship of Samen return to the Beta Israel, and this was in the hands of a family of Christian converts epitomized by *dejazmach* Webe, who had little to do with traditional Beta Israel society.[200]

A higher degree of acculturation was also occurring in Samen than in some other places. The dominant language of Lamalmon by the 1770s was already Amharic, though their indigenous language was still spoken in many more remote locations, in Samen and elsewhere.[201] It may be inferred that the mid-eighteenth century was a period of increased conversions to Christianity in Samen since nearly half the one hundred churches there were founded from the 1730s to 1770s.[202]

In general, during the Gondar era, incorporation occurred only to a limited extent on certain levels. It mainly characterized the greater Gondar region and, in a different form, the Samen area. At the present state of documentation, less is known about processes elsewhere in the areas inhabited by the Beta Israel. Most likely, those regions continued to be dominated by the Beta Israel religious hierarchy of monks and priests. Qwara and Hohwara, for example, each were said to have had over 250 Beta Israel monks during this era.[203] So there was to some extent a rural-urban bifurcation with secular officials coming to the fore in the urban environment.

The incorporation was also restricted mainly to what I have called the institutional level. From both Abyssinian and Beta Israel perspectives, there remained a great desire to maintain social separation and prevent a high degree of social incorporation from occurring.

The evidence indicates not many Beta Israel converted or lost their language, even those nearest to the Christian center of power and religious influence at Gondar. The Beta Israel maintained their prayer houses, priests, and schools even in their enclaves near Gondar, where they were still observed in the nineteenth century.[204] Though some conversions probably occurred, their traditions maintain that even those who received appointments did not convert to Orthodoxy.[205]

A tradition recorded in the nineteenth century clearly suggests the continuing high value the Beta Israel placed on their religion during the Gondar era. In that tradition, a Gondar king was said to have had five hundred Kayla in his army when some rebels attacked them on a Saturday, knowing that was their holy day. Disregarding the pleading of the king, they refused to fight and began praying instead. God rewarded their religious steadfastness by granting them victory over their opponent, even without fighting.[206]

The Beta Israel to some extent maintained their indigenous Agaw language. In the seventeenth century, some Portuguese observers mistakenly called it Hebrew, by which they simply meant it was not Amharic, which they would have recognized. All the evidence suggests this was a dialect of the Agaw, not Hebrew, which the Beta Israel never spoke before the twentieth century.[207] In the eighteenth century, James Bruce collected some word lists and a short text in an Agaw dialect that he called "Falashan."[208] He also observed that although Amharic was gradually replacing "Falasha," the latter was still spoken in many villages of Dambeya and east of Tana.[209] Use of this language was still widespread in the nineteenth century, though Amharic was becoming more common.[210]

In summary, in the words of their only written chronicle, "during the reign of all the kings of Gondar, Israel lived in peace and welfare."[211] They developed new skills and were rewarded with land and titles that facilitated their institutional incorporation. But they maintained a high degree of cultural integrity. Most did not change religions, either under duress or voluntarily. Especially in the urban setting, they had become an integral part of the evolving Ethiopian political economy and class structure, but simultaneously held themselves, and were held by the dominant Abyssinian element, apart from the society. Particularly in the Gondar region, their position and security was dependent on their close relationship with a strong monarchy, a typical occurrence in Ethiopia.[212] All these factors demonstrate their gradual evolution toward a caste relationship within northwest Ethiopia, performing essential work while remaining socially separated. Such a relationship was fully elaborated and crystallized during the next century of turmoil.

Gondar viewed from the Royal Compound in 1975.

Gondar castles.

Beta Israel weaver in Dambeya.

Priests and people of Endabaguna, Tigray.

Synagogue in Endabaguna, Tigray.

Menstrual house in Tigray.

Beta Israel woman in Azazo.

Abba Gete Asrass, Ambobar.

Elders in Wefdar, Wagara.

4. The Consolidation of Caste Formation, 1755–1868

The consolidation of Beta Israel caste formation was completed during the early nineteenth century era of political instability and localization known as the *zamana masafent* ("era of the princes"). The decline in imperial power and bankruptcy of the imperial ideology, increased warfare and insecurity, and the fall in Gondar's population adversely affected the construction industry, causing the Beta Israel to revert to ironworking and pottery-making as their main craft activities.

Though respected among their own people, these were lower prestige tasks in the dominant Abyssinian society. The Beta Israel were no longer rewarded with land grants or the more prestigious titles of *azmach* or *azaj*. Instead, they became scapegoats for the problems of the times, increasingly stereotyped by the *buda* ("evil eye") syndrome. In addition, both Orthodox Christians and foreign Protestants stepped up proselytization, providing other challenges to Beta Israel society.

As in previous times of internal crisis and external threats, the Beta Israel responded with a religious revival that culminated in a dispute with Orthodox officials argued before Tewodros's court in 1862. The main consequence of the revival was to rigidify their ideology of social separation. The Beta Israel saw themselves as having a greater religious purity and higher morality than Orthodox society. To protect themselves in a time of crisis, they consolidated and fully invoked the rules of social separation originally developed by *abba* Sabra in the fifteenth century.

Thus, Orthodox society reinforced the ideology and practice of social separation of the Falasha blacksmith/potter-*buda,* while the Beta Israel maintained separation on the grounds of moral and religious purity. Each perspective strengthened the caste nature of the relationship. Hence, the political-economic, social, and religious changes of this period marked the last stage of the caste formation process. By the 1860s, the Beta Israel–Abyssinian caste relationship was characterized by a common political-economic structure, similar cultural practices, birth-ascribed occupational specialization, and fixed rules and patterns of social interaction that were maintained by separationist ideologies on each side.[1]

A Century of Conflict: *Zamana Masafent* and Tewodros, 1755–1868

The breakdown in central government or the *zamana masafent* ("era of the princes") was caused by both immediate and long-range structural factors.[2] The forbidding Ethiopian geographic features provide only the background but not the explanation for the breakdown, since the geography was constant whether in periods of unity or disunity. These features include a plateau cut by steep escarpments and deep river valleys and a rainy season that cuts off communications for several months of the year. Although Ethiopia did not yet possess a technology sufficient to overcome these disunifying factors,[3] the Abyssinian regions nevertheless had been previously much more united than they became during this period, so that historical analysis must supplement geographical and technological factors.

Structural Transformations

The underlying explanation for disunity must be sought in the nature of the Abyssinian institution of kingship, the personal characteristics of the Gondarine kings, changes in the political and economic relationship of the kings to the provinces, and an apparent transformation in Abyssinian social structure during the eighteenth and nineteenth centuries.

In general, Abyssinian kingship was "weakly institutionalized"[4] and relied for its actual power—as opposed to its theoretical authority—on a continuing process of military expansion that provided a steady source of land and booty to be redistributed as royal patronage. The relatively fluid, achievement-oriented Abyssinian society meant each king had to legitimize his own rule and rebuild his personal coalition upon ascending to office by allocating titles and land in his name and, in the Gondar period especially, by building castles and churches.[5] The weak-willed kings after Fasiladas, except for Iyyasu I (1682–1706), found it difficult to strengthen the institution of kingship by consolidating their power and authority.[6]

Long-range structural changes at both the national and provincial levels were the main causes of disunity. At the king's court, as early as the Order of Precedence of 1690, military leaders had achieved a preeminence over clerical officials. Gradually, each king permitted the devolution of many of his military and administrative functions into the hands of a favorite lieutenant whose office of *ras* ("head") or *ras-behtewaddad* ("beloved head") acquired the authority of "first minister" and who became the real power behind the throne.[7]

Crucial developments at the provincial level accompanied these changes at the center. As noted previously, during the period of large-scale Oromo migrations in the sixteenth and seventeenth centuries, the kings gradually lost control of their frontier regiments of professional soldiers called *chewa*.[8] The *chewa* slowly became autonomous in the frontier provinces with their own control over local land and warfare. By the time of Iyyasu I, *chewa* units were refusing his summons to war, desiring to campaign on their own.[9]

Since they campaigned independently, the *chewa* controlled the rewards of booty and land, thus depriving the kings of an important source of revenue and the wherewithal to build their own power bases. Hence, the *chewa* transformed themselves from a professional soldiery dependent on the monarchy for land and titles into an autonomous provincial nobility. By the eighteenth century, *chewa* could be translated as "gentry," or in other words, they had become a part of the nobility, just below the *makwannent* or "great nobles."[10]

A comparable process of localization took place in the central provinces as, already by the early to mid-seventeenth century, certain "ancient and illustrious families" claimed the hereditary right to both lands and titles, especially in Tigray and Dambeya.[11] By 1730, outlying provinces such as Damot made the same claim, as local nobles refused to accept two royal appointees as governors because they did not come from that province. Thus, the king had to appoint a local noble as governor.[12]

In the northern province of Tigray, through which the principal international trade routes ran, the acquisition of local control extended to the customs revenues as well. Though Iyyasu I tried to attack that problem, in general, the kings suffered an erosion of control over customs duties. As early as the eighteenth century, this erosion allowed the Tigrayan rulers, such as *ras* Mika'el, to build up a significantly larger stock of firearms than any other leader, including the king at Gondar.[13]

Recent stimulating research by Donald Crummey has gone some distance toward providing empirical support for the hypothesis that the eighteenth-century Abyssinian nobility at both the national and provincial levels was emerging as a self-conscious class, increasingly in opposition to the interests of the monarchy, and also trying to assert itself against the peasantry. In the Abyssinian ideological and social charter, offices and *gult*, or the right to collect tribute from certain pieces of land, were to be allocated by the king and were neither hereditary nor permanent. In institutions and practices during the eighteenth century, both the *chewa* ("gentry") and the *makwannent* ("upper nobility") began to arrogate unto themselves the right to overturn these royal prerogatives. They did this through the practice of land sales and the institution of the *alaqenat*.

The practice of land sales apparently began around 1730 and steadily increased thereafter.[14] These sales were carried out mainly by the lesser nobility, or "gentry."[15] Selling land contravened both the practice of awarding *gult* rights by the king and to some extent the inheritance of direct access to the land by the peasantry through the institution of *rest*.

The institution of the *alaqenat* emerges from documents on marriage and inheritance during the eighteenth century. *Alaqa* was a title, generally rendered as "leader," but in this case, it meant "something rather different: the right of seniority, precedence or leadership amongst a group of heirs or claimants."[16] In these documents the *alaqenat* appears as an "institution of inheritance which favored one child over the others by giving that child a substantially larger, and better-defined, share of the inheritance."[17] The inheritance in the documents cited included *gult* and *rim* land as well as cattle and other movable property.[18]

By the eighteenth century, the nobility was accumulating material rights within transgenerational families. This process, hence, was in contradistinction to the traditional prerogatives of the king, as well as in opposition to the principles of ambilineal inheritance that tended toward the fragmentation of land, other material goods, and even the family structure. Though less well-documented, these processes of land sales and the institution of the *alaqenat* also appear to be in opposition to the tradition direct access to the land enjoyed through the *rest* system by the peasantry. To the extent that the same noble families inherited *gult* and *rim* land rights over several generations, would not that process tend to consolidate their interests over these same pieces of land whose *rest* rights were being passed down within particular peasant families?

Thus, particularly vis-à-vis the monarchy, but one may hypothesize also vis-à-vis the peasantry, a "national ruling class"[19] was developing in the eighteenth century. Its increasing economic and local political power reached its apogee with the acquisition of national political power during this period. Nevertheless, this political power was always somewhat limited by the power struggle within the nobility and by the continuation of the monarchical form even without the substance. The *masafent* were competing with each other for the position of kingmaker rather than king. To see how this competition developed, an analysis of the short-range factors that led to a power struggle in the mid-eighteenth century is necessary.

Transition to the *Zamana Masafent*

The immediate origins of the "era of the princes" lay in the reigns of Iyyasu II (1730–55) and his son Iyo'as (1755–69). Although the issues that began the *zamana masafent* have sometimes been cast in ethnic-religious terms as a struggle by the Christian Abyssinians (Amhara and Tigrayan) against Muslim "Galla" (Oromo) domination, the actual situation was both simpler and more complex. Ethnic-religious motivations and more especially propaganda were certainly present, but the precise alignment of forces fluctuated. The real dynamics were the struggle for personal power by key individuals which occurred within the context of the long-range structural changes already discussed.[20]

During the reign of Iyyasu II, a "first minister" rose to be the real power behind the throne, along with the king's mother Mentewwab, who was crowned empress simultaneously with the accession of her son. Her elder brother, Walda Le'ul, climaxed a brilliant career by obtaining the appointment of *ras-behtewaddad*, or "first minister," in 1733 and remained in that office until his death in 1767.[21] His rise was part of that long-range structural transformation described above in which military appointees achieved precedence over the clerical, but it was also an example of the means by which Mentewwab had woven a web of political power since the death of her husband Emperor Bakaffa in 1730, using her family from Qwara and marriage alliances with other groups.

Mentewwab's desire to keep personal power prevented her son, Iyyasu II, from ever achieving power in his own right. On his premature death in 1755 at the age of 32,[22] she had his child, Iyo'as, appointed king. Iyo'as's mother Wabi was the daughter of a Wallo Oromo chief whose marriage to Iyyasu had been arranged by Mentewwab. On the accession of Iyo'as, Wabi's brothers, Lubo and Birale, rose in influence at the court.[23]

Both the major claimants to replace Walda Le'ul as first minister were sons-in-law of Mentewwab: Ya-Maryam Barya, the governor of Begamder, and Mika'el Sehul of Tigray. Mika'el's son was also married to Mentewwab's daughter.[24] They had become the two major territorial lords and had been competing for control of Lasta province since 1765. Each tried to manipulate his connection to Mentewwab and to the Wallo Oromo to become first minister, but Mika'el won out.

Lubo, the brother of the king's wife, dominated the court after the death of Walda Le'ul in 1767. He appointed his brother Birale, governor of Begamder and Mika'el, to the position of *ras-behtewaddad,* or first minister.[25] These appointments sparked a revolt by Ya-Maryam Barya, who defeated and killed Birale in 1768 before Mika'el and the king suppressed his rebellion and executed him the next year.[26]

This revolt by Ya-Maryam Barya has sometimes been seen as a defense of Amhara Christianity against Muslim "Galla" influence at court.[27] But it would be more accurate to say that both Ya-Maryam Barya and Mika'el were trying to use the Oromo to further their own interests and power. Ya-Maryam Barya, in fact, urged Lubo to become the first minister himself rather than appoint Mika'el.[28] It was basically a struggle between two powerful individuals who mobilized whatever ethnic, religious, and personal ties they had as motivational and propagandistic tools.

During these conflicts, the king became worried about the growing power of Mika'el and ordered him to return to Tigray. Mika'el, however, ignored the order, marched into Gondar, and had the king assassinated. Mika'el then placed two kings on the throne in quick succession, but was himself defeated at the battle of Sarbakusa in 1771.

For more than a decade after this, provincial governors fought for control of the court through a series of shifting alliances. *Ras* Ali the Great of the Warrashek family from Yajju, whose father Gwangel had earlier supported *ras* Mika'el, finally won these struggles by 1784 and established the ruling dynasty of kingmakers that lasted until the defeat of *ras* Ali II by Kassa-Tewodros in 1853.[29]

The Yajju have often been referred to as "Galla" (Oromo) and Muslim,[30] but their actual ethnic-religious identity by the eighteenth century is problematical. Though the area of Yajju had had Muslim and Oromo influences, research suggests the area was Semitic-speaking in the sixteenth century; their oral traditions also do not indicate that they saw themselves as Galla.[31] Even one chronicler, who was often critical of the increased "Galla" influence during this era, referred to *ras* Ali, the founder of the dynasty, as a new Constantine, a convert to Christianity who built many churches and upheld the faith.[32] The dominant figures in this dynasty and their ruling years included the first Ali (1784–88), Gugsa (1803–25), Mareyye (1828–31), and Ali II (1831–53).[33]

But despite their role as kingmakers and their dominance over the central provinces of Begamder-Amhara, these Yajju rulers were never able to consolidate control over the whole country. Tigray remained autonomous under Sabagadis from the 1820s until his death at the battle of Dabra Abbay in 1831, and then under Webe until 1855.

The third major power in the highlands was the kingdom of Shawa, which had been tributary to the king during the Gondar era. But by the reign of Sahle Sellase (1813–47), Shawa had grown in size and prosperity and had become completely autonomous from Gondar and the Yajju kingmakers.[34]

The rulers of the lesser provinces of Gojjam, Damot, Lasta, and Qwara contributed to the power struggles by supporting one side or the other in the shifting coalitions. But until the rise of Kassa-Tewodros of Qwara, none could make a bid for national power nor were they permanently controlled by the Yajju dynasty. As the chronicler lamented: "Those were the days not of kings, but of the servants."[35] Not only had "masters . . . become servants, and the servants masters," but the servants were in disarray and fighting among themselves.[36]

Urban Decline and Rural Instability

The kingmakers and would-be kingmakers fought numerous wars that ravaged the countryside and depleted the population of some major cities, such as Gondar. Of course, other cities flourished, such as the new Yajju capital, Dabra Tabor. But the decline of royal power and bankruptcy of the imperial ideology meant the kings of the period had neither the means nor interest in the large-scale stone construction that each Gondar king had carried out to establish and legitimize his own personal rule.[37]

In rural areas, Abyssinian soldiers historically had lived off the land, seizing crops and cattle as needed. The disturbed conditions of these times made farming more difficult for the peasantry, especially those living along the main roads that were likely to be plundered by every passing army.[38] Much of the violence occurred between soldier and peasant rather than simply between the soldiers of rival armies. Governors sent expeditions to collect tribute and assert their authority over areas they claimed, even if they could not control them completely. In the 1830s, for example, *ras* Ali was said to have invaded Lasta and Wag, "devastating those districts which admitted of access" when he could not thoroughly conquer them.[39]

In the Gondar area, a critical transitional period began with the death of the Yajju kingmaker Gugsa (reigned 1803–25), which unleashed a power struggle and a period of extreme instability for the next six years. Some of the contenders, such as *ras* Mareyye (1828–31), specifically encouraged their soldiers to plunder so that they could share in the booty.[40] Although Gondar remained somewhat important, it declined in population and significance from the warfare and loss of imperial power. The city was sacked and parts of it burned many times.[41] Its population declined from the 40,000 to 80,000 estimated at its peak[42] to the 6,000 to 18,000 who lived there from the 1830s to 1860s.[43] Even by 1838, observers saw how "war can desolate a capital. The debris of its houses and of its palaces litters its vast streets or remains hidden under the filthy grass; . . . every evening all the public places are abandoned to the hyenas and jackals."[44]

By the 1860s, the city had deteriorated further: "I am already in the streets of Gondar, but I perceive nothing yet that indicates a city. I see five or six large villages, separated by some vacant ground strewn with ruins, cut by low walls of dry stone. There is thus the capital of Suseneyos and of Fasiladas!"[45] The peripheries of the city were particularly affected. Kayla Meda, for example, had been a traditional gathering place in which proclamations were issued, theological disputes debated, and armies had gathered to go off to war.[46] But in these times, battles were fought there and at other areas in and around the city.[47]

Gondar's smaller population needed fewer houses. And because of the decline of the monarchy, no large-scale stone construction was undertaken after the reign of Iyyasu II (1730–55). The great castles and churches of Gondar were falling down for lack of repairs. By 1771, even Fasiladas's great palace was partially in ruins, though some rooms on the lower floors were still usable.[48] Smaller houses of wood and clay with thatched roofs had been built near the large palace and given the names of its former rooms.[49] By the middle of the nineteenth century, Fasiladas's palace had further deteriorated and was almost entirely uninhabitable.[50] During the power struggles following the death of Gugsa, conditions worsened. Mennen, the mother of *ras* Ali II (reigned 1831–53) deliberately tore down parts of Fasiladas's palace and had only one church repaired.[51] Of the other buildings in the royal compound, only a few were in good condition by the 1840s.[52] Mentewwab's castle to the west and the Ras Gemb north of the royal compound were also in disrepair.[53]

The only new construction was churches and houses, but these structures were simple affairs compared to the great buildings of Egzi'abher Ab, Dabra Berhan Sellase, and Dabra Sahay Qwesqwam. In the place of those great stone edifices built between 1667 and 1755 were the seven smaller churches built by Takla Haymanot II (1769–77) and those of two other late eighteenth-century kings.[54] In the early nineteenth century, fewer churches were built or even repaired, and no more than half of Gondar's reputed forty-four churches were in good condition.[55]

Builders to Blacksmiths: Beta Israel Occupations to 1868

In response to the decreasing construction opportunities after 1755, the Beta Israel began to reorient their occupational emphases. In urban areas during the Gondar era, they had been masons and carpenters as well as blacksmiths, potters, and weavers. But, during the *zamana masafent,* especially after the key transitional period of 1825–31, they reverted more completely to their pre-Gondarine roles as blacksmiths, potters, and weavers, even in the Gondar area. Though some still worked as builders up through the early twentieth century, this was no longer their main occupation, nor were all the builders Beta Israel.[56]

Evidence for this transformation is found in the direct testimony of outside observers. In the 1770s, for example, Bruce mentioned "several small villages" just north of Gondar inhabited entirely by Beta Israel masons and roof thatchers who worked in Gondar.[57] This evidence is not unambiguous, since Bruce did not refer to these villages by name, but no subsequent visitor who followed the same route to Gondar mentioned these villages just to the north—unless Bruce meant Abba Entonyos, which is more to the west than north—suggesting they ceased to exist following the 1770s.[58]

The Beta Israel enclaves nearest the city were Abwara, Dafacha, and Kayla Meda. In these areas, up to the 1830s, the Beta Israel were referred to mainly as builders and masons. Thus, in 1815 and 1830, they were considered to be the best builders[59] and the "architects of Gondar" who built "most of the houses" of the city.[60] Also in Tigray in 1805 the "main employment" of the Beta Israel near the village of Antalo, the governor's capital, was building and thatching houses.[61]

From the mid-1830s to the 1860s, however, observers noted the occupations of blacksmith, potter, and weaver as often as those of mason or carpenter, even for those Beta Israel in the vicinity of Gondar.[62] In rural areas, such as in Dambeya and Gojjam, they were almost entirely blacksmiths, potters, or weavers, and in some cases, entire villages were devoted to one of those crafts.[63] By the 1860s, the occupation of blacksmith was "almost exclusively" carried out by the Beta Israel.[64] Besides the Gondar area, Beta Israel blacksmiths were observed in several locations in Tigray, Walqayt, Samen, and Gojjam.[65]

Of course, blacksmithing was not a new occupation for the Beta Israel. Even during the Gondar era, probably almost all of the blacksmiths in the central and northern parts of the country were Beta Israel. The point here is that to the extent construction work was no longer a viable occupation, smithing and potting became even more significant.

As building opportunities disappeared and the overall population of Gondar declined, the Beta Israel population on its peripheries also decreased. Again, a key period was the second quarter of the century. On the southwest edge, Abwara fell from about 300 to 400 people with sixty houses in the 1830s[66] to an area of only thirty houses by 1860.[67] On the eastern edge of the city, Dafacha experienced a parallel decline from about four hundred people in 1815[68] to about forty families (or about 200 to 250 people) in 1860.[69] The third area, Kayla Meda, probably also declined similarly, especially since it was an area specifically referred to as a battleground at various times during this period.[70]

An occupational alternative to construction work could have been agriculture. But the political instability and the tenuous relationship of the Beta Israel to the land meant agriculture could not be an adequate substitute for building. The Beta Israel had been completely dependent on the Gondar kings not only for construction work but also for the beginning steps to reacquire land-use rights they had lost in the pre-Gondarine conquest era. But with the decline of the monarchy, they could not obtain new land grants, and some evidence suggests their few land rights began to be encroached upon by the *masafent*.

Though the direct evidence is fragmentary, the insecurity of the times, the erosion of the monarchy, the monetization of society, and the increased wealth and power of the nobility all suggest that the disruption, confiscation, or purchase of Beta Israel land was a common phenomenon during this era. Beta Israel traditions assert the Abyssinian nobility, once it had escaped royal control, began to reclaim land they regarded as rightfully theirs.[71] The increased monetization of society and the land sales that had begun in the mid-eighteenth century also allowed wealthy nobles to purchase new pieces of land. Land charters record at least one instance specifically involving the Beta Israel, in which Walda Sellase purchased "five parcels" of land from "Falasha *medr*" ["field"] as part of a package he then granted to the Cathedral of Aksum.[72] The location of this purchase is unknown. Though the phrase *Falasha medr* might suggest the area of Kayla Meda near Gondar, most likely this land was located in Tigray, where many Beta Israel also lived, such as near Walda Sellase's capital of Antalo.[73]

While the nobles were encroaching upon their land-use rights, they were not able to acquire new land either. After the reign of Iyyasu II, they were no longer paid for craftwork with land grants, except in isolated cases.[74] Instead of land, they were said to have been paid in money and slaves. In 1815, one builder would work for six days for one Maria Theresa dollar.[75] Also during the time of Gugsa, slave-raiding expeditions produced a surplus so that some slaves were given to Beta Israel workers as payment for repairing or constructing houses.[76] Beta Israel traditions deny ever having received slaves, but admit they did have servants.[77] Such traditions indicate the sensitive nature of the subject but also suggest the relative insignificance of the occurrence.

In any case, their payments in whatever form were probably not sufficient to enable them to acquire land by purchase, even if they had been allowed by Abyssinian society to do so. They only made one dollar in six days, hardly enough to obtain a surplus for land purchases, whose typical price was one dollar per parcel.[78] And if they did acquire the use of servants or slaves within the family, they certainly did not become international slave dealers and obtain money to purchase land in that manner. The subject of slavery in Ethiopia needs more study, but the skimpy evidence available suggests the institution mainly involved household servants who might eventually be incorporated into the society, much as was the case in some other African societies.[79]

Thus, although many Beta Israel continued to survive as tenant farmers, they had to supplement that income with craftwork. And since construction opportunities were declining, an increasing number had to revert to blacksmithing and potting.

Internal societal characteristics facilitated this transformation. The Beta Israel called a person who was too lazy or unskilled to do good work *enchet menchet,* referring to a pot made of wood, that is, a useless article.[80] The high, though not necessarily equal, value the Beta Israel placed on all types of work, including ironworking, agriculture, and building meant there were few internal constraints on switching occupations as dictated by external conditions. Though Beta Israel priests could not be blacksmiths simultaneously, in general, the Beta Israel respected blacksmiths as wise men.[81] Construction work and particularly agriculture were more respectable occupations to both Beta Israel and Abyssinian society, as illustrated by the grants and titles awarded during the Gondar era.

As the situation changed in the early nineteenth century, the Beta Israel adapted to circumstances by reemphasizing smithing, potting, and weaving instead of masonry and carpentry. This occupational transformation allowed them to survive economically but had significant political and social implications.

Political, Cultural, and Social Changes to 1868

The political, cultural, and social consequences of the transformation in Beta Israel occupations further illustrates their consolidation into an occupational caste. Politically, the Beta Israel secular elite lost their formerly prominent leadership roles in the general society as they changed from war leaders to artisans. Accompanying this was some account of cultural-linguistic change. But despite heightened acculturation, the principal social structural characteristics of the period were an increasing degree of separation and the delineation of clearly defined rules of interaction between Beta Israel and non–Beta Israel.

Political Titles: From *Azmach* to *Bejrond*

Politically, the Beta Israel were in transition from a position of some political influence to a status virtually outside the political leadership structure of the general society. Though it is not well-documented, Beta Israel oral traditions suggest that despite the loss of independence in the seventeenth century, their elite had continued to play a prominent political-military role in Gondar society.[82] Vestiges of that type of role as war leaders, administrators, and soldiers remained during the early nineteenth century, as illustrated in their relationship with *dejazmach* Webe.[83] But, in general, the Beta Israel elite no longer played any significant political role in the general society during the *zamana masafent*.

Their transition to a position of little political importance is illustrated by the changes in the types of appointments and recognition the Beta Israel secular elite received during this era. During the Gondar period, the Beta Israel had been soldiers and war leaders as well as respected builders and artisans. Correspondingly, their elites had received land grants and appointments, both of a general political-military nature, such as *azmach* or *azaj*, and those derived chiefly from their artisan functions, such as *bejrond*, which for the Beta Israel had the connotation of "chief of the workers." Their traditions emphasize the higher status and larger number of *azmaches/azajes* than *bejronds* during that period.[84]

During the nineteenth century, however, they began to be known almost exclusively as *bejrond* rather than by any other title. This change was a natural consequence of their increasingly rigid occupational identification only as low-status artisans.[85] Beta Israel traditions recorded the transformation quite explicitly: "They [*azmach* and *azaj*] commanded everybody in town. Later, they were replaced by *bejronds*."[86]

The *azmach,* and to a lesser extent, the *azaj,* were titles given to war leaders, district governors, and in general, those who commanded other people ("everybody in town"). On the other hand, the Beta Israel *bejrond* was only "the leader of the pottery workers, masons, blacksmiths, and all other workers."[87] As another informant stated: "The *azmach* was a government administrator for many people, but the *bejrond* was only concerned with the Beta Israel."[88]

Contemporary observations confirm this. In the 1840s, for example, d'Abbadie said, "The Falasha being all workers, that is to say, potters, masons, or carpenters, seek to be employed by the king, which authorizes them to 'wear a shirt' and [have] the title of *bejrond*."[89] "To wear a shirt" refers to the Amharic, *baʿala shamiz* ("owner of a shirt"), indicating someone with a royal appointment. The statement thus indicates not only their historic connection to and dependence on the monarchy, but also that the title of *bejrond* was the main title to which the Beta Israel could aspire by the early nineteenth century. For the Beta Israel, it was a lower-level and, more specifically, occupationally defined title than either *azmach* or *azaj*.

This gradual change in type of political appointment illustrates the narrowing options available to the Beta Israel as they became almost exclusively defined by particular occupations. This political change was, therefore, a part of the hardening Beta Israel occupational relationship to Abyssinian society.

This transition to *bejrond* was begun, but not completed, during the early nineteenth century. Several secular leaders whose names are known from the reign of Tewodros (1855–68) and earlier were *bejronds,* such as *bejrond* Eyrusalem of Abwara.[90] Many people are recalled by name as *bejrond* from the reigns of Yohannes IV and Menilek II, as this title became increasingly typical for Beta Israel secular leaders.[91]

The transitional nature of this era is further illustrated by the relationship of the Beta Israel to *dejazmach* Webe. This relationship was a vestige of the former Beta Israel role as war leaders and soldiers. Webe was the illegitimate second of several sons by different women of *dejazmach* Hayla Maryam, the ruler of Samen and Walqayt. The third son, Merso, was his designated successor instead of the older Webe, apparently because Webe's mother, *waizero* Mentaye, was of "humble birth."[92] She was said to be a beautiful widow from Janamora district in Wagara with whom Hayla Maryam spent a rainy afternoon while out hunting.[93] Beta Israel oral traditions dating from the 1840s, supported by testimony from the 1970s, indicate that on his father's side Webe descended from a branch of the Beta Israel ruling family which converted to Christianity after the fifteenth-century defeat in Wagara by King Yeshaq.[94]

After the death of his father, Webe became involved in a power struggle with his half-brother Merso for the governorship of Samen. He built a power base in Walqayt, Samen, and Wagara through alliances with some of his father's former generals who were also from his mother's land.[95] "Half the army" and many of the officers in Webe's force were Beta Israel from Walqayt; he also had a Beta Israel "captain of riflemen" from Samen.[96] With this power base, he defeated Merso and claimed the governorship of Samen, Walqayt, and eventually Tigray as well, with his capital at Amba Hay in Samen.[97]

This case study of Webe illustrates that a man of Beta Israel ancestry and even immediate descent could still play a prominent political-military role in northern Ethiopia and that some Beta Israel were still soldiers and war leaders. These, however, were the exceptions and even in these cases, the limitations on the Beta Israel political role are apparent. In no sense was Webe fighting for the Beta Israel as such. In his wars—for example, the battle of Dabra Tabor against *ras* Ali in 1842—he had the support of the *abun* and was considered to be the defender of Christendom against the Muslim upstarts.[98] In this sense, as well as in view of the fact that the Beta Israel did not play a prominent role as fighters for other warlords of the period, this case was atypical of the Beta Israel political role during the *zamana masafent*.[99]

Linguistic Acculturation

As political roles deteriorated, the Beta Israel came under increasing pressure from Abyssinian society that affected aspects of their culture, such as language. The process of linguistic acculturation was long and gradual. During the earlier centuries of conquest and urban interaction, the Beta Israel began to learn Amharic but also maintained their Agaw language, variously called Hwarasa, Felashinya, Felashan, Falasha, or Kaylinya.[100] The gradual spread of Amharic in the northwest by the 1770s was captured by Bruce in his reference to the village of Dingleber in Dambeya: "The language here is Falasha, though only used now by the Jews who go by that name: it was anciently the language of all the province of Dembea, which has here its southern boundary."[101] At another time, Bruce was again traveling in the same region: "The inhabitants of this and the neighboring villages speak Falasha, the language anciently of all Dembea, which as has already been observed, in most of the plain country, has now given place to Amharic."[102]

These comments suggest that, in the 1770s, the Beta Israel still mainly spoke their own language but that the region was becoming more Amhara ethnically (which included the absorption of some Beta Israel, too), and therefore, the use of Amharic was spreading, especially in non–Beta Israel areas.

By the second quarter of the nineteenth century, Amharic was becoming the first language of the Beta Israel as well. Thus, in 1830, the Beta Israel were said to use their own language among themselves, but except for a few women they were all able to speak Amharic with "some ease and accuracy."[103] By the 1840s at Gondar, whereas the older people still spoke their own indigenous language, the children of the Beta Israel spoke "only Amharic" and had forgotten the language of their parents.[104] By the 1860s, even in rural areas apart from Gondar, the Beta Israel all spoke Amharic as well as the Amhara.[105] By the early twentieth century, the Beta Israel in Gondar knew only Amharic, except for a few old people.[106]

Although the causes of this linguistic change cannot be documented precisely, it is possible to reconstruct the broad outlines of the process. During the Gondar dynasty, the men—who had the highest degree of interaction with Abyssinian society as builders, soldiers, and war leaders—learned the most Amharic. But they also retained their indigenous language because they had learned it in their families as children, especially from their mothers. The women would have had little use for Amharic because their only interaction with the general society was to sell and buy a few goods at the market. Since one pottery market was within Kayla Meda itself,[107] they did not even have to leave their district to sell the pottery.

Perhaps in the more precarious economic situation of the early nineteenth century, including the breakdown of large-scale group occupations such as masonry and carpentry, both men and women found it economically necessary to interact individually with the Amhara in order to make their living. Whereas in a group of Beta Israel builders only their leader would have had to deal much with non–Beta Israel, smithing and potting were more individualized occupations, requiring a one-to-one relationship between the artisan and his or her customer. This type of interaction may have led to more Beta Israel learning Amharic.[108]

Social Separation: The *Buda* Phenomenon

Despite some degree of linguistic acculturation, social separation rather than Beta Israel incorporation characterized this period. These separatist patterns included three main aspects: the Beta Israel became more specifically defined as a unique group within the general society; they declined in social status from their previous position during the Gondar era; the rules of interaction rigidified, based on increasingly negative stereotyped attitudes by each group toward the other.

Social separation was increasingly supported by specific policies and ideologies on the part of both the Beta Israel and the dominant society. Abyssinians called the Beta Israel *buda* and treated them with a mixture of fear and repugnance, while the Beta Israel considered themselves morally superior and underwent a religious revival in defense of their ideology and practice of social separation.

A *buda* ("evil eye") was considered to be both the spirit which possessed a person and the person capable of causing the spirit to posses one. Several variations on the actions of the *buda* were known from northwestern Ethiopia.[109] At night, the *buda* could turn itself into a hyena and roam about digging up graves and devouring the cadavers.[110] It was believed that if a hyena were harmed, the same injury would appear on the *buda*-person the next day.[111] Conversely, small gold earrings worn by certain suspected *budas* during the day were also found on hyenas shot during the night.[112]

During the day, a *buda* could possess another person and cause him or her to turn into a hyena,[113] a donkey,[114] or other animals, such as cows or cats, or even stones.[115] The *buda* could also cause death or illness by using his or her evil eye to enter another person and drink the person's blood or eat the entrails.[116]

In the northwest, the main *buda*-persons were Beta Israel, especially blacksmiths or potters,[117] but other peoples might also be considered *buda*. At times, even Christians were called *buda*.[118] People from Gojjam were often suspected of being *budas,* but it is not clear if those accused were Beta Israel, Agaw, or Christian Amhara.[119] At times also, Wayto, Muslims, the Qemant, or other groups might be called *buda*.[120] Of course, among other peoples in other parts of the country, such as the Oromo, Gurage, and in Harar, ironworkers and other artisans such as leatherworkers and potters were often considered *buda* or sorcerers.[121] In addition, many Muslims and even some Beta Israel believed in the *buda* phenomenon, fearing its power as much as did the Christians.[122]

Since non–Beta Israel were occasionally called *buda,* while Beta Israel and others were themselves afraid of the *buda,* the epithet was obviously not applied only to the Beta Israel. But in the Beta Israel heartland of northwestern Ethiopia, the *buda* attribute gradually became almost exclusively assigned to Beta Israel blacksmiths and potters in a rigid equation: blacksmith/potter = *buda* = Falasha [Beta Israel].

As explained above, the Beta Israel increasingly became identified as blacksmiths and potters. To complete the equation, several sources noted that the dominant society identified both the Falasha and blacksmiths or potters as *buda.* Christians in Gondar said the Beta Israel were "wizards and cannibals—eating men by some secret process of sorcery," or that they were "looked upon as witches."[123] A well-known Beta Israel woman in Gondar was called the "Queen of the *Boudas.*"[124]

In Tigray, the "*buda* or blacksmith" were equated.[125] Gafat near Dabra Tabor was said to be inhabited by a "population of blacksmiths who passed for *buda,* sorcerers."[126] In general: "the class or workers in iron are universally and without exception honoured with the title [of *buda*], insomuch that the terms are synonymous."[127] Another observer noted: "In Abyssinia the trade of blacksmith is hereditary, and considered as more or less disgraceful, from the fact that blacksmiths are, with very rare exceptions, believed to be all sorcerers, and are opprobriously called 'Bouda.'"[128]

The Beta Israel themselves saw the *zamana masafent* as critical in the development of the *buda* phenomenon: "The Galla came and magnified the insults. They began to call us *buda.* They talked about it very much. That is when the insult *buda* began. They even said the Falasha kill men."[129] According to the evidence, however, this was not the period when the *buda* insult, the idea of *buda* sorcery, or even the association of *buda* with Falasha originated. It was also obviously not the beginning of Beta Israel segregation. But it does seem to have been a period when the *buda* phenomenon intensified, and the rules of social separation were more fully elaborated and enforced than previously.

Over the centuries, the experience had varied. In the fifteenth century, Zar'a Ya'eqob was said to have executed blacksmiths at his court, accusing them of sorcery, and it was said to have happened in the seventeenth century as well.[130] Also in the seventeenth century, a popular notion of the Falasha was of men who "spat fire and were bred up in hell"[131] and who had to live in segregated quarters.[132] But also in the seventeenth century, several Christians denied that *budas* existed, stating that to believe such a power could exist outside the will of God was to believe there were two Gods and therefore such a belief was un-Christian.[133] This view was congruent with Beta Israel traditions, which state they successfully defended themselves against *buda* accusations at that time.[134] These ambiguities in the sources may reflect the relative fluidity of Abyssinian social structure and the Beta Israel position within it during the seventeenth century. But by the late eighteenth century, the association of Falasha with *buda* and the were-hyena was renewed.[135]

Abyssinian prayers against the *buda* as part of the corpus of magical and other prayers in Ethiopic manuscripts over the centuries suggests the long-standing existence of the phenomenon.[136] Some of these prayers explicitly equate Falasha, blacksmith, *buda,* and evil eye.[137] They cannot be dated precisely in most cases, but the early nineteenth century was a key period.[138]

How can the ebb and flow of the *buda* phenomenon over the centuries be explained? Part of the explanation may lie in the nature and extent of the sources. The numerous European observers in the early nineteenth century were struck by this phenomenon, perhaps because it confirmed preexisting views of African "magic." Perhaps the experience was not only more prevalent in that period but also more widely observed and documented.

But an overall explanation must consider the broad historical, social, and psychological factors within Ethiopia and particularly the changing position of the Beta Israel in Abyssinian society. The roots of the attitude may lie in the mystery surrounding the process of transforming earth into pottery and "rock" into iron in the context of a peasant and technologically relatively simple society.[139] In such a society, those who can work such transformations are naturally assumed to have supernatural help. Such beliefs, which often result in either an extraordinarily high social position and an attitude of awe and reverence, or a very low social position and an attitude of fear and repugnance toward the blacksmith, in particular, have been common to many African societies.[140]

A reconstruction based on historical data as interpreted by ethnographic studies suggests that the *buda* phenomenon served the socio-psychological function of maintaining the solidarity of Amhara and, more broadly, Abyssinian society during times of crisis.[141] The presumed magical powers of blacksmiths are the psychological bases of the dominant society's attitudes toward them. In general, Amhara society was characterized by intense rivalry between status equals, especially in competition for land-use rights, within the context of the ambilineal descent system.[142] In such a social system, the existence of the *buda* enabled the threats or rivalry to be projected outward, thereby strengthening internal social and psychological solidarity.[143]

A historical period of internal disruption with a high degree of competition for power would be a likely time to expect increased levels of *buda* belief manifestation. The *zamana masafent* was such a time, characterized by endemic warfare exacerbated by ethnic and religious conflicts, changes in the land tenure system, and increased economic competition.

In this period, from the perspective of the dominant society, the Beta Israel were both feared and despised: "few people will venture to molest or offend a blacksmith, fearing the effects of his resentment."[144] In some cases, fears toward the *buda*-blacksmith resulted in violence. In Gojjam, Goshu Beru was said to have executed hundreds of suspected *budas*.[145] In the Maqdala crisis during the last days of Tewodros, people living in fear of the "hyenas of the Buda" armed themselves and killed vast numbers of hyenas.[146]

The more common consequence of the *buda* phenomenon for the Beta Israel, however, was a redefinition of their position in society. They were evolving from a low-ranking class within the general society to an occupational caste position. During the Gondar era, although they generally ranked low, many had achieved a limited upward mobility to middle-level positions and received titles and land grants. During the nineteenth century, as they reverted to blacksmith and potter occupations and the *buda* epithet developed, such mobility was no longer possible.

The relative prestige and the resulting treatment for different occupations was obvious to some observers: "Those who work in silver and gold, in brass or at the carpenter's trade, are esteemed as persons of high rank; but those who work in iron or pottery are not allowed the privilege even of being in common society."[147] Those held apart from "common society" (blacksmiths and potters) were especially the Falasha *buda*, who supposedly had supernatural powers such as the ability to turn into hyenas.

As an occupational caste, the Beta Israel were treated as one group vis-à-vis Abyssinian society. Blacksmiths, for example, were considered to be "servants of all without being [servants] of one man in particular." In an army camp, they were not considered a part of the army itself and, hence, could not follow that traditional Ethiopian path toward upward social mobility. They even had a lower rank than such people as butchers, who, although regarded as "proverbially gross," were tied to a particular master within the system of clientage and thus "could hope for advancement."[148] Such hope for upward mobility was unlikely for blacksmiths, who were frozen into a fixed position in the social structure.

A few observers used the terminology of caste to interpret the Beta Israel position in society. One referred to the "stranger castes" grouped around Gondar, stating that "the most important of these castes is that of the Falashas, or Jews."[149] Others noted that the Falasha "had perpetuated their caste without mixture through the ages,"[150] that "blacksmiths constituted a kind of hereditary caste," and that the Falasha could be likened to the "inferior castes of Hindustan."[151]

The consolidation of the occupational caste relationship crystallized clear rules regulating the degree and types of social interaction which could take place between the Beta Israel and Abyssinian society. These rules were determined and reinforced by sanctions imposed by each side. The Beta Israel were to be entirely avoided except for the necessary exchange of goods in the marketplace.[152] Christians would "neither enter their homes nor eat with them."[153] And the Beta Israel were "obliged by their occupations to live together."[154]

As noted above, these practices of social separation were not entirely new in the nineteenth century. But this was a period of renewed separatism, reinforced by Abyssinian society through the intensification of the *buda* epithet.

The Beta Israel reinforced social avoidance through regulations regarding contact with non–Beta Israel which were just as rigid and more detailed than those of Christian society, especially concerning the sanctions imposed for noncompliance. For the Beta Israel, these regulations were based on their moral and religious beliefs and practices.

Beta Israel Religion: Conflict and Revival, 1800–1868

The Beta Israel used their religion to provide the ideological justification for caste separation by viewing their beliefs and practices as purer than those of Christian Orthodoxy. On the other hand, the religious and broad cultural similarities between the two by the early nineteenth century suggests they should be analyzed in the context of one culture, rather than as two separate cultures. This common cultural context makes possible the use of caste analysis as the most useful framework for understanding the social relationship between the two separate groups within a broader Abyssinian society.

The Old Testament ambiance of early nineteenth-century highland Abyssinian society—including both Orthodoxy and the Beta Israel—has led many observers to emphasize the Orthodox-Falasha religious similarities. Contemporary observers noted that the Falasha religion was half Christian, or that Orthodoxy was simply "a coarse mixture of Judaism and Christianity."[155] An early missionary visitor felt the Orthodox Christians "observe the Jewish religion with more exactness than all the Jews throughout the world."[156] Such formulations assume the similarities resulted from borrowing between two different religions and societies. As already noted, however, recent scholarship has suggested the "Judaic" elements in Ethiopian Orthodoxy were probably not due to the Falasha, while the Beta Israel similarities to Orthodoxy were probably due to the intensive interaction and influences acquired during the fourteenth to sixteenth centuries.[157]

Whatever the ultimate source of the similarities, the mid–nineteenth-century Beta Israel religious leaders who led a revival during this period tried to have it both ways. On the one hand, they argued that their practices were based on and justified by the Old Testament—the same book fundamental to Abyssinian Christianity—and therefore, on the other hand, they should be allowed to maintain their own practices and beliefs, and remain distinct and independent from Abyssinian Christianity. That is, they were attempting to argue their legitimacy on the basis of a degree of religious congruency, while manipulating that cultural similarity to maintain social separation.[158]

There were many similarities in the two religions, especially in the manner in which beliefs were manifested through complex cycles of feasts and fasts. But a Beta Israel religious revival in mid-century—which was a response both to the processes of political breakdown and socioeconomic transformation and to the direct threats to their religion—had the effect of strengthening the moral basis of the caste relationship with Abyssinian society by leading the Beta Israel to turn inward. The revival reinforced the Beta Israel ideology of separation and rigidified the patterns and rules of caste interaction with the dominant society.

Beta Israel and Orthodox Religion and Culture

Despite acculturation and proselytization, the Beta Israel developed and maintained their religious institutions, beliefs, and practices through the centuries. Most details are lacking on these practices for any period before the nineteenth century. By that time, their religious practices were characterized chiefly by a complicated and overlapping cycle of weekly, lunar, monthly and yearly fasts and feasts; by the rigid observance of the Saturday Sabbath; and by the use of sacrifices at major feasts. Their religious year was complex since they used both a lunar calendar and the Ethiopian (solar) calendar. They also commemorated the most important yearly holy days with lunar or monthly remembrances on the same day of each lunar month that the main ceremony was held.[159] Some of the feasts and fasts were to be observed by the total population, and others were followed only by the priests and monks. These complex observances obviously required a careful vigilance and regulation on the part of their religious leaders in order to keep them in effect. Of course, the travelers who reported these ceremonies could only state the ideal as they were told it but did not usually observe what was actually carried out by the Beta Israel.

The Beta Israel were particularly known for their striking and rigid observance of the Sabbath from sunset Friday to sunset Saturday. The laws to be followed on that day are given in detail in the Beta Israel writing, *Te'ezaza Sanbat* ("Commandments of the Sabbath").[160] During the afternoon on Friday, enough food was prepared for that evening and the next day, and then everyone went to a stream to wash, first the men and then the women. They extinguished all fires by sunset Friday. During the Sabbath day, they could not work, light a fire, or draw water; people could leave their houses only to go to the prayer house; they could not cross any rivers or streams and were supposed to speak in soft voices. The Sabbath was so important to the Beta Israel that it was personified as a female intermediary to God,[161] and it took precedence over other religious observances. For example, even if the important yearly fast of Astasreyo fell on a Saturday, the fast was broken for the Sabbath.[162] Indeed, among the prohibitions in the *Te'ezaza Sanbat* was the injunction against fasting on the Sabbath.[163]

Their yearly schedule of fasts and feasts, based mainly on the lunar calendar as reported by observers between the 1840s and 1860s, were extensive and detailed. Among the most significant observances then were Passover (*fasika*), the Harvest Festival (*ma'rar*), the Fast of Ab (*soma ab*), the Fourth (*barabu*), and the Day of Atonement (*astasreyo*), but there were several other important fasts and feasts as well. In most cases, some reason for the observances and a description of the obligations of each were told to foreign travelers.

Passover (*fasika*), which the Beta Israel also called Feast of Joy (*ba'ala tafsiht*), was held in the lunar month of Nisan, the first moon of the lunar year. It celebrated the Exodus of Jews from ancient Egypt under Moses. For three days before 14 Nisan, people were to eat only roasted grain. They sacrificed a lamb on the evening of the fourteenth, and for the next seven days (the 15th to the 21st) ate only unleavened bread. The twenty-second day was called *buho* ("fermented dough"), the first day when regular bread made from fermented dough could be eaten again. The priests read to the people passages from Exodus 12 and 13 and Numbers 9.[164]

The Harvest Festival (*ma'rar*) was celebrated on the twelfth day of the third moon, Sivan, which fell fifty days after Passover, that is, during May and June. Two reasons were given for its observance: the time of "first-fruits" and the reception of the Ten Commandments by Moses on Mount Sinai. The priests read from Leviticus 23 and Psalms 1, 32, and 48. People were also to bring grain to the prayer house, but since this was not in accordance with the agricultural season in Ethiopia, another Harvest Festival was celebrated on the 12th of the tenth moon (Tavt) which fell about November. Ethiopian Orthodox Christians celebrate 12 Hedar (November) as the day honoring Saint Michael.[165]

An apparently minor fast was held the first nine days of the fourth moon, Tomos, and a very important fast during the first seventeen days of Ab, the fifth moon, was called the Fast of Ab (*soma ab*). Though there is some discrepancy in the sources, the main reason for it was to commemorate the fall and burning of Jerusalem by Nebuchadnezzar (in 586 B.C.E.). Judged by the obligations imposed, this was the most important fast of the year for the Beta Israel in the 1840s since everyone was expected to fast, not just the monks, priests, and pious elders, as was the case with most other fasts. Moreover, for the first ten days, no one could eat meat, milk, or butter. During the last seven days, they followed their usual method of fasting, which meant not eating before sundown, but in the evening they could eat any food in a regular meal.[166]

The fourth Saturday of Ab, the fifth moon, was the holy day of *barabu* (Ge'ez: "the fourth"), considered to be "the greatest Saturday of the year."[167] This is the same day known in Amharic as *ya sanbat sanbat* ("Sabbath of Sabbaths"), but the Beta Israel seem to have used only the Ge'ez term in the 1840s.[168] On this day, of course, people followed all the usual Sabbath observances, but in addition, they walked around saying "Absolve me" (literally, "open me," *yeftan*), expecting to receive absolution from God on this day because of their good works during the year.

The Fast of Lul was during the first ten days of Lul, the sixth moon. It was said to have been begun by Jeremiah at the time of his imprisonment.[169]

A much more important series of observances were in Tahasaran, the seventh moon. The first day was the Feast of Drums (*ba'ala matki*). The first nine days (apparently, however, excluding the first feast day) was the Fast of Tahasaran, said to have been started by Esdras after his return to Jerusalem. Then on the tenth of Tahasaran was one of the most important celebrations of the year, the Day of Atonement (*astasreyo*), today referred to as Yom Kippur. This was a day for the expiation of sins, marking the time when God appeared to Jacob. Priests were said to read the Beta Israel book *Mashafa As-ta-serit* to the people.[170]

The Feast of Tabernacles (*ba'ala matsallat*) was celebrated on the fifteenth day of Tahasaran, the seventh moon. The priests read Leviticus 23 and 24 and Psalms 49–91. The holiday was said to be a commemoration of the feast Joseph gave his father. The Beta Israel were familiar with the prescriptions of Leviticus 23 but said since they had no citrus fruits they could bring only leafy branches from palm, willow, and cypress trees.[171]

Other yearly observances were mentioned but not described in detail, and the dates are not congruent in different sources. These included *amata so* on the last day of the ninth moon; a fast of ten days in the tenth month, possibly called the Fast of Tavt or the Fast of Heddar; and the Fast of Esther during the first ten days of the eleventh moon. The day of *amata so,* not further described, was said to be a time of pilgrimage to a nearby mountain.[172] Hence, it probably was the predecessor of the twentieth-century celebration, *segd,* or Fast of Supplication (*mehlella*), which had become a major holy day by the 1970s.[173] The Fast of Heddar was supposed to have been instituted by *abba* Sabra in the fifteenth century, but its date of celebration was not at all clear.[174]

Another important commemoration for which conflicting dates were given was the remembrance of Abraham. It was held either on the 28th of Nahase,[175] or the 18th of Yekatit,[176] both dates, interestingly, are given according to the Ethiopian (solar) rather than the Beta Israel (lunar) calendar. The two times are about six months apart, and Yekatit is the sixth solar month, while the 28th of Nahase is near the time of the sixth moon of the lunar calendar. Again, perhaps the differences were due to the different location of d'Abbadie's informants: in 1842, he was a "learned Falasha" from Kayla Meda near Gondar, while in 1848, he was a monk from the ancient monastic center of Hohwara.[177] Another day mentioned in passing was the *tazkara Abraham,* said to be the first day of one moon, but again, the specific time reference was not clear.[178]

In addition to the yearly ceremonies, the Beta Israel followed a strict schedule every moon. The first day of every new moon was a Feast of the

New Moon. Several days each moon served as reminders of important holy days during other moons of the year. The 10th day (*ceki asart*) of each moon was observed as a reminder of Astasreyo on the tenth day of the seventh moon.[179] This term is a composite of two words for ten: *ceki* in Qwarenya, and *asart* in Ge'ez.[180] The fifteenth day (*ceki ankwa* in Qwarenya) of each moon was celebrated as a reminder of Passover on the 15th of Nisan, and the Feast of Tabernacles on the 15th of Tahasaran.[181]

The 12th day of each new moon was celebrated, apparently as a holy day of Saint Michael, which had previously been celebrated on the 12th day of each month. According to d'Abbadie, Christians objected to the Beta Israel use of the same day they followed, and hence, the Beta Israel moved their observance to a lunar rather than a monthly schedule.[182] The tenth of each *month,* called *arfe asart,* was also remembered, said to have been established by the priests who survived the destruction of the temple (i.e., in 586 B.C.E.).[183]

Finally, the 29th (and 30th, when applicable) days of the moon were times of watching and preaching for the new moon. They fasted on the last day of the moon.[184]

The weekly cycle in the 1840s included fasts on Monday, Thursday, and Friday. The Thursday fast was especially emphasized and was said to have been begun by Isaiah. A man named *abba* Battui was said to have started the Monday fast, and Moses the Friday fast. The Beta Israel method of fasting was to eat nothing during the day, but there were no restrictions on the kind of food eaten after sunset. This was different from the Christian practice of eating no meat or milk on their fast days of Wednesday and Friday.[185]

This section is not meant to be a detailed comparison of specific Christian and Beta Israel fasts and feasts, although such a thorough comparative historical analysis would facilitate an increased understanding of each group. In general, there were many broad similarities, especially in the way they practiced their religions. Both religions based themselves on a set of written texts. More specifically, most Beta Israel religious texts were written in Ge'ez and were derived from Christian sources.[186] The Beta Israel respect for the written word explains their eagerness to acquire the Bible distributed by the Protestant missionaries, even if only the New Testament were available.[187]

They each had the same types of religious practitioners, referred to by the same terminology, such as prophets, monks, priests, *dabtaras,* and some minor figures that included "spirit-raisers," soothsayers, and hail and rain conjurors.[188] Both Christian and Beta Israel priests could marry but monks could not.[189] Both religions shared a belief in certain spirits and beings, such as the *zar* and *buda*. They both believed in the coming of a Messiah who would be called Tewodros.[190]

Many aspects of the religiously sanctioned life-cycle ceremonies were similar but with variations. The place of birth was considered unclean by both groups. For Christians, the birthing room and everything in it was unclean until properly purified. This seems to have occurred after about three days, at which time the mother's clothes were washed in a brook. But any man who entered the birthing room before purification would be considered unclean for forty days. In previous centuries, the practice may have been more rigid, as it was said the mother was unclean and unable to attend Church for forty days after the birth of a male and eighty days after the birth of a female.[191] For the Beta Israel, of course, birth was carried out in a separate building, not just a separate room, and the mother had to remain isolated in that building for forty days if the child were a boy and for eighty days if a girl.[192]

Both groups practiced the circumcision of boys and the excision of girls, generally on the eighth day after birth.[193] Some observers indicated the Beta Israel ceremony was on the seventh rather than the eighth day.[194] One observer mentioned that Christians also had previously used the seventh instead of the eighth day for this practice.[195]

The periods of forty days for a male and eighty days for a female were significant to both groups. In Christian society, the baptism of each was performed at this time.[196] Among the Beta Israel, the mother had to stay isolated for forty days or eighty days in a separate hut. After that time, the naming ceremony, *arde'et* was performed. The child was immersed in water and the formula "Blessed be God, the Lord of Israel," was uttered, the child was named, and then the mother could return to live in her own house. The Beta Israel specifically denied the similarity of this ceremony to the Christian baptism and called it a "purification" instead.[197]

With regard to marriage and the family, it was noted, "an Abyssinian betrothal . . . differs very little amongst Falashas and Christians."[198] Among both groups, marriages were arranged by the parents, performed before the elders, seemed to distinguish between civil and religious contracts, upheld monogamy, and allowed divorce, though each religion reproved it.[199] Both groups had substantial roles during the wedding ceremony for the bridegroom's best man, who was called "wedding brother" by the Beta Israel and "bridesman" by the Christians.[200] In both cases, the woman was expected to be a virgin before marriage, and adultery, especially by women, was punished.[201] In general, the Beta Israel seem to have married about the same age as Christians.[202]

The Beta Israel as well as Christians believed in individual immortality and in the necessity of confession by a dying person. Without confession, a person would go to hell and would have no *tazkar* ("memorial service") performed for him or her in the future. Formerly, one was supposed to confess one's sins every evening, but by the 1840s, confession once a year and just before death was considered sufficient.[203]

The *tazkar* was a similar type of memorial service among both groups. It was supposed to be performed for Christians on the third, seventh, twelfth, thirtieth and fortieth days, one year after death, and every year thereafter. For the Beta Israel, it was performed on the third and seventh days, after one year, and then annually.[204] No *tazkar* was performed among the Beta Israel for one who had not confessed one's sins just before death, nor for an adulterous woman.[205]

In general, both groups followed the same Old Testament food restrictions. Both slaughtered animals while uttering a religious formula and would only eat meat slaughtered by their coreligionists.[206] Both apparently held negative views of tanners, who were considered to be impure.[207]

Sacrifices and offerings to God were made by both groups. The Beta Israel called them *qwerban,* the Ge'ez word for "offering" or "sacrifice," but used by Christians to refer specifically to Holy Communion. The extent of Beta Israel sacrifices by the early nineteenth century is somewhat unclear, but it was a fundamental part of their religious practice. The main sacrifice was at the time of Passover, but the evidence suggests the practice had previously been much more extensive than it had become by the early nineteenth century.[208] D'Abbadie stated a sacrifice of a year-old lamb and an offering of pure wheat bread was made at each new moon and at each "great festival."[209] Stern said sacrifices were only "capriciously offered," with the exception of the lamb at Passover.[210] Halévy said they were made twice a year, at Passover and at the Tazkara Abraham, but he was referring specifically only to the Sagade region.[211] Flad suggested there were many occasions for offerings or sacrifices by both Christians and Beta Israel. The latter were said to observe a bread or meat offering every Sabbath, a sacrifice of a young heifer every new moon, a lamb at Passover, an offering at the Harvest Festival, and others periodically, such as burnt offerings, thanks offerings, and offerings in times of trouble. In addition, both Christians and the Beta Israel observed "non-Biblical" sacrifices, such as offerings for the sick, in times of drought, in a new house, at the Tazkar, and the "sacrifice of the barns."[212] Christians also were said to offer sacrifices for "those afflicted with the devil,"[213] apparently referring to cases of spirit possession.

On a more mundane level, the clothing of both groups was similar. The principal Abyssinian article of dress was the *shamma*, the typical toga-like cotton clothing worn by both rich and poor. The Beta Israel wore their *shamma* in the same way and used it for the same occasions, such as to show respect, as did the Christians. *Shamma* styles varied more by social class than by ethnic or religious group. Priests (*qes*), a term used by both groups, wore the turban.[214]

Their shared religious and cultural milieu is illustrated by the mutual veneration of certain holy places. One such place containing hot springs was called *amba* or *abba* Mahari after the famous Beta Israel monk of that name.[215] Likewise, the prominent Beta Israel monk *abba* Yeshaq, who lived at Hohwara in the 1840s, was well regarded and respected by Christian "professors of theology" who asked him to interpret some religious books for them.[216] And some Beta Israel prayer houses were said to be considered holy places by Christians as well.[217]

It is suggested here not that the two religions were the same, but that they existed in a common Old Testament cultural milieu, as a result of centuries of religious and cultural interaction. It was this common background that the Beta Israel priests attempted to manipulate in defending their right to remain separate from Orthodoxy during the increasingly virulent attacks on their religion and society that characterized this period.

Ethiopian and Foreign Threats

Despite the cultural and religious similarities, the Beta Israel position in Abyssinian society was redefined into increasingly restricted roles. As their occupations narrowed to blacksmiths, potters, weavers, and sometimes builders, they were often blamed for the problems of the times and attacked as *buda*.

In addition, they faced direct religious threats, both internal and external. The upstart Yajju, heavily influenced by Islam, but many of whom had converted to Christianity, were the catalysts for these attacks. *Ras* Ali I had been seen by a royal chronicler as a "new Constantine," but many of his successors were viewed as somewhat less than true believers by Christian society.[218] The evidence from Beta Israel traditions suggests the Warrashek dynasty may have tried to compensate for their Islamic background by becoming zealous Christian proselytizers, trying to gain greater acceptance by the Abyssinian power structure. In the words of a Beta Israel document: "At the time of the princes called *ras* Mareyye, *ras* Gugsa, and *ras* Ali, the religion of Israel disappeared again, and this decline lasted twenty years."[219]

Beta Israel oral traditions also recall that during the *zamana masafent*, "our religion was lost for forty years."[220] Forty years rather than twenty years, as stated above, is perhaps more accurate, though it is difficult to gain any more detailed information or corroboration as to just what constituted the decline or loss of the religion. As documented above, it was a time when the harshness of *buda* accusations increased. In the 1830s, other observers noted that the Beta Israel, "exposed to continual harassment, are rather disposed to abandon their faith."[221] One observer felt the process had intensified in the eighteenth century, and that "now many of them have exchanged the Jewish faith for the Mahomedan."[222] Their traditions assert that those who did not convert were often forced to disperse to outlying areas, a reenactment of the fourteenth- to seventeenth-century conflicts.[223] Even if not very many people actually converted to Christianity or were forced to disperse to outlying areas, statements in their oral traditions, as transmitted by monks and priests, concerning the loss or decline of their religion could be simply referring to a less-than-faithful observance of their cycle of feasts and fasts during this period.

Evidence suggests, for example, that probably due to increased poverty in the community, the use of sacrifices and offerings was less frequent than in previous years. In addition, some penalties imposed for transgressing religious laws were less severe than previously. For example, d'Abbadie was told in 1848 that formerly people who ate leavened bread during the seven days of Passover had been thrown out of the community and even stoned to death, but that now they only had to do penance.[224]

Because of the nature of the sources, it is much easier to document the existence of the external religious threat that clearly exacerbated the internal problems. During the reign of Tewodros (1855–68), European Protestant missions to the Falasha were established. After a few scattered individual efforts, three separate missions were established in the area: Gafat near Dabra Tabor and Jenda and Darna (both in Dambeya).[225]

These missions received the official support of Tewodros and *abuna* Salama, the head of the Orthodox Church. Some observers emphasized Tewodros "was an advocate for converting all the world to the religion of his forefathers."[226] In 1850, Tewodros was quoted as saying, "I have often taken trouble to convince the Falashas that Jesus Christ is the Son of God and the Savior of the world, but I have never succeeded. The Jews are hardened, and they are the born enemies of Christ."[227] In a letter to the missionaries in 1857, the *abun* stated that Tewodros's policy was to convert all Muslims, Beta Israel, Qemant, and Oromo.[228] When Henry Stern of the London Society for Promoting Christianity Amongst the Jews first arrived in 1860, Tewodros expressed approval.[229] The *abun* supported the conversion of the Beta Israel as long as a new Protestant Church was not established and the converts were all baptized into the Ethiopian Church.[230]

On the other hand, Tewodros's efforts were really rather moderate and ambiguous. He was willing to allow missionaries to teach and attempt to persuade, but he was against any forced conversions.[231] His actual behavior, as opposed to some of the things he was quoted as saying or what others said about him, was "classical," to be compared with that of the Gondar kings or with Menilek after him. He was willing to tolerate some diversity as long as he could maintain order and control and obtain certain benefits from the missionaries.[232]

Tewodros's main interests were to obtain the use of the missionaries' artisan skills to improve Abyssinian technology, especially military technology. For this reason, he was particularly sympathetic to the lay artisan missionaries at Gafat: "As the King was a friend to both civilization and our Mission, he loved and supported us, and gave us many hundreds of Abyssinian workmen—Christians, heathens, Jews, and Mohammedans—whom we instructed in arts, and in true religious principles."[233] His relatively favorable view of the Gafat mission spilled over to the missions of Flad at Jenda and the Scottish mission of Staiger and Brandeis at Darna,[234] who enjoyed the king's support until the dispute with Stern erupted later.[235]

The three missions had a limited degree of success among the Beta Israel in the Dambeya-Gondar region. Schools were started for them in Dafacha and Abwara near Gondar, as well as at Jenda. Altogether, there were about fifty Beta Israel converts during the Tewodros years.[236]

Beta Israel Religious Revival

According to internal Beta Israel sources, their religious revival began before the Protestant missions' efforts started, but the main details of that revival are illustrated in two events that took place in the 1860s as part of the Beta Israel response to the missions. The revival began perhaps by the 1840s through the efforts of monks in outlying regions. Supposedly, ten years before the reign of Tewodros, *abba* Wedaje, the chief monk of Qwara, was said to have "brought his people back to their religion." Wedaje was viewed as the legitimate successor to the great fifteenth-century monk, *abba* Sabra, remembered as the originator of Beta Israel monasticism.[237]

The sources do not specify just how Wedaje "brought his people back," but it must have consisted of a reemphasis on the regular cycle of fasts and feasts which would have required the active participation of local priests and monks. In several outlying areas in the 1840s, Beta Israel monks and high priests were working to perpetuate their religious traditions and institutions deriving from the fifteenth century.[238] By the 1860s, the four main religious leaders were the monks *abba* Mahari in Qolla Wagara (originally from Dambeya), *abba* Gedewon in Samen, *abba* Yeshaq in Hohwara, and *abba* Simon in Qwara.[239] There were also monks elsewhere as well as priests and *dabtaras* in nearly every small village, and schools for boys in the immediate vicinity of Gondar.[240] A link between the phases of the revival of the 1840s and the 1860s exists in that one of the main Beta Israel protagonists of the 1860s dispute was *abba* Simon, the student, protégé, and successor of *abba* Wedaje, the chief figure in Qwara in the 1840s.[241]

These traditional religious figures came into direct conflict with the first converts of the Protestant missionaries in the 1860s. The early converts, though few in number, were fervent believers and began to criticize certain Beta Israel religious practices. The missionary Flad said a "wholesome crisis" had occurred in the rainy season of 1861, and his coworker Bronkhorst said a "great division" had arisen, especially between some of the community and their monks.[242] But the main argument broke out in June 1862 between a young Beta Israel convert and his uncle, who was a Beta Israel monk at Jenda. That monk, and three others, excommunicated the young convert along with his mother and father. The convert then swore in the name of the king (*ba Tewodros yemut!*) that the Beta Israel should stop their practice of sacrifices unless they could prove it was ordained by the Old Testament. Sacrifices were an integral part of the Beta Israel religion at that time, so this was a serious interdiction.[243] Excommunication, of course, meant total exclusion from the society, not just the religion.

As this dispute continued, Tewodros was drawn in. On 1 July 1862, a letter from the king gave his consent to the baptism of the converts. On 21 July the first twenty-two converts were baptized and were promptly excommunicated by the Beta Israel monks.[244] A second letter from Tewodros on 25 July stated his view that he "did not intend to force any Falasha to change his religion, but it was his desire that all those who from conscientious motives wanted to become Christians should not be hindered or molested by their relatives."[245]

Though the dispute had begun as an argument among the Beta Israel, it quickly broadened to a controversy between the Beta Israel and the Orthodox Church. As the Ethiopian Church entered on the side of the missionaries and converts, the specific issues changed from the sacrifice controversy to include a theological debate on the nature of the Godhead and the Trinity.

In September, the sacrifice dispute had been heard by the local governor in Gondar, but he decided to refer it to Tewodros. In the meantime, the Beta Israel contacted the king and claimed the missionaries were trying to convert them by force, which was clearly against his policy.[246]

Finally, on 7 and 9 October 1862, the dispute reached a climax in a debate before Tewodros, held at his camp in the Macha area south of Lake Tana. According to the missionary records, the main protagonists were the Beta Israel monks and the leader of the converts, Beru Webe. *Abba* Salama was apparently not present, but was consulted later by Tewodros.[247]

According to the internal Beta Israel document based on oral traditions that were written down in the reign of Menilek (1889–1913), the *abuna* Salama was present at the debate and took an active part in the controversy as the issues broadened. Oral traditions collected in the 1970s also confirm the Beta Israel interpretation that their opponents were not only the missionaries and a few converts, but included the Ethiopian Orthodox Church itself.[248]

In the missionary records, a connection between the two issues was made by Beru Webe, but the emphasis was on the sacrifice question:

> Your majesty, . . . when we were Falashas, we very strictly observed the law, and all the ordinances of our priests, hoping that we should thereby inherit everlasting life. We were so ignorant, that we did not even know what was written in our own books. But when the missionaries came, we received the Amharic Bible, and one after another our errors were disclosed to us. We found a Triune God, and found that Christ, whom we had abused, or at best thought a creature like ourselves, was the very Son of God. We found that since God has given His well-beloved son, to be our all-sufficient ransom for sinners, it was an abomination in His sight to offer sacrifices at this time and place.[249]

In the Beta Israel document and in other oral traditions, the main issue was the nature of God. Again, the main protagonist was Beru Webe, who, speaking for the converts, quoted Genesis 1:26, "Let *us* make man in *our* image, after *our* likeness," as proof of the Trinity. *Abba* Simon countered, however, with the passage from Genesis 1:27 that states: "*He* created man in *His* image."[250]

The *abun* entered the argument and exchanged insults with *abba* Simon, after which Tewodros became angry with the squabbling in front of him and exclaimed: "It is I who have the power to split and to cut." *Abba* Simon remained steadfast, telling Tewodros: "It is my flesh that you can split and cut, but you cannot touch my soul."[251] A longer version of this part of the dispute was collected from Beta Israel recollections a few years later by the Jewish traveler Halévy:

> When the King saw that our faith was firm as rock, he became wroth and threatened us all with instant execution. . . . At this terrible command all trembled; the missionaries themselves were frightened, for they knew that Theodore was a man who did not hesitate in carrying out his threats. Abba Simeon arose, and said resolutely to the King, "In matters of death, O Theodore, thou art master on earth, but there is another Master in heaven. Here thou hast full power over my body, above in heaven thou hast no power over me." At the same time we all got up from the ground, and cried out, "Kill us, we are willing to die for the faith of our fathers."[252]

Tewodros's decision was sufficiently ambiguous to have satisfied all sides and to have left corresponding ambiguities in the sources. He did not resolve the religious issues but tried to reestablish peace among the factions. According to Beta Israel oral traditions, as recorded in the recollections in Halévy, the Beta Israel document from the era of Menilek, and my more recent collection, "the king showed favor to *abba* Simon," as Tewodros's advisors urged moderation on him. He was said to have awarded the Beta Israel some cattle and stated they would not be forced to convert, though in Halévy's account he gave them four years to think about it and urged them to convert peacefully.[253] Flad felt the decision was "indisputably a victory" for the missionaries and converts.[254] Indeed, they still had complete freedom to preach and teach, and two months after this debate, Tewodros finally gave permission to the Scottish mission, the third Protestant group in the area.[255]

Interestingly, the theological question of the nature of God had often been disputed in Ethiopia, and the specific terms in which it was argued replicated the debate at the fifteenth-century court of Zar'a Ya'eqob, when the monarch had taken the position of the Trinity, citing Genesis 1:26, while the dissidents had taken the position of *abba* Simon and the Beta Israel in the nineteenth century. These parallels probably suggest the continuity of the issues in the Ethiopian religious and cultural milieu rather than any direct line of descent between the fifteenth-century anti-Trinitarians and the nineteenth-century Beta Israel, though the strong similarities are intriguing.[256]

Shortly after the end of this debate, the second stage of the Beta Israel religious revival occurred with a millennial "back to Jerusalem" movement. The origins of this movement are obscure. In October 1862, probably just after the culmination of the dispute heard before Tewodros in early October, a Beta Israel priest named *abba* Sagga Amlak wrote a letter to a man he considered the head of the Jewish community in Jerusalem asking advice about whether the Beta Israel should "return" to Jerusalem:

> Has the time arrived that we should return to you, [to] our city, the holy city of Jerusalem? For we are a poor people and have neither prince nor prophet and if the time has arrived send us a letter which will reach us. . . . Tell us and inform us of all that will happen to us. But as for us, a great agitation has disturbed our hearts, for they say that the time has arrived: the men of our country say, "Separate yourselves from the Christians and go to your country, Jerusalem, and reunite yourselves with your brothers and offer up sacrifices to God, Lord of Israel, in the Holy Land."[257]

Apparently, the advice was requested because another Beta Israel priest, *abba* Mahari, was trying to convince the community to return to Jerusalem. Though an answer was never received to *abba* Sagga Amlak's letter, a group of Beta Israel did attempt to journey to Jerusalem.

The recollections collected by Halévy a few years later give the following account:

> Some of the [Beta Israel] priests who had been ordered to appear at Gondar to assist at the controversy, and who had feared a fatal termination, fell subsequently into a singular state of religious exaltation. According to Jewish traditions, a great calamity must precede the advent of the Messiah; they believed that the behests of Theodore were the harbingers of deliverance, and that the time had arrived for a return to Jerusalem, and for a recovery of the inheritance of their ancesters. All shared in this hope of speedy redemption, and a crowd of poor, simple-minded individuals resolved to start for Jerusalem, which they knew to be situated beyond the Red Sea.[258]

The Beta Israel belief in a Messiah named Tewodros—a belief shared by Ethiopian Christians—may have contributed to the millennial and even messianic aura of this event, though the actual role of Emperor Tewodros vis-à-vis the Beta Israel was not so positively unambiguous.[259]

The main leader of the expedition was *abba* Mahari of Dambeya. He and other leaders exhorted the Beta Israel to follow them to the promised land, promising that the great miracles of the Old Testament would reoccur, including the opening of the Red Sea, and that like the ancient Jews they would find deliverance in Jerusalem. The group crossed the Takkaze

River and reached the vicinity of Aksum, but after several years of hardship, many of the people perished and others settled in Tigray. *Abba* Mahari survived and returned to the lowland Qolla Wagara to live out his days, though later he moved closer to Gondar.[260]

In summary, both phases of the Beta Israel religious revival—the theological debate and the millennial movement—illustrate aspects of the religious milieu shared with Orthodox Abyssinians. Ethiopian Christianity was heavily oriented toward the Old Testament, and both religions appealed to that book as the authority. On the other hand, the religions were fundamentally different despite external similarities, and the main effect of this religious revival was ultimately to emphasize the divisions between the two groups. As the Abyssinians used the *buda* syndrome to maintain separation, the Beta Israel viewed themselves as morally superior and, on that basis, also desired separation from Abyssinian Christian society.

The Moral Basis of a Caste Relationship

The caste relationship consolidated by the mid-nineteenth century was supported by ideologies of separation on each side. Abyssinians feared and resented the Falasha blacksmith/potter-*buda* and held themselves apart. But the Beta Israel religious and moral code demanded separation just as strongly.

The Beta Israel view of Christian Orthodoxy and Abyssinian society in general was negative and scornful. Abyssinians were seen as both impure and immoral compared to their own religion and culture. This view was based on laws concerning food, sex, birth, and death. Although both groups based their practices in this area on Old Testament interdictions and, hence, had many similarities, the Beta Israel practices seem somewhat stricter. The Beta Israel certainly viewed their own practices as stricter and more moral than those of the Christians.

The Beta Israel thought, for example, that the Abyssinian practice of eating raw meat was a "barbarous custom,"[261] and "compared those gluttonous savages to dogs."[262] Moreover, the Beta Israel would not eat meat offered them by a Christian or cattle killed or injured by wild beasts instead of slaughtered by prescribed rituals, while according to some accounts, Christians would eat meat killed by a lion or leopard because those animals were considered Christian, although they would not eat those killed by a hyena.[263] The more restrictive Beta Israel food practices provide a contrast with the case of castes or low status groups in southern Ethiopia, where the higher status group avoided more foods than the lower group; with the Beta Israel, it was just the opposite.[264]

Reproductive practices were also stricter. Beta Israel women had to live in separate houses during menstruation and for forty days following the birth of a boy and eighty days after the birth of a girl, somewhat stricter than Christian practice. Divorce, though possible, was strongly reproved, and an adulterous woman could be killed,[265] a stricter practice than that generally followed by Christian society. Although the church did not approve of adultery, either polygyny or concubinage was said to be common among the Abyssinians, and the punishment for adultery did not seem very severe.[266] The offspring of a Beta Israel adulterous union could not enter the prayer house.[267]

A person on his deathbed would be moved to a tent outside so that death would not occur in the house.[268] Grave diggers were considered unclean for seven days after digging a grave and could not enter the prayer house during that time.[269] Among the Christians, those who had recently touched carrion or dead bodies could not enter the church, but the injunction does not seem to have lasted as long as seven days.[270]

Though Orthodox Abyssinians had historically venerated the Sabbath (Saturday) as well as Sunday, by the nineteenth century, Beta Israel observances were much stricter. As noted above, on that day no fire was lit, and they could not work or even travel if that necessitated crossing any streams. In connection with this veneration of the Sabbath, there were strict rules prohibiting people with various degrees of impurities from attending the prayer house service on that day. The following categories were considered impure: lepers; those with a year-old wound, very dark skin (indicating an adulterous birth), or "very small, partly closed eyes"; tanners; Oromo slaves; renegades who changed back and forth between the Beta Israel and Christian religions; girls raped and not pardoned by their parents; men bitten by a hyena; or those who had sexual intercourse on either Thursday or Friday before the Sabbath.[271]

These distinctions indicate various degrees of physical, sexual, and religious impurities and were probably different in degree rather than in kind from Christian practices. Tanners, for example, were probably negatively viewed by the Amhara as well, though the direct evidence is from the early twentieth century.[272] Amhara practice forbade sexual intercourse the night before a holy day, in this case, Sunday, rather than on both days before the Sabbath.[273] Also in terms of personal and ritual cleanliness, Christians were all supposed to wash at least near the beginning of a New Year on Saint John's day in the evening, and one observer stated some people only washed that one time during a year.[274] In contrast, the Beta

Israel were required to wash at least once a week before the Sabbath and any other time when they needed purification.

The relatively stricter rules of the Beta Israel were doubly significant: on the one hand, their priests and monks emphasized Christian impurities as a means of maintaining a high degree of separation from Abyssinian society; on the other hand, at times, Christians themselves were attracted to the Beta Israel religion because of its high standards of morality, holiness, and asceticism. The possibility of conversion was enhanced by the existence of specified procedures by which a person could be incorporated into Beta Israel society and religion.[275]

Despite this possibility of individual conversions, however, the stricter Beta Israel standards mainly reinforced their separation from other groups. As already indicated, this separation was not a new phenomenon in the nineteenth century. Over the centuries, various degrees of incorporationist or separationist forces operated between the two societies. But during the first two-thirds of the nineteenth century, separatism was exacerbated from each perspective and was relatively well documented compared with other eras.

A separatist code was developed to prohibit or strictly regulate relations with non–Beta Israel persons. Intermarriage with a non–Beta Israel was "strictly interdicted."[276] If a Beta Israel should happen to visit the house or even meet and converse with non–Beta Israel, he or she had to wash his or her body and clothes before reentering his or her own house.[277] Beta Israel people did not permit anyone to visit their houses or to touch them or their clothes; if someone entered their house, they would desert it, and if they touched their clothes they would wash in running water.[278] For this reason, they had always lived close to a river or spring, as is illustrated by their settlement patterns in the Gondar region. Even articles bought in the market had to be washed before using them, and money they were paid for their craft goods was received in a dish full of water.[279]

While traveling, the Beta Israel could only accept uncooked food, such as dried chick-peas (*shembra*), unground grain, salt blocks, and water or beer for which they provided their own cup or drank out of their hands.[280] If they had to eat at the house of a Christian, they were required to eat only chick-peas for six days thereafter, drink a purgative on the seventh day, and have chicken broth on the eighth day.[281] They felt it was "forbidden by Moses' law to come near an Amhara," and some observers noted one reason they had started making their own clothes and tools was to avoid contact with strangers.[282] In general, they said concerning Christians: "We speak with them, but do not eat with them, or partake of anything that comes from them. If we meet with them, we wash ourselves and our clothes seven times. We never allow them to enter our houses."[283]

Regulations regarding contact with non–Beta Israel were even stricter for the monks. When *abba* Mahari received a Bible and white clothes from Stern, the articles had to be put first in a bag held by another priest and then given to Mahari so that he did not receive them directly from a "polluted" hand.[284] Monks had to obey all the interdictions with regard to non–Beta Israel as the other Beta Israel; in addition, they had to live apart from other Beta Israel, grinding their own grain and making their own food, each one living in a separate house and remaining celibate.[285]

Summary: Beta Israel Caste Formation

In summary, the late eighteenth to mid-nineteenth century was a key period in the consolidation of the caste relationship between the Beta Israel and the dominant Abyssinian society. The breakdown of the central government, economic changes, and religious proselytization during the "era of the princes" resulted in an increased persecution and repression of the Beta Israel. They were increasingly stereotyped as *buda,* or carriers of the "evil eye," and relegated to a more restricted role in society than had been the case during the Gondar era.

On the other hand, they responded with a religious revival which led them to turn inward and reinforce the degree of social separation between themselves and Orthodox Abyssinian society. Thus, a combination of factors over the centuries since the 1300s had brought the Beta Israel into a caste position within the emerging Ethiopian society of the nineteenth century. This last stage of the process was characterized by the final elaboration of a separatist code of interaction reinforced by mutual ideologies of separation. Abyssinian society both feared and reviled the "Falasha-*buda*" while the Beta Israel defended themselves as legitimate followers of Old Testament prescriptions and as morally purer and hence superior to Orthodoxy.[286]

This high sense of self-worth and moral superiority despite persecution attracted Protestant missionaries to the group. Some Beta Israel responded favorably to the fervor of missionaries, such as J. M. Flad, while others tried to reinforce their traditional beliefs and practices. Still another external factor in Beta Israel history was that of Western Judaism. Their great influence later was foreshadowed in these years by the interest of Luzzatto in the 1840s and 1850s and the trip by Halévy in the 1860s. In the coming decades, these external forces caused increasing divisions among the Beta Israel as they tried to cope with change and the continuing need for self-definition.

5. Splintering of the Beta Israel, 1868–1920

Internal disruption and external influences on the Beta Israel increased during the late nineteenth and early twentieth centuries, eventually creating a badly splintered group and eroding the caste-based relations with Abyssinian society. While the Protestant mission to the Falasha faced the handicaps of inadequate financial resources and the lack of strong imperial support, the Falasha-Christians managed to survive and even increase in number. Imperial power struggles, rebellions, foreign invasions, disease, and famine made life more difficult for all rural dwellers in the Begamder region, whether Christian, Beta Israel, or Protestant-Falasha, particularly in the late 1880s and 1890s. Local and imperial rulers' demands for Beta Israel building skills, particularly in the new capital area of Entotto and Addis Ababa, took many men of Begamder away from their families and further divided the society economically and socially. Revived European Jewish interest in the Beta Israel, particularly by Jacques Faitlovitch, undermined the credibility of many traditional Beta Israel religious practices, even though Faitlovitch attempted to rejuvenate the society to save it from the missionaries.

By the early twentieth century, Beta Israel society had splintered into several distinct religious and cross-cutting socioeconomic groups. The religious divisions were three: the Falasha-Christian converts to Protestantism, the Western Jewish-influenced Beta Israel, and the more traditionalist Beta Israel, especially in outlying rural areas that were still not influenced much by either foreign group. In broader socioeconomic terms, a new educated elite was emerging—whether Protestant or Jewish—which would play a role mainly as bureaucrats, envoys, and interpreters in the modernizing Ethiopia of the first half of the twentieth century. On the other hand, the masses of Beta Israel remained rural tenants and artisans as before. Despite a temporary demand for Beta Israel carpenters and builders, their craft skills were not used as an indigenous base for the technological transformation of Ethiopia.

Armies, Disease, and Famine, 1868–1900

"The people of Ethiopia were the slaves . . . of soldiers," wrote Afewarq Gabra Iyyasus (1868–1947) during the reign of Menilek II.[1] For the Ethiopian rural peasantry of whatever religion or ethnic group, it usually made little difference whether an army had come to attack or protect them. In either case, the main impact on the peasantry was predatory. Despite initial efforts by Tewodros to create a regular salaried army, neither he nor his successors were able to escape the traditional means of provisioning a large army by plundering or seizing supplies from the peasantry, whether friendly or rebellious.[2] In addition to plunder and living off the land, banditry (*sheftanet*) by local or would-be national nobles, up to and including aspiring emperors, was an accepted means of political advancement in Ethiopia. Two emperors were crowned as a result of such efforts, and numerous other officials rose and fell by these means in this period. Whatever the results of individual power-seeking, the effects on the peasantry were devastating.[3]

For the rural Beta Israel, the late nineteenth century was a time of horrors. Predatory armies, whether of rebels, rulers, or invaders, combined with the impact of disease and famine to disrupt and temporarily depopulate large areas of the countryside.

Shortly after the suicide of Tewodros on 13 April 1868, Wagshum Gobaze occupied Gondar and proclaimed himself Emperor Takla Giyorgis. This declaration followed Gobaze's successful battles earlier in 1868 against rivals who controlled Walqayt, Wagara, Chelga, and Balasa. Gobaze's estimated 60,000-man army lived off the land in Begamder, creating hardship among the local population. In addition, his entire three-year reign was marked by rebellion and opposition as he was never able to consolidate his hold over more than Begamder, and even that was not very secure. These rebellions and efforts to subdue them ended with Takla Giyorgis's defeat in 1871 by Kassa of Tigray, who was crowned Emperor Yohannes IV in January 1872.[4]

Emperor Yohannes IV of Tigray established a capital at Dabra Tabor in the Greater Begamder region in order to be more centrally located to control Begamder, Gojjam, and Lasta and to keep an eye on Shawa. During the first years of his reign, he was faced with several local rebellions and the overall threat of Menilek of Shawa as a rival claimant to the throne. Rebellions against Yohannes or his appointees took place in Begamder-Samen and other nearby regions between 1872 and 1876, some of which were fomented or supported by Menilek.[5]

Local reports as early as 1872 referred, in general, to "the political disorder of our unhappy country,"[6] and to a specific rebel in 1874 who was "overrunning Dambeya, plundering, and murdering."[7] A letter from Dambeya in October 1874 stated, "The political state of the country is getting every day more gloomy. Rebels arise everywhere against King John, and all of them torment the poor country people."[8] But it was also clear that the soldiers sent to put down rebellions were just as harsh on the local population as the rebels: "Our community was in great trouble and financial loss by soldiers being quartered with them. You know how badly Abyssinian soldiers behave. They take away everything they can get hold of."[9] Other reports referred to the "savage soldiers" quartered among them in Dambeya.[10] The list of problems suffered by the rural population by 1876 in Dambeya included the "bloody war," famine, cattle plague, rabies, the quartering of soldiers, and exorbitant taxes.[11]

Even after the settlement of the near war between Yohannes and Menilek in 1878, following the movement of troops into Begamder by each in 1877, peace did not come to the area.[12] Conditions remained "unsettled" and in a state of "disorder" through the early 1880s, with reports of further rebellions and troop movements in the region.[13]

By the early 1880s, the region of Begamder was reported to be politically calm, but natural difficulties persisted. Although the Great Famine that affected Ethiopia in the late nineteenth century is usually said to have occurred between 1888 and 1892,[14] local reports in the Begamder region refer to natural calamities as early as 1879, with reports of "plague," and seeds being eaten by insects, "pestilence," and "great famine" in 1879, 1880, and 1882. In the north in general, famine had already begun by 1882.[15]

Foreign invaders, and the Ethiopian efforts to repel them, wrought more havoc on the countryside of northwestern Ethiopia between 1885 and 1892. In March 1885, Mahdist forces from the Sudan occupied Matamma and in June invaded the Chelga region, burning churches, plundering, killing, and setting off a "spiral of punitive violence" between Ethiopia and the Mahdists.[16] In January 1886, they invaded Qwara, burned houses, churches, and the Monastery of Mahbera Sellase, and murdered many monks. In January 1887, King Takla Haymanot of Gojjam burned Matamma in retaliation for the attack on Mahbera Sellase, but in order to reach the border area, his army "devastated the whole of Dambeya," living off the land.[17]

In April 1887, the Mahdists reoccupied Matamma, and Takla Haymanot was ordered by Yohannes to protect the western borders. But in January 1888, Takla Haymanot was defeated by a Mahdist army that "may have been the largest army to invade Ethiopia in the nineteenth century."[18] The invaders under Abu Anja advanced all the way to Gondar, making "all the province of Dembea a wilderness." In Gondar, they destroyed forty of the city's forty-seven churches and took thousands of captives.[19]

Yohannes ordered Menilek's army to Begamder in February, but he moved it very slowly, arriving at Azazo just south of Gondar only on 18 April. Though too late to fight the Mahdists, who had withdrawn, Menilek's very large army proceeded to "eat up the country" in the whole region until ordered by Yohannes to leave.[20]

A new Mahdist invasion left Matamma in June 1888, plundered the areas of Balasa and Begamder, and sacked Gondar again in August, before withdrawing to Matamma. By early 1889, Yohannes had finally resolved his conflict with Takla Haymanot and decided to postpone a confrontation with Menilek to move decisively against the Mahdists. He concentrated a large imperial army in Dambeya and attacked Abu Anja at Matamma in March. Wounded on 9 March, the emperor died on 10 March 1889.[21] Other Mahdist invasions of the region occurred, including one in January 1892.[22]

Several years of political unrest in Begamder followed Menilek's accession to power, as nobles vied with each other for superiority in the region and influence at court. *Ras* Walda Sellase was appointed governor in June 1889, but rebelled in December. In March 1890, Zewde was appointed Governor of Begamder and Dambeya and ordered to capture Walda Sellase. By July, he had done so and was promoted to *ras*, but in January 1891 he rebelled too. *Ras* Zewde's rebellion "devastated the whole country," especially near Dabra Tabor, making the famine in the region worse. Later, he fled to Chelga and "devastated" that region, trying to survive against the forces Menilek sent against him.[23] By January 1892, Wale, the brother of Empress Taytu, had finally captured Zewde and brought him to Menilek.[24] All these conflicts over appointments and rebellions had a negative effect on the peasantry, who had to support the maneuvering of large armies through the countryside.

Between 1888 and 1892, famine ravaged much of the country, killing an estimated third of the population. This famine began with a rinderpest epidemic among the cattle and oxen that were brought by the Italians through their movements into Eritrea. It was probably carried to Begamder by the king's armies fighting the Mahdists during 1888–89. Many oxen were also killed directly by the Mahdist invaders.[25]

The rinderpest epidemic and killing of livestock in Begamder left few plow oxen to cultivate the land and resulted in famine, refugees, and an inflation of food prices. Some people ate human flesh, hyenas, or dead asses to avoid starvation.[26] Beta Israel refugees fled Qwara to the southwest and fled Dambeya to the east and northeast, going as far as Gaynt, Lasta, Wagara, and Sallamt.[27] The impact on Dambeya was devastating:

> Alas! This beautiful country, Dembea, has for the last three years become a perfect wilderness, with only here and there a few inhabitants. Agriculture and cattle breeding, which used to flourish throughout the country, are nowhere to be seen; hyenas, leopards, and lions are nearly the only inhabitants of the country between Ferka and Dingel Ber.[28]

By 1890, prices of grain had increased, and by 1891 they had quadrupled from the previous year.[29]

The worst effects were over by 1893, when prices began to decline and some people were returning home, though others were still scattered. By 1894, it was said "starvation is over, but great poverty still exists."[30] There is evidence that certain areas in the greater Begamder region never recovered their previous prosperity, even ten years later: "Sakalt is a very fertile, healthy country. Before the Dervishes came it was very rich, like Dembea, but now it is poor and very thinly populated. Thousands of Falashas formerly lived in Sakalt, but now only a few hundreds in all."[31]

The years of power struggles, famine, disease, and Mahdist invasions marked the end of the northwestern region's status as a national political power center. The period was also a turning point for the Beta Israel, particularly the years 1888–92, still remembered in traditions as the *kefu qan* ("bad days").[32] A letter from the Falashas a few years later noted, "Formerly we were very numerous; formerly there were 200 synagogues, now only 30 remain. In the time of the Dervishes a frightful number of people died from famine. . . . We are in great misery. Our books have been destroyed; the Dervishes burnt them by fire. We have no longer any schools; they are destroyed."[33] From this time on, it became increasingly difficult to sustain the institutions and practices of traditional Beta Israel society.[34]

Construction Work and Migration

During the late nineteenth century, the Beta Israel continued to be the main skilled artisans as masons, carpenters, blacksmiths, potters, and weavers in the Begamder-Gondar region. But except perhaps for the brief claim to reign by Takla Giyorgis (1868–71), little of the construction activity was actually carried out in Gondar itself, where major building had been in abeyance for a hundred years, until after the turn of the century. Therefore, even when there was construction work, the impact was further to divide Beta Israel society, as skilled artisans were taken throughout the empire and tended to remain in their new locations permanently or at least all year long except for the rainy season (July–August). Whereas during the Gondar dynasty construction work had enhanced the wealth and prestige of the Beta Israel in the Gondar region, during this period such work contributed to the overall splintering of the group, geographically and often religiously as well.

Takla Giyorgis was said to have begun "restoring" the churches of Gondar in 1868, but it is not clear whether this restoration only meant replenishing their endowments or included physical reconstruction.[35] In any case, he was not even in nominal power long enough to have any impact on the construction activities of the Beta Israel.

Gondar was mostly ignored by the next kings. Its buildings deteriorated or were destroyed by the Mahdists, and its Beta Israel artisan community declined in numbers. The population of the whole city was estimated at no more than 4,000 in the 1880s, even before the Mahdist invasion, and only about 1,000 in the early twentieth century.[36] The Gondar Beta Israel enclave, Abwara (also called Falasha-Bet), had long been the center of the masons and carpenters and was the residence of the head of the workers, *bejrond* Eyrusalem, during the reign of Tewodros.[37] That enclave continued to exist during the late nineteenth century, even after the Mahdist invasion, but it was much reduced in size, as masons and carpenters were taken from there to other places in Ethiopia.[38] If it had not been "entirely destroyed" by the first decade of the twentieth century, there certainly was not much left of it.[39]

Due in particular to the skills of the Beta Israel builders, the houses, churches, and palaces were historically the best built in the country, even as late as the 1870s, when it was already in decline. But by the end of the century, the city was described as "a heap of stones."[40] Although some masons and carpenters continued to live there, by the beginning of the twentieth century there were so few artisans left that Empress Taytu was said to have ordered some of the Samen Beta Israel to Gondar to begin its reconstruction. These masons established the new village of Qeddus Yohannes, about a half-hour walk from Gondar, and constituted the main artisans in the vicinity.[41] Walaka, on the northern edge of the city, was another new Beta Israel village established near Gondar in the early twentieth century. It was inhabited mainly by weavers, farmers, and some masons, who had been used by *ras* Gugsa to build his residence at Dabra Tabor. The head of the community there was a *bejrond* Barkoligne.[42] As late as 1930, however, it was said that the Beta Israel quarter at Gondar "had its *start* when Empress Zawditu ordered Falasha workmen to that city to repair the churches." The Italian consul in the city in the 1920s had also used Beta Israel builders to construct his house and other buildings.[43] Obviously, this was only a rebirth, not the beginnings of such a community at Gondar! But such expressions show how far Gondar had fallen.

The pattern of Beta Israel construction activity for the next several years was set as early as the 1870s. Several "masons and carpenters" were taken from Abwara by *ras* Adal Tessema, governor of Gojjam (and the future King Takla Haymanot), to build a church. These craftsmen were away from their homes the whole year except for the rainy season.[44]

The chronicle of Yohannes IV mentions a palace built at Aksum in the early 1880s, though other sources omit its mention.[45] The major construction ordered by Yohannes was a new castle at Maqale. The supervisor of the work there, which was completed in 1886, was an Italian carpenter, Giacomo Naretti, accompanied by his half-Ethiopian assistant, Engidashet Schimper.[46] "Skillful masons and carpenters" assisted them.[47] These skilled artisans were Beta Israel, probably brought either from Gondar, or from elsewhere in Tigray where there were already Beta Israel builders. The leader of the Beta Israel workers at Maqale was a *bejrond* Tasfa Issayas.[48]

The major stone construction during the late nineteenth century was, of course, that ordered by Menilek II (1889–1913) and/or his consort, Empress Taytu. Oral traditions suggest there were Beta Israel workers in or taken to Samen, Dabra Tabor, Dambeya, Walqayt, Sagade, Azazo, Wagara, Saqqalt, and Gondar.[49] A regular procedure developed to utilize teams of workers. Masons and carpenters and sometimes blacksmiths were taken between September and the next July, during which they were separated from their wives and children. They were given food to live on and, according to some traditions, forty dollars per year for this work. At first, they had to work on Saturdays, but after protest, a proclamation by Menilek stopped this practice. Informants praised Menilek for his equitable treatment of the Beta Israel, but some still felt this migrant situation was bad since it separated families for most of the year. Some workers never returned home, and many converted to Christianity even though they were not forced to.[50]

The names of many leaders and workers are remembered, but the principal one was the carpenter *qanazmach* Desta Maru, said to have been taken to Shawa with a group of workers by *ras* Wale, the brother of Empress Taytu. *Qanazmach* Desta was variously said to have been originally from Azazo or Dabra Tabor, but after going to Shawa he remained there, apparently converted to Christianity, and was eventually rewarded with eighty *gashas* of land, probably in the Yajju region of Wallo province, which was *ras* Wale's home district.[51] By the turn of the century, Yajju was a peaceful and prosperous place in which the people lived in stone houses and manufactures were well developed. *Ras* Wale's house was, according to a foreign observer, "the best I have seen in Abyssinia." Some Beta Israel families lived under the control of *ras* Wale in and near Dessie, the main city in the region.[52]

The first area of construction ordered by Menilek and particularly encouraged by his consort, Taytu, was at Entotto, a new settlement in the 1880s. Menilek began building a new palace, and later Taytu had the churches of Maryam and Saint Raguel built there. Several thousand houses were also built in 1882, and the Church of Maryam was completed in 1887. A master craftsman and nine artisans were brought from Gondar to oversee the work, while thousands of laborers were drafted from the surrounding area.[53] It is probable that Desta Maru was, indeed, the master craftsman referred to in the written sources, since traditions name him and nine others who went with him to Shawa at some point.[54]

"Gondari craftsmen" (that is, Beta Israel) built a church at Dabra Libanos.[55] Sahla Sellase, King of Shawa (1813–47), had brought *anhase* (carpenters and masons) from Gondar (i.e., Beta Israel) to build the church of Madhane Alam at Ankobar, which by the early twentieth century was still considered to be the best-constructed building there. The Beta Israel continued to live at several locations in the Ankobar area, especially Let Marefiya, and the men mostly worked for the king in Addis Ababa during the reign of Menilek.[56]

By the late 1880s, construction on the new capital, Addis Ababa, had begun. For a while, it appeared the Addis Ababa area might not have enough trees to support a large population, and Menilek contemplated moving west to a new area called Addis Alam. Beta Israel masons built a palace for him there, and by the early twentieth century, there were about fifty Beta Israel inhabitants in Addis Alam.[57] But the main imperial residence and hence capital remained Addis Ababa.[58]

In Addis Ababa, the king sponsored artisan shops near the new palace, which included workshops for blacksmiths and carpenters.[59] Of course, not all of these artisans were Beta Israel, since people from all over the expanding empire were brought or attracted to the capital. The predominant peoples among the workers were Gurage, Oromo, Wallamo, and others, but the Beta Israel were prominent as masons, carpenters, and blacksmiths.[60] The main Beta Israel residential area in Addis Ababa was called the workers' quarter, or *anasi safar* ("carpenters' quarter"), and was also known as Abware, in memory of the Beta Israel quarter at Gondar. It was located near Menilek's palace. By the early twentieth century, there were estimated to be 100 to 250 Beta Israel residents in the city.[61]

At the turn of the century, a small community of Beta Israel blacksmiths lived at Dire Dawa.[62] Although not stated, perhaps its function involved railroad work as the line from Djibouti had reached Dire Dawa in 1902.

Of course, Beta Israel, or groups apparently descended from earlier Beta Israel migrants, lived all over historic Abyssinia, and do not date from this new dispersal of artisans during the late nineteenth century. Some of these examples probably include the *tabiban* in the Ankobar region of Shawa, whose continued existence was noticed again.[63] Another example may include the "gypsy encampment" southwest of Saqota in Lasta, where there had probably been a Beta Israel presence for centuries.[64] Gojjam was another area with a long-standing Beta Israel population that has not been sufficiently studied. That area may have been augmented by the artisans brought from Gondar but had probably been in existence for centuries.[65]

Despite the existence of these ancient communities, the main impact of increased demands for Beta Israel craft skills in the late nineteenth century was to create a new dispersal of the people. Many of the Beta Israel artisans moved to the new center of the empire, the Shawan Entotto–Addis Ababa–Addis Alam axis. But despite the critical demands for their skills, the rewards received by this new Beta Israel artisan community did not compare with their position in the old imperial capital of Gondar. In Shawa, they were just another group among many involved in building and working in the city, and could not dominate that process as they had in Gondar. They could also not compete technologically with the new groups of foreigners who played such an increasingly important role in Menilek's court as technical advisors, gradually bringing running water, electricity, and new construction methods to the capital.[66] In the first stages of the migrations, men were cut off from their families, at least temporarily. If they stayed in their new locations, they presumably sent for their families, but they still comprised isolated groups cut off from the main Beta Israel cultural and religious supports in northwestern Ethiopia. As small enclaves cut off from their own society, they had little leverage in getting benefits from Menilek, and little success even in maintaining their own culture and religion. Many apparently converted, at least nominally, to Orthodox Christianity.

So, when Jacques Faitlovitch became active in Ethiopia with his first trip in 1904–5, he began to advocate founding schools to prevent further conversions, including those among the children of the scattered artisans as in Addis Ababa. But this topic is part of the larger story of efforts to convert the Beta Israel that had begun in the mid-nineteenth century.

Imperial Policies Toward Religion and Missionaries

The religious policies of the Ethiopian emperors, Yohannes IV (1871–89) and Menilek II (1889–1913), are often contrasted. Yohannes has been seen as rigid, dogmatic, and even fanatical, while Menilek has been seen as more flexible and tolerant. Despite some recent efforts to moderate the hyper-critical view often drawn of Yohannes,[67] which was probably often based on exaggerated statements by European travelers, a difference in style and approach between the two was evident, particularly regarding Ethiopian Muslims. But with regard to their concrete actions, in contrast to various statements concerning efforts to convert the Beta Israel, they were not entirely different.

Religious Policies of Yohannes IV

Yohannes was a deeply religious person, beginning with his very early life. It has been suggested that he took Yohannes as a throne name after John the Baptist, not only because of his piety but because he intended to baptize the unbelievers.[68] It appears, however, that his religious priorities were, first, to establish doctrinal unity within the Orthodox Church; second, to prevent political intrigues by foreign missionaries by expelling or keeping them out of Ethiopia; and, third, to worry about internal proselytization, and then only mainly with regard to Ethiopian Muslims.

He worked assiduously to strengthen the Ethiopian Church. His major success was in acquiring a new *abun,* the head of the Church, from Egypt. In fact, he had four bishops sent simultaneously in 1882[69] to prevent long periods when there would be no bishop in the country, one of the great problems of Ethiopian religious administration for centuries. He was also deeply concerned about establishing doctrinal unity, for political as well as religious reasons, since different views had historically been supported in different provinces.[70]

With regard to foreign missionaries, he was mainly concerned about the Catholics in the north, whom he felt were not just missionaries but political intriguers who wanted a pro-French Ethiopia. As early as 1869, even before he became emperor, he supported the order of *abuna* Atnatewos that all Ethiopian Catholics should be chained and their goods confiscated.[71] In 1871, he felt there was sufficient evidence that Catholics were inciting a rebellion against him to send troops into Akala Guzay to burn the churches and houses of Catholic priests and missionaries and to chain the inhabitants and pillage the villages.[72]

He justified his policy of not allowing foreign missionaries to enter the country by stating *abuna* Atnatewos would excommunicate them if he did allow them entry.[73] After his 1878 agreement with Menilek and the Council of Borumeda, Yohannes pressured Menilek to expel foreign missionaries from Shawa as well.[74] This policy affected the Protestant mission to the Beta Israel by keeping foreign missionaries, in particular J. M. Flad, out of the country throughout Yohannes's reign.

Although Yohannes was "far from being the fanatic that Europeans judged him to be,"[75] he nevertheless did pursue "the spirit of Ethiopian Christian nationalism."[76] He was concerned that Ethiopian Muslims would support their coreligionists involved in attacks on Ethiopia, such as the Egyptians in 1875–76 and the Mahdists after 1888. But regardless of foreign threats, his policies were also stimulated by a desire for an internal religious-based political unity.[77]

Various proclamations giving Yohannes's views have been preserved, such as the following: "Let any Moslem who does not like Christianity be exiled to his country, Egypt. Let everybody who likes Christianity be baptized."[78] He specifically ordered Menilek to "convert the Moslems to Christianity and divide pieces of land among the converts."[79] A joint Yohannes-Menilek proclamation after the historic Council of Borumeda provided the rationale for conversion of Muslims throughout the greater Wallo area:

> We are your apostles. All this used to be Christian land until Gran ruined it and misled it. Now let all, whether Muslim or Galla [pagan] believe in the name of Jesus Christ! Be baptized! If you wish to live in peace preserving your belongings, become Christians. . . . Thereby you will govern in this world and inherit the one to come.[80]

Although an early campaign in 1872 against the Muslim Oromo of Azebo, just south of Tigray, apparently did not use the tactic of forced conversion, later campaigns in Yajju and Wallo used a combination of force and coercion, especially manipulation of land-use rights and office-holding privileges.[81] Military and political measures were accompanied by church-building and proselytization, especially among the elite, as the Wallo leaders Muhammad Ali and Abba Watew were converted and renamed Mika'el and Hayla Maryam, respectively.[82]

Yohannes IV and the Beta Israel

The policies of Yohannes toward the Beta Israel were not as unambiguous as the general proclamations stating that all non-Christians had to convert would leave one to believe. Overall, his policies seem similar to those of Tewodros before him. The only Beta Israel written document on this topic viewed their relations with Yohannes as follows:

> At the time of the Emperor Yohannes, a proclamation was issued as follows: "May all worship and believe in what I believe." The Moslems were converted, the Wayto were baptized, but Israel refused to be baptized. The [Beta Israel] priests called *abba* Eli, *abba* Samu'el, *abba* Kidanu, were imprisoned and stayed in prison for six months. The people took the *orit* [with them] and fled from the province. The learned [Christian] persons of Gondar, of the monastery of Waldebba, [and] the monks of Mahbara Sellase gathered, read the *orit*, commented [on] it, and reported to the Emperor Yohannes. The Emperor then said: "These should not be compelled to adopt our religion. They did not have a [good] judge. It is rather they who should bring us over to [their religion]." He released the imprisoned priests, but did not give the *orit* back to them and kept it for himself.[83]

As was the case during the 1862 controversy argued before Tewodros, the Beta Israel resisted conversion using a textual study of the Old Testament as their defense, even if in this case it was carried out by Christian priests and monks. And Yohannes, like Tewodros, is remembered in this document as having refused to compel the Beta Israel to convert.

Oral traditions, particularly those collected in Tigray, recall a Beta Israel defense of their beliefs: "Like most previous kings, Yohannes also tried to persuade the Beta Israel to convert to Christianity, but a group of prominent Beta Israel priests from Walqayt, Dambeya, and Samen went to Yohannes where he was living in Dabra Tabor and appealed to him that the Beta Israel wanted to retain their own religion. The leader of this prominent group was *abba* Mahari."[84] Another statement that dates to the reign of Menilek supports the generally positive official view of the Beta Israel:

> Very late in the reign of King Theodore [Tewodros], and King John [Yohannes IV] in our days, when the Christians began to force the Mohammedans to be baptized there were some attempts by the lower classes of people against the Falashas also; but both the kings and the priests prevented them, and said: "No man has right to blame the laws of Moses, because he is the inventor of the real worship of the true God." Thus, the Falashas are proud and honoured among the great and learned Abyssinians.[85]

Information recorded in missionary sources do not contradict the somewhat positive view of the Beta Israel held by Yohannes, but they also justify his permission given the mission to work to convert them. In a meeting with Yohannes and the ***abun*** in 1874, J. M. Flad, the European advisor to the Falasha converts, asked the emperor whether he would allow the four new converts Flad had just brought back with him to teach and preach among the Beta Israel:

> He [Yohannes] replied that he loved the Falashas because they were the descendants of Abraham, and that if they would become Christians, he would love them as brethren in Christ. "If those who are my subjects," he said, "teach them, and bring them for baptism into our Church, I shall be happy, and promise to give them my protection; but I do not wish to have any Europeans in my country."[86]

A few years later, another missionary account of Yohannes's relations with the Beta Israel further justified their work among them:

> Some time ago the king issued a decree requiring all the Mohammedans, Kamants (heathens), and Jews in his realm to be forthwith baptized and become Christians. The first two and a portion of the Jews complied with the order, and the king had a church built at Gondar especially for these proselytes from the Mohammedans, Kamants and Falashas. Abuna Joseph, the spiritual advisor of the late Abuna Salama, our kind friend, on hearing this, told the king not to have the Jews baptized without instruction, as *we were there especially for the purpose of teaching them* previous to baptism; on which the king rescinded the decree as far as the Jews were concerned, and gave us full permission to continue the work of preaching and teaching the Jews, without let or hindrance.[87]

In fact, there were two clear restrictions on the mission to the Beta Israel: that no European missionaries were allowed into the country and that the converts could not establish a new Protestant church, but had to join the Ethiopian Orthodox Church. The convert teachers, however, during Flad's meeting with the bishop and emperor in 1874, were granted the privilege of exemption from payment of taxes.[88] This privilege was tested a few years later by a local chief who demanded that taxes be paid, but the privilege was upheld on appeal all the way to the emperor, who remembered his promise of 1874.[89] The converts were also allowed to open two new stations, at Azazo and in the Dagusa area, to go with the long-established headquarters at Jenda in Dambeya.[90]

Menilek II and the Beta Israel

Menilek's policies with regard to efforts to convert the Beta Israel were not really substantially different from those of Yohannes, but he has a much better reputation among the nonconverts. The Beta Israel chronicle written during Menilek's reign puts the matter succinctly: "After that, the Emperor Menilek reigned, and a time of peace came. He proclaimed that everyone should adhere to the religion of his ancestors. The Beta Israel were happy, and the Moslems were happy. We live to this day saying: 'May God show mercy to Menilek.'"[91]

Recent oral traditions remember a similar proclamation that the Beta Israel under Menilek were not forced to convert, but could live and worship as their ancestors had lived: "'Live as your fathers lived.' He said they had the choice to convert or not to convert. They should not be forced to convert. They could practice their fathers' religion. We lived well during Menilek's reign."[92] In general, Menilek's reign was seen as a good time for the Beta Israel.[93]

Menilek expressed his personal views on the Beta Israel in a letter to an English missionary, cited in 1896:

> Not only do European Christians practice violence against their own countries, but even at home they persecute the Hebrews, who also are Christian souls, and to whom we owe our Saviour. In my kingdom dwell many Jews, who enjoy complete liberty, and are loyal and industrious subjects. They never conspire, pay all due tribute, and respect our priests. If they are worse in Europe, it is because the Christians there are worse. Our Lord pardoned the Jews on the cross, then why should they be any longer persecuted?[94]

Like the other kings before him, however, Menilek allowed the mission activities to continue. He was described in 1890 as being "favorable to the Falashas having teachers."[95] The mission continued, but was in disarray during the Mahdist invasions and the Great Famine. During the period of recovery, two converts journeyed to Addis Ababa in 1895 to seek Menilek's permission to reopen their mission stations. He gave them such permission to operate "anywhere in Western Abyssinia" and exempted them from all taxes and from the obligation of quartering soldiers.[96] But despite Flad's hopes and requests, no European missionary received permission to work among the Beta Israel until 1926. The Beta Israel mission remained in the hands of the converts, even though some European missionaries such as John Mayer, who had been expelled during Yohannes's reign, were allowed to return to Shawa after Menilek became Emperor.[97]

Protestant Missionaries and Beta Israel Responses

The Protestant mission to the Beta Israel, which formally began in the late 1850s, had the effect of further splintering Beta Israel society. The new converts were neither assimilated completely into Amhara Orthodox society nor did they totally lose their Beta Israel identity. Rather, they became known as a new group of Falasha-Christians, or more colloquially as *Yaaito Flad Letshotsh* or *Ya Ato Flad lejoch* ("Children [or adherents] of Mr. Flad"),[98] after Johann Martin Flad, the originator, inspiration, and spiritual advisor to the mission. Though not significant during these years in the total number of converts, the new movement was highly important in stimulating debate, controversy, and divisions within both the Beta Israel and Orthodox communities, as was evident in the controversy already discussed during the 1860s.

Purpose and Methods

As early as 1838, Reverend Samual Gobat of the Church Missionary Society urged the establishment of a mission to the Beta Israel whom he had found receptive on his previous visits to Ethiopia.[99] From his position as Anglican Bishop in Jerusalem after 1846, Gobat's prodding eventually resulted in the establishment of two missions: the Pilgrim Mission in 1856, employing men trained in artisanry and pietism by the Saint Chrischona Institute at Basel, and the Falasha Mission, after 1859 formally under the auspices of the London Society for Promoting Christianity Amongst the Jews (hereafter known as the London Society).[100] The Church of Scotland also authorized a Falasha Mission in 1860 that began work in November 1862.[101]

From the beginning, the dream of Protestant missionaries to the Beta Israel had been not only to convert Jews to Christianity but to use the new converts to revive the Ethiopian Orthodox Church, which was uniformly seen as unenlightened and backward, if not corrupt and morally bankrupt. A typical view was that of Stern, as expressed in his initial visit in 1860:

> This is certain, that the Falashas are far superior to their Christian neighbours in industry, honesty, and purity of life: all that they want is Gospel light and spiritual life, and if, by the blessing of God, we can communicate to them these Divine gifts, we may perhaps prepare the best agencies for emancipating this part of Africa from a thraldom and bondage far more grinding and grevious than ever the white man inflicted.[102]

Later, Stern wrote a whole essay on this topic, concluding that "The introduction into the Abyssinian Church of a body of men who would combat error and satisfy inquiry was, under existing restricted circumstances, the best leaven to move an idolatrous, corrupt mass."[103] Though Stern was more flamboyant, outspoken, and arrogant than anyone else, similar views concerning the possible role of the Beta Israel were expressed by others, such as Flad: "Yet who knows but that a reformation of the Church itself may, perhaps, be best brought about through converted Falashas?"[104]

These missionary views, shared by their converts, continually exacerbated tensions between the new Christians and the Orthodox Church. *Abuna* Salama in the 1860s had given his assent to the missions only on condition that a separate Protestant Church would not be established. In 1874, *abuna* Athanasius laid down the same condition, which was renewed later.[105]

The converts, therefore, never could establish a separate church, but had to be baptized within the Orthodox Church. Nevertheless, though they were in it, they followed Stern's strictures by effecting only a "nominal unity" rather than a "conformity" to Orthodoxy.[106] As the converts reported in 1874, "the priests are piqued because the proselytes do not become members of their Church, though baptized in it."[107] Thus, the converts' position in society, as well as their relative fewness in numbers, did not allow them to become the agents of transformation that the missionaries had envisioned, though they did cause a degree of tension within both traditional Orthodox and Beta Israel communities.

From 1868 to 1926 the Falasha Mission was carried out without the presence of any European missionaries inside the country. The mission survived and even expanded despite tremendous obstacles, owing to the skill and devotion of its Ethiopian proselytes and the constant spiritual and monetary support of J. M. Flad, the London Society, and the British and Foreign Bible Society, which provided thousands of tracts and Bibles. Although Flad was never given permission to return to live and missionize inside Ethiopia, he did visit the borders to meet with his proselytes, either at Matamma or near Massawa, at least five times (1870–71, 1874, 1880–81, 1890, and 1894).[108] One proselyte also visited him in Europe twice, in 1885 and 1893.[109]

The support of Flad was crucial. He brought money and books, as well as organizational and moral support. He intervened successfully to mediate crises that threatened to end the mission, particularly in the 1890s. The only time during these visits when he actually crossed the border was his 1874 meeting with Yohannes and the bishop, when he also brought back with him four new trainees from Saint Chrischona. It was for good reason that the converts were called Flad's children.

But the day-to-day mission work was carried out by the Ethiopian converts. Even in the 1860s, during the imprisonment of the missionaries, the converts carried on.[110] The behavior of the converts, especially those such as Beru and Kindy Fanta was considered "irreproachable."[111] They remained steadfast in their faith despite difficulties and the loss of their worldly goods: "Beroo especially . . . is still found faithful and glorifies the Gospel amidst his brethren by his consistent and holy conversation."[112]

After the freeing of the missionaries and the death of Tewodros in 1868, the converts were entirely on their own. Beru continued to earn his living as a weaver, while proselytizing among the Beta Israel on Saturdays and among the Ethiopian Christians on Sundays.[113] During Flad's meeting with the converts at Matamma in 1870–71, Beru was appointed "scripture reader and superintendent of all the converts" at a salary of twenty-one pounds per year. Kindy Fanta was appointed his assistant with a salary of fifteen pounds per year.[114]

These salaries freed the converts for more frequent missionary trips to other areas away from their headquarters at Jenda in Dambeya.[115] They began to have some success outside of Dambeya, as five Beta Israel were baptized at Dagusa in 1871 and two of those began to preach there.[116]

In 1874, the mission received a boost when Flad brought back four trained proselytes from Saint Chrischona Institute at Basel.[117] By 1875, the mission had expanded to three stations—Jenda, Azazo (near Gondar), and Dagusa (west of Lake Tana)—and employed eight "native assistants" as well as four teachers.[118] By 1876, Flad estimated 220 converts were currently living.[119] In 1877, two of the Chrischona graduates who had returned in 1874, Agashy and Samany, died.[120] Their losses were partially offset by the return of Gobbaw Desta, another Chrischona graduate, in 1878.[121]

By the mid-1880s, further missionary visits had been made to Qwara and to the Agawmeder and Macha areas of Gojjam, as well as into Wagara and Balasa.[122] Beru felt that 800 converts had been baptized by 1880.[123] Michael Aragawi estimated that by 1885, there had been 800 to 900 converts since the 1860s.[124]

By the late 1880s and lasting until after 1894, the mission was in a severe state of crisis, caused mainly by the Mahdist invasions and various Ethiopian armies' attempts to defeat them, and by the severe rinderpest epidemic and famine that ravaged the country. Many converts and several teachers or agents, including Beru in 1890, had died or migrated out of western Ethiopia during this period. After Beru's death in 1890, Michael Aragawi himself, the acknowledged leader of the agents, suggested candidly in a letter to Flad in August 1892, "I do not see how the Mission can be continued under such trials."[125] Flad was inclined to agree.[126]

In 1893, Aragawi went to Europe to discuss the situation with Flad,[127] and in March 1894, Flad held a conference with the agents at the Swedish mission at Monkullo near Massawa. At the Monkullo conference, Aragawi was appointed head of the mission, which had been reduced to a total of six agents. The converts had all withdrawn to Dabra Tabor and Abu Harra, away from the invasions and famine in Dambeya. It was estimated at the conference that there had been a total of 1,470 conversions by the mission since the 1860s.[128]

Despite the difficulties, the mission survived and began to expand again, under the new leadership of Michael Aragawi. By mid-1895, many refugee Falasha converts had returned to Dambeya.[129] Aragawi, accompanied by two agents, visited Menilek at Entotto in 1895, apparently to defend themselves against accusations. They stayed a month, during which the king and bishop renewed their permission for them to proselytize.[130] Another trip to Menilek in 1899 renewed permission again.[131]

During the 1890s, missionary trips were renewed, and eventually Jenda, which was still in ruins in 1897, was rebuilt, as were other stations.[132] In 1904, a new factor arrived with the first trip to Ethiopia by Jacques Faitlovitch, whose work on behalf of western Judaism began to slow down the conversions of the Beta Israel. Nevertheless, by 1908, it was estimated that about 1,800 Falasha converts had been baptized since the beginning of the mission.[133]

Convert Biographies

The impact of the Mission on the Beta Israel was more qualitative than quantitative. With less than 2,000 total converts in fifty years of work, out of a total Beta Israel population estimated at 80,000 to 200,000 at the most in mid-century, this 1.0 to 2.5 percent conversion rate does not seem very significant.[134]

In the present state of the documentation, an overall demographic, quantitative analysis of the converts cannot be provided. But anecdotal and brief biographical evidence suggests, unsurprisingly, that the young and/or literate were more likely to convert. According to a few brief biographies of converts who became mission agents, a critical factor was often a disrupted childhood that led to an early association either with missionaries or at least placement in an educational environment.

The principal convert, who became the leader and inspiration of the "Native Agents" from the time of his conversion in the early 1860s to his death in 1890, was *dabtara* Beru Webe.[135] Beru's father was a Beta Israel priest and weaver and had cattle herds. He was well-off until his relative wealth aroused the jealousy of local officials. The family was persecuted, and not long afterward, Beru's father died in a fire. Beru learned weaving to supplement his mother's pottery-making and from a young age followed religiously the Beta Israel cycle of fasts and feasts. He also learned Ethiopic (Ge'ez) from a local Christian *dabtara* and eventually became known as *dabtara* himself, translating the *orit* from Ethiopic to Amharic at Beta Israel services.

It was only in 1860 or 1861, at the mature age of around 30, that he came into contact with Flad and the new Protestant mission at Jenda.[136] After a day-long disputation with Flad, probably in 1861, he was said to have been convinced and was among the first group to be baptized in 1862.[137]

Unlike Beru, many of the other converts who became mission agents came under the influence of the missionaries as young children. Michael Aragawi, for example, the man who, after Beru, was the most talented and respected leader, was raised by Flad himself from early childhood. Unlike the other best-known converts, Aragawi (as he was consistently known) was of an Amhara Christian, not a Beta Israel, family.

Aragawi was born between 1848 and 1853 in Dambeya. His father was a former servant of Reverend J. Nicholayson in Jerusalem who accompanied Flad as a cook and servant to Ethiopia on Flad's first trip in 1855. In the late 1850s, Aragawi's father asked Flad to take complete charge of raising him, and he henceforth grew up in the household of Flad and his wife. He was educated in Europe, and after 1866, at Baden and Basel, spending 1869 to 1874 at Saint Chrischona Institute. Subsequently Flad brought him back to Ethiopia. Aragawi, thus, was brought up in a missionary environment, and he remained true to that calling until his death in 1931.[138]

Samany Daniel was raised at Azazo, near Gondar, where his father was a weaver. There, at the age of four, he was sent to a Jewish school where he learned to read and memorized the Psalms of David. But his father died while he was still a child, leaving the family in poverty. His mother was a potter, and at the age of ten he learned weaving. A year later, she moved the family to Jenda. He began to attend *dabtara* Beru's school and by age 12 was seriously studying the Bible and began to attend Flad's religious services. Finally, he was baptized after running away from home, and he then appealed to the missionary Waldmeier for support. He stayed with Waldmeier, who was at Gafat. After the release of the captives in 1868, Flad brought him to Saint Chrischona, where he was educated further and returned to proselytize in 1874.[139]

Samany's brother Sanbatoo was sent as a child by his mother to live in Waldmeier's orphanage at Gafat. From there, Waldmeier took him to Jerusalem, where he stayed three years at Bishop Gobat's school, and then in 1871 to Saint Chrischona, where he stayed until returning to Ethiopia in 1874.[140]

Hailu Wosan from Saqqalt was born about 1855. His father died when Wosan was only ten. While watching their cattle one day, soldiers of Tewodros took him, the cattle, and his sister and kept them about six months. Upon being released by the soldiers, he was near Gafat and sought refuge with the missionaries. Waldmeier took him in and in 1868 took him to Jerusalem. In 1871, he entered Saint Chrischona but died of consumption on 26 April 1872.[141]

Many other cases, whose brief biographies are available, could be cited, such as Agashy, Goshu Mersha, Negoosie, Meherat, and Beleta Goshu.[142] In most cases, the converts were exposed to education at a very early age, either through an Orthodox school or a Mission school, such as that of Beru at Jenda. Often, their families had suffered hardship, and the children used education and conversion as a path for advancement.

The Missionary Message and Conversions

The early age at which many came under missionary influence through the schools was, of course, a very important factor in the conversion process, particularly since there were few, if any, Beta Israel schools to counteract these influences. Some of the converts, however, came from priestly Beta Israel families, and some, such as Beru, were already seeking learning on their own and had contact with the missionaries as mature adults, not merely as impressionable and vulnerable youths. As they read the Bible and/or had it explained to them, they began to raise questions that could not be answered through the traditional Beta Israel formulas.

The missionary message to the Beta Israel comprised several aspects that were appealing to some of the community. Missionary preaching emphasized two main theological themes: that the coming of Jesus really was the fulfillment of Old Testament prophecies concerning the Messiah and that Jesus' sacrifice on the cross obviated the need for any other earthly sacrifices. These themes had been evident already in the religious controversy of 1862 when Beru Webe argued Christ was the Son of God who had made the ultimate sacrifice and that, therefore, the sacrifices offered by the Beta Israel were an "abomination."[143]

With great consistency, the same religious arguments were made for the next half-century. Isaiah 53 was a favorite text the preachers used to argue against sacrifices, from Stern in 1864[144] to a convert agent in 1904.[145] They also argued that sacrifices were completely forbidden even according to the Old Testament, because according to Deuteronomy 12:14, sacrifices could only be offered in one place. Since the Temple had been destroyed, there was no longer any place where sacrifices legitimately could be offered.[146] The agents also spoke against the belief in intercession by saints, such as the Beta Israel "goddess of the Sabbath" (*Sanbatitoo*).[147]

Such arguments against the mediating role of saints were most commonly used by the convert agents when preaching among Ethiopian Christians. They particularly criticized the Ethiopian Church's veneration of Saint Mary,[148] and for that reason were regularly called "enemies of the Virgin Mary."[149] Preaching to Ethiopian Christians was one of the aims of the mission from the beginning, despite Church and state opposition to that practice and despite the requirement that all converts had to become members of the Ethiopian Church.[150]

The convert agents presented their message in typical Protestant terms as the need for inner faith and true spiritual conversion. Their message offered not only fulfillment of Old Testament prophecies but also demanded a higher level of individual commitment and morality. The Ethiopian Christians were correct in their suspicion concerning the nature of the converts' Christianity. Since traditional Beta Israel already regarded themselves as purer in belief and practice than the Orthodox Christians, the missionary message was attractive to some as a logical extension of the level of commitment and pure faith they felt they already exhibited.

Thus, the convert agents and several potential converts were quoted by mission sources as being attracted to the message but repulsed by the formal requirement of joining the Orthodox Church.[151] The feeling was returned by the Orthodox Church and many local government officials who were highly suspicious. They accused the converts of being "Protestants," "English Protestants," or "English Christians" and "hated" their "Bible teaching."[152] The new Bishop who arrived in Adwa in 1869, with the approval of Kassa, issued a letter "prohibiting the Abyssinians [Orthodox Christians] reading the Protestant Bible."[153] The converts felt that "the Abyssinian Christian Debteras hate us"[154] and that more opposition came from the "Abyssinian priesthood" than from the Beta Israel.[155]

In 1876, charges were brought against the convert agents by Orthodox priests, accusing them of being "heretics" because they did not venerate the saints. The converts "testified openly" before the judges that to venerate the saints was against the word of God. The priests then forbade them to visit Orthodox Churches and the local governor, *ras* Walda Sellase, issued an order prohibiting them from preaching to Ethiopian Christians.[156]

Several years later, when Michael Aragawi returned from a visit to Europe in 1885, he was arrested and imprisoned in a "subterranean dungeon" for two weeks. He was accused of being a Protestant, a pupil of the English, an enemy of the Virgin Mary, and of leaving the country without permission. He was eventually freed after Beru's appeal to the governor of Gondar.[157]

Although tensions between the two Christian communities continued throughout the period, some positive interaction also occurred. There is little information on the existence of the *buda* accusation during this period, but one convert agent felt the significant conversions to Christianity in the Dambeya region had led Christians to stop calling the Beta Israel *buda* in that region, though the practice continued elsewhere.[158] Some Orthodox Christians came or sent their children to mission schools or prayer services despite Orthodox priestly opposition.[159] A few Orthodox *dabtaras* and priests joined the mission and taught in their schools.[160] In general, despite a few examples of positive cooperation or interaction between the two Christian groups, tensions, conflicts, and suspicion continued and prevented the assimilation of the converts into the Orthodox community.

Despite the formal requirement that converts be baptized in Orthodoxy, they continued to form a separate group, not assimilated into either the Ethiopian Church or Amhara culture.[161] In fact, both the convert agents and Flad were highly critical of any converts who attached themselves too closely to the Ethiopian Church. One agent wrote to Flad that

"We have frequently been disappointed by some of the baptized Falashas, who have a love of the world, and prefer attaching themselves to the Abyssinian Church, whereby they are misled into many evils and vices."[162]

Two years later, just before returning to the Ethiopian borders, Flad expressed similar doubts about the mission as a whole:

> Their work is but imperfect and I feel and fear they have accommodated themselves so much to the Abyssinian Church that they are no more a light in it. It may prove the best thing to give up the whole mission, for there are plenty of baptized Abyssinians. If the Falashas are wishful of being baptized only without being converted, it is better that they remain Falashas.[163]

Though the references above to the "love of the world" by some baptized Beta Israel and to their alleged desire to be baptized without being (truly) converted inwardly are vague, these brief statements may relate to the larger issue of possible material incentives and rewards for becoming officially Orthodox Christian. Several years earlier, Flad alleged that Tewodros had offered ten German crowns to every Falasha worker at Gafat who would convert to Orthodoxy.[164] During the late 1870s, especially after the Council of Borumeda and the reconciliation with Menilek in March 1878, was precisely the time when Yohannes was pushing for proselytization of Orthodoxy. In that push, one of the tools used was access to *rest* land-use rights by those who converted.[165] The documentation here refers to the conversion of Ethiopian Muslims. But with some exceptions, Beta Israel, like Muslims, were deprived of inheritable *rest* rights. Perhaps the "love of the world" referred to by a convert agent in 1878 meant a desire to obtain land rights. An accommodation with Orthodoxy, even if only nominal, might be a step in that direction.

The early 1890s crisis of invasion and famine was another period of increased nominal conversion. Beru wrote about the hard times that caused more Beta Israel to seek a better life at the mission.[166] Aragawi described how the disruptions of the period had forced many Beta Israel into closer relations with Christians as they scattered around the country seeking means to survive and had to eat, drink, and live with the majority Christian population. During this time many were baptized, but in Aragawi's view, they knew nothing of "true conversion and regeneration." Instead, they had become "proud, puffed-up and light-minded."[167]

The sources, thus, merely hint at what may have been the much larger phenomenon of nominal conversion. The converts were often considered by the pro-Falasha activists such as Faitlovitch and Marguiles as *marranos,* after the Jews who converted nominally to Christianity under duress in medieval Spain.[168] Recent scholarly analysis confirms the view that in the 1960s there may have been 50,000 former Beta Israel who called themselves Christian, even taking the appellation *Maryam Wodet*—short for *Maryam Wededoch* ("lovers of Mary")—in order to distinguish themselves from the Protestant converts, called by their Orthodox opponents "enemies of Mary."[169] Although they called themselves Christian, they maintained some of the traditional Beta Israel practices, such as the veneration of the Saturday Sabbath. Oral testimony from some of these people in 1962 elicited the motivation for their ancestors' conversion as the desire to obtain land, and now they did have their own land.[170]

This evidence is so far only suggestive, and only further investigation would document the phenomenon of nominal conversion more completely. It is indicative, however, of another aspect of the splintering of Beta Israel society in the late nineteenth century.

Resistance of the Traditional Beta Israel

Followers of the traditional Beta Israel religion used several arguments and methods to defend their religion in the face of Protestant and Orthodox pressures to convert. They fought part of the battle at the level of religious doctrine and practice. As had been the case for centuries, the Beta Israel argued for the "unity of the Godhead"; one *dabtara* stated that the anti-Trinitarian doctrine was his main argument against Christianity.[171] As a Beta Israel priest stated: "We will never believe in a Trinity nor in Christ. 'Hear O Israel, the Lord Our God is One Lord.' That's our creed."[172]

Though those who converted were attracted to the argument that Christ was the Messiah promised in the Old Testament, most Beta Israel, especially their priests and *dabtaras,* remained unconvinced. Beta Israel priests argued against Christianity on the grounds that Christians eat human flesh and drink human blood, their explanation of Christian Communion.[173]

The priests also defended their continued use of sacrifices. During the 1862 controversy, Beru had pronounced a ban on their use. Even after Tewodros's decision, which at least partially satisfied the Beta Israel, the practice of sacrifices apparently fell into disuse. But after Tewodros's death, some Beta Israel priests approached Beru, asking him to lift his ban on sacrifices. Beru replied, "As long as you leave me, and those of the Falashas who wish for instruction and Baptism, undisturbed, you may do as you like."[174]

Although, over the years, the number of sacrifices declined, they remained an essential part of Beta Israel practice. By the end of the century, a Beta Israel priest defended the practice of sacrifices during celebration of the feast of Maorer (*ma'rar*), by shouting to his congregation: "My children, our faith is the true faith, and our bloody sacrifices have been ordered to us by Moses. We will remain what we are."[175] Even in the small Beta Israel settlement in Addis Ababa at the turn of the century, sacrifices were said to be an integral part of their religion.[176]

In general, Beta Israel priests and monks defended their beliefs. Sometimes they agreed to listen to the mission agents or to let their people listen, as the great leader *abba* Simon of Qwara allegedly stated in 1878. But Simon was unimpressed by the converts' Biblical readings, saying he already knew all those, but he desired to die in the "faith of my fathers."[177]

Other elders, such as one who had argued with Flad in his 1874 visit, refused even to listen any more. When the convert agents try to visit him, "He trembles in his rage, and wishes much to beat and kill us, exclaiming, 'Do not enter my house, you have nothing to do with me; and I desire to know nothing of you, nor of Jesus Christ [of] whom you preach.'"[178]

As one High Priest in Saqqalt stated in 1898: "We have now heard a great many things of your religion, and of your Jesus. We Falashas don't want a Jesus who died on the cross. Are not the Christians of this country worse than we are? God gave us the law by Moses, and commanded us to make sacrifices for our sins. More we don't want."[179]

Similar sentiments were expressed by the High Priest *abba* Maru, "A great many of my people you have taken from me. . . . Others will follow, but we priests are deaf—entirely deaf—to your teaching. We Falashas are better people than all the Abyssinian Christians. We are, and remain, and will die Falashas, with the words on our lips: 'Hear O Israel, the Lord our God is One Lord.'"[180] In general, such traditionalist arguments held the day, despite the dedication of the mission convert agents and their relatively larger, though still meager, monetary resources.

Despite the best efforts of the mission agents and the depredations and problems of the times, the traditional Beta Israel religious beliefs and practices continued to be upheld, though with great difficulty. Oral traditions remember the active efforts of Beta Israel monks and priests in several locations, including Qwara, Wagara, Saqqalt, Hohwara, and Samen. The best known included *abba* Simon at Qwara; and *abba* Mahari at Qwara, Dambeya, Qolla Wagara, and later Abba Entonyos, near Gondar, who had both achieved prominence during the reign of Tewodros. Later, prominent individuals included Kidanu at Hohwara; Kendaye, Gedewon, and Tamenu in Samen; two Warqnehs, Alazar and Aytegab, in Wagara; Nega and Dejen at Saqqalt, and many others.[181]

Social pressure was an important factor in the defense of Beta Israel society. The initial pressure came from family and friends.[182] Very strong societal pressure came from the sanctions imposed by Beta Israel priests and monks or from their threat of sanctions. Sometimes they threatened a whole village with excommunication for listening to the mission agents preach. At other times, they banned parents from sending their children to the mission schools.[183] Sometimes, the threatened excommunication was against an individual, such as a father, for talking to a convert son,[184] or to an individual considering conversion but who was afraid of the priests' condemnation.[185]

Legal or judicial sanctions were attempted against the converts or the agents. At times, these sanctions were brought by Ethiopian Christians, such as when Aragawi was arrested (see above). At other times, the Beta Israel tried to get the converts to stop their activities by appealing to local governors, as when "Aba Teesasu" (*abba* Tezazu), "a converted Falasha priest," was accused of being an enemy of the Beta Israel by some Beta Israel in Wagara.[186]

When religious disputation, societal pressure, or judicial accusations were not sufficient, physical means were sometimes used to resist proselytization. One Beta Israel youth who got up early to go to church for baptism was stopped along the way, beaten, and carried back to his house.[187] Thirteen Beta Israel priests came to bring one of their brethren, *abba* Elias, back.[188] A more typical physical response was a variety of avoidance behaviors, either refusing to talk to the missionaries or leaving an area while they were there.[189]

A more extreme form of avoidance was threatened by the famous *abba* Mahari, who had led the abortive millennial movement to Jerusalem in the 1860s.[190] When Flad entered the country for a short visit in 1874, *abba* Mahari said he had heard Flad had permission from Emperor Yohannes to convert all the Beta Israel by force if necessary and issued the following proclamation: "Aba Maharee invites all those who wish to die as Falashas to leave West Abyssinia, and to follow him to a place of refuge. Those who do not care for their fathers' religion may remain; but let them remember that there is only one true religion—that of Moses."[191]

The place of refuge was to be Qolla Wagara, the hot lowland west of the Wagara escarpment. Flad, however, wrote to Mahari stating that he was only there to preach peacefully and not convert anyone by force. Mahari sent a message back that, in that case, he would call off his retreat. Several years later, Mahari was reported to remain "as hardened as ever," and was living at Abba Entonyos, a Beta Israel settlement just outside of Gondar.[192] Despite all the problems, the Beta Israel maintained their traditional beliefs and practices, such as a strict monotheism, the practice of the Sabbath and other festivals, the laws of purification, fasting on Monday and Thursday, and some sacrifices, especially a lamb on Passover. Monasticism continued even through the Italian occupation, and of course, their oral liturgy and oral historical traditions continued to be remembered and passed down to future generations.[193]

Western Jewish Impact to 1920

Direct, personal contacts between Western Jews and the Beta Israel started later than contact with Christian missionaries and developed more slowly. Gradually, Western Jews became concerned with the missionary impact on the Beta Israel and began to devise strategies to "save" them from conversion. This effort was colored, however, by two questions that have continued to affect the group and to create divisions among those attempting to assist them up to the present: the question of whether the Beta Israel were "real" Jews, and the question of the kind of strategies needed to assist them.

Though a Jew from Vienna named Solomon or Abraham visited the court of Suseneyos in seventeenth-century Ethiopia, he apparently had no impact on the Beta Israel.[194] Various scholars and travelers, such as Ludolphus, Bruce, Gobat, Antoine d'Abbadie, and Luzzatto, had done much to inform Western Jews about the existence of the Beta Israel, but the first European Jew to visit the Beta Israel in their villages was Joseph Halévy in 1867–68. Even at that late date, his efforts were ignored until his student Jacques Faitlovitch made his first visit to Ethiopia in 1904–5. The full consequences of Western Jewish interest in the Beta Israel are only reaching fruition today in Ethiopia and Israel.[195]

Background: Pre-Faitlovitch Contacts

The initiative for contact with the outside world was actually taken by the Beta Israel themselves. The Beta Israel had long had an interest in and concern with Jerusalem. Contact with missionaries further stimulated that interest. In connection with the crisis of the 1860s, a back-to-Jerusalem millennial movement was started by some Beta Israel priests. Although that expedition never got out of Ethiopia, there had already been some contact with Jerusalem. As early as the 1850s, at least one Beta Israel had traveled to Jerusalem and left his son there to study for some time. In October 1862, another Beta Israel priest, one *abba* Sagga Amlak, wrote a letter to the Jewish community in Jerusalem, asking them if the time were ripe for a return.[196] The missionary Bronkhorst was apparently to be the intermediary and deliver this letter. Though the letter was not delivered to its addressee and had no immediate effect, its existence indicates a Beta Israel interest in external contact.

At the same time in Europe, events were leading to the first direct contact of the Beta Israel community with a Western Jew. European Judaism was becoming gradually and slowly aware and concerned about the Beta Israel, as well as Jews in other parts of the world. In Paris, l'Alliance israélite universelle (AIU) was founded and began sending expeditions to various Jewish communities to investigate their conditions and implement means of assistance. For example, the Semitic linguist Joseph Halévy was sent by the AIU to Morocco in 1861.[197] The Orthodox German rabbi Israel Hildesheimer, after investigating the question, published a statement in the *Jewish Chronicle* of London in 1864 stating that the Beta Israel were authentic Jews, and he called for Western Jews to assist them.[198]

After undertaking his own investigation of the question, Joseph Halévy proposed to the AIU that they support his mission to the Beta Israel to find out more about their situation. The AIU eventually agreed; additional support was found in England, and by October 1867, Halévy arrived in Massawa.[199] His arrival coincided with the development of the British Napier expedition to free the missionaries and other Europeans being held captive by King Tewodros. Halévy's original plan had been to follow the Napier expedition into the interior, expecting it would go to the Gondar area, and from there make contact with the Beta Israel. But Napier was taking too long in getting started, and Halévy found his route was not going to take him through Gondar, so he decided to strike out on his own.

Eventually, Halévy spent several months visiting the Beta Israel in their villages in Walqayt and near the ancient monastic center of Mount Hohwara. He was not able, however, to visit Gondar, Samen, or Qwara due to unrest in the region. Despite these geographic limitations, he returned with invaluable historical, religious, and cultural information concerning the people, not all of which was believed by the European Jews. He also brought with him a Beta Israel youth named Daniel, whom he hoped to educate in Europe and return to his people. Another Beta Israel, named *dabtara* Feroo, started to accompany him but was obliged by the climate in the Sudan to turn back.[200] The AIU did not follow through on the education of Daniel but rather sent him to Cairo, where he died soon afterward.[201]

Halévy recommended in his report to the AIU that assistance should be given to the Beta Israel, whom he believed to be undoubtedly authentic Jews.[202] He felt the Beta Israel were eager for contact with the West, particularly for education and spiritual assistance. AIU leaders, however, were not convinced, and some went so far as to question whether Halévy had even been to Ethiopia and to assert that the young man he brought back was an African from the Sudan, not a Beta Israel.[203]

Suspicions remained during the next decades among AIU leaders and among other European Jews that the Beta Israel were not authentic Jews, and therefore, it was more convenient to ignore them. Despite Halévy's urgings, no further expeditions were sent until the abortive attempt of 1896. At that time, owing to the incessant efforts of Halévy, the AIU decided to send a Dr. Rappoport on a new mission to the Beta Israel. He got only as far as Cairo, however, before he was recalled.[204] No further efforts were made until the first trip by Jacques Faitlovitch, a student of Halévy, in 1904–5.

Impact of Jacques Faitlovitch

Faitlovitch, like Halévy, was born in Poland and came to France to study. Halévy, who was fifty-three years older, succeeded in firing Faitlovitch's imagination concerning the Beta Israel. In 1904, Faitlovitch, supported by the Baron Edmond de Rothschild, began his exploratory voyage to Ethiopia. Thus began his career devoted to the improvement and well-being of the Beta Israel that did not end until his death in 1955.[205]

Faitlovitch's work may be accurately seen in terms of the concept of "culture broker."[206] In his view, he was trying to preserve and "save" the Beta Israel from the deprecations of the missionaries and their convert agents. But in order to do that, he felt he needed to educate the people in the ways of the Western world and, in particular, to reform their Judaism to make it conform to contemporary Western practices. So, in order to preserve Beta Israel culture and save the people from extinction, it was necessary to encourage a careful process of change. The tension between these two forces has characterized Beta Israel history for the succeeding eight decades.[207]

Faitlovitch's overall aims were to impede the process of conversion to Christianity pushed by the convert agents, to establish contact with and support from Western Judaism which would encourage and revitalize Beta Israel religion, resulting in the reform of certain religious practices, and to create a cadre of Western-educated Beta Israel teachers who could carry on this process. During his first trip between January 1904 and August 1905, he sought to build a relationship of trust and caring in the villages he visited. As the country was more peaceful than it had been in the time of Halévy, he was able to visit nearly all the main Beta Israel areas, coming through Tigray to Walqayt, Samen, Wagara, Gondar, Dambeya, Begamder, and back through Lasta.[208]

As a first step toward establishing schools for the Beta Israel, he took back with him to Europe for further education two Beta Israel youths, Gette Jeremias and Taamrat Emmanuel. Gette was from the village of Fenja in Dambeya, and Taamrat was originally from a family of converts in Saqqalt but was at the Swedish Protestant mission at Asmara when Faitlovitch made contact with him. During this first trip, he conceived the idea of starting a school for the Beta Israel, perhaps in Asmara.[209]

He also made contact with some of the Falasha-Christians, the products of the Protestant mission supported by Flad. One of the convert agents reported in a letter to Flad a confrontation with Faitlovitch, apparently at Jenda in Dambeya, the center of the Christian mission. Faitlovitch said he had come "to become acquainted with the 'children of Flad.'" He asked whether all the people in that village had converted. The agent answered: "Yes, . . . we were all Falashas, and now we have become Christians and are called Flad's children." In the conclusion to this letter, the convert agent summarized Faitlovitch's efforts and his own reaction:

> As we heard, he visited many Falasha villages, distributed much money, visited the high-priest and said to all, "Do not listen to these deceivers, these fellows ought to be hanged." He took with him two Falasha youths, whom he will send back with rabbis to instruct the Falashas in Judaism, and in the Talmud, and also to try and convert back us proselytes. This visit reminded me of our Lord's warning (Mathew vii, 5), "Beware of false prophets, which come unto you in sheep's clothing, but inwardly they are ravening wolves."[210]

At a village in Balasa, convert agents were told about the impact of Faitlovitch after he had returned to Europe: "We have heard you now, but we were told that a French Jew at Gondar said to our people, 'Remain what you are, don't believe the teaching of Mr. Flad's children, for they are apostates.' . . . That French Jew promised us teachers and plenty of money."[211]

Though the convert agents cited here may not have been personally affected by Faitlovitch's message, it appears he did have an important impact on impeding proselytization. Faitlovitch himself claimed to have stopped conversions to Christianity for four years following his first visit.[212] The convert agents, such as Michael Aragawi, the head of the mission, admitted that Faitlovitch had had an effect, though they tended to equate his success with the distribution of money and promise of further assistance to reconstruct prayer houses and establish schools.[213] Contrary to some assertions, the contemporary missionary records indicate that a few conversions continued, but the process was slowed down by the impact of Faitlovitch.[214]

Faitlovitch also had to deal with conservative opposition to his innovations in making Beta Israel practice conform to contemporary Judaism. One such instance was reported by Aragawi: "Not all Falashas, however, are in favour of this French Jew, and his teaching Talmudic doctrine in Abyssinia. Some monks in Wogera would not have anything to do with him and literally chased him away."[215] The Beta Israel were particularly resistant to some of the demands for religious change made by Faitlovitch, such as the use of sacrifices, deeply engrained in Beta Israel religion and which they had strenuously supported against the Protestant missionaries.

One informant remembered the debates about sacrifices that Faitlovitch's efforts had sparked. Faitlovitch told the monks that it was forbidden to perform sacrifices anywhere except Jerusalem. One monk argued with him stating that the *orit* sanctioned sacrifices anywhere that "God chose," even in "barren lands." Faitlovitch said that was no longer the case, and the monk said that he had been following the *orit,* but if it were forbidden, they would stop: "because they had been forbidden to make sacrifices, the priests were weeping [and saying], 'God's sacrifice is lost, Jerusalem is lost.' They said, 'Cry for Jerusalem and God's sacrifice' . . . as they made their last sacrifices. It was forbidden thereafter."[216] In reality, sacrifices continued, though gradually greatly diminished in number (for economic reasons in particular).[217]

The Beta Israel also scrutinized Faitlovitch's personal habits carefully. They were critical of his practice of chain-smoking, since the Beta Israel along with Orthodox Ethiopians condemned smoking as a Muslim practice.[218] Such careful scrutiny was congruent with Faitlovitch's role as a culture broker; in order to legitimize his desire to change aspects of their religion, he first had to gain their trust. In general, he was highly successful in doing that through his obvious and demonstrated desire to help them. His fluency in Amharic and Ge'ez and his observance of some important practices, such as not traveling on the Sabbath, went a long way toward increasing his legitimacy in the eyes of the Beta Israel.

Faitlovitch realized that the changes he felt were necessary in order to revitalize the Beta Israel would only come about through a long-term effort. Such an effort required the mobilization of international Jewish support for the people and an internal education process carried out by Western-educated Beta Israel. He began to put both aspects into effect upon his return to Europe in 1905, after his first trip to Ethiopia. He enrolled the two Beta Israel youths he brought back with him in the École Normale of the AIU near Paris, though one was transferred to Florence later.

He also went on a lecture tour of Europe and began to organize the network of "Pro-Falasha Committees" that were to play such an important role in mobilizing international support for his efforts. Such committees were eventually set up in several countries, including Germany, Italy, and the United States. In Germany, he persuaded the Hilfsverein der Deutschen Juden, which had been organized in 1901 on the lines of the French AIU, to sponsor the education of several Beta Israel at its school in Jerusalem.[219]

Since the AIU offered Faitlovitch only a subordinate position in their new expedition, which was to be led by Rabbi Nahum, he demurred and his second trip to Ethiopia was sponsored by the Florence Pro-Falasha Committee, headed by Rabbi Marguiles. This trip had the specific aims of widening and deepening the relationship with the Beta Israel; distributing among them a brochure assuring them of the sympathy of European Jews and including a letter in Hebrew signed by many rabbis in different countries; preparing to erect a Falasha school; and bringing more youths out of Ethiopia to be educated by the Hilfsverein der Deutschen Juden in Jerusalem.[220] He brought Gette Jeremias back with him as proof of his good intentions.

This trip covered some of the same ground as his first one but also included a trip to the holy site of Mount Hohwara, a visit with King Menilek, and a return through Wallo, Yajju, and Tigray. His account of this trip between April 1908 and June 1909 contains the German version of the letter to the Beta Israel signed by forty-four rabbis throughout Europe and the Amharic text and German translation of an answer signed by many Beta Israel leaders. During his trips, Faitlovitch collected several letters and statements by the Beta Israel, which he published in Amharic with European translations.[221] His efforts succeeded in improving mutual knowledge and connections between European and Ethiopian Judaism. Faitlovitch viewed these connections as essential to the effort to bring the Beta Israel into congruence with Western Jewry.

His biggest problems had to do with splits within Western Judaism on views toward the Falasha and what, if anything, should be done to assist them. Rabbi Nahum, the chief rabbi of Turkey, had been sent by the AIU to visit the Falasha, and he returned with a very negative report, stating there were only 6,000 to 7,000 left, that they lived in dispersed settlements and, therefore, that establishing a school in a particular place such as Eritrea would not be practical. He concluded that nothing should be done by Jewish organizations to assist the Falasha. Another position was expressed by Rabbi Zepin, who felt that, at the most, "industrial education" of the type advocated at the time by Booker T. Washington for African-Americans would be the most that could be done for people of "primitive mental attainments."[222]

Despite such opposition, during the next several years Faitlovitch made a start on his aim to establish schools headed by well-trained Beta Israel in order to help improve their quality of life and reform their Judaism. Although Gette Jeremias accompanied him to Ethiopia during the 1908–9 trip, he went back overseas for more training after that and took with him his cousin Solomon Isaac. They both went to the Hilfsverein der Deutschen Juden school in Jerusalem, where Taamrat Emmanuel was still being educated. In 1913, Faitlovitch brought Gette back with him during his third trip to Ethiopia, and Gette became the first Beta Israel teacher to begin the modern education of his people at a school established in Asmara.[223]

World War I interrupted Faitlovitch's trips, but he returned in 1920, bringing with him Taamrat Emmanuel and Solomon Isaac and taking out four more youths, including Yona Bogale, a very important leader in future years. Taamrat was appointed the director of a school for the Beta Israel in Addis Ababa in 1920, though an actual institution does not seem to have existed until 1923. Temporary quarters were obtained for a few years, until land was acquired in 1928 to build school buildings and a dormitory that at its peak had about eighty students.[224]

In Addis Ababa, Taamrat and Faitlovitch made a conscious effort to promote the interaction of Beta Israel and foreign Jews, particularly from Yemen and Aden. For example, in 1924, Beta Israel and some foreign Jews met with Faitlovitch and formed a provisional committee of the Jews of Addis Ababa. A week later, these seven people signed a document registering the purchase of land for a Jewish cemetery, thus officially inaugurating the Jewish Community of Addis Ababa. The formation of such a community was part of Faitlovitch's overall effort to increase contact and interaction between Ethiopian and foreign Jews as one means of inducing change within Ethiopia.[225]

Thus, by the 1920s the efforts of Faitlovitch had begun to bear some fruit. The impact was still very limited, however. A few dozen people received some training at the schools in Asmara or Addis Ababa, or abroad. Little was done to have any impact in the countryside of northwestern Ethiopia or even within Gondar itself, hundreds of kilometers from either school. The beginnings of a Western-educated Beta Israel elite were created. Some of this elite continued to work among the Beta Israel in educational efforts, but many entered government service and became another splinter in the fragmenting Beta Israel community during the early twentieth century.

Summary: The Splintering of Beta Israel Society

A half-century of Ethiopian and foreign influences on Beta Israel society created a badly splintered group. The devastating diseases, wars, and famine during the late nineteenth century helped undermine the economic and cultural viability of rural Beta Israel society. Thousands died and others migrated away from their traditional settlements. In some instances, the exigencies of the struggle to survive resulted in increased cultural interaction and mixing. Starving people could not be choosy about how or from whom they acquired food.

Added to these natural pressures was the impact of the Protestant convert agents. Though the converts suffered from famine and warfare too, they did receive some external support to help mitigate the effects of the devastation. They managed to keep some of their convert communities together, or at least in existence, by moving to places such as Dabra Tabor and Abu Harra, away from the main location of the wars and famines. They also tried to attract the nominal Beta Israel converts to their brand of inner-committed Christianity.

Western Jewish influence was nonexistent until the work of Faitlovitch started in 1904–5. Thereafter, his attempts to "save" the Falasha resulted in the formation of a new group of Beta Israel oriented toward Western Judaism and eventually toward Israel. Though the full impact of this influence did not occur until after World War II, and especially after 1974, its roots lie in the early twentieth-century efforts of Faitlovitch and his early students.

Foreign influences, whether Protestant or Jewish, had a socioeconomic impact that went beyond their particular religious agendas. Western education resulted in the formation of a new elite that often began to express itself in a secular orientation, particularly in government service in a society starved for the skills they could offer. At least eight Beta Israel students of Faitlovitch rose to high government positions after World War II.[226] Of course, the secularization of Ethiopian education, in general, was a trend that started in the early twentieth century and affected the role and influence of the Orthodox Church schools as well as the traditional Beta Israel institutions.[227]

The Protestant mission school and the Jewish schools for the Falasha had some similar secular effects. An interesting comparison, for example, is found in the careers of the Protestant-educated Beta Israel, Gobbaw Desta (*kantiba* Gabru) (1855–1950), and the Jewish-educated Beta Israel, Taamrat Emmanuel (1887–1968). After receiving foreign education, both returned to teach among their people but then moved into careers in government service as diplomats and officials. Both advocated education for Ethiopia as a whole as the main means for the development of the country and, coincidentally, for the improvement of the Beta Israel people. Gabru seems to have moved away very early from any particular concern with the Beta Israel, while Taamrat maintained his concern but saw the problem in broad national development terms rather than focusing on the narrower religious questions concerning the Beta Israel.[228]

Meanwhile, in rural northwestern Ethiopia, the Beta Israel had to try to cope with the new pressures and situations. Although it is difficult to document substantial religious and cultural change between 1868 and 1920, it seems the stage was being set for the undermining of the viability of traditional institutions. Their religion was under attack by Protestants and Western Jews. Ironically, both agreed on some of their agenda, such as abolishing Beta Israel sacrifices.

A turning point for the survival of traditional Beta Israel educational and religious training was the disruption caused by the Mahdist invasions of 1888 and after. Many schools and prayer houses were destroyed, never to be rebuilt. Though Beta Israel monasticism survived beyond World War II, the number and influence of monks had been declining since the turn of the century. Since the monks were the traditional guardians of the religious cycle of feasts and fasts, the veneration of the Sabbath, the laws of purity, and the social segregation from Christian society on the basis of an ideology of moral superiority, when their influence began to decline, so did these crucial defining characteristics of traditional Beta Israel society and religion.

Traditional secular leaders, such as the head artisans—in particular masons and carpenters—also declined in influence in northwestern Ethiopia. Many migrated out of the region. Traditional building in the Gondar area did not revive, despite some efforts made by Taytu and later Zawditu to encourage it. After the Italian occupation and World War II, new methods and materials bypassed the building skills of the Beta Israel. In rural areas, farmers still needed the skills of Beta Israel blacksmiths, potters, and weavers, but these activities had never been as prestigious or as well-rewarded since the Gondar dynasty. Their usefulness in scattered rural villages only allowed them to survive but did not result in enough influence to be able to redevelop their society.

Ironically, the few benefits by way of schools and clinics brought to the rural Beta Israel by Western Jewish organizations after World War II often sparked new antagonism and sometimes violence on the part of their rural Christian neighbors. The revival of Protestant missionary efforts to the Beta Israel, including the first involvement of European missionaries in Beta Israel areas since their expulsion in 1868, which began in the 1920s under Haile Sellassie, renewed such pressures on the Beta Israel.

Conclusion

This study has aimed to shed light on the controversial and fascinating story of the Beta Israel–Falasha. It has emphasized the necessity of seeing their history within the broader context of Ethiopian history. Both the "persecuted Jews" perspective and the assimilationist view—which have dominated the literature over the years—provide only partial glimpses of the true dynamics of their historical evolution. Certainly, the group was conquered, their land confiscated; many people were killed or forced to convert; others moved away or were absorbed into the larger society. Later, they faced derogatory insults, threats, and persecutions for presumably having the evil eye, and they were kept in a subordinate social position. On the other hand, despite the severe forces working against them, the Beta Israel were also the agents of their own history. In that sense, they provide an exciting and inspiring example of perseverance and cultural creativity in the face of extreme hardship.

The Ethiopian Jews of today have a long and honorable history, though the details are still obscure in many important places, and hence will always be open to varying interpretations. Scholars, activists, and the interested public have argued vehemently about the question of Falasha origins and identity. Concerned with questions of religious and ethnic identity, Jewish and other scholars of differing perspectives have debated whether the Falasha were direct descendants of one of the original Lost Tribes of ancient Israel or primarily descendants of Agaw converts to Judaism. Concerned primarily with questions of race and Black identity, African-Americans have written about "Black Jews" everywhere, including the Falasha.[1] Concerned with nationalism and national unity, the dominant Ethiopian interpretation has seen the Falasha as Christian renegades and rebels against the centralizing government and society. These have all been partial interpretations of a much more complex reality.

As I have argued in Chapter 1, it seems to me that neither the Lost Tribe nor the Convert nor the Rebel perspective provides the total picture of Falasha identity. Based on the Judaic-Hebraic influences still evident in

Ethiopian Orthodox Christian culture and the Ge'ez language, there does appear to have been some sort of Jewish group or influence in ancient Aksum, though another interpretation suggests these influences could have been carried by a Jewish-Christian group. But even if there was a specific Jewish group in Aksum, the Falasha—a name which originated only in the fifteenth or sixteenth century—are not their direct, unaltered descendants.

Rather, the Falasha developed as an identifiable group through a complex and still obscure process. At some point before the fourteenth century, when the documents first speak of them, groups of *ayhud* had emerged and were then living in such provinces as Begamder, Samen, Wagara, and even Shawa. To the dominant Christian culture by that time, *ayhud* meant "Jews" or "Jewish group," but what "Jews" meant to fourteenth-century Ethiopian Christians is not entirely clear. At a minimum, however, it meant those who had specifically rejected the concept that Christ was the son of God. Owing to the influence of the Solomonic legend among the Christian ruling elites, these elites distinguished themselves, whom they called *esra'elawi* ("Israelites"), from those who had refused to accept Christ, whom they called *ayhud*. In other words, the *ayhud* were interpreted by the Christians to be not simply followers of an ancient belief but those who had specifically rejected or rebelled against the new belief system. But whether the *ayhud* were simply descendants of an ancient pre-Christian group or rebels against an original Jewish-Christian group or some combination of both, the development of the Falasha clearly involved a further evolutionary process.

The Falasha, as we see them emerging in the fifteenth and sixteenth centuries, were formed from a combination of influences, including the coalescence of some *ayhud* after their conquest by the Christian state, but who were also joined by renegade monks from Christianity who brought the main elements of Falasha literature and liturgy in Ge'ez, the calendar for the celebration of holy days, and the institution of monasticism. Despite these serious influences from Ethiopian Christianity, the Falasha since the fifteenth century defined their history, culture, social institutions, and new material bases of artisanship in ways to maintain their separation and integrity from Christian Orthodoxy, as they saw themselves as the true *beta esra'el* ("House of Israel"). They were a part of the Christian-dominated society but held themselves apart from it.

In other words, the Beta Israel–Falasha created their own identity from the *ayhud* and Old Testament Christian material at hand under the constraints of a powerful centralizing state reinforced by a persuasive imperial ideology. This identity and their partially autonomous material base allowed them to survive as a group despite conquest, land confiscation, forced conversion attempts, and derogatory epithets. The development of their history cannot be understood properly outside the broader Ethiopian context.

In this sense, my study is congruent with recent societal and historical scholarship on Ethiopia.[2] The peoples who make up what became Greater Ethiopia were not simply conquered, submerged, and assimilated into a common externally imposed framework. Rather, they each had their own histories before conquest or incorporation, and they maintained a degree of integrity and even influenced the central tradition after their incorporation. The histories of each people that make up the mosaic of what became Ethiopia must be understood on their own terms but also within the context and constraints of the broader framework.

In developing this relationship with the broader framework, I have found caste analysis to be a useful organizing tool. Caste analysis allows us to see both the internal dynamics of Beta Israel history and the construction of the broader framework within which they had to operate. Caste formation occurred in this case through a dialectical process that included both violent conquest and peaceful incorporation.

The reasons given for the original conquest of *ayhud* groups in the fourteenth and fifteenth centuries were mainly political-economic: the refusal to pay tribute or revolts against the central power, as can be seen in the oral and written traditions concerning the wars by Amda Seyon and Yeshaq. In later conflicts, such as those against Sarsa Dengel and Suseneyos in the sixteenth and seventeenth centuries, a political-economic element also was significant, but an overt religious basis for the conflicts was more obvious. By that time, the Falasha had elaborated a religious identity that they used to maintain their integrity and separation from the dominant society. Suseneyos in particular seemed to be not merely interested in putting down rebels but also in changing their religion. He forced the Falasha in "all the regions of his reign" to convert to Christianity and was said to have "erased the memory of Judaism from his empire."[3] Although other Ethiopian kings from time to time urged conversion to Christianity, in general, the kings were tolerant of diverse beliefs so long as the people paid tribute and were peaceful. Suseneyos was something of an aberration in this regard, no doubt owing to the advice and influence of his fellow Catholics who had always criticized Ethiopian Orthodoxy itself for being too "Jewish."

The strong self-image of the Beta Israel, of which their religion was an essential part, allowed them to survive through the next several centuries. Their sense of identity, the developing ideology of separation, and their partially independent material base as artisans were all aspects of the emerging caste relationship of the Beta Israel with the dominant society. This caste relationship prevented their assimilation and disappearance into Christian society to a greater extent than occurred with other groups in the northwest, such as the Qemant, Zalan, Agaw, Oromo, and various "slave" categories. Of these, the Zalan, who were a recognizable group of cattle-keepers in the early nineteenth century, have completely disappeared. Various Agaw and Oromo migrants to the region have been assimilated, as to a lesser extent have the "slave" groups. The Qemant by the late twentieth century were still distinguishable as a group, but were highly acculturated and rapidly disappearing as a separate people. The Muslim group in the region was most similar to the Beta Israel in terms of their relationship to the dominant society. Their distinctive religion, landlessness, and hence practice of trading and artisan activities provided them with a separate material basis and ideology of separation similar to the Beta Israel.

The case of the Beta Israel is also significant for an elaboration of the relationship of small groups with a dominant state. Ironically, except for the initial period in which the *ayhud*-Falasha were conquered, the group benefited more from a strong state than from a weak one. During the Gondar era, they flourished (at least in the greater Gondar region) from their close relationship to a strong central state. The state provided them work as skilled artisans and soldiers and payment with land-use rights and some titles. When the central state deteriorated in the next period of the *zamana masafent,* the Beta Israel caste lost the shield that had protected them from persecution by Abyssinian society.

During the political period beginning with Tewodros's attempts to recentralize the government and lasting up to the revolution of 1974, the role of the state was more ambiguous. Although some of the kings, such as Tewodros to some extent and Yohannes IV to a greater extent, were interested in converting all non-Christians, the Beta Israel were generally able to defend their beliefs successfully against Orthodox Christianity. Menilek essentially practiced toleration, though he allowed internal mission activities led by the Falasha converts to continue. Under Haile Sellassie, missionary activities were stepped up, including the reappearance of European missionaries among the Beta Israel for the first time since the 1860s. But the real concerns of both Menilek and Haile Sellassie were elsewhere. Although attempting to rebuild and centralize a strong state, as well as improve the society's technological capability, neither king was much concerned with the Beta Israel. Unlike the Gondar kings, who tried to build upon internal technological skills—and therefore greatly utilized the Beta Israel—the state since Menilek oriented itself more toward Western education and technology and hence essentially ignored the Beta Israel. Particularly under Haile Sellassie, the Beta Israel felt they were again being persecuted by local powers as well as the increased role of foreign missionaries, but they had no recourse and no protection from the central government.

During the Ethiopian Revolution that began in 1974, the Beta Israel position in Ethiopian society became increasingly precarious. After a first year or so of cautious optimism in which they were hopeful of benefiting from the land reform declaration of March 1975, their position became untenable. In historical perspective, this recent period seems analogous to the *zamana masafent* era, when the local population and local rulers took it upon themselves to vent their frustrations against the Falasha, who were caught in the various crossfires of competing power struggles. As in the earlier period, the Falasha suffered more when the central state was weak and insecure than when it was strong.

In such a revolutionary upheaval, the trend that had been developing since Jacques Faitlovitch's first visit to the country in 1904–5 began to bear fruit. From one perspective, the exodus to Israel of thousands of Falasha from Ethiopia in the 1980s and 1990s marks a final stage in the splintering of the group that has been occurring since the late nineteenth century. From another view, it is the fulfillment of a back-to-Jerusalem dream that was first expressed in the 1860s. In any case, the exodus marks another and perhaps decisive stage in the process of continual evolution and redefinition of *ayhud*–Falasha–Beta Israel–Ethiopian Jewish society and religion that has characterized the group since it first emerged in the historical record in the fourteenth century.

Abbreviations

AA	*American Anthropologist*
AB	*Analecta Bollandiana*
AE	*Annales d'Ethiopie*
AJS	*American Journal of Sociology*
AL	*Afroasiatic Linguistics*
APSR	*American Political Science Review*
ARIV	*Atti del Reale Istituto Veneto*
ASE	*Annuario di studi ebraici*
ASP	*Actes de la société philologique*
ASR	*African Studies Review*
BAIU	*Bulletin de l'Alliance Israélite Universelle*
BIFAN	*Bulletin de l'Institut Fondamental d'Afrique Noire*
BO	*Bibliotheca Orientalis*
BSG	*Bulletin de la société de géographie*
BSGI	*Bolletino della Reale Societa Geografica Italiana*
BSOAS	*Bulletin. School of Oriental and African Studies*
CAA	*Cahiers de l'Afrique et de l'Asie*
CEA	*Cahiers d'études africaines*
CSCO	*Corpus Scriptorum Christianorum Orientalium*
CSSH	*Comparative Studies in Society and History*
DA	*Das Ausland*
EGJ	*Ethiopian Geographical Journal*
EJE	*Ethiopian Journal of Education*
EMML	Ethiopian Manuscript Microfilm Library
EO	*Ethiopia Observer*
ES	*Economy and Society*
GLECS	*Groupes linguistiques d'études Chamito-Sémitique*
GSAI	*Giornale della Societa Asiatica Italiana*
HA	*History in Africa*
IESS	*International Encyclopedia of the Social Sciences*
IJAHS	*International Journal of African Historical Studies*
JA	*Journal asiatique*

JAAS	*Journal of Asian and African Studies*
JAH	*Journal of African History*
JC	*Jewish Chronicle*
JES	*Journal of Ethiopian Studies*
JHSN	*Journal of the Historical Society of Nigeria*
JI	*Jewish Intelligence*
JJS	*Journal of Jewish Studies*
JMAS	*Journal of Modern African Studies*
JMI	*Jewish Missionary Intelligence*
JQR	*Jewish Quarterly Review*
JR	*Jewish Records*
JRA	*Journal of Religion in Africa*
JRGS	*Journal of the Royal Geographical Society*
JSA	*Journal de la société des africanistes*
JSS	*Journal of Semitic Studies*
MRAL	*Memorie della Reale Accademia dei Lincei*
NA	*Nouvelles annales des voyages et des sciences géographiques*
NAMSL	*Nouvelles archives des missions scientifiques et littéraires*
NAS	*Northeast African Studies*
OC	*Oriens Christianus*
OCA	*Orientalia Cristiana Analecta*
OCP	*Orientalia Cristiana Periodica*
OLP	*Orientalia Lovaniensia Periodica*
OM	*Oriente Moderno*
PGM	*Petermanns Geographische Mitteilungen*
PP	*Past and Present*
PRGS	*Proceedings of the Royal Geographical Society*
RA	*Rural Africana*
RDM	*Revue des deux mondes*
REJ	*Revue des études juives*
Report	*Report of the Society for the Promotion of Christianity amongst the Jews*
RI	*Rivista Israelitica*
RO	*Rocznik Orientalistyczny*
RRAL	*Rendiconti della Reale Accademia Nazionale dei Lincei*
RS	*Revue sémitique*
RSE	*Rassegna di studi etiopici*
RSO	*Rivista degli studi orientali*
SJA	*Southwestern Journal of Anthropology*

SNR	*Sudan Notes and Records*
TBGS	*Transactions of the Bombay Geographical Society*
TJH	*Transafrican Journal of History*
TMIE	*Travaux et mémoires de l'Institut d'Ethnologie*
ZA	*Zeitschrift für Assyriologie*
ZAE	*Zeitschrift für Allgemeine Erdkunde*
ZDMG	*Zeitschrift der Deutschen Morgenlandischen Gesellschaft*
ZS	*Zeitschrift für Semitistik*

Notes

Preface

1. See Chapter 1 on terminology.

2. Though his oral traditions see Sunjata, the founder of the Mali Empire, primarily as a practitioner of (indigenous) supernatural powers, they also provide him with a suitable Islamic genealogy: D. T. Niane, ed., *Sundiata: An Epic of Old Mali* (London, 1965), p. 2. For a view of Sunjata's powers from within the society, see Patrick McNaughton, *The Mande Blacksmiths* (Bloomington, 1988), pp. 61–63. The manipulation of indigenous traditions by the influence of Islam is documented by David Conrad in "Islam in the Oral Traditions of Mali: Bilali and Surakata," *JAH* 26 (1985): 33–49. In East Africa, traditions linking Swahili city-states with Islamic founders has complicated unraveling the actual history of the states: Derek Nurse and Thomas Spear, *The Swahili* (Philadelphia, 1985). The case of Solomon and Sheba in Ethiopia is discussed below.

3. Zewde Gabre-Sellasie, *Yohannes IV of Ethiopia* (Oxford, 1975), p. 1. This statement is illustrative of a common view and not unique.

4. Donald Donham and Wendy James, eds., *The Southern Marches of Imperial Ethiopia* (Cambridge, 1986).

5. Cf. ibid., preface, p. xiv.

6. See Chapter 1 below and my earlier formulations: James Quirin, "The Beta Israel (Felasha) in Ethiopian History: Caste Formation and Culture Change, 1270–1868" (Ph.D. dissertation, University of Minnesota, 1977), pp. 26–31.

7. Kay Shelemay, *Music, Ritual, and Falasha History* (East Lansing, Mich., 1975); Steven Kaplan, forthcoming book and several articles.

Introduction

1. Though contemporary research is used for this section, an effort is made not to succumb to the fallacies of the "ethnographic present." See Jan Vansina, "Anthropologists and the Third Dimension," *Africa* 39 (1969): 62–67; and Chapter 4 below for details.

2. Frederick J. Simoons, *Northwest Ethiopia. Peoples and Economy* (Madison, Wisc., 1960); Simon Messing, "The Highland-Plateau Amhara of Ethiopia" (Ph.D. dissertation, University of Pennsylvania, 1957); Mesfin Wolde Mariam, *An Atlas of Ethiopia* (Addis Ababa, 1970), pp. 11–12; James McCann, *From Poverty to Famine in Northeast Ethiopia* (Philadelphia, 1987), p. 25.

3. On *tef* (*Eragrostis Tef*), the most prestigious grain of northern Ethiopia, see Simoons, *Northwest Ethiopia,* p. 103; A. Haudricourt, "L'histoire du tef," *Revue du botanique appliquée et d'agriculture tropicale* 21 (1941): 128–30; Solomon Deressa and Gedamu Abraha, "Non Sequitor, An Historical Experiment," *Addis Reporter* 1/27 (4 July 1969): 14–18, 1/28 (11 July 1969): 13–16.

4. Imperial Ethiopian Government, Central Statistical Office, *Report on a Survey of Gondar* (Addis Ababa, 1966), p. 3.

5. Joseph Halévy, "Essai sur la langue Agaou, le dialecte des Falachas (Juifs d'Abyssinie)," *ASP,* 3/4 (November 1873): 155.

6. Charles Beke, "Abyssinia—being a Continuation of Routes in that Country," *JRGS,* 14 (1844): 8; Taye Reta, "Gojam Governorate General," *EGJ* 1 (1963): 25–26; *JI,* 21 (June 1881): 166; Aragawy letter in *Report,* 74 (1882): 140; ibid., 76 (1884): 122–24; *JMI,* 15 (November 1899): 169–71.

7. The missionary J. L. Krapf, for example, visited the *tabiban* (plural of *tabib,* "artisan" or "metalsmith") at "their monastery, called Mantek," near Ankobar in Shawa in 1840. Outwardly, they seemed to be Christians, but he supposed they were Jews or Falasha. This group and others near Ankobar and elsewhere in Shawa were noticed by other travelers in the twentieth century as well, but their history is obscure. See: J. L. Krapf, and K. W. Isenberg, *Journals* (London, 1843), pp. 238–40 and also pp. 74, 88–89, 142, 151, 157–58; J. L. Krapf, "Extracts from a Journal," *JRGS* 10 (1841): 473, 478; William Cornwallis Harris, *The Highlands of Aethiopia,* 3 vols. (2nd ed., London, 1844), 2:363–64; Jacques Faitlovitch, *Quer durch Abessinien* (Berlin, 1910), pp. 136–39; Marcel Cohen, "Rapport sur une mission linguistique en Abyssinie 1910–1911," *NAMSL* n.s. 20/6 (1912): 35–38; Deborah Lifchitz, "Un sacrifice chez les Falacha, juifs abyssins," *La Terre et la Vie* 9 (1939): 116; Donald Levine, "On the History and Culture of Manz," *JSS,* 9 (1964): 204, note 3. See below on terminology of *tabib.* Other references have been made to obscure groups sometimes alleged to be Falasha in Lasta and even among the Oromo or Gurage. See Faitlovitch, *Quer durch,* p. 150; Diana Spencer, "Trip to Wag and Northern Wallo," *JES,* 5/1 (1967): 96; A. Z. Aescoly, "Notices sur les Falacha ou Juifs d'Abyssinie, d'après le 'Journal de Voyage' d'Antoine d'Abbadie," *CEA* 2 (1961): 91; Antoine d'Abbadie, "Extrait d'une lettre de M. Antoine d'Abbadie sur les Falacha ou Juifs d'Abyssinie," *BSG,* ser. 3, 4 (1845): 45.

8. Donald Levine, *Greater Ethiopia* (Chicago, 1974), appendix.

9. On the other hand, there are traditions of dispersal after conquest among the Beta Israel, and the actual history of such groups in Shawa, Lasta, and Gojjam, for example, is virtually unknown. Anthropological accounts note that the local Amhara see these people as non-Amhara strangers who came into the area at some unknown time in the past: Ronald Reminick, "The Structure and Functions of Religious Belief among the Amhara of Ethiopia," in Harold Marcus, ed., *Proceedings of the First United States Conference on Ethiopian Studies, 1973* (East Lansing, Mich., 1975): 33–34. Some distant connection with the conquered *ayhud* of northwestern Ethiopia cannot be entirely ruled out, pending further investigation.

10. Henry Stern estimated around 250,000: *Wanderings among the Falashas in Abyssinia* (London, 1862), p. 194; idem., in *JI* n.s. 1 (1861): 132; J. M. Flad estimated 200,000 in the 1860s, *The Falashas (Jews) of Abyssinia* (London, 1869), p. 14, or

150,000 in his reflections years later: *Sechzig Jahre in der Mission unter den Falaschas in Abessinien* (Giessen, 1922), p. 20. James Bruce suggested there were 100,000 in the 1770s, but he did not visit their villages: *Travels to Discover the Source of the Nile,* 5 vols. (Edinburgh, 1790), 1:486; Antoine d'Abbadie estimated 80,000 in the 1860s: *L'Abyssinie et le roi Théodore* (Paris, 1868), pp. 15–16. But later in the century, an accepted figure was about 200,000: *JI,* n.s. 8 (September 1892): 146–49.

11. A. Z. Aescoly, *Recueil de textes falachas, TMIE* 55 (1951): 1. But an unsympathetic observer said there were only 6,000 to 7,000!; see H. Nahoum, "Mission chez les Falachas d'Abyssinie," *BAIU,* ser. 3, 33 (1908): 135.

12. About 28,000 was the generally accepted figure among Jewish organizations assisting them in 1975.

13. Donald Crummey, "Abyssinian Feudalism," *PP* 89 (November 1980): 118–20.

14. The Abyssinian cultivator was clearly a "peasant" in the anthropological usage: Eric Wolf, *Peasants* (Englewood Cliff, N.J., 1961); Lloyd Fallers, "Are African Cultivators to be called Peasants?" *Current Anthropology* 2 (1961): 108–110; Frederick Gamst, *Peasants in Complex Society* (New York, 1974); idem., "Peasantries and Elites Without Urbanism: The Civilization of Ethiopia," *CSSH* 12 (1970): 373–92.

15. Allan Hoben, *Land Tenure among the Amhara of Ethiopia* (Chicago, 1973), p. 256; idem., "Family, Land, and Class in Northwest Europe and Northern Highland Ethiopia," in Harold Marcus, ed., *Proceedings of the First United States Conference on Ethiopian Studies, May 1973* (East Lansing, Mich., 1975), pp. 157–70; Crummey, "Abyssinian Feudalism."

16. Hoben, *Land Tenure,* pp. 14–15.

17. Ibid., p. 13.

18. Ibid., p. 6.

19. Ibid., pp. 48–49, 137–38; Mahteme Sellassie Wolde Maskal, "The Land System of Ethiopia," *EO,* 1/9 (October 1957): 287. See also Gedamu Abraha on the significance of land rights: "Wax and Gold," *EO,* 11/3 (September 1968): 233–36.

20. Donald Crummey, "Gondarine Rim Land Sales," in R. Hess, ed., *Proceedings of the Fifth International Conference on Ethiopian Studies, Chicago, 1978* (Chicago, 1979), p. 472. See also Ignazio Guidi, *Vocabolario Amarico-Italiano* (Rome, 1901), p. 121; Mahteme Sellassie, "Land System," p. 287.

21. Mahteme Sellassie, "Land System," p. 285; Hoben, *Land Tenure,* p. 188; Messing, "Highland-Plateau Amhara," pp. 248–52; Wolfgang Weissleder, "The Political Ecology of Amhara Domination" (Ph.D. dissertation, University of Chicago, 1965), pp. 109–10. On variations in land systems, see also Gebre-Wold-Ingida Worq, "Ethiopia's Traditional System of Land Tenure and Taxation," *EO* 5 (1962): 302–39; Berhanou Abbebe, *Évolution de la propriété foncière au Choa (Ethiopie) du regne de Menelik à la constitution de 1931* (Paris, 1971); J. Mantel-Niecko, *The Role of Land Tenure in the System of Ethiopian Imperial Government in Modern Times* (Warsaw, 1980).

22. On the other hand, there is the possibility that some of the Gondar era land rights were in the form of long-term tenancy rights on *rim* land held by various churches. See Donald Crummey, "Some Precursors of Addis Ababa: Towns in Christian Ethiopia in the Eighteenth and Nineteenth Centuries," in Ahmed Zekaria

et al., eds., *Proceedings of the International Symposium on the Centenary of Addis Ababa, November 1986* (Addis Ababa, 1987), p. 24; V. L. Grottanelli, *Ricerche geografiche et economiche sulle popolazione,* vol. 2 of *Missione di Studio al Lago Tana* (Rome: Accademia d'Italia, 1939), pp. 112, 238. Further investigation into the land records of Gondar churches such as that currently being carried out by Donald Crummey may shed more light on this situation.

23. Extensive documentation of the following is in Chapter 4.

24. See Chapter 4 and the excellent recent survey by Kay Shelemay, *Music, Ritual.*

Chapter 1

1. Levine, *Greater Ethiopia* discusses various paradigms but creates his own as well.

2. A lack of explicit evidence for any of these views had led to rife speculation. See the sensible comments by Steven Kaplan, "The Origins of the Beta Israel: Five Methodological Cautions," *Pe'amim* 32 (1987). Though I had written my views on this question before reading Kaplan's account, I thank him for making an English version available to me. For summaries of previous views, see Aescoly, *Recueil de textes Falachas,* 1–4; Leslau, *Falasha Anthology* (New Haven, Conn., 1951), p. xliii; Robert Hess, "Towards a History of the Falasha," in D. F. McCall et al., eds., *Eastern African History. Boston University Papers on Africa,* vol. 3 (New York, 1969), pp. 110–11; Steven Kaplan, "A Brief History of the Beta Israel," in *The Jews of Ethiopia. A People in Transition* (New York: The Jewish Museum, 1986), p. 11.

3. In one account it was even asserted that "10,000 Jews" mixed with "4,000 Syrians" were established in Ethiopia already by 330 B.C.E.; Louis Marcus, "Notice sur l'époque de l'établissement des Juifs dans l'Abyssinie," *JA,* 3 (1829), 414.

4. Faitlovitch, "The Falashas," *The American Jewish Year Book 5681* 22 (1920–21): 80; Henry Stern, *Wanderings among the Falashas of Abyssinia* (London, 1868), p. 197.

5. Personal observations during fieldwork. Most recent observers have generally agreed; see Wolf Leslau, *Falasha Anthology* (New Haven, Conn., 1951), p. xii; Michele Dacher, "Les Falasha, Juifs noirs d'Ethiopie," *Nouveau cahiers* 18 (1969): 44.

6. Tel Hashomer Government Hospital, "A Survey of some Genetical Characters in Ethiopian Tribes," *American Journal of Physical Anthropology,* n.s. 20 (1962), 208A.

7. Even Faitlovitch had to admit there had been some such mixture: "The Black Jews of Abyssinia," *American Hebrew and Jewish Messenger* 97/16 (August 20, 1915): 382.

8. Louis Rapoport, *The Lost Jews* (New York, 1980, 1983), pp. 200–12; David Kessler, *The Falashas* (New York, 1982), pp. 147–71; Kay Shelemay, *Music, Ritual,* p. 37, note 73; Tudor Parfitt, *Operation Moses* (London, 1985); Leon Wieseltier, "Brothers and Keepers," *The New Republic* (11 February 1985), pp. 21–23; David Kessler and Tudor Parfitt, *The Falashas* (London: Minority Rights Group, 1985).

9. Witold Witakowski, "The Origins of the Jewish Colony at Elephantine,"

Orientalia Suecana [Uppsala], 27–28 (1978–79), 34, 40; J. Halévy, "Inscription araméenne d'Éléphantine," *RS* 16 (1908), 95–99, 224–40; A. E. Cowley, *Aramaic Papyri of the Fifth Century* B.C. (Oxford, 1923); Albert Vincent, *La religion des judéo-araméens d'Éléphantine* (Paris, 1937); Bezalel Porten, *Archives from Elephantine* (Berkeley and Los Angeles, 1968).

10. A specific version of the view supporting diffusion through Egypt argued for the spread to Ethiopia between 643 and 330 B.C.E.; see Marcus, "Notice sur l'époque de l'établissement des Juifs," p. 414. Another account argued they were descended from "Hellenistic Jews" who came from Egypt through Meroe in the third century B.C.E.; see P. Luzzatto, *Mémoire sur les Juifs d'Abyssinie, ou Falashas* (Paris, 1852–53), p. 12. The missionary Flad argued for the diffusion from Israel through Egypt and up the Nile after the Assyrian conquest or the Babylonian conquest (eighth to sixth centuries B.C.E.): *The Falashas,* pp. 2–3. He felt the existence of Beta Israel landownership (*rest*) in Qwara province, the Ethiopian region closest to the Sudan, supported their early and first settlement in that region (ibid., p. 6). Faitlovitch, similarly, argued that after the destruction of the First Temple, Jews migrated to Egypt and then to Sudan and entered Ethiopia through Qwara, where they learned Qwarenya, still spoken by some in the early twentieth century: "The Falashas," pp. 95–98. Some traditions exist of the Beta Israel drawing inspiration from early Jewish battles against Vespasian and Titus up to the destruction of the Second Temple in 70 C.E.; see Conti Rossini, ed., *Historia Regis Sarṣa Dengel, CSCO* 3 (1907): 101, 171, 182 (trans.); Halévy, ed., "La guerre de Sarsa-Dengel contres les Falashas," *RS* 15 (1907): 151. A written tradition of their origins refers to the same time period; see Conti Rossini, "Note di agiografia etiopica ('Abiya-Egzi, Arkaledes e Gabra Iyesus')," *RSO* 17 (1938): 446–49, but Conti Rossini is probably more correct in his supposition that this tradition derives from the "History of the Jews" by Joseph ben Gorion (Josephus) [*Zena Ayhud la-Yosef Walda Koreyon* in Ge'ez] than that it reflects an internal Beta Israel tradition. For this book in Ge'ez, see EMML 21. In English, see Josephus, *The Jewish War,* trans. G. A. Williamson (Harmondsworth, England, Penguin, 1978). For migration after the fall of Elephantine, see Ignazio Guidi, *Storia della Letteratura Etiopica* (Rome, 1932), pp. 95–97, note 2; Jean Doresse, *L'empire du Prêtre-Jean,* 2 vols. (Paris, 1957), 2:198.

11. On Elephantine practices, see B. Porten, *Archives,* pp. 248–52; Kessler, *Falashas,* pp. 42–44. On Ullendorff's contrary view, see *Ethiopia and the Bible* (London, 1968), pp. 16–17. The major problem with Kessler's lengthy reconstruction of the view of migration from Elephantine is the lack of any direct documentation of movement to Ethiopia: Kessler, *Falashas,* pp. 24–57. See reviews by Getatchew Haile, in *JRA* 17 (1987): 187–88, and Quirin, in *IJAHS* 16 (1983): 743–46.

12. Joseph Halévy, *Mélanges d'épigraphie et d'archéologie sémitique* (Paris, 1874), pp. 129–31; idem., "Excursion chez les Falacha en Abyssinie," *BSG,* ser. 5, 17 (1869): 285.

13. Conti Rossini, "Piccole note falascia," *ASE* (1935–37): 107–8; "I Falascia," *La Rassegna mensile di Israel,* ser. 2, 10 (1936): 372; idem., "Appunti di storia e letteratura Falascia," *RSO* 8 (1919–20), 605; "Nuovi Appunti sui Guidei d'Abissinia," *RRAL* 29 (1922): 225–27.

14. Carl Rathjens, *Die Juden in Abessinien* (Hamburg, 1921), pp. 92–94;

Leslau, *Anthology,* p. xliii; idem., *Coutumes et croyances des Falachas, TMIE* 61 (1957): 1; Ullendorff, *Bible,* pp. 17–23. On the contacts see L. Duchesne, "Note sur la massacre des chrétiens himyarites au temps de l'Empereur Justin," *REJ* 20 (1890): 220–24; Conti Rossini, "Expéditions et possessions des Habasat en Arabie," *JA* 18 (1921): 5–6, 30–32; Maxime Rodinson, "Sur une nouvelle inscription du règne de Dhou Nowas," *BO* 26 (1969): 26–34.

15. The Jewish ancestors of Ras Amdu migrated from Yemen but at some point converted to Ethiopian Christianity: "The Abbots of Dabra-Hayq, 1248–1535," *JES* 8/1 (1970): 112–14; Getatchew Haile, "The *Kalilah wa-Dimnah* and the *Mazmura Krestos,*" in Robert Hess, ed., *Proceedings of the Fifth International Conference on Ethiopian Studies, Session B, Chicago 1978* (Chicago, 1979), p. 376; idem., *A Catalogue of Ethiopian Manuscripts* (Collegeville, Minn., 1981), 5:241–42 (on EMML 1768), 452 (on EMML 1943). See also Shelemay, *Music, Ritual,* p. 30, note 13.

16. Rodinson argued that Judaism was not well-established in South Arabia until 375 C.E., thereby leaving insufficient time for any direct *Judaic* influences on Ethiopian Christianity: "Review of Edward Ullendorff, *The Ethiopians* (London, 1960)," in *Bibliotheca Orientalis* 21 (1964): 239. But most scholars have agreed Jews were there by the second century C.E.; see Conti Rossini, "Nuovi appunti sui Guidei," pp. 226–27; Solomon D. Goitein, *Jews and Arabs. Their Contacts through the Ages* (New York, 1955), p. 47; H. S. Lewis, *After the Eagles Landed: The Yemenites of Israel* (Boulder, 1989), p. 17.

17. Ullendorff, *Bible,* pp. 115–18.

18. Veronika Krempel, "Die soziale und wirtschaftliche Stellung der Falascha in der christlich-amharischen Gesellschaft von Nordwest Athiopien," (Ph.D. dissertation, Free University of Berlin, 1972), pp. 266–67 and *passim.*

19. Ibid., p. 9; idem., "Eine Berufskaste in Nordwest-Athiopien—die Kayla (Falascha)," *Sociologus,* n.s. 24 (1974): 39–40. Though she and I have both employed the tool of analysis of "occupational caste," we arrived at that position independently, but through an apparent common concern with the context of Ethiopian social history. See Quirin, "The Beta Israel (Felasha) in Ethiopian History: Caste Formation and Cultural Change, 1270–1868" (Ph.D. dissertation, University of Minnesota, 1977); idem., "The Process of Caste Formation in Ethiopia: A Study of the Beta Israel (Felasha), 1270–1868," *IJAHS* 12 (1979): 235–58.

20. See Chapter 2 and Maurice Gaguine, "The Falasha Version of the Testaments of Abraham, Isaac, and Jacob" (Ph.D. dissertation, University of Manchester, 1965); Leslau, *Anthology;* Joseph Halévy, *Te'ezaza Sanbat (Commandements du Sabbat)* (Paris, 1902); Steven Kaplan, "Te'ezaza Sanbat: A Beta Israel Work Reconsidered," *Studies in the History of Religions,* vol. 1 (Leiden, 1987), 107–24 (reprinted in *Truman Institute Reprints*).

21. Shelemay, *Music, Ritual;* idem., "Jewish Liturgical Forms in the Falasha Liturgy? A Comparative Study," *Yuval* 5 (1986): 372–404.

22. Halévy, "Excursion chez les Falacha," p. 287.

23. Asmarom Legesse, *Gada* (New York, 1973). The use of "Beta Israel" for the group within Ethiopia and "Ethiopian Jews" for those in Israel has since become widely accepted; see Michael Ashkenazi and Alex Weingrod, eds., *Ethiopian*

Jews and Israel (New Brunswick, N.J., 1987); *The Jews of Ethiopia: A People in Transition* (New York, 1986).

24. James Bruce, *Travels to Discover the Source of the Nile,* 5 vols. (Edinburgh, 1790), 1:485.

25. Examples in the chronicle and hagiographic literature are numerous and unanimous; see C. Foti, "La cronaca abbreviata dei Re d'Abissinia in un manoscritto di Dabra Berhan di Gondar," *RSE* 1 (1941): 97; J. Perruchon, ed., "Le règne de Lebna Dengel," *RS* 1 (1893): 279 (text), 285 (trans.) (on Lebna Dengel); Getatchew Haile, "Inside the Royal Confinement," *NAS* 4/1 (1982): 19 (on Zar'a Ya'eqob); Taddesse Tamrat, "Problems of Royal Succession in Fifteenth Century Ethiopia: A Presentation of Documents," *IV Congresso Internazionale di Studi Etiopici* (Rome, 1974), p. 507.

26. As explained to Samuel Gobat, *Journal of Three Years' Residence in Abyssinia* (New York, 1850 [orig. ed., 1834]), p. 241. See below for further analysis of "Jew" (*ayhud*).

27. Leslau, *Coutumes et croyances,* pp. 1–2; idem., *Anthology,* p. ix; Conti Rossini, "Nuovi appunti sui Giudei d'Abissinia," p. 227; Edward Ullendorff, "Review of Wolf Leslau, *Falasha Anthology* (New Haven, 1951)," in *BSOAS* 15 (1953): 174.

28. Joseph Tubiana "Note sur la distribution géographique des dialectes Agaw," *Mer rouge, Afrique orientale, CAA* 5 (1959): 303–4; Robert Hetzron, "The Agaw Languages," *AL* 3/3 (June 1976): 4. "Hwara which is Qwara" appears in the short chronicle as well; see J. Perruchon, "Règne de Sarṣa-Dengel ou Malak-Sagad I (1563–1597)," *RS* 4 (1896): 181 (text), 275 (trans.).

29. Hetzron, "Agaw Languages," p. 4. This transference has been questioned, however, by another linguist; personal communications with Getatchew Haile, 26 April 1980, and 26 July 1989. Another approach was developed by Aescoly, who objected to the simple assumption of the equivalency of "Falasha" ("go over there," "cross over") and "Falasyan" ("foreigner") in the traditional Ge'ez etymology; see A. Z. Aescoly, "Falascha-Ibrim," *American Journal of Semitic Languages and Literature* 51 (1934–35): 127–30. Getatchew also sees the derivation of Falasha from *falasi* ("immigrant" or "exile") as an example of folk etymology; see "Review of David Kessler, *The Falashas,*" in *JRA* 17 (1987): 187–88. See also Krempel, "Die soziale und wirtschaftliche Stellung," pp. 187–91. Some wilder etymologies in the past attempted to connect the Falasha with the Shona of Zimbabwe or the Fulani of Nigeria; se Harald von Sicard, "The Derivation of the Name Mashona," *African Studies* 9 (1950): 138–43; M. D. W. Jeffreys, "L'origine du nom fulain," *Bulletin de la société d'études camerounaises* 5 (1944): 523, cited in Wolf Leslau, "A Supplementary Falasha Bibliography," *Studies in Bibliography and Booklore* 3 (1957): 22, #221a.

30. The term was used in the early sixteenth century in Ethiopic, Arabic, and Hebrew: *Gadla Gabra Masih,* Steven Kaplan, "The Falasha and the Stephanite: An Episode from the *Gadla Gabra Masih,*" *BSOAS* 28 (1985): 278–84; Chihab Ed-Din Ahmed ben 'Abd el-Qader (Arab Faqih), *Histoire de la conquête de l'Abyssinie (XVI siècle),* ed. René Basset (Paris, 1897–1901), pp. 456–59; Abraham Levi, a sixteenth-century kabbalist, cited in A. Neubauer, "Where are the Ten Tribes," *JQR* 1 (1889): 196–97.

31. "Tarika Nagast," EMML 7334, Ff. 28a–28b; "Tarika Negest," Paper

manuscript, Dabra Sege, cited in Taddesse, *Church and State,* p. 201. These two manuscripts are probably the same source.

32. Interview with Berhan Beruk on 20 August 1975. In this interview, the informant stated both that the name Falasha began at the time of Yeshaq's war with Gedewon (see Chapter 2) in the early fifteenth century, and that it began when the "Israelites" left [ancient] Israel.

33. Antoine d'Abbadie, "Réponses des Falasha dits juifs d'Abyssinie aux questions faites par M. Luzzatto, orientaliste de Padoue," *AI* 12 (1851): 240; See also Rathjens, *Die Juden,* p. 62. A later linguistic analysis of the term "Kayla" argued that it was not the negative of *kaya* "to cross" in Agaw languages but rather that it was simply the way of forming the plural in several related Agaw languages; Conti Rossini, "Piccole note," p. 110.

34. F. M. Esteves Pereira, *Chronica de Susneyos, Rei de Ethiopia,* 2 vols. (Lisbon, 1892–1900), 1:307 (text). See Chapter 2 below.

35. Ignazio Guidi, ed., *Annales Iohannis I, Iyasu I, Bakaffa. CSCO,* ser. alt., Script. Aeth. 5 (1903): 8. See also Chapter 3 below.

36. Halévy, "Excursion chez les Falacha," p. 287.

37. On *tabib,* see Krapf, *Journals,* p. 240; C. T. Lefebvre, *Voyage en Abyssinie,* 6 vols. (Paris, 1845–51), 3:245; A. Z. Aescoly, "Notices sur les Falacha ou Juifs d'Abyssinie, d'après le 'Journal de voyage' d'Antoine d'Abbadie," *CEA* 2 (1961): 90, 99. See Chapter 4 below for analysis of *buda.*

38. Halévy, "Excursion chez les Falacha," p. 287.

39. See Chapter 2 below and also Quirin, "The *'Ayhud* and Bēta 'Esrā'ēl-Falāshā in Fifteenth-Century Ethiopia: Oral and Written Traditions," *NAS* 10 (1988): 89–104, for further analysis of connections between the *ayhud* and those who later became known as Falasha, Kayla, or Beta Israel.

40. Esteves Pereira, ed., *Susneyos,* 1 (text): 150–51, 154–56, 177, 189, 271, 278–80, 282–84, 307, especially pp. 155, 282. For Yohannes I, see Guidi, ed., *Annales Iohannis I,* p. 8.

41. Edward Ullendorff, "Hebraic-Judaic Elements in Abyssinian (Monophysite) Christianity," *JSS* 1 (1956): 229–31; A. Z. Aescoly, "Les noms magiques dans les apocryphes chrétiens des Ethiopiens," *JA* 220 (1932): 87–137; Frank Hallock, "Review of A. Z. Aescoly, 'Les noms magiques dans les apocryphes chrétiens,'" in *Aethiopica* 1 (1933): 52; Deborah Lifchitz, *Textes éthiopiens magico-religieux. TMIE* 38 (1940); Jacques Mercier, *Ethiopian Magic Scrolls* (New York, 1979); Stefan Strelcyn, "Les écrits médicaux éthiopiens," *JES* 3/1 (1965): 82–103; idem., "Prières magiques éthiopiennes pour délier les charmes," *RO* 18 (1955): I–LXXVI, 1–498; Quirin, "New Archival Sources."

42. Ullendorff, "Hebraic-Judaic Elements," pp. 235–53. See also Rodinson, "Influences juives"; Ernst Hammerschmidt, "Jewish Elements in the Cult of the Ethiopian Church," *JES* 3/2 (1965): 1–12; Ullendorff, *Bible;* Samuel Mercer, *The Ethiopic Liturgy* (New York, 1970 [orig. 1915]); Harry Hyatt, *The Church of Abyssinia* (London, 1928); Ephraim Isaac, *The Ethiopian Church* (Boston, 1967); Aymro Wondmagegnehu and Joachim Motovu, eds., *The Ethiopian Orthodox Church* (Addis Ababa, 1970), pp. 123–24.

43. Bishop Sawirus, *History of the Patriarchs of Alexandria,* vol. 2, pt. 3, p. 330,

cited in Taddesse, *Church and State,* p. 209 and n. 1–2. The practice of sacrifices by the Ethiopian Church was also mentioned in the thirteenth century: Abu Salih, *The Churches and Monasteries of Egypt and Some Neighbouring Countries,* ed. by B. T. A. Evetts (Oxford, 1895), p. 291.

44. Ullendorff, *Bible,* pp. 36–62.

45. Michael A. Knibb, ed., *The Ethiopic Book of Enoch,* 2 vols. (Oxford, 1978), 2:37–46. This was a suggestion already made by Ullendorff and now demonstrated more thoroughly by Knibb, especially through the use of the Dead Sea Fragments of the Book of Enoch in Aramaic. See Ullendorff, "An Aramaic 'Vorlage' of the Ethiopic Text of Enoch?" in Ullendorff, *Is Biblical Hebrew a Language?* (Wiesbaden, 1977), pp. 172–81. See also J. Hallevi [Halévy], "Recherches dur la langue de la rédaction primitive du Livre d'Enoch," *JA,* ser. 6, 9 (1867): 352–95.

46. Rodinson, "Review of Edward Ullendorff, *The Ethiopians* (London, 1960)," in *BO* 21 (1964): 238–45.

47. Ephraim Isaac, "An Obscure Component in Ethiopian Church History," *Le Muséon* 85 (1972): 237–45. Though Ephraim is critical of Rodinson's "non-contact" theory that "Jewish" elements could be explained simply by the Old Testament emphasis of Ethiopian Christianity, the two ideas are not in conflict. Rodinson even hinted at the possible role of "Judeo-Christianity" in transmitting these influences to Ethiopia—"Influences juives," p. 19—a suggestion Ephraim does not acknowledge. On ancient Jewish-Christianity in general, see Jean Danielou, *The Theology of Jewish-Christianity* (Chicago, 1964).

48. H. J. Polotsky, "Aramaic, Syriac, and Ge'ez," *JSS* 9 (1964): 10. See also Wolf Leslau, *Hebrew Cognates in Amharic* (Wiesbaden, 1969); Ullendorff, *Bible,* pp. 36–62.

49. Getatchew Haile, "The Forty-Nine Hour Sabbath of the Ethiopian Church," *JSS* 33 (1988): 243.

50. Ullendorff, *Bible,* p. 38; Getatchew, "Forty-Nine Hour Sabbath," p. 245. The best short introduction to the Ethiopian Church is by Getatchew Haile, "Ethiopian Church," in M. Eliade, ed., *Encyclopedia of Religion* (New York, 1987), 5:173–77.

51. W. H. Schoff, ed., *The Periplus of the Erythraean Sea* (London, 1912), p. 23; J. McCrindle, ed., *The Christian Topography of Cosmas* (London, 1897), pp. 57–68, 120; Getatchew, "Forty-Nine Hour Sabbath," pp. 245–46.

52. Murad Kamil, "An Ethiopic Inscription Found at Mareb," *JSS* 9 (1964): 56–57.

53. Getatchew, "The Forty-Nine Hour Sabbath," p. 245.

54. Ibid., p. 246.

55. Donald Levine, "Menilek and Oedipus: Further Observations on the Ethiopian National Epic," in Harold Marcus, ed., *Proceedings of the First United States Conference on Ethiopian Studies, 1973* (East Lansing, Mich., 1975), p. 12.

56. Carl Bezold, *Kebra Nagast* (Munich, 1909); E. A. Wallis Budge, ed., *The Queen of Sheba and Her Only Son Menyelek . . . A Complete Translation of the* Kebra Nagast (London, 1922); D. A. Hubbard, "The Literary Sources of the *Kebra Nagast*" (Ph.D. thesis, St. Andrews University, 1956); Edward Ullendorff, *Bible;* Irfan Shahid, "The *Kebra Nagast* in the Light of Recent Research," *Le Muséon* 89

(1976): 133–78; Meredith Spencer, "Structural Analysis and the Queen of Sheba," in R. L. Hess, ed., *Proceedings of the Fifth International Conference on Ethiopian Studies, Chicago, 1978* (Chicago, 1979), pp. 343–58; L. Ricci, "Edipo e Storia," *Paideuma* 24 (1978): 169–77.

57. Conti Rossini used the words "enigmatic" and "obscure" in "I Falascia," p. 373. See also idem., "Leggende geografiche giudaich del IX secolo (*Il Sefer Eldad*)," *BSGI,* ser. 6, 2 (1925): 160–90.

58. A. Neubauer, "Where are the Ten Tribes," *JQR* 1 (1889): 100. The names of the seven kingdoms are not identifiable, though some are closer to names in Nubia, also known as Cush, than they are to names in Ethiopia; ibid., 100; "Eldad the Danite" in Elkan Adler, ed., *Jewish Travellers* (London, 1930), p. 11. Al-Masudi's tenth century list of "Ethiopian Provinces" are probably also references to Nubia and two of them are close to Eldad's names: Al-Masudi, *Prairies d'or,* 9 vols. (Paris, 1861–77), 3:37–38; A. J. Arkell, *A History of the Sudan* (London, 1961), pp. 66, 154, 189; Sergew, *Ancient and Medieval,* p. 222.

59. Max Schloessinger, *The Ritual of Eldad ha-Dani Reconstructed and Edited from Manuscripts and a Genizah Fragment* (Leipzig, 1908); E. David Goiten, "Note on Eldad the Danite," *JQR,* n.s., 17 (1926–27): 483. I thank Tamara Kaigalithe of the University of Minnesota for translating the Hebrew passages. One scholar felt the account was "fanciful throughout"; see Neubauer, "Where are the Ten Tribes?" p. 109.

60. J. Perruchon, "Vie de Cosmas, patriarche d'Alexandrie de 923 à 934," *RS* 2 (1894): 78–93; Sergew, *Ancient and Medieval,* pp. 205–25.

61. Sawirus, *History of the Patriarchs of the Egyptian Church* vol. 2, pt. 2, pp. 171–72, cited in Sergew, *Ancient and Medieval,* p. 223.

62. Jewish: Ignazio Guidi, "Due notizie storiche sull'Abissinia," *GSA* 3 (1889): 176–78; Agaw: J. Halévy, "Appendice," *REJ* 21 (1890): 77–79; idem., book review in *RS* 4 (1896): 94; southern Cushitic: Conti Rossini, *Storia d'Etiopia* (Bergamo, 1928), p. 286. See also W. A. Wallis Budge, *The Book of the Saints of the Ethiopian Church* (London, 1928), 1:233–34; J. Perruchon, "Lettre addressée par le roi d'Éthiopie au roi Georges de Nubia sous le patriarcat de Philothée (981–1002 ou 1003)," *RS* 1 (1893): 71–76, 359–72.

63. Chronicle from *qes gabaz* Takla Haymanot of Aksum, text and translation by Sergew, *Ancient and Medieval,* pp. 226–28; Conti Rossini, "Les listes des rois d'Aksoum," *JA,* ser. 10, 14 (1909): 266–69.

64. Ludolphus uses the name "Essat" and refers to her as a "wicked woman" but does not call her Jewish: *New History* (London, 1682), p. 168; Budge, *History of Ethiopia,* 279; A. Dillmann, "Zur Geschichte des abyssinischen Reichs," *ZDMG* 7 (1853): 350; Basset, ed., "Études sur l'histoire," pp. 428–30, note 60. Local traditions throughout northern Ethiopia echo this interpretation and make her responsible for churches that were still blackened by her fires, for example: Paul Henze, *Ethiopian Journey, Travels in Ethiopia, 1969–1972* (London, 1977), pp. 74–75.

65. Abu al-Qasim Muhammad Ibn Hauqal, *Configuration de la terre (Kitab surat al-Ard),* trans. J. H. Kramers and G. Wiet, 2 vols. (Paris, 1964), 1:16, 56. Sergew leans toward this interpretation in *Ancient and Medieval,* pp. 230–32; idem., "The Problem of Gudit," *JES* 10/1 (January 1972): 113–24. See also Taddesse, *Church and State,* pp. 38–39; Conti Rossini, *Storia d'Etiopia,* p. 286.

66. I have used the translation made from the Hebrew by Robert L. Hess, "The Itinerary of Benjamin of Tudela," *JAH* 6 (1965): 16. See also another version by Marcus N. Adler, "The Itinerary of Benjamin of Tudela," *JQR* 18 (1906): 677; and the same text in Elkan Adler, *Jewish Travellers,* p. 60.

67. Hess, "The Itinerary of Benjamin of Tudela," pp. 15–24. Also on the Beja see Andrew Paul, *A History of the Beja Tribes of the Sudan* (Cambridge, 1954). One interpretation saw this account as referring to the Falasha, but the evidence is very ambiguous; see Conti Rossini, "Piccoli studi etiopici," *ZA* 27 (1912): 358–65.

68. Marco Polo, *The Travels,* trans. Ronald Latham (Harmondsworth, England, 1958), pp. 303–4.

69. On the conquest of Samen by the Aksumites as well as their use of the area as a place of exile, see E. A. Wallis Budge, *A History of Ethiopia,* pp. 237–41; Sergew, *Ancient and Medieval,* pp. 62–63; McCrindle, ed., *Christian Topography,* pp. 61–62, 67. Archaeological research shows Semitic influence had reached Lake Tana by ca. 1100: Joanne Carol Dombrowski, "Excavations in Ethiopia: Lalibela and Natehabiet Caves, Begemder Province" (Ph.D. dissertation, Boston University, 1972), p. 160. Local traditions assert the early inhabitants of Samen were Agaw who were driven out by the Aksumites: Nur Hussein A. Kadir, "Land Use Study of Ten Farmers at Adi Arkay" (B.A. Thesis, Department of Geography, Haile Sellassie I University, 1972), pp. 12–13. Aksumite influence up to Lake Tana is recorded in diverse sources: Taddesse, *Church and State,* p. 190 and notes 4 and 5; Sergew, *Ancient and Medieval,* p. 166; Conti Rossini, "Il convento di Tsana in Abissinia e le sue Laudi alla Vergine," *RRAL,* ser. 5, 29 (1910): 582–83; Kobishchanov, *Axum,* pp. 65, 120. William Winstanley, *A Visit to Abyssinia,* 2 vols. (London, 1881), 2:115, was told by the Governor of Dambeya that the island of Dek was where many "illustrious Jewish prisoners" were kept after the "final defeat of mosaic pretensions to the throne." Tana Cherqos island was said by local priests to contain several "Jewish relics"; see Paul Henze, "Patterns of Cultural Survival on the Islands in Ethiopia's Highland Lakes," *EO* 16 (1973): 95. On the Qemant, another Agaw people in the area, see Frederick Gamst, *The Qemant* (New York, 1969); and James Quirin, "The Beta Israel in Ethiopian History," pp. 269–302.

70. Interviews with Gete Asrass on 3 June 1975, with Berhan Beruk on 3 July 1975, with Menase Zammaru and Wande Iyyasu on 13 October 1975, and with Yeheyyeis Madhane and Yalaw Siyamer on 27 October 1975.

71. *Travels* 1:484–85.

72. Antoine d'Abbadie, "Réponses des Falasha," p. 183; idem., "Extrait d'une lettre de M. Antoine d'Abbadie sur les Falacha ou Juifs d'Abyssinie," *BSG,* ser. 3, 4 (1845): 51, 69, 71–72, 73. See also Neubauer, "Where are the Ten Tribes?" pp. 24–25.

73. Samuel Gobat, *Journal,* pp. 278, 331.

74. C. Mondon-Vidailhet, ed., "Une tradition éthiopienne," *RS* 12 (1904): 259–68. This manuscript is said to date from before the invasion of Ahmad "Gragn" and was saved because it had been hidden on the island of Dabra Sina in Lake Zway, from which it was taken during the conquest by Menilek II in 1890. I collected similar information from a manuscript in the possession of Jammara Wande in Gondar in 1975 called the "History of the Kings" (*Tarik Zanagast*). See also A. Caquot, "Titre et fonctions des grands officiers venue de Jerusalem avec Menilik," *AE* 2

(1957): 191; Shelemay, *Music, Ritual,* pp. 224–25, note 9. Getatchew Haile notes a similar terminology about the division of the land is used in other manuscripts: personal communication, August 1990.

75. In terms of territory, the only exception was Qwara, granted to Het instead of Gedewon. See below for other Beta Israel Gedewons. Aescoly also suggested "Gideon" may have been a title: "Notice sur les Falacha," p. 94.

76. Joseph Varenbergh, ed., "Studien zur abessinischen Reichsordnung (*Ser'ata Mangest*)," *ZA* 30 (1915–16): 11, 29.

77. Ignazio Guidi, "Contributi alla Storia Letteraria di Abissinia: Il 'Ser'ata Mangest,'" *RRAL,* ser. 5, 31 (1922): 68–69 and note 1. Guidi's footnote denying the "Falasha" in the manuscript referred to the same group called the Falasha people is unnecessary: it simply means the Christians saw the Falasha group as Jews and applied the word to the ancient context. See also EMML 6574 for another version of the *Ser'ata Mangest,* which, however, does not refer to the Falasha.

78. This is also the view of the chronicles. See Chapter 2.

79. In a genealogy of Takla Haymanot, it is stated his ancestors "came forth from Egypt with Israel [*esrā'ēl*] into the land of Ethiopia"; see EMML 1834, *Gadla Takla Haymanot* (Dabra Hayq version), f. 76a. See also description in Getatchew Haile and William Macomber, eds., *A Catalogue of Ethiopian Manuscripts* 5:310–11.

80. Bruce, *Travels,* 1:485. Oral traditions mention war with Ezana: interview with Gete Asrass, 9 November 1975.

81. Getatchew Haile, "An Anonymous Homily in Honor of King—Ǝlla Asbaha of Axum, EMML 1763, Ff. 34v–35v," *NAS* 3/2 (1981): 30.

82. Ibid., pp. 25–27; idem., "Frumentius," pp. 312–13. Interviews with Berhan Beruk on 20 August, Menase Zammaru on 15 October, and Gete Asrass on 9 November 1975.

83. Getatchew, "An Anonymous Homily," p. 30.

84. Budge, *History of Ethiopia,* p. 265.

85. Getatchew Haile, "A New Look at Some Dates of Early Ethiopian History," *Le Muséon* 95 (1982): 311–12.

86. Sergew, *Ancient and Medieval,* pp. 162, 163, 166; idem., "New Historical Elements in the 'Gedle Aftse,'" *JSS* 9 (1964): 200–203; idem., "A History of Aksum: The Successors of Caleb," *RA* 11 (Spring 1970): 30–36; Budge, *History of Ethiopia,* p. 265.

87. Sergew, *Ancient and Medieval,* pp. 159–60.

88. Sergew makes this point: *Ancient and Medieval,* p. 161. On the king's lists, see Conti Rossini, "Les listes des rois d'Aksoum," *JA,* ser. 10, 14 (1910): 263–320; C. F. Rey, *The Real Abyssinia* (2nd ed., New York, 1969 [orig. 1935]), appendix: "List of the Sovereigns of Abyssinia," pp. 265–81; Sergew, *Ancient and Medieval,* photo facing pp. 160 and 161; A. Mordini, "Appunti di Numismatica Aksumita," *AE* 3 (1959): 182, 184, plate 79d; Francis Anfray, "Les rois d'Axoum d'après la numismatique," *JES* 6/2 (1968): 1–5.

89. See the fascinating play by the well-known Ethiopian playwright, Tsegaye Gabre-Medhin, *Collision of Altars* (London, 1977), who sees a Christian-Jewish-Pagan struggle during this era.

90. Conti Rossini, ed., *Gadla Yared seu Acta Sancti Yared, CSCO,* ser. alt., 17

(1904); R. Basset, ed., "La vision de Saint Iared," in Basset, ed., *Contes populaires d'Afrique* (Paris, 1903), pp. 124–26; Sergew, *Ancient and Medieval*, pp. 164–66, based on *Gadla Yared* and other local sources and traditions.

91. Interview with Berhan Beruk on 20 August 1975. In less detail, another Beta Israel informant said both Kaleb and Gabra Masqal fought wars against the Beta Israel: Interview with Menase Zammaru on 15 October 1975.

92. Suggested by Getatchew, "New Look at Some Early Dates," p. 320. Another suggestion was that the reign of Kaleb may have been a key to the beginning of the *Kebra Nagast:* Shahid, "The *Kebra Nagast* in the Light of Recent Research"; Taddesse Tamrat, "The Sheba Legend and the Falasha: Problems of Ethiopian Historiography," presented to African Studies Program, University of Illinois, Urbana-Champaign, 11 February 1986.

93. Getatchew suggests the name "Gedewonites" in "New Look at Some Early Dates," p. 320. Another source mentioned the name "Gedewon" as the founder of the clergy of Aksum: "he was from the genealogical line of Gedewon (of the clergy) of the Church of Aksum"; see Getatchew, "On the Identity of Silondis and the Composition of the Anaphora of Mary Ascribed to Hərəyaqos of Bəhansa," *OCP* 49 (1983): 385. In another context, he cited a conflict between two *Christian* sects: the *Negusites* (followers of the King), who favored a Sunday Sabbath, and the *Oritites* (followers of the Old Testament), who favored a Saturday Sabbath; see EMML 1763, F. 46r in Getatchew Haile, "A Study of the Issues Raised in Two Homilies of Emperor Zär'a Ya'əqob of Ethiopia," *ZDMG* 131 (1981): 106. See also Chapter 2 below.

94. The tradition that Yared was allowed to go to Samen as a favor from King Gabra Masqal may have arisen to soften the impression of what may have been a forced exile. See *Acta Yared* and Sergew's long quotation from it on the traditional story.

95. Ethiopian social history is in its infancy, but some examples include: Ulrich Braukamper, *Geschichte der Hadya Sud-Athiopiens* (Wiesbaden, 1980); Alessandro Triulzi, *Salt, Gold, and Legitimacy* (Naples, 1981); Donham and James, eds., *Southern Marches;* McCann, *From Poverty to Famine.*

96. Crawford Young, *The Politics of Cultural Pluralism* (Madison, Wisc., 1976); Donald Horowitz, *Ethnic Groups in Conflict* (Berkeley and Los Angeles, 1985).

97. Aidan Southall, "The Illusion of Tribe," *JAAS* 5/1–2 (1970).

98. On "primordialism," see Clifford Geertz, "The Integrative Revolution. Primordial Sentiments and Civil Politics in the New States," in C. Geertz, ed., *Old Societies and New States* (New York, 1963), pp. 155–57, and *passim.* See also Edward Shils, "Primordial, Personal, Sacred and Civil Ties," *British Journal of Sociology* (June 1957), 130–45; Harold Isaacs, *Idols of the Tribe* (New York, 1975); idem., "Basic Group Identity: The Idols of the Tribe," *Ethnicity,* 1 (1974): 15–41; A. L. Epstein, *Ethos and Identity* (London, 1978).

99. Robert Bates, "Modernization, Ethnic Competition, and the Rationality of Politics in Contemporary Africa," in Donald Rothchild and Victor Olorunsola, eds., *State Versus Ethnic Claims* (Boulder, Colo., 1981); Abner Cohen, *Custom and Politics in Urban Africa* (Berkeley and Los Angeles, 1969); A. L. Epstein, *Politics in an Urban African Community* (Manchester, 1958); Nelson Kasfir, "Cultural Sub-

Nationalism in Uganda," in Victor Olorunsola, ed., *The Politics of Cultural Sub-Nationalism in Africa* (Garden City, N.J., 1972), pp. 51–148.

100. Benedict Anderson, *Imagined Communities* (Ldon, 1983); Jean-Loup Amselle and E. M'Bokolo, eds., *Au coeur de l'Ethnie* (Paris, 1985); Belinda Bozzoli, ed., *Class, Community and Conflict: South African Perspectives* (Johannesburg, 1987); Terence Ranger, "The Invention of Tradition in Colonial Africa," in T. Ranger and E. Hobsbawm, eds., *The Invention of Tradition* (Cambridge, 1983), pp. 247–62; John Illife, *A Modern History of Tanganyika* (Cambridge, 1979), pp. 318–41; Leroy Vail, ed., *The Creation of Tribalism in Southern Africa* (Berkeley and Los Angeles, 1989).

101. On the relationship of Islam to "tribal" categories, see J. Trimingham, *Islam in Ethiopia* (New York, 1952), pp. 147–224; on ignoring ethnic fluidity, see Donald Crummey, "Society and Ethnicity in the Politics of Christian Ethiopia During the Zamana Masafent," *IJAHS* 8 (1975): 266–78.

102. Donham and James, *Southern Marches,* pp. 4–17; Messing, "Highland-Plateau Amhara," pp. 63–67.

103. Trimingham, *Islam in Ethiopia,* pp. 150–53, 193–99; personal observations; McCann, *From Poverty to Famine,* pp. 25–27.

104. Crummey, "Abyssinian Feudalism," pp. 118–20. On the role of the Agaw, see also Taddesse Tamrat, "Processes of Ethnic Interaction and Integration in Ethiopian History: The Case of the Agaw," *JAH* 29 (1988): 5–18.

105. Donham and James, *Southern Marches,* pp. 12, 34–35; Allan Hoben, *Land Tenure.*

106. The following were the most useful sources in arriving at these criteria: Max Weber, "The Development of Caste," in Reinhard Bendix and Seymour Lipset, eds., *Class, Status and Power* (New York, 1966), pp. 28–36; A. L. Kroeber, "Caste," in Edwin Seligman and Alvin Johnson, eds., *Encyclopaedia of the Social Sciences* (New York, 1935), 3:254–56; Gerald Berreman, "Caste: the Concept of Caste," *IESS* 2 (1968): 333–39; K. C. Roser, "Caste," in *Dictionary of the Social Sciences* (New York, 1964), pp. 75–77; Adrian Mayer, "Caste: The Indian Caste System," *IESS* 2 (1968): 339–44; Edmund Leach, "Caste, Class and Slavery: The Taxonomic Problem," in Edward Laumann et al., eds., *The Logic of Social Hierarchies* (Chicago, 1970), pp. 83–94; idem., "Introduction: What Should We Mean by Caste?" in Leach, ed., *Aspects of Caste in South India, Ceylon and North-West Pakistan* (London, 1960), pp. 1–10; Louis Dumont, *Homo Hierarchus* (Chicago, 1970).

107. See especially Dumont, *Homo Hierarchus;* George DeVos and Hiroshi Wagatsuma, *Japan's Invisible Race* (Berkeley, 1967).

108. McKim Marriott, "Interactional and Attributional theories of Caste Ranking," *Man in India* 39 (1959): 92–107; idem., "Caste Ranking and Food Transactions, a Matrix Analysis," in Milton Singer and Bernard Cohn, eds., *Structure and Change in Indian Society* (Chicago, 1968), pp. 133–71; Adrian Mayer, "Some Hierarchical Aspects of Caste," *SJA* 12 (1956): 117–44; Harold Gould, "Castes, Outcastes, and the Sociology of Stratification," *International Journal of Comparative Sociology* 1 (1960): 220–38; David Pocock, "The Movement of Castes," *Man* 55 (1955): 71–72; William Rowe, "Mobility in the Nineteenth-Century Caste System," in Milton Singer and B. Cohn, eds., *Structures and Change in Indian Society,* pp. 201–7.

109. On "castes" in Africa, see McNaughton, *Mande Blacksmiths;* Robert Launay, "Manding 'Clans' and 'Castes'" Conference on Manding Studies, School

of Oriental and African Studies, London, 1972; M. Sidibe, "Les gens de caste ou Nyamakala au Soudan Français," *Notes africaines* 81 (1959): 13–17; Nehemia Levtzion, *Ancient Ghana and Mali* (London, 1973), pp. 119–20; James Vaughn, "Caste Systems in the Western Sudan," in Tuden and Plotnicov, *Social Stratification in Africa,* pp. 59–92; Walter Cline, *Mining and Metallurgy in Negro Africa* (Menasha, Wisc., 1937), comparative table, pp. 128–39; S. M. Cissoko, "Traits fondamentaux des sociétés du Soudan occidental du XVIIe au début du XIXe siècle," *BIFAN,* ser. B, 31 (1969): 1–30; B. Appia, "Les forgerons du Fouta-Djallon," *JSA* 35 (1965): 317–52; N. Echard, "Note sur les forgerons du l'Ader (Pays Hausa, République du Niger)," *JSA* 35 (1965): 353–72; Abdoulaye-Bara Diop, *La société Wolof: Tradition et changement* (Paris, 1981); L. Tauxier, *Moeurs et histoire des Peuls* (Paris, 1937). For East Africa, see Jacques Maquet, *Power and Society in Africa* (New York, 1971), pp. 137–90; idem., "Rwanda Castes," in Tuden and Plotnicov, *Social Stratification in Africa,* pp. 93–123; René Lemarchand, "Power and Stratification in Rwanda: A Reconsideration," *CEA* 6 (1966): 592–610; Jose Kagabo et Vincent Mudandagizi, "Complainte des gens de l'argile, les Twa du Rwanda," *CEA* 14 (1974): 75–87.

110. See the summary in Levine, *Greater Ethiopia,* appendix, pp. 195–97; Herbert Lewis, "Historical Problems in Ethiopia and the Horn of Africa," *Annals of the New York Academy of Sciences* 96 (1962): 504–11; William Shack, "Notes on Occupational Castes among the Gurage of South-West Ethiopia," *Man* 54 (1964): 50–52; C. R. Hallpike, "The Status of Craftsmen among the Konso of South-West Ethiopia," *Africa* 38 (1968): 258–69; Enrico Cerulli, "The Folk-Literature of the Galla of Southern Abyssinia," in E. A. Hooton and Patricia Bates, eds., *Harvard African Studies, Varia Africana* (Cambridge, Mass., 1922), vol. 3, appendix: "The Watta. A Low Caste of Hunters," pp. 200–214; Herbert Lewis, "Wealth, Influence and Prestige among the Shoa Galla," in Plotnicov and Tuden, eds., *Social Stratification in Africa,* pp. 163–86; G. W. B. Huntingford, *The Galla of Ethiopia* (London, 1955), pp. 16–17, 28, 35, 63, 83, 103, 131, 136, 139–40; Karl Knutsson, *Authority and Change,* pp. 89, 145–46. For an approach that emphasizes the attributional and "outcaste" characteristics, see Eike Haberland, "Zum Problem der Jäger und besonderen Kasten in Nordost- und Ostafrika," *Paideuma* 8 (1962): 136–55; idem., "Eisen und Schmiede in Nordost-Afrika," *African Abstracts* 14 (1963): 9; idem., "Special Castes in Ethiopia," in Robert Hess, ed., *Proceedings of the Fifth International Conference on Ethiopian Studies, Session B, Chicago, 1978* (Chicago, 1979), pp. 129–32; idem., "Caste and Hierarchy Among the Dizi (Southwest Ethiopia)," in Sven Rubenson, ed., *Proceedings of the Seventh International Conference of Ethiopian Studies, Lund, 1982* (Uppsala, Sweden, 1984), pp. 447–450.

111. Herbert Lewis, "Historical Problems in Ethiopia"; S. F. Nadel, "Caste and Government in Primitive Society," *Journal of the Anthropological Society of Bombay* 8 (1954): 9–22; Levine, *Greater Ethiopia,* pp. 45–46. Those emphasizing a conquest approach include Cerulli, "The Folk-Literature of the Galla," and J. Maquet, *Power and Society in Africa* (New York, 1971).

112. Crummey, "State and Society: Nineteenth-Century Ethiopia," in Crummey and C. C. Stewart, eds., *Modes of Production in Africa* (Beverly Hills, 1981), p. 228.

113. Allan Hoben, "Social Stratification in Traditional Amhara Society," in Plotnicov and Tuden, eds., *Social Stratification in Africa,* pp. 203–4, 192.

114. Crummey, "Abyssinian Feudalism," p. 134.

115. Addis Hiwet *Ethiopia: From Autocracy to Revolution* (London, 1975), p. 27, and below.

116. Crummey, "Abyssinian Feudalism," pp. 127–34; Hoben, "Social Stratification in Amhara Society," pp. 191–205; Gene Ellis, "Feudalism in Ethiopia: A Further Comment on Paradigms and their Use," *NAS* 1/3 (1979–80): 91–97; but see the contrasting view of Addis Hiwet, *Ethiopia*.

117. See studies of peoples in the region: Frederick Gamst, *The Qemant;* idem., "Wayto Ways: Change from Hunting to Peasant Life," in R. Hess, ed., *Proceedings of the Fifth International Conference on Ethiopian Studies, Chicago, 1978* (Chicago, 1979), pp. 233–38; R. Pankhurst, "The History of the Bareya, Shanqella and other Ethiopian Slaves from the Borderland of the Sudan," *SNR* 59 (1977): 1–43.

118. On class analysis, see Emmanuel Terray, "Classes and Class Consciousness in the Abron Kingdom of Gyaman," in Maurice Bloch, ed., *Marxist Analyses and Social Anthropology* (New York, 1975), pp. 85–135; Karl Marx, *Pre-Capitalist Economic Formations,* ed., by E. J. Hobsbawm (New York, 1964).

119. Claude Meillassoux, "Are There Castes in India?" *ES* 9 (1973): 89–111; Donham and James, *Southern Marches,* p. 12.

120. On the ambiguity of blacksmiths in Mande society, see McNaughton, *Mande Blacksmiths,* pp. 1–21.

121. Interviews; see Chapter 4.

122. Mahteme Sellassie, "Land System," p. 285. Messing asserted the Falasha told him in the 1950s they had been given this type of land by Menilek ("Highland-Plateau Amhara," p. 252), but it seems most likely to have begun during the Gondar era (see Chapter 3).

123. Studying the manipulation of marriage and sexual relations across ethnic or racial lines is one way of analyzing the role of gender; see George Frederickson, *White Supremacy: A Comparative Study in American and South African Society* (New York, 1981); Carl Degler, *Neither Black nor White* (New York, 1971); Angela Davis, *Women, Race and Class* (New York, 1983); Bell Hooks, *Ain't I a Woman: Black Women and Feminism* (Boston, 1981).

124. Crummey, "Women and Landed Property in Gondarine Ethiopia," *IJAHS* 14 (1981): 444–65; idem., "Family and Property Amongst the Amhara Nobility," *JAH* 24 (1983): 207–20; Chris Prouty Rosenfield, "Eight Ethiopian Women of the *Zemene Mesafint* (c. 1769–1855)," *NAS* 1/2 (1979): 63–85.

125. See details in Chapter 4.

126. Jan Vansina, *Oral Tradition as History* (Madison, Wisc., 1985), pp. 197–98.

127. See Chapter 2. See an analogous situation in Janet Ewald, "Experience and Speculation: History and Founding Stories in the Kingdom of Taqali, 1780–1935," *IJAHS* 18 (1985): 265–87, where the heightened detail of traditions suggested the beginning of a new regime.

128. James McCann, "The Ethiopian Chronicles: An African Documentary Tradition," *NAS* 1/2 (1979): 47–61; Vansina, *Oral Tradition,* (Chicago, 1965), pp. 84–87.

129. McCann, "The Ethiopian Chronicles," p. 55.

130. André Caquot, "Les 'chroniques abrégée' d'Ethiopie," *AE* 2 (1957): 187–92. The main examples which have been published are: René Basset, "Études sur

l'histoire d'Éthiopie," *JA,* ser. 7, 17 (1881): 315–434; 18 (1881): 93–183, 285–389; Francesco Beguinot, ed., *La cronaca abbreviata d'Abissinia* (Rome, 1901); Jules Perruchon, ed., in *RS* [see bibliography for each listing]. These are currently being re-edited by Manfred Kropp, with a German translation in the *CSCO* series, beginning with Lebna Dengel: *Die Geschichte des Lebna-Dengel, Claudius und Minas, CSCO* 83 (1988) [text], 84 (1988) [trans.].

131. Steven Kaplan, "Hagiographies and the History of Medieval Ethiopia," *HA* 8 (1981): 107–23.

132. Carlo Conti Rossini, "L'agiografia etiopica e gli atti del santo Yafqeranna-Egzi," *ARIV* 96/2 (1936–37): 403–33; Taddesse Tamrat, *Church and State,* pp. 1–4; idem., "Hagiographies and the Reconstruction of Medieval Ethiopian History," *RA* 11 (1970): 12–20; Steven Kaplan, *The Monastic Holy Man and the Christianization of Early Solomonic Ethiopia* (Wiesbaden, 1984); idem., "Iyasus-Mo'a and Takla Haymanot: A Note on a Hagiographic Controversy," *JSS* 31 (1986): 47–56.

133. Vansina, *Oral Tradition,* p. 114.

134. Stefan Strelcyn, "Prières magiques éthiopiennes pour délier les charmes," *RO* 18 (1955): I–LXXVI, 1–498. For a preliminary effort to suggest their use as historical sources, see James Quirin, "A Preliminary Analysis of New Archival Sources on Daily Life in Historical Highland Ethiopia," in Sven Rubenson, ed., *Proceedings of the Seventh International Conference of Ethiopian Studies, Lund, 1982* (Uppsala, Sweden, 1984), pp. 393–410.

135. For example, *alaqa* Tayya Gabra Maryam, *Ya-Iteyopeya Hezb Tarik* [*History of the Peoples of Ethiopia*], trans. Grover Hudson and Tekeste Negash (Uppsala, Sweden, 1987).

136. Wolf Leslau, ed., "A Falasha Religious Dispute," *Proceedings of the American Academy for Jewish Research* 16 (1947): 71–95.

137. Interview with Admas Chakkol, 16 December 1975.

138. On the use of oral material in interpreting written documents, see LaVerle Berry, "The Solomonic Monarchy at Gonder, 1630–1755: An Institutional Analysis of Kingship in the Christian Kingdom of Ethiopia" (Ph.D. dissertation, Boston University, 1976); Donald Crummey, Shumet Sishagne, and Daniel Ayana, "Oral Traditions in a Literate Culture: The Case of Christian Ethiopia," paper presented to the International Symposium on Unwritten Testimonies of the African Past, University of Warsaw, 7–8 November 1989.

139. As noted even by some other researchers, whose focus was not on this group; ibid., p. 390.

140. Vansina, *Oral Tradition as History,* pp. 59–63.

Chapter 2

1. Taddesse Tamrat, *Church and State,* pp. 53–66; Sergew, *Ancient and Medieval,* pp. 239–87; George Gerster, *Churches in Rock* (London, 1970); J. Perruchon, *Vie de Lalibela* (Paris, 1892).

2. Donald Levine, "Menilek and Oedipus," p. 12. But see L. Ricci, "Edipo e Storia," *Paideuma* 24 (1978): 169–77.

3. On the *Kebra Nagast,* see Chapter 1.

4. Al-Masudi, *Les Prairies d'or,* ed. C. Barbier, 9 vols. (Paris, 1861–77), 1:230–31, 1:266, 1:272, 1:281, 3:34; Ibn Hauqal, *Configuration de la Terre,* ed. J. H. Kramers and G. Wiet, 2 vols. (Paris, 1964), 1:10, 54; Umarah, *Yaman, Its Early Mediaeval History,* ed. H. C. Kay (London, 1892), p. 10.

5. J. Perruchon, "Histoire des guerres d'Amda Syon," *JA,* ser. 8, 14 (1889): 280 (text), 328 (trans.).

6. Arab traveler cited in Franz Rosenthal, "A Fourteenth Century Report on Ethiopia," in S. Segert and A. J. E. Bodrogligeti, eds., *Ethiopian Studies, Dedicated to Wolf Leslau* (Wiesbaden, 1983), p. 499. Taddesse Tamrat labels this period one of "territorial expansion" (*Church and State,* pp. 119–55), while Getatchew Haile sees the conflicts in terms of rebellions against legitimate Ethiopian authority: "Some Notes on the History of Ethiopia: A Re-examination of the Documents," in P. Adwoa Dunn, ed., *Quo Vadis Ethiopia? Conference Proceedings, November 3, 1982* (Washington, D.C., 1983), pp. 7–38. Both views appear to have validity: the Christian state had always claimed sovereignty over these areas but, on the other hand, had not actively controlled them for centuries.

7. Ibn Khaldun, *Histoire des Berbères,* 3 vols. (Paris, 1927), 2:108; Taddesse, *Church and State,* pp. 122–28.

8. Historical note in Iyyasus Mo'a, "The Four Gospels," MS at Dabra Hayq, f. 25b, cited in Taddesse Tamrat, "The Abbots of Dabra-Hayq 1248–1535," *JES* 8/1 (1970): 96.

9. Perruchon, "Amda Seyon," p. 280 (text), p. 328 (trans.). Collecting booty also occurred; see Getatchew Haile, "A Note on Writing History from Forgotten Documents," *NAS* 2/1 (1980): 73–74.

10. Perruchon, "Récit d'une ambassade envoyée au roi d'Éthiopie Sayfa-Ar'ad sur l'ordre du sultan d'Egypte," *RS* 1 (1893): 179 (text), 181 (trans.).

11. Chihab ed-Din Ahmed ben Abd el-Qader (Arab Faqih), *Histoire de la conquête de l'Abyssinie,* ed. R. Basset (Paris, 1897–1901), p. 146.

12. Perruchon, "Amda Syon," pp. 293, 339–40; Taddesse, *Church and State,* pp. 190–91.

13. Taddesse, *Church and State,* pp. 23–25, 107.

14. Stanilas Kur, ed., *Actes de Iyasus-Mo'a,* in *CSCO* 49, 50 (1965); C. Conti Rossini, ed., *Il 'Gadla Takla Haymanot,'* in *MRAL,* ser. 5, 2/1 (1894): 97–143; E. A. Wallis Budge, ed., *The Life and Mysteries of Takla Haymanot* (London, 1906); Taddesse, *Church and State,* pp. 114–17, 158–69, 174–77; idem., "Abbots of Dabra-Hayq," pp. 88–91; Getatchew Haile, "The Monastic Genealogy of the Line of Täklä Haymanot of Shoa," *RSE* 29 (1982–83); Steven Kaplan, "Court and Periphery in Ethiopian Christianity," *Asian and African Studies* 20 (1986): 149; C. Conti Rossini, ed., *Acta S. Basalota-Mika'el et S. Anorewos, CSCO* 20 (1905).

15. Steven Kaplan, *The Monastic Holy Man,* pp. 36–38, 59.

16. Ibid., pp. 50–54; Getatchew Haile, "From Strict Observance to Royal Endowment: The Case of the Monastery of Däbrä Halle Luya," *Le Muséon* 93 (1980): 163, 169–71. *Abuna* Ya'eqob was sent back to Egypt! See Taddesse, *Church and State,* p. 118.

17. René Basset, ed. "Études sur l'histoire d'Éthiopie," *JA* 17 (1881): 324 (text), 18 (1881): 93–94 (trans.).

18. As Getatchew Haile points out, "there is not in fact a single new heresy in the writings of Zär'a Yaʿəqob known to me that has not been mentioned before his time"; see his "A Study of the Issues Raised in Two Homilies of Emperor Zär'a Yaʿəqob of Ethiopia," *ZDMG* 131 (1981): 102. On the "Judaic" ambiance of Ethiopian Orthodoxy, see Chapter 1 above. On Ewostatewos's career, see: Taddesse, *Church and State,* pp. 206–19.

19. Zar'a Ya'eqob, *Mashafa Berhan,* pt. 2; C. Conti Rossini and L. Ricci, eds., *Il libro della luce del Negus Zar'a Ya'qob (Mashafa Berhan),* in *CSCO,* v. 261–62, Script. Aeth., v. 51 (text), v. 52 (trans.), p. 82; Taddesse, *Church and State,* pp. 206–10.

20. EMML 1763 as cited by Getatchew, "Two Homilies," p. 106 (trans.) and note 113 (text). See also Edward Ullendorff, *Bible,* pp. 109–13.

21. EMML 1763, in Getatchew, "Two Homilies," p. 106. The Sabbath was debated during the reign of Amda Seyon: EMML 1202, Ff. 16v–17r; Taddesse, *Church and State,* p. 208; Enrico Cerulli, "Gli Atti di Zena Marqos," *Studi e testi,* 219 (1962): 198.

22. Taddesse, *Church and State,* pp. 216–31. On Giyorgis, see Getatchew Haile, "*Fəkkare Haymanot* or the Faith of *abba* Giyorgis Saglawi," *Le Muséon* 94 (1981): 255 and n. 49; Conti Rossini, "Due Capitoli del Libro del Mistero di Giyorgis da Sagla," *RSE* 7 (1948): 13–53; Giyorgis of Gasecca/Sagla, *Mashafa Mestir:* EMML 1831, described in Getatchew Haile, *A Catalogue of Ethiopian Manuscripts* (Collegeville, Minn., 1981), 5:286–92; EMML 1838, "Gadla Giyorgis"; Getatchew Haile, "On the Writings of *abba* Giyorgis Saglawi from Two Unedited Miracles of Mary," *OCP* 48 (1982): 65–91; Sergew Hable Sellassie, "Giorgis Zegasitcha: Teacher and Author," *EJE* 8/1 (November 1975): 15–32.

23. Quotation from Taddesse, *Church and State,* p. 219; Getatchew Haile, ed., "The Letter of Archbishops Mika'el and Gäbrə'el concerning the Observance of Saturday," *JSS* 26 (1981): 73–78. Getatchew says the council was in 1449 (ibid., 73, n. 3), not 1450, the date given by Taddesse: *Church and State,* p. 230. On the Sabbath question, see also Getatchew Haile, "The Homily of *Aṣe* Zär'a Yaʿəqob of Ethiopia in Honour of Saturday," *OLP* 13 (1982): 185–231; idem., "The Forty-Nine Hour Sabbath of the Ethiopian Church," *JSS* 33 (1988): 233–54.

24. Getatchew Haile, "The Cause of the Ǝstifanosites: A Fundamentalist Sect in the Church of Ethiopia," *Paideuma* 29 (1983): 104.

25. Taddesse Tamrat, "Some Notes on the Fifteenth Century Stephanite 'Heresy' in the Ethiopian Church," *RSE* 22 (1966): 103–15; Robert Beylot, "Le Millénarisme, Article de Foi dans l'Église Éthiopienne, au XVe siècle," *RSE* 25 (1971–72): 32–34. On the new cult of Mary, see Enrico Cerulli, *Il libro etiopico dei Miracoli di Marie e le sue fonti nella letteratura del Medio Evo latino* (Rome, 1943); Getatchew Haile, "Documents on the History of Aṣē Dawit (1382–1413)," *JES* 16 (1983): 25–35.

26. Getatchew, "The Cause of the Ǝstifanosites," pp. 102–3; J. Perruchon, ed., *Les chroniques de Zar'a Ya'eqob et de Ba'eda Maryam, rois d'Éthiopie de 1434 à 1478* (Paris, 1893), pp. 69–70.

27. André Caquot ed., "Les actes d'Ezra de Gunda-Gunde," *AE* 4 (1961): 75 (text), 97 (trans.). See also Kaplan, *Monastic Holy Man,* pp. 41–44.

28. EMML 4 (*Gadla Abaw wa-Ahaw za Dabra Garzen*), an internal chronicle

of Zar'a Ya'eqob's persecution of them, cited in Getatchew Haile, "A Preliminary Investigation of the *Ṭomara Təsbə't* of Emperor Zär'a Ya'əqob of Ethiopia," *BSOAS* 43/2 (1980): 227.

29. C. Conti Rossini, "Il convento di Tsana in Abissinia e le sue Laudi alla Vergine" *RRAL,* ser. 5, 29 (1910): 611 and n. 3: According to Conti Rossini, this is an allusion to Estifanosites.

30. Taddesse, "Stephanite 'Heresy,'" pp. 114–15; Getatchew, "The Cause of the Ǝstifanosites," p. 111.

31. Steven Kaplan, "The Falasha and the Stephanite: An Episode from *Gadla Gabra Masih,*" *BSOAS* 48 (1985): 278–84.

32. Caquot, "Gadla Ezra," pp. 75 (text), 97 (trans.).

33. Getatchew Haile, "Review of Steven Kaplan, *The Monastic Holy Man,*" *JRA* 16 (1986): 237.

34. Kaplan, "The Falasha and the Stephanite," p. 280.

35. Getatchew, "The Cause of the Ǝstifanosites," p. 107. The works cited by Getatchew are *Gadla Abakerasum* and *Gadla Abaw wa-Ahaw.*

36. Ephraim Isaac, *A New Text-Critical Introduction to Mashafa Berhan* (Leiden, 1973), pp. 54–75; Marilyn Heldman, "Jewish Christianity and Medieval Ethiopian Illumination," *Manuscripta* (March 1976): 13–14.

37. The *historical* formation of "Falasha"-like landless, endogamous "caste" groups observed later in Shawa and Lasta needs further investigation. See Chapter 1 above.

38. Cerulli, "Gli atti de Zena Marqos," p. 195; EMML 2136, F. 15v; EMML 3987, Ff. 17v–19r; Getatchew Haile, "Monastic Genealogy of Täklä Haymanot," p. 25, n. 20. Scholars have not previously fully recognized the significance of the *Gadla Zena Marqos,* available in several manuscripts, the following of which I have used: EMML 932, 3987, 4741, 4922, and 6678. Cerulli's Vatican manuscript apparently did not mention the *ayhud.* See James Quirin, "*Ayhud* in Fourteenth-Century Ethiopia: Data from the *Gadla Zena Marqos*" (forthcoming).

39. EMML 4741, Ff. 46r–51v. Sege Berhan collaborated with Gabra Maryam in writing the *Mahelete Sege.* On Gabra Maryam, see Getatchew, "Monastic Genealogy of Täklä Haymanot," p. 30, n. 41; Taddesse, *Church and State,* p. 176; Sergew Hable Sellassie, "Giorgis Zegasitcha," p. 20. The Mahelete Sege has been edited by A. Grohmann, *Aethiopische Marienhumnen. Abhandlungen der Philologisch-historischen Klasse der Sachsischen Akademie der Wissenschaften* 33 (1919).

40. J. L. Krapf, "Extracts from a Journal," *JRGS* 10 (1841): 473, 478; Krapf and K. W. Isenberg, *Journals* (London, 1843), pp. 239–40; and see Chapter 4 below.

41. "Falasha" were said to live in both areas in the nineteenth and twentieth centuries: Charles Beke, "Abyssinia—being a Continuation of Routes in that Country," *JRGS* 14 (1844): 8, 56; Mikael Aragawy, in *Report* 74 (1882): 140–41; and Diana Spencer, "Trip to Wag and Northern Wallo," *JES* 5/1 (1967): 96; James McCann, *From Poverty to Famine,* p. 27.

42. Taddesse, "Abbots of Dabra Hayq," pp. 95–96; idem., *Church and State,* pp. 186–96; J. Perruchon, "Amda Seyon," p. 309.

43. My translation from Perruchon, "Amda Seyon," 293 (text). I thank Taddesse Tamrat for assistance. As Taddesse pointed out, Perruchon's French version (pp. 339–40) is inaccurate in making it appear to be a revolt of the governor of

Begamder: *Church and State,* p. 192. See also the paraphrase by Conti Rossini which seems to state the war was against the population of Begamder: "Appunti di Storia di Letteratura Falascia," *RSO* 7 (1920): 565. Dillmann's translation is more accurate: *Die Kriegsthaten des Konigs 'Amda-Sion gegen die Muslim. Sitzungsberichte der Koniglich Preussischen Akademie der Wissenschaften zu Berlin* 43 (1884): 1,017. There is no evidence in the sources of explicit Muslim-*ayhud* cooperation in their revolts, despite Trimingham's assertion, *Islam in Ethiopia* (London, 1952), p. 71.

44. For example, Zar'a Ya'eqob "unmasked the Jews who call themselves Christians"; see J. Perruchon, ed., "Histoire d'Eskender, d'Amda-Seyon II et de Na'od, rois d'Éthiopie," *JA*, ser. 9, 3 (1894): 350 (text), 365 (trans.).

45. *Gadla Yafqeranna 'Egzi':* I. Wajnberg, ed., "Das Leben des hl. Jafqerena 'Egzi'," *OCA* 106 (1936): 50–58; Conti Rossini, "Note di agiografia Etiopica ('Abiya-Egzi', 'Arkaledes e Gabra-Iyasus)," *RSO* 17 (1938): 439–51.

46. *Gadla Gabra-Iyyasus,* fol. 143r: Conti Rossini, "Note di agiografia," pp. 444–45. The Ethiopic text from B.M. Or. 705, an eighteenth century redaction, is not printed by Conti Rossini, but large extracts appear in his Italian translation interspersed with his own commentary. The original *gadl* was said to have been lost during the wars with Ahmad Gragn, but was rewritten from memory in the sixteenth century. For accounts of the important role later of Enfraz (or Emfraz), see the references in Richard Pankhurst, *A History of Ethiopian Towns From the Middle Ages to the Early Nineteenth Century* (Wiesbaden, 1982), pp. 94–100.

47. *Gadla Gabra-Iyyasus:* Conti Rossini, "Note di agiografia," pp. 445–46.

48. Interview with Berhan Beruk on 20 August 1975, and Webe Akale on 27 December 1975. No details are remembered and the traditions in general of this period are very vague.

49. *Gadla Gabra-Iyyasus:* Conti Rossini, "Note di agiografia," pp. 446–47.

50. Ibid., p. 448. Conti Rossini noted that "King Ya'eqob" also married a Falasha (ibid., p. 449), but this seems to be a confusion between Ya'eqob the son of Lebna Dengel (1508–40), who did apparently marry a Falasha woman but who never became king, and Ya'eqob, who was the (natural) son of Sarsa Dengel and his Falasha mistress and who did become king briefly (1597–1603, 1605–7). See my account of these cases below. In any case, such examples were not unheard of.

51. Ibid., p. 451. For the usage of the formula in Falasha texts, see J. Halévy, ed., *Te'zaza Sanbat (commandements du Sabbat)* (Paris, 1902), pp. 41, 80, 97, 108; Wolf Leslau, *Anthology* (New Haven, Conn., 1951), pp. 11, 107.

52. *Gadla Yafqeranna-Egzi',* I. Wajnberg, ed., "Das Leben des Hl. Jafqerana 'Egzi'," p. 50. See also C. Conti Rossini, "Appunti di storia e letteratura Falascia," pp. 572–77.

53. Taddesse, *Church and State,* p. 115, and references in notes 4–7; Conti Rossini, "Appunti di storia e letteratura Falascia," p. 573, n. 1. See also *Gadla Gabra-Iyyasus,* Conti Rossini, "Note di agiografia," p. 444.

54. *Gadla Yafqerrana Egzi',* Wajnberg, "Das Leben," pp. 52–55. See comments by Conti Rossini, "Note di agiografia," p. 433.

55. *Gadla Yafqeranna Egzi',* p. 56. My translation from the Ge'ez.

56. Ibid., p. 58. The "prophecy" was that Qozmos would become an *ayhud* and destroy Enfraz (p. 52). My translation; I thank Getatchew Haile for suggestions.

57. For variations on the dates of the reigns of Dawit, Tewodros, and Yeshaq,

see Taddesse, "Problems of Succession," pp. 506–11; idem., *Church and State,* pp. 279–80, n. 3; R. Schneider, "Notes Ethiopiennes," *JES* 16 (1983): 106–10.

58. On the title *kantiba,* see LaVerle Berry, "The Solomonic Monarchy at Gondar, 1630–1755: An Institutional Analysis of Kingship in the Christian Kingdom of Ethiopia" (Ph.D. dissertation, Boston University, 1976), pp. 266–67. Conti Rossini suggested migrations from both Tigray and Shawa accompanied these conversions: "L'agiografia etiopica e gli Atti del Santo Yafqeranna-Egzi'," *ARIV* 96/2 (1937): 424.

59. Francisco Alvares, *The Prester John of the Indies,* ed. C. F. Beckingham and G. W. B. Huntingford, 2 vols. (Cambridge, 1961), 1:248. On *gult* see also Chapter 1 above.

60. Ibid., 1:173. On the "traditional" land tenure systems, see Mahteme Sellassie Wolde Maskal, "The Land System of Ethiopia"; Gebre-Wold-Ingida Worq, "Ethiopia's Traditional System of Land Tenure"; Berhanou Abebe, *Evolution de la propriété;* Mantel-Niecko, *Role of Land Tenure.* See Chapter 1 above.

61. Alvares, *Prester John,* 1:69–70, 2:412, 428, 430, 464; G. W. B. Huntingford, ed., *The Land Charters of Northern Ethiopia* (Addis Ababa, 1965), pp. 40–59. On Ethiopian or "Abyssinian" feudalism, see Donald Crummey, "Abyssinian Feudalism," *PP* 89 (November 1980): 115–38; Gene Ellis, "The Feudal Paradigm as a Hindrance to Understanding Ethiopia," *JMAS* 14 (1976): 275–95. Most such accounts are very present-oriented.

62. "Tarika Nagast," EMML 7334, Ff. 28a–28b. I am indebted to Getatchew Haile for this reference. This seems to be the same document used by Taddesse: "Tarika-Nagast," paper MS, Dabra Sege, pp. 53–54, cited in *Church and State,* p. 200. The name is also written as Bit-Ajir (EMML 7334), or Bet-Ashur (Conti Rossini, "Appunti di storia e letteratura Falascia," p. 567). If this name is the same as the "Abet-Ajer" said to be from Agaw which appeared in a soldier's song from the reign of Amda Seyon, perhaps it was either a common name among the Falasha Agaw, or a title among them; I Guidi, "Le Canzoni Ge'ez-Amarina in onore di re abissini," *RRAL,* ser. 4, 4 (1889): 62; and G. W. B. Huntingford, ed., *The Glorious Victories of Amda Seyon,* pp. 129, 132–33.

63. Interviews with Berhan Beruk on 3 July and 20 August 1975, Gete Asrass on 11 June and 9 November 1975, Menase Zammaru and Wande Iyyasu on 13 October 1975, Menase Zammaru on 15 October 1975, Yeheyyes Madhane and Yalew Siyamer on 27 October 1975, Enneyaw Tarraqagne on 30 December 1975. A nineteenth-century oral tradition collected by Antoine d'Abbadie has comparable information: Antoine d'Abbadie, "Réponses des Falasha dits Juifs d'Abyssinie," *AI* 12 (1851): 267–68. The greatly increased detail of the oral traditions beginning with Yeshaq's reign suggests this was a turning point in Beta Israel history, which may be analogous to interpretations of oral traditions elsewhere: Janet Ewald, "Experience and Speculation: History and Founding Stories in the Kingdom of Taqali, 1780–1935," *IJAHS* 18 (1985): 268, note 11.

64. Ferret and Galinier, *Voyages en Abyssinie* 3 vols. (Paris, 1847), atlas.

65. Mansfield Parkyns, *Life in Abyssinia* (London, 1868), map.

66. René Basset, ed., "Études sur l'histoire," 17:325–26 (text); 18:95 (trans.); Guidi, "Le Canzoni," p. 62.

67. Interview with Enneyaw Tarrekagne, 30 December 1975.

68. Interview with Berhan Beruk, 20 August 1975.

69. Recorded from a Falasha from Dafacha, on the outskirts on Gondar in 1848 by d'Abbadie: "Réponses," pp. 267–68.

70. Basset, "Études sur l'histoire," v. 17, pp. 325–26, v. 18, p. 95.

71. "Tarika Nagast," EMML 7334, F. 28b.

72. Admas Chakkol, "Attempts to Exterminate The Beta Israel," unpublished manuscript in possession of James Quirin, p. 3; interview with Admas Chakkol on 16 December 1975. The alleged role of Muslims is probably anachronistic and would date only to the Islamic conflict of the sixteenth century.

73. Interviews with Gete Asrass on 9 November 1975, Berhan Beruk, 20 August, 1975. See also Basset, "Études sur l'histoire," p. 95; "Tarika Nagast," EMML 7334, F. 28b. In the 1430s Elijah of Ferrara, a Jewish traveler in Jerusalem heard from a "young Jew" about his coreligionists in "Habesh" (Abyssinia) who fought constant wars with the Christians. This is probably referring to the wars against Yeshaq, though it may be a reference to wars during the unsettled interregnum between Yeshaq and Zar'a Ya'eqob (1430–34); Eliakim Carmoly, *Itinéraires de la Terre Sainte des XIV, XV, XVI, et XVII siècles, traduits de l'hébreu* (Brussels, 1847), p. 334; "Elijah of Ferrara (1434)," in Elkan Adler, ed., *Jewish Travellers* (London, 1930), pp. 151–55.

74. Basset, "Études sur l'histoire," p. 95; James Bruce, *Travels,* 2:65–66; Antoine d'Abbadie, "Journal et mélanges," unpublished manuscript in Bibliothèque nationale, FNA 21300, pp. 253–54; interviews with Berhan Beruk on 20 August 1975, Ayyallegn Adgwachaw and Kebrate Samu'el on 26 October 1975, Yeheyyes Madhane and Yalew Siyamer on 27 October 1975, and Gete Asrass on 3 June 1975.

75. Interview with Berhan Beruk on 20 August 1975, Jammara Wande on 21 July 1975, and Admas Chakkol on 16 December 1975.

76. Interview with Admas Chakkol on 16 December 1975.

77. "Tarika Nagast," EMML 7334, F. 28b. See also "Tarika Nagast," MS Dabra Sege and "Mar Yeshaq," MS Dima, ff. 171b–112a [*sic:* 172a], cited in Taddesse, *Church and State,* p. 201.

78. Admas Chakkol, "Attempts to Exterminate the Beta Israel," p. 3; interview with Admas Chakkol on 16 December 1975.

79. Interview with Berhan Beruk on 20 August 1975.

80. Interviews with Gete Asrass on 3 June and 9 November 1975, Berhan Beruk on 3 July and 20 August 1975, Yeheyyes Madhane and Yalew Siyamer on 27 October 1975. Conti Rossini emphasized the significance for the Christians of controlling the rich land of Wagara: "Appunti di storia e letteratura Falascia," pp. 566–67.

81. Interview with Admas Chakkol on 16 December 1975. In the nineteenth century, the Beta Israel of Walqayt and Sagade were known as *foggara,* suggesting a dispersal from the area called Fogara, east of Lake Tana, at some unknown time; see J. Halévy, "Excursion chez les Falacha en Abyssinie," *BSG* 17 (1869): 287.

82. Taddesse, *Church and State,* p. 103, and see pp. 98–102; Conti Rossini, "I loggo e la legge dei loggo Sarda," *GSAI* 17 (1904): 31–35. This issue is certainly complex and warrants further research. Taddesse's reconstruction perhaps does not explain adequately what happened to the previous *rest*-holders when the new layer

of *gult*-holders was imposed on them: Donald Crummey, personal communication, 21 November 1989. On the other hand, it is clear many of the "pagan" or *ayhud* Agaw in the region had their land taken away, others moved out of the area, and others assimilated.

83. The etymology of the Amharic *rest* is the Ge'ez *warasa,* meaning "to inherit." Attempts have been made to derive *rest* from the Ge'ez *rasata,* meaning land conquered and occupied by force which a new settler takes up and begins to farm: Aleme Eshete, "General Examination of Ethiopian Feudalism," paper presented to Conference on Ethiopian Feudalism, Institute of Ethiopian Studies and Historical Society of Ethiopia, March 1976, p. 3. Although Aleme cites Conti Rossini (*Principi di Diritto Consuetidinario dell'Eritrea* (Rome, 1916), p. 114) in support of this etymology, Conti Rossini actually denied such a derivation, saying it was "absolutely false"; ibid., p. 115, note 2.

84. *Gadla Takla Hawāryāt:* Conti Rossini, ed., *Vitae Sanctorum Indigenarum T. Acta Santi Abakerazun, II. Acta Santi Takla Hawaryat, CSCO,* Scrip. Aeth., 25 (1954): 104 (text).

85. Ibid., p. 105. Takla Hawaryat's life ended in a political conflict with Zar'a Ya'eqob, probably in 1455: Taddesse Tamrat, "Problems of Royal Succession in Fifteenth Century Ethiopia: A Presentation of the Documents," in *IV Congresso Internazionale di Studi Etiopici* (Rome, 1974): 519–25. See also A. Caquot, ed., "Histoire amharique de Gran et des Gallas," *AE* 2 (1957): 139–40.

86. The "princesses" were the women Zar'a Ya'eqob had appointed to provincial governorships as a means of governmental reorganization: Perruchon, *Chronique de Zar'a Ya'eqob,* p. 95.

87. My translation from ibid., pp. 96–97. The *ma'etab* was a colored cord Christians wore around their necks as a symbol of their religion. "Amhara" in this passage means, more generally, "Christian."

88. *Gad* derives from the Amharic *gadd* ("luck"), and the original form of "Yestan" was apparently *yest* ("let him give"). Thus, the word has no relationship to the coincidentally similar word *Gad* used in some early accounts of "Jews" in Ethiopia; "Eldad the Danite," in Elkan Adler, ed., *Jewish Travellers* (London, 1930), p. 11; A. Neubauer, "Where are the Ten Tribes?" *JQR* 1 (1889): 196–97.

89. Perruchon, *Chronique de Zar'a Ya'eqob,* p. 103.

90. On "religious nationalism," see Taddesse, *Church and State,* pp. 206–47; Getatchew argues for the significance of the theological challenges of the *ayhud:* "Two Homilies," p. 91, n. 40. Portuguese sources later speculated Zar'a Ya'eqob was seen as anti-*ayhud* because he was said to have executed many blacksmiths: Almeida, "Do emperador Zara Jacob" extract from *Historia de Ethiopia,* MS 9861, British Museum, in Perruchon, ed., *Chronique de Zar'a Ya'eqob,* appendix, pp. 199–205. See also Emmanuel Barradas, *Tractatus Tres Historico-Geographici,* in C. Beccari, *Rerum Aethiopicarum Scriptores Occidentales Inediti a Saeculo XVI ad XIX,* 15 vols. (Rome, 1903–17), 4:61.

91. *Gadla Giyorgis:* Gérard Colin, ed., *Vie de Georges de Sagla, CSCO,* Script. Aeth., 81 (1987): 26–27 (text), 82 (1987): 19–20 (trans.) [utilizing EMML 1838, F. 23r, and citing John 11:34 and Genesis 3:9, 18:9]. See also Sergew Hable Sellassie, "Giorgis Zegasitcha" pp. 20–21, 30, notes 52 and 54.

92. Colin, *Vie de Georges,* v. 81, pp. 27–30 (text), v. 82, pp. 20–22 (trans.). See

also Getatchew Haile, "Two Homilies," pp. 102–3; idem., "Fəkkare Haymanot or the Faith of *Abba* Giyorgis Saglawi," p. 254; Giyorgis Gasecha, *Mashafa Mestir,* EMML 1831, Ff. 45a–53b, cited in EMML *Catalogue,* vol. 5, p. 287; C. Conti Rossini, "Due capitoli del Libro del Mistero di Giyorgis da Sagla," *RSE* 7 (1948): 39–53.

93. Cited in Getatchew Haile, "Two Homilies," pp. 86–87.

94. Zar'a Ya'eqob, *Mashafa Berhan* in *CSCO,* Script. Aeth. 52 (1965): 74. For the controversies, see Getatchew Haile, "Religious Controversies and the Growth of Ethiopic Literature in the Fourteenth and Fifteenth Centuries," *OC* 65 (1981): 108–9, and *infra.* They are considered "Jewish-Christian" by Ephraim Isaac, *A New Text-Critical Introduction,* pp. 54–75. For early background on these issues see: Timothy Ware, *The Orthodox Church* (London: Penguin, 1984 [orig. 1963]), pp. 216–42. For a study of the "Mikaelites" in a later period, see Enrico Cerulli, *Scritti teologici ethiopici dei secoli XVI–XVII. Studi e testi,* no. 198 [Vatican], 1958).

95. Getatchew Haile, "The Homily of Zär'a Yaʿəqob in Honour of St. John the Evangelist, EMML 1480, Ff. 48r–52v," *OC* 67 (1983): 144–66; idem., "The Homily of *Aṣe* Zär'a Yaʿəqob of Ethiopia in Honour of Saturday," *OLP* 13 (1982): 185–231.

96. Getatchew, "The Homily in Honour of Saturday," pp. 196 (text), 220 (trans.).

97. Ibid., pp. 210–11 (text), 231 (trans.).

98. "Zamika'el, who agrees with him [Gamaleyal], is not (now) in Dabra Seyon to seduce the Christians from the Orthodox Faith with the wickedness of his heart": Zar'a Ya'eqob, *Tomara Tesbe't,* cited in Getatchew Haile, "A Preliminary Investigation of the *Ṭomara Təsbə't* of Emperor Zär'a Yaʿəqob of Ethiopia," in *BSOAS* 43, pt. 2 (1980): 218 and note 77. Getatchew Haile, in "The End of a Deserter of the Established Church of Ethiopia," G. Goldenberg, ed., *Ethiopian Studies. Proceedings of the Sixth International Conference, Tel-Aviv, 1980* (Rotterdam: Balkema, 1986), p. 195, says this miracle of Mary is about the exile, capture and execution of Zamika'el, and suggests another manuscript (EMML 1480) concerns the similar end of Gamaleyal.

99. *Ṭomara Təsbə't* (in EMML 1480), as edited by Getatchew, "A Preliminary Investigation," p. 219 (twice), 210, 226.

100. Ibid.

101. Ibid., p. 210.

102. Ibid., p. 226. Getatchew is preparing a complete edition of this important work of Zar'a Ya'eqob.

103. *Gadla Abaw wa-Ahaw za-Dabra Garzen:* EMML 4, cited in ibid., p. 227.

104. Zar'a Ya'eqob, *Mashafa Milad:* Kurt Wendt, ed., *Das Mashafa Milad (Liber Nativitatis) und Mashafa Sellase (Liber Trinitas) des Kaisers Zar'a Ya'qob. CSCO,* Scrip. Aeth. 41–42 (1962).

105. Perruchon, *Chronique de Zar'a Ya'eqob et de Ba'eda Maryam,* pp. 96–97, 142–43, 172–73; C. Conti Rossini, ed., *Historia Regis Sarṣa Dengel (Malak Sagad), CSCO,* Script. Aeth. 3 (1907): 110. See also J. B. Coulbeaux, *Histoire politique et religieuse d'Abyssinie,* 3 vols. (Paris, 1929), 2:50–51; Getatchew Haile, "Power Struggle in the Medieval Court of Ethiopia: The Case of Bätärgēla-Maryam," *JES* 15 (1982): 37–55; G. Ellero, "Il Uolcait," *RSE* 7 (1948): 94.

106. "Tarika Nagast," MS Dabra Ṣegē, p. 56, cited in Taddesse, *Church and*

State, p. 291. On the regency and power struggles, see Perruchon, ed., "Histoire d'Eskender, d'Amda Ṣeyon II et de Na'od," *JA,* ser. 9, 3 (1894): 339 (text), 354 (trans.); Taddesse, *Church and State,* pp. 286–87, 290–92; idem., "Problems of Royal Succession," pp. 526–35. The regent, Amda-Mika'el, or Ras Amdu, had Jewish ancestors from Yemen who entered Ethiopia during Zagwe times and soon converted to Christianity: Taddesse, "The Abbots of Dabra Hayq" *JES* 8/1 (1970): 113.

107. Alvares, *Prester John,* 2:357. See also Taddesse, *Church and State,* p. 291; E. A. Wallis Budge, *A History of Ethiopia, Nubia and Abyssinia* (Oosterhout, 1970 [orig. ed. 1928]), pp. 179–80, 322, on Pedro de Covilham.

108. "The Letters of Obadiah Jare da Bertinaro (1487–90)," in Elkan Adler, ed., *Jewish Travellers,* pp. 238–39; Conti Rossini, *Sarṣa Dengel, CSCO,* Script. Aeth. 3 (1907): 107.

109. Stanilas Kur, ed., *Actes de Marha Krestos, CSCO,* Script. Aeth. 62 (1972): 101–2 [text], 63 (1972): 92–93 [trans.).

110. EMML 1874, F. 150r, my translation. I thank Getatchew Haile for the reference. See also Conti Rossini: "Il Convento di Tsana," *RRAL,* ser. 5, 29 (1910): 581–621.

111. *Gadla Abunā Habta Māryām,* EMML 2142, F. 24v. That Habta Māryām was the father confessor of King Nā'od is revealed in another historical document, EMML 1515, p. 163. See also Getatchew Haile, ed., *A Catalogue of Ethiopian Manuscripts,* 5:17–18, 6:254–55.

112. Chihab, *Histoire de la conquête,* p. 458; J. Perruchon, ed., "Histoire d'Eskender," pp. 350–51 (text), 365–66 (trans.); Conti Rossini, *Sarṣa Dengel,* p. 107; Neubauer, "Where are the Ten Tribes," pp. 196–97; Steven Kaplan, ed., "Some Hebrew Sources on the Beta Israel (Falasha)," in Taddesse Beyene, ed., *Proceedings of the Eighth International Conference of Ethiopian Studies, Addis Ababa, 1984,* 2 vols. (Addis Ababa, 1988), 1:203–5.

113. *Gadla Zēnā Mārqos* [see note 38 above]; *Gadla Yāfqerrana Egzi'* [see note 45 above].

114. Obadiah Jare of Bertinaro, in Adler, ed., *Jewish Travellers,* pp. 238–39; Obadiah in Enrico Cerulli, *Etiopia in Palestina,* 2 vols. (Rome, 1943), 1:323–24; Elijah of Ferrare, in Adler, *Jewish Travellers,* 153; Rabbi David ibn Zimri in Solomon B. Freehof, "Marriage with Falashas," in Freehof, ed., *A Treasury of Responsa* (Philadelphia, 1963), p. 125.

115. On inference for *mehellanna* and also on speaking Agaw, see *Gadla Takla Hawāryāt* [note 84 above], which has been pointed out by Steven Kaplan as noted by Shelemay, *Music, Ritual,* p. 64, note 55, p. 60, note 4. That the *ayhud* observed a "Fast of Esther" as the Falasha were known to do later is inferred from the statements by Jewish observers that they possessed the Book of Esther, where the events and reasons for the observance are laid down: "Elijah of Ferrare" in Adler, *Jewish Travellers,* p. 153; Elijah in Cerulli, *Etiopi in Palestina,* 1:236; Elijah of Pesaro in A. Neubauer, "Where are the Ten Tribes?" *JQR* 1 (1889): 200. But the Falasha did not call this Purim until the early twentieth century. See description of Leslau, *Falasha Anthology,* p. xxxv; and Shelemay, *Music, Ritual,* p. 50. On the lack of Hebrew, Chanukah, or the Talmud, see Rabbi David ibn Zimri in Freehof, "Mar-

riage with Falashas," p. 125; "Elijah of Ferrare," p. 153; Elijah of Pesaro, in Neubauer, "Ten Tribes," p. 200.

116. Shelemay, *Music, Ritual,* pp. 48, 50.

117. On "Kings," see "Obadiah of Bertinaro" in Adler, *Jewish Travellers,* pp. 238–39; Abraham ben Eliezer Ha-Levi, in Steven Kaplan, "Some Hebrew Sources on the Beta Israel (Falasha)," 1:203–5. The reference to Falasha as shepherds here and to the *ayhud* in Begamder as having herds of cattle in the *Gadla Gabra Iyyasus* probably refers to the practice of mixed cultivation and herding common to highland Ethiopia, though it may also be a confusion of the *ayhud*-Falasha with other groups of herders in the region, who were called "Zalan" in the nineteenth century (see Chapter 4 below). On the regalia of kingship during the reign of Sarsa Dengel, see J. Perruchon, "Règne de Sarṣa-Dengel ou Malak-Sagad I (1563–1597)," *RS* 4 (1896): 180 (text), 275 (trans.); and see Halévy's comments: "La guerre de Sarsa-Dengel contre les Falashas," *RS* 15 (1906): 155–63.

118. For example, Yuri Kobishchanov, *Axum* (University Park, Penna., 1979), pp. 132–42.

119. Interview with Berhan Beruk on 3 July 1975; Louis Rapoport, *The Lost Jews* (New York, 1980 and 1983), pp. 97–114, has greatly oversimplified these issues. On "Gudit," see Chapter 1 above. A traveler was told a "Falasha carpenter" built a church just east of Lake Tana during the reign of Dawit, but this is very shaky evidence; see Paul Henze, *Ethiopian Journeys* (London, 1977), p. 184.

120. D'Almeida, cited in J. Perruchon, *Chronique du Zar'a Ya'eqob,* appendix, pp. 199–205; *Gadla Marha Krestos:* Stanilas Kur, ed., *Actes de Marha Krestos, CSCO* 63 (1972): 10–11 (text), refers to a blacksmith with an "evil eye" (*ekuy ayn*) but does not use the word "Falasha," or the word *buda,* which was applied to the Falasha later. The editor (p. 10, n. 1) says that blacksmiths were *buda,* which was true, at least later, but is not in the text here. Kaplan infers *buda* is implied here; see Kaplan, *Monastic Holy Man,* p. 112. For documentation on *buda,* see Chapter 4 below. Lebna Dengel's proclamation is contained in a note in EMML 2490; see Getatchew Haile and William Macomber, *A Catalogue of Ethiopian Manuscripts,* 6:526. For the seventeenth century, see Balthazar Tellez, *The Travels of the Jesuits in Ethiopia* [1660] (London, 1710), p. 38; Job Ludolphus, *A New History of Ethiopia* (London, 1682), pp. 390–91.

121. Perruchon, "Amda Seyon," pp. 352, 355, 441–42; Taddesse, *Church and State,* pp. 92–94.

122. Maqrizi, *Al-Ilmam,* p. 4, cited in J. S. Trimingham, *Islam in Ethiopia,* p. 75; al-Umari, *Masalik,* p. 36, cited in Richard Pankhurst *An Introduction to the Economic History of Ethiopia* (London, 1961), p. 289; G. Wiet, "Les relations égypto-abyssines sous les sultans mamelouks," *Bulletin de la Société d'archéologie copte* 4 (1938): 126, cited in Pankhurst, *Economic History,* p. 289; Taddesse, *Church and State,* p. 154; Pankhurst, "Misoneism and Innovation in Ethiopian History," *EO* 7 (1964): 287–90.

123. See note 120 above. For blacksmiths at the royal court, see also F. Alvares, *Prester John,* 2:243–45.

124. Interviews with Yeshaq Iyyasu on 15 December 1975, Gete Asrass on 9 November 1975, Admas Chakkol on 16 December 1975; joint interview with Yeheyyes Madhane and Yalew Siyamer on 27 October 1975.

125. Halévy, "Excursion chez les Falacha, en Abyssinie," *BSG,* ser. 5, 17 (1869): 287.

126. Perruchon, "Amda Syon," pp. 339–40.

127. See above. Such dispersals were comparable to other cases of highlanders being pushed down into marginal land, for example, in Shawa, Volker Stitz, *Studien zur Kulturgeographie Zentraläthiopiens* (Bonn, 1974). For one popular account of the survival of enclave cultures, see Paul Henze, "Patterns of Cultural Survival on the Islands in Ethiopia's Highland Lakes," *EO* 16 (1973): 89–96.

128. The *Gadla Aron* shows the importance of these monasteries as self-sufficient agricultural communities: B. Turaiev, ed., *Acta S. Aronis et S. Phillipi, CSCO* 20 (1905): 146–48, cited in Kaplan, *Monastic Holy Man,* p. 49. The extent to which these Beta Israel monks founded complete monastic communities in the fifteenth century is unknown, but several locations in the nineteenth and twentieth centuries contained many monks, not just individual leaders; see Chapter 4, below.

129. Kaplan, *Monastic Holy Man,* p. 40.

130. Wolf Leslau, "Taamrat Emmanuel's Notes of Falasha Monks and Holy Places," in *Salo Wittmayer Barron Jubilee Volume, American Academy for Jewish Research* (Jerusalem, 1975), pp. 624–25. This important text is a translation from Italian of notes written by Professor Taamrat, a Falasha student of Jacques Faitlovitch, apparently after years of gathering the information from Falasha elders. For the tradition that *abba* Sabra spent some time at Yeshaq Dabr, see interview with Yeshaq Iyyasu, 15 December 1975. His name is written inconsistently: Ṣabrā, Ṣebrā, Sabrā, or Sebrā: Leslau, "Taamrat," p. 624. A location in Samen was called Sabra; see Pedro Paez, *Historia Aethiopiae,* in Beccari, *Rerum Aethiopicarum,* 3:348; Conti Rossini, "La cronaca reale abissina dall'anno 1800 all'anno 1840," *RRAL,* ser. 5, 25 (1916): 864. He is also called *abba* Sura by Halévy, *Travels,* p. 230.

131. James Quirin, "The *'Ayhud* and Bēta 'Esrā'ēl-Falāshā in Fifteenth-Century Ethiopia: Oral and Written Traditions," *NAS* 10 (1988): 89–104. Interview with *qes* Yeshaq Iyyasu, 12 December 1975; interview with Wubshet Atagab, 17 July 1980, cited in Shelemay, *Music, Ritual,* p. 218, note 20. *Qes* Yeshaq pushed back *abbā* Ṣabrā's time to the alleged origins of Jews in Ethiopia, suggesting perhaps his importance as a founding figure. Professor Taamrat, in his notes published by Leslau, suggested sometime after 1550 as a likely date for *abbā* Ṣabrā, due to the movement of the Ethiopian capital to northwestern Ethiopia after that time, thus leading to increased Jewish-Christian contacts. I have already documented, however, the increasing intensity of conflicts with the reign of Yeshaq. The reign of Zar'a Ya'eqob, or possibly beginning during the last part of Yeshaq's reign seems the most logical time to posit the efforts of *abbā* Ṣabrā.

132. Leslau, "Taamrat," p. 624; Halévy, *Travels,* p. 227; Faitlovitch, *Quer Durch,* pp. 88–89; J. M. Flad, *The Falashas,* p. 29; Luzzatto, *Mémoire,* pp. 96–97.

133. Leslau, "Taamrat," p. 625.

134. Faitlovitch, *Quer Durch,* p. 89; Max Wurmbrand, "Fragments d'anciens écrits juifs dans la littérature Falacha," *JA* 242 (1954): 83–100.

135. D'Abbadie, "Réponses des Falasha," p. 237.

136. Leslau, "Taamrat," p. 625; idem., *Falasha Anthology,* p. xl.

137. Quirin, "The *'Ayhud* and Bēta 'Esrā'ēl-Falāshā." The tradition was first recorded in the early nineteenth century by Antoine d'Abbadie by the Beta Israel's

chief priest at the time who lived at Hohwara, *abba* Yeshaq: Antoine d'Abbadie, "Journal et mélanges," pp. 464, 473; idem., "Réponses des Falasha," p. 184; idem., "Extrait d'une lettre," pp. 49, 72. They were also heard and referred to briefly by Flad (*The Falashas,* p. 29), Halévy (*Travels,* pp. 229–30), and Faitlovitch, *Quer Durch,* p. 89. Conti Rossini noted that d'Abbadie had mentioned the existence of a *gadl* of *abbā* Ṣabrā, but seemed doubtful that such a manuscript existed: "Appunti di storia e letteratura Falascia," p. 579. If it exists it has not been found.

138. EMML 2058, ed. Getatchew Haile, "The End of a Deserter of the Established Church of Ethiopia," in Gideon Goldenberg, ed., *Ethiopian Studies. Proceedings of the Sixth International Conference, Tel-Aviv, 1980* (Boston, 1986), 193–203.

139. Ibid., p. 195 citing EMML 6343, Ff. 120b–121a; Getatchew, personal communication, 7 September 1982. Kay Shelemay suggested the Miracle may record the story of Qozmos (personal communication).

140. See Leslau, *Falasha Anthology,* p. xxxvi, and interview with Kebrate Samu'el and Ayyallegn Adgwachaw on 26 October 1975.

141. Halévy, *Prières des Falashas* (Paris, 1877), cited by Leslau, *Falasha Anthology,* pp. 115, 182, note 2; Leslau, "Taamrat," pp. 626–27, notes 18 and 21; d'Abbadie, "Réponses des Falasha," p. 184 and note 1; Carlo Viterbo, "Nuovi manoscritti Falascia," *ASE* (1935–37): 117; Monica Devens, "Remarks on a Falasha Liturgical Text for the Sanbata Sanbat," in Sven Rubenson, ed., *Proceedings of the Seventh International Conference of Ethiopian Studies, University of Lund, April 1982* (Addis Ababa, 1984), pp. 121–23; Halévy, *Travels,* p. 230. The Aksumite king, Ezana, was said to be of the Halen, a Cushitic-speaking ethnic group: Leslau, op. cit; d'Abbadie, op. cit; Sergew, *Ancient and Medieval,* p. 92.

142. Carl Rathjens, *Die Juden in Abessinien* (Hamburg, 1921), p. 82; Conti Rossini, "Appunti," p. 584, note 1. See also Leslau, *Falasha Anthology,* pp. 77–91.

143. E. A. W. Budge, ed., *The Book of the Saints of the Ethiopian Church* (Hildesheim and New York, 1976 [orig. ed., 1928]), p. 666; Shelemay, *Music, Ritual,* p. 69, note 116; Getatchew Haile, "On the Identity of Gorgoryos and the Provenance of His Apocalypse," paper presented to the Eleventh International Conference of Ethiopian Studies, Addis Ababa, 1991.

144. Robert Hess, "An Outline of Falasha History," in *Proceedings of the Third International Conference of Ethiopian Studies, Addis Ababa, 1966* (Addis Ababa, 1969), 1:102; Shelemay, *Music, Ritual,* p. 211.

145. Halévy, *Travels,* p. 227; Leslau, *Falasha Anthology,* p. xii.

146. Oral traditions emphasized the part importance of Qwara and Samen and also mentioned other locations and lists of monks of uncertain antiquity: Interviews with Menase Zammaru and Wande Iyyasu on 13 October 1975, Ayyallegn Adgwachew and Kebrate Samu'el on 26 October 1975, Yeheyyes Medhane and Yalew Siyamer on 27 October 1975.

147. Edward Ullendorff, *Ethiopia and the Bible,* pp. 31–62.

148. M. A. Knibb, ed., *The Ethiopian Book of Enoch,* 2 vols. (Oxford, 1978, 1982), 2:1–47. See also Oesterley, Introduction to R. H. Charles, ed., *The Book of Enoch* (Oxford, 1893), p. xviii.

149. Box, introduction to R. H. Charles, ed., *The Book of Jubilees or the Little Genesis* (London, 1917), pp. x–xiii.

150. *Gadla Yafqerrana 'Egzi':* Wajnberg, ed., "Das Leben," p. 56; Conti Rossini, "Appunti di storia e letteratura Falascia," pp. 567–77; and see above.

151. Leslau, "Taamrat," p. 625, and see above.

152. Leslau, *Falasha Anthology,* pp. 3–39; Joseph Halévy, ed., *Te'ezaza Sanbat (Commandements du Sabbat)* (Paris, 1902), pp. 1–40 (text), 133–64 (trans.); Charles, ed., *Jubilees,* Book 50, pp. 211–13; Chaim Schwarzbaum, "Jewish and Moslem Sources of a Falasha Creation Myth," *Studies in Biblical and Jewish Folklore,* no. 13 (1960): 41–56; Jean Doresse, "Survivances d'écrits Gnostiques dans la littérature Gueze," in *Proceedings of the Third International Conference on Ethiopian Studies, Addis Ababa, 1966,* 3 vols. (Addis Ababa, 1969–70), 2:213–16; Getatchew Haile and William Macomber, *A Catalogue of Ethiopian Manuscripts,* 5:12 describing EMML 1512; Max Wurmbrand, "Le *Dersana Sanbat*—une homélie éthiopienne attribuée à Jacques de Saroug," *L'Orient Syrien* 8 (1963): 343–94; Steven Kaplan, "Te'ezaza Sanbat: A Beta Israel Work Reconsidered," *Studies in the History of Religious,* vol. 1 [*Truman Institute Reprints*], 107–24.

153. Antoine d'Abbadie, "Extrait d'une lettre de M. Antoine d'Abbadie sur les Falacha ou Juifs d'Abyssinie," *BSG,* ser. 3, 4 (1845): 56–57; Luzzatto, *Mémoire,* pp. 46–47; Getatchew Haile, "The Forty-Nine Hour Sabbath of the Ethiopian Church," *JSS* 33 (1988): 243–44. The "Anaphora of St. Athanasius," a part of the Christian liturgy, addresses the Sabbath as a person; see Marcus Daoud, *The Liturgy of the Ethiopian Church* (Addis Ababa, 1954), p. 153. See also Ernst Hammerschmidt, *Stellung und Bedeutung des Sabbats in Athiopien* (Stuttgart, 1963), p. 63; and Kay Shelemay, "Music and Text of the Falasha Sabbath," *Orbis Musicae* 8 (1982–83): 3–22.

154. Its originality was previously noted: Leslau, *Falasha Anthology,* pp. xxxviii, 3–10; Conti Rossini, "Appunti di storia e letteratura Falascia," pp. 584–85. But see Kaplan, "The Te'ezaza Sanbat." The continuing significance of this work was clear when I observed the celebration of the Astasreyo holiday in 1975 in a village in Wagara where the *qes* read from some works, including the *Te'ezaza Sanbat,* translating to Amharic as he went along.

155. On Arabic influences in Ethiopian literature transmitted through the Egyptian Christians, see Leslau, *Anthology,* p. 10; Edward Ullendorff, *The Ethiopians* (2nd ed., London, 1965), p. 146. The mention of "King Gabra Masqal" is problematical since it could refer to the sixth century king, or that king's reign might have been the ninth century, or it could refer to the throne name of several kings including Lalibela, Amda Seyon, or Yeshaq; see Halévy, ed., *Te'ezaza Sanbat,* p. xii, 158; Leslau, *Anthology,* pp. 34, 154, note 264; Sergew, *Ancient and Medieval,* pp. 162–64; Getatchew Haile, "A New Look at Some Dates of Early Ethiopian History," *Le Muséon,* 95 (1982): 315–20; Jean Doresse *L'empire du Prêtre-Jean,* 2 vols. (Paris, 1957), 2:196.

156. Leslau, *Falasha,* p. 113; A. Z. Aescoly, *Recueil de textes Falachas,* pp. 40–46.

157. Halévy, "Nouvelles prières des falachas," *RS* 19 (1911): 96–104, 215–18, 344–64; Devens, "Remarks on a Falasha Liturgical Text," p. 121; Viterbo, "Nuovi manoscritti Falascia."

158. See notes 130 and 131 above on Ṣabrā and Ṣaggā Amlāk; Aescoly, *Recueil de textes,* p. 201, Halévy, *Te'ezaza Sanbat,* pp. 108 (text), 220 (trans.); Max Wurmbrand,

"Fragments d'ancien écrits." A Christian model was found for a prayer at first thought to be an original Falasha creation: Conti Rossini, "Appunti di storia e letteratura falascia," 593–97; Stefan Strelcyn, "Sur une prière 'falacha' publiée par C. Conti Rossini dans les 'Appunti di storia e letteratura falascia,'" *RSE* 8 (1949): 63–82. On magical prayers, see Strelcyn, "Prières magiques éthiopiennes pour délier les charmes," *RO* 18 (1955): xiii, note 2.

159. Leslau, *Falasha,* pp. 40–49, 77–91; Halévy, *Te'ezaza Sanbat,* pp. 41–50, 165–72; Wurmbrand, *Death of Aron* (Tel Aviv, 1961), cited in Shelemay, *Music, Ritual,* p. 58. See note 143 above.

160. Leslau, *Falasha,* pp. 50–76, 92–111; Halévy, *Te'ezaza Sanbat,* pp. 51–56, 80–96, 173–77, 196–209; Edward Ullendorff, "The 'Death of Moses' in the literature of the Falashas," *BSOAS* 24 (1961): 419–43; Max Wurmbrand, "Remarks on the Text of the Falasha, 'Death of Moses,'" *BSOAS* 25 (1962): 431–37; Maurice Gaugine, "The Falasha Version of the Testaments of Abraham, Isaac and Jacob, A Critical Study of Five Unpublished Ethiopic Manuscripts" (Ph.D. dissertation, University of Manchester, 1965).

161. Leslau, *Falasha,* pp. 62–64.

162. Stefan Strelcyn, "La littérature falacha: état de la question," *Studi e materiali di storia dell religioni* 26 (1955): 106–13.

163. Maxime Rodinson, "Sur la question des 'influences juives' en Ethiopie," *JSS* 9 (1964): 11–19; Maurice Gaguine, "The Falasha Version of the Testaments of Abraham, Isaac and Jacob," p. 51.

164. Bengt Sundkler, *Bantu Prophets in South Africa* (London, 1961); Vittorio Lanternari, *The Religions of the Oppressed* (New York, 1963); James Cone, *A Black Theology of Liberation* (Philadelphia, 1970), pp. 17–22, 92–96; Michael Walzer, *Exodus and Revolution* (New York, 1985). Gaugine goes too far, however, in suggesting some apparent "Christological" terms were understood in a pre-Christian sense and hence were not erased by Beta Israel copyists: Gaugine, "Falasha Version," p. 12 and n. 4; p. 45.

165. Leslau, "Te'ezaza," in *Falasha,* p. 16.

166. Ibid., pp. 37–38.

167. Some of the liturgy is provided in the *Te'ezaza Sanbat:* Shelemay, *Music, Ritual,* pp. 139, 159, note 5.

168. Ibid., pp. 153–54, and *passim.*

169. Ibid., pp. 44–56; Otto Neugebauer, *Ethiopic Astronomy and Computus* (Vienna, 1979), pp. 7–10, 15–16, 21–23, 28, 92–94, 109–11, 228–29.

170. Veronika Krempel, "Die soziale und wirtschaftliche Stellung der Falascha."

171. Jean Doresse, *L'empire du Prêtre-Jean,* 2:323.

172. For overviews, see Mordechai Abir, "Ethiopia and the Horn of Africa," in Richard Gray, ed., *The Cambridge History of Africa,* vol. 4, *From 1600 to 1790* (Cambridge, 1975), pp. 537–77; Richard Pankhurst, *Introduction to Economic History,* pp. 322–37.

173. Girma Beshah and Merid Wolde Aregay, *The Question of the Union of the Churches in Luso-Ethiopian Relations (1500–1632)* (Lisbon, 1964). For background, see Taddesse, *Church and State,* pp. 248–67.

174. Mohammed Hassen, *The Oromu of Ethiopia: A History, 1570–1860* (Cambridge, 1990); Merid Wolde Aregay, "Southern Ethiopia and the Christian Kingdom, 1508–1708, with Special Reference to the Galla Migrations and their Consequences," (Ph.D. dissertation, University of London, 1971); Bahrey, "History of the Galla," in C. F. Beckingham and G. W. B. Huntingford, eds., *Some Records of Ethiopia, 1593–1646* (London, 1954), pp. 111–29; A. Caquot, ed., "Histoire amharique de Gran et des Gallas," *AE* 2 (1957): 123–43; H. S. Lewis, "The Origins of the Galla and Somali," *JAH* 7 (1966): 27–46; idem., "Historical Problems in Ethiopia."

175. Ralph A. Austen, "The Islamic Red Sea Trade: An Effort at Quantification," in Robert L. Hess, ed., *Proceedings of the Fifth International Conference on Ethiopian Studies, Session B, Chicago 1978* (Chicago, 1979), pp. 461–63, and Table 4: from an average of 3,100 people exported per year in the 1200–1500 period, it increased to 4,500 per year in the 1500–1700 period. This study supersedes all previous ones, such as those by Pankhurst, *Introduction to Economic History,* pp. 372–88; idem., "The Ethiopian Slave Trade in the Nineteenth and Early Twentieth Centuries: A Statistical Inquiry," *JSS*. See also Mordechai Abir, "The Ethiopian Slave Trade and Its Relation to the Islamic World," in John Ralph Willis, ed., *Slaves and Slavery in Muslim Africa,* 2 vols. (London, 1985), 2:124. Much more work on the Ethiopian slave trade in all eras is needed. On the Funj, see Jay Spaulding, "The Funj: A Reconsideration," *JAH* 13 (1972): 39–53.

176. "Nine-tenths" of the population converted, a gloss meaning a great number; William Conzelman, ed., *Chronique de Galawdewos (Claudius)* (Paris, 1895), p. 123. See also Chihab, *Conquête;* Asa J. Davis, "The Sixteenth Century Jihad in Ethiopia and the Impact on its Culture," *JHSN* 2 (1963): 567–92; 3 (1964): 113–28; Robert Ferry, "Quelques hypothèses sur les origines des conquêtes musulmanes en Abyssinie au XVI siècle," *CEA* 2 (1961): 24–36; J. S. Trimingham, *Islam in Ethiopia* (London, 1952), pp. 84–91.

177. Perruchon, ed., "Le règne de Lebna Dengel," *RS* 1 (1893): 282–83; Chihab, *Conquête,* pp. 453–55.

178. Chihab, *Conquête,* pp. 455–56. My translation from French.

179. Bahr Amba was a royal stronghold and also the name of troops stationed there. Its exact location is uncertain. The chronicle of Zar'a Ya'eqob suggests Tigray, while the editor of the chronicle of Ahmad's conquest assumes it was in Samen, and the editor of Suseneyos's chronicle asserts it was in Sallamt, a region south of the Takkaze, between Samen and Tigray. See Perruchon, *Chronique du Zar'a Ya'eqob,* p. 47; Chihab, *Conquête,* pp. 277 and note 1, 407 and n. 2; C. Conti Rossini, *Sarṣa Dengel,* pp. 100, 102; J. Halévy, ed., "La guerre de Sarsa-Dengel contre les Falashas," *RS* 15 (1906): 127; F. M. Esteves Pereira, *Chronica de Susenyos,* 2 vols. (Lisbon, 1892, 1900), 2:437. Perhaps the name was originally in one of these areas (such as Tigray) and moved with people who migrated from one region to another; personal communication with Getatchew Haile, 12 September 1989.

180. Chihab, *Conquête,* pp. 456–59. My translation from French.

181. The service of Falasha as soldiers and *azmaches* for the kings is well-documented for later kings, see below. In this case, I owe the suggestion that Sa'ul may have been a Falasha to Getatchew Haile (personal communication, August 1989).

182. Chihab, *Conquête,* pp. 459–67. Similar assistance was given Ahmad by local people, usually Muslims, see ibid., pp. 426–30; Basset, "Études sur l'histoire," v. 18, p. 98; Trimingham, *Islam in Ethiopia,* p. 92.

183. Perruchon, "Le règne de Lebna Dengel," pp. 277 (text), 283 (trans.); Basset, "Études sur l'histoire," v. 17, pp. 329–30 (text), v. 18, p. 100 (trans.); F. Beguinot, *La cronaca abbreviata d'Abissinia* (Rome, 1901), p. 21; F. Dombrowski, *Tanasee 106* (Wiesbaden, 1983), pp. 41 (text), 164 (trans.); Manfred Kropp ed., *Die Geschichte des Lebna-Dengel, Claudius und Minas, CSCO,* Script. Aeth., 83 (1988): 17 (text), 84 (1988): 16 (trans.); C. Foti, ed., "La cronaca abbreviata dei Re d'Abissinia in un manoscritto di Dabra Berhan di Gondar," *RSE* 1 (1941): 98.

184. Basset, "Études sur l'histoire," p. 148, note 159.

185. James Bruce, *Travels,* 2:165.

186. Eduard Rüppell, *Reise in Abyssinien,* 2 vols. (Frankfurt am Main, 1838–40), 2:359, referring to a chronicle he calls, "Ueber die Abyssinische Geschichte bis zum Jahre 1769"; also cited in F. M. Esteves Pereira, ed., *Chronica de Susneyos, Rei de Ethiopia,* 2 vols. (Lisbon, 1892, 1900), 1:vii, and by Luzzatto, *Mémoire,* p. 25. Among the editors of the chronicles cited (note 183 above), only Beguinot (p. 21, note 4) commented specifically on the *ḥamāta negus* phrase, by suggesting the "king" referred to might be Gedewon, the Falasha leader, making Yodit his mother-in-law ("suocera"). I disagree because *negus* was not used to refer to a Falasha leader, but only to the Ethiopian kings. The German translation by Kropp also has "mother-in-law" (*Schwiegermutter*). The two French translations of this short chronicle by Basset and Perruchon both translate *ḥamāta* as *bru* ("daughter-in-law"), while Dombrowski, the editor of a German translation, does not translate it. The Ge'ez word derives from *taḥāmawa* ("to acquire an in-law") and hence could refer to either mother- or daughter-in-law. What seems most likely in this case is that either Yodit (also possibly known as Wesenabi) or Yodit's daughter, Wesenabi, married Ya'eqob, the son of Lebna Dengel. In the latter case, Yodit would, of course, become the mother-in-law of Ya'eqob, not Lebna Dengel, while in the former, she would become the daughter-in-law of Lebna Dengel. In either case, there was a marriage relationship between the two families. Gedewon was probably Yodit's brother. Another chronicle does not have this phrase: Conti Rossini, ed., "Storia di Libna Dingil, Re d'Etiopia," *RRAL,* ser. 5, 3 (1894): 617–40.

187. Zar'a Ya'eqob, for example, had married a Hadeyya princess: Perruchon, *Chronique de Zar'a Ya'eqob,* p. 59; and Sarsa Dengel had a Beta Israel mistress (see below). Beta Israel traditions mention several other cases of marriage or concubinage relationships between Ethiopian kings and Beta Israel women. Most scholars have not commented upon this case.

188. Miguel de Castanhoso, *The Portuguese Expedition to Abyssinia in 1541–1543* ed., R. S. Whiteway (London, 1902), pp. 56–65, 73–75, and "Introduction" by editor, pp. lviii–lxii; Bruce, *Travels,* 2:188–89; D. Joao Bermudez, "This is a Short Account of the Embassy which the Patriarch D. Joao Bermudez brought from the Emperor of Ethiopia," in R. S. Whiteway, ed., *The Portuguese Expedition,* pp. 162, 176–78. The short chronicles state that the people of Samen and Sallamt supported Galawdewos but do not specifically name the Falasha; see Foti, "La cronaca," p. 101; Basset, "Études sur l'histoire," v. 18, pp. 104 and 151, note 174. See also Charles Rey,

The Romance of the Portuguese in Abyssinia (New York, 1969), pp. 175–77, 186–87; Clements Markham, "The Portuguese Expedition to Abyssinia in the Fifteenth, Sixteenth and Seventeenth Centuries," *JRGS* 38 (1868): 6.

189. Pedro Paez, *Historia Aethiopiae,* Chapter 23, in Camillo Beccari, ed., *Rerum Aethiopicarum scriptores occidentales inediti a saeculo XVI ad XIX,* 15 vols. (Rome, 1903–17), 2:314–15. The story is retold in almost the same detail by Ludolphus, *New History,* pp. 223–24, with some differences. Paez calls the *amba,* Wati, while Ludolphus calls it "Jews Rock."

190. Basset, "Études sur l'histoire," pp. 104–5 and p. 154, notes 181 and 182.

191. Interview with Berhan Beruk, 20 August 1975.

192. Conzelman, *Galawdewos,* pp. 141, 144, 151–57.

193. Interview with Berhan Beruk on 20 August 1975.

194. Interview with Admas Chakkol on 16 December 1975.

195. Conzelman, *Galawdewos,* p. 148. For general assessments of Galawdewos, see Merid Wolde Aregay, "Southern Ethiopia," pp. 107–18, 159–94, 230 ff.; Conzelman, "Introduction," *Galawdewos,* and p. 188, note 1. See also the comments on this chronicle by James McCann, "The Ethiopian Chronicles as Documentary Tradition: Description and Methodology," in R. L. Hess, ed., *Proceedings of the Fifth International Conference on Ethiopian Studies, Chicago, 1978* (Chicago, 1979), p. 390.

196. Conzelman, *Galawdewos,* pp. 141, 149–51, 163; J. Perruchon, ed., "Le Règne de Galawdewos (Claudius) ou Asnaf-Sagad," *RS* 2 (1894): 269–70. See also Richard Pankhurst, *History of Ethiopian Towns* (Wiesbaden, 1982), p. 48.

197. Letter of Goncalo Rodrigues, 3 February 1556, to fathers and brothers of Society of Jesus in Europe, MS 49-IV-50, fol. 67–83, of *Jesuitas na Asia,* in Biblioteca de Ajuda, cited in Merid Wolde Aregay, "Southern Ethiopia," p. 165; Conti Rossini, ed., "L'autobiografia di Pawlos monaco Abissino del secolo XVI," *RRAL,* ser. 5, 27 (1918): 285 (text), 291 (trans.).

198. "Fulgentius Freire ad Ioannem Nunez patriarcham Aethiopiae, 12 augusti 1560," in Beccari, *Rerum Aethiopicarum,* 10:105.

199. Perruchon, ed., "Règne de Minas ou Admas-Sagad (1559–1563)," *RS* 4(1896): 89–90; Basset, "Études sur l'histoire," p. 110; Foti, "La cronaca," p. 106; Bruce, *Travels,* 2:206; F. M. Esteves Pereira, *Historia de Minas* (Lisbon, 1888), pp. 28 (text), 46 (trans); M. Kropp, *Lebna-Dengel, Claudius und Minas,* pp. 54–55; Paez, *Historia,* in Beccari, *Rerum Aethiopicarum,* 3:54–55. See also Diogo de Couto, *Da Asia,* dec. VII, liv. VIII, cap. IX, p. 233, cited in Merid, "Southern Ethiopia," p. 179, n. 1.

200. Luzzatto, *Mémoire,* pp. 22–23, citing Bruce, *Travels.*

201. Conti Rossini, *Sarṣa Dengel,* 2:50–51, 53–57, 60–61, 63–89; Marius Saineano, "L'Abyssinie dans la seconde moitié du XVI siècle. Le règne de Sartsa-Dengel (Malak Sagad) (1563–94), d'après des annales éthiopiennes inédits," (Inaugural-dissertation, University of Leipzig, 1892), pp. 35, 38; Ludolphus, *New History,* p. 175; Abir, "Ethiopia and the Horn of Africa," pp. 538, 544–46, who asserts some of the Tigrayan nobility wanted "independence or at least autonomy" from the royal dynasty; Merid Wolde Aregay, "Southern Ethiopia," pp. 265, 303–4 and *passim.*

202. Conti Rossini, *Sarṣa Dengel,* 2:50; Pankhurst, *Ethiopian Towns,* pp. 94–95.

203. Conti Rossini, *Sarṣa Dengel,* 2:133. On the question of who had Guzara built, see note 221 below.

204. For a few examples in his chronicle in which enslaving the defeated was specifically mentioned, see Conti Rossini, *Sarṣa Dengel,* pp. 43, 52–53, 96. Merid interprets most of his campaigns as essentially slave raids: "Southern Ethiopia," pp. 284–87, and also makes the assertion about opening up relations with Funj, pp. 303–4.

205. The dates in the chronicles do not always agree with each other. I have followed the chronological reconstruction made by Merid, "Southern Ethiopia," pp. 285–86. For an overview of these battles with the Beta Israel, see also Pedro Paez, *Historia* in Beccari, *Rerum Aethiopicarum,* 3:141–45.

206. Conti Rossini, *Sarṣa Dengel,* pp. 96–97, 112–13; Saineano, "Sartsa-Dengel," p. 43; Halévy, "La guerre," pp. 139–40.

207. Interview with Berhan Beruk, 20 August 1975.

208. Conti Rossini, *Sarṣa Dengel,* pp. 97–98.

209. Conti Rossini, *Sarṣa Dengel,* pp. 99–101; Halévy, "La guerre," pp. 122–27; Saineano, "Sartsa-Dengel," p. 44; Paez, *Historia,* in Beccari, *Rerum Aethiopicarum,* 3:141. For the story of the woman throwing herself and her captor to death, see also interview with Gete Asrass on 11 June 1975.

210. Conti Rossini, *Sarṣa Dengel,* pp. 102–12; Halévy, "La guerre," pp. 128–41; J. Perruchon, "Règne de Sarṣa-Dengel ou Malak-Sagad I," *RS* 4 (1896): 275; Basset, "Études sur l'histoire," 18: 111–12.

211. Conti Rossini, *Sarṣa Dengel,* pp. 108–14.

212. Perruchon, "Sarṣa-Dengel," p. 275.

213. Conti Rossini, *Sarṣa Dengel,* pp. 116–21, 167–68; Halévy, "La guerre," pp. 143–44; Paez, *Historia,* in Beccari, *Rerum Aethiopicarum,* 3:143.

214. Conti Rossini, *Sarṣa Dengel,* pp. 121–25; Halévy, "La guerre," pp. 144–54 (quotation on p. 150); Saineano, "Sartsa-Dengel," pp. 47–48; Perruchon, "Sarṣa-Dengel," p. 275; Paez, *Historia,* in Beccari, *Rerum Aethiopicarum,* 3:144.

215. J. Perruchon, ed., "Le Règne de Yaqob et Za-Dengel (1597–1607)," *RS* 4 (1896): 358 (text), 361 (trans.); Conti Rossini, "Due squarci inediti di cronica etiopica," *RRAL,* ser. 5, 2 (1893): 806, 810; Stephen Wright, *Catalogue of the Ethiopic Manuscripts in the British Museum,* p. 317a; Merid, "Southern Ethiopia," pp. 356–59. Her name is spelled as Harago (Pereira, 1:282); as Ḥarago (Perruchon, 358; Conti Rossini, 806); as Ḥargo (Perruchon, 356); or as Ḥaragwē (Wright, 317a). Esteves Pereira said her name was a shortened form for Ḥarago Amlāk in *Chronica Susneyos,* 2:376–77. She is called a "new Christian" (recent convert), but her name is not given in the Portuguese sources; see Paez, *Historia,* in Beccari, *Rerum Aethiopicarum,* 3:209; Emmanuel d'Almeida, *Historia Aethiopiae,* in Beccari, *Rerum Aethiopicarum,* 6:41.

216. Perruchon, "Le Règne de Yaqob," p. 355 says Ya'eqob was seven when he came to power on Sarsa Dengel's death in 1597. See below for further documentation on these sons.

217. Bruce, *Travels,* 2:231.

218. Perruchon, "Le Règne de Sarsa Dengel," pp. 275–76.

219. Conti Rossini, *Sarṣa Dengel,* p. 173.

220. Perruchon, *Chronique de Zar'a Ya'eqob,* pp. 71 and 93 where they constructed a new church at Dabra Berhan, and whom the editor identified as "builders or architects" (p. 71, note 2). Conti Rossini, the editor of Sarsa Dengel's chronicle, also identified the *agēt zar* as "a corps of masons and artisans which followed the royal court": *Sarṣa Dengel,* p. 185. See also ibid., pp. 7–8, 35, 60, 63.

221. On the architectural style of Guzara, see Alberto Pollera, *Storie, leggende e favole del paese dei negus* (Florence, 1936), p. 226–28; G. Annequin, "Château de Gouzara," *AE* 5 (1963): 23–24. The ruins of the palace were still visible when I observed them in 1968. A recent account doubts whether this castle was really built by Sarsa Dengel and suggests the reigns of some king after Suseneyos (e.g., Fasiladas, Yohannes I, or Iyyasu I were more likely; see Francis Anfray, "Les monuments Gondariens des XVIIe et XVIIIe siècles. Une vue d'ensemble," in Taddesse Beyene, ed., *Proceedings of the Eighth International Conference of Ethiopian Studies, Addis Ababa, 1984,* 2 vols. (Addis Ababa, 1988), 1:17, 24. Even if Sarsa Dengel was not responsible for building the palace whose remains still exist in Guzara, the chronicle suggests he did have something built in that region.

222. Conti Rossini, *Sarṣa Dengel,* pp. 96–97.

223. Saineano, "Sartsa-Dengel," p. 52.

224. Abir, "Ethiopia and the Horn of Africa," p. 545.

225. Merid, "Southern Ethiopia," pp. 284–87. Merid fits this into his general interpretation of Sarsa Dengel whom he sees as weak, erratic, and prone more to slave-raiding and pillaging than effective military action and who in particular ignored the "Galla threat" to the empire, pp. 230–87.

226. Interview with Berhan Beruk on 20 August 1975. See above.

227. See above and Esteves Pereira, *Chronica Susneyos,* 1:viii (introduction), 1:101, 282 (text), 2:376–77 (editor's note); Perruchon, "Le Règne de Yaqob," pp. 356–61; C. Conti Rossini, "Due squarci inediti di cronica etiopica," *RRAL,* ser. 5, 2 (1893): 806, 810; Paez, *Historia,* in Beccari, *Rerum Aethiopicarum,* 3:209; Almeida, *Historia,* in Beccari, *Rerum Aethiopicarum,* 6:42–43; Telles, *The Travels of the Jesuits,* pp. 162–63; Merid, "Southern Ethiopia," pp. 356–57; Girma and Merid, *The Union of the Churches,* pp. 70–71; J. B. Coulbeaux, *Histoire politique et religieuse,* 2:173–74.

228. Perruchon, "Le Règne de Yaqob," pp. 359, 361; Conti Rossini, "Due squarci," p. 811; Esteves Pereira, *Chronica Susneyos,* 2:39; Almeida, *Historia,* in Beccari, *Rerum Aethiopicarum,* 6:59; Berry, "The Solomonic Monarchy," pp. 127–28; Merid, "Southern Ethiopia," pp. 354–70.

229. Berry, "The Solomonic Monarchy," p. 128. Berry, however, is wrong in stating his mother was the queen, Sarsa Dengel's former wife, and does not consider a possible concern by the nobles of Ya'eqob's half-Falasha origins.

230. Jules Perruchon, ed., "Règne de Susneyos ou Seltan-Saggad (1607–1632)," *RS* 5 (1897): 76, 78; Aloisius de Azevedo to Provincialem Goanum, Fremona, 22 July 1607, in Beccari, *Rerum Aethiopicarum,* 11:135. See also Ludolphus, *New History,* 178.

231. Ludolphus, *New History,* pp. 183–84; F. A. Dombrowski, "Observations on Crown-Pretendership in Seventeenth Century Russia and Ethiopia," in Sven Rubenson, ed., *Proceedings of the Seventh International Conference of Ethiopian Studies,* pp. 235–38.

232. Esteves Pereira, *Chronica Susneyos,* 1:101 (text).

233. Ibid., 1:128–31 (text).

234. Ibid., 1:150; Ignazio Guidi, "Di due frammenti relativi alla storia di Abissinia," *RRAL,* ser. 5, 2 (1893): 593–94; Paez, *Historia,* in Beccari, *Rerum Aethiopicarum,* 2:19, 3:348. He is called Amdo in the source used by Bruce: *Travels,* 2:288–89. See also Basset, "Études sur l'histoire," p. 122; Dombrowski, "Crown-Pretendership," p. 237.

235. Esteves Pereira, *Chronica Susneyos,* 1:150.

236. Ibid., 1:152–53; Paez, *Historia,* in Beccari, *Rerum Aethiopicarum,* 3:349; Bruce, *Travels,* 2:290–91; Perruchon, "Règne de Susneyos," p. 183; Basset, "Études sur l'histoire," p. 122; Foti, "La cronaca," p. 112. Sagannat is southwest of Mount Ras Dashan in Samen: Hormuzd Rassam, *Narrative of the British Mission to Theodore,* 2 vols. (London, 1869), vol. 1, map.

237. Esteves Pereira, *Chronica Susneyos,* 1:177. Yamana's proposal was also reported by Paez, who said, however, that it was Gedewon's son Walaye who was going to marry Yamana's daughter: *Historia,* in Beccari, *Rerum Aethiopicarum,* 3:362.

238. Esteves Pereira, *Chronica Susneyos,* 1:155–56; Bruce, *Travels,* 2:292–93. Bruce conflated this episode with a later revolt in which Gedewon was killed. Gedewon was not mentioned at all in connection with this massacre and mass conversion in 1617 in the long chronicle. Paez said the order to convert all Jews of Dambeya occurred in 1616: *Historia,* in Beccari, *Rerum Aethiopicarum,* 2:19.

239. Bruce, *Travels,* 2:292, note.

240. Perruchon, "Règne de Susneyos," pp. 183–84. This was during the revolt of Yolyos described below, so it may have been in 1618, not 1616.

241. Galawdewos wrote a defense of Ethiopian Christianity to justify his anti-Catholic stance; see Girma and Merid, *The Union of the Churches,* appendix I, pp. 107–10; Lino Lozza, "La confessione di Claudio Re d'Etiopia," *RSE* 5 (1946), 67–78.

242. Esteves Pereira, *Chronica Susneyos,* 1:253–54.

243. Perruchon, "Règne de Susneyos" pp. 183–84; Girma and Merid, *The Union of the Churches,* pp. 80–85.

244. Esteves Pereira, *Chronica Susneyos,* 1:271, 278–79. *Mesgada* refers to a Falasha prayer house.

245. Ibid., 1:281–82; Foti, "La cronaca," p. 113 and note 4. And see *Tarika Nagast,* a Ge'ez chronicle at Dabra Berhan Sellasse Church, Gondar, copied by And Alem Mulaw, translated to Amharic by Ato Garima Taffara, MS 361, Institute of Ethiopian Studies, Addis Ababa, p. 42; Almeida, *Historia,* in Beccari, *Rerum Aethiopicarum,* 6:413, 442–44. Gedewon's final defeat also resulted in attempts to disperse them out of Samen and Sallamt; see Almeida, *Historia,* in Beccari, *Rerum Aethiopicarum,* 6:444.

246. Esteves Pereira, *Chronica Susneyos,* 1:283; Basset, "Études sur l'histoire," pp. 124, 179 and note 263; Perruchon, "Susneyos," 186; Almeida, *Historia,* in Beccari, *Rerum Aethiopicarum,* 6:475–77.

247. Conti Rossini, "Piccole note falascia," *ASE* (1935–37): 107–11. See also Mendez, *Expeditions aethiopicai, liber I et II,* in Camillo Beccari, ed., *Rerum Aethiopi-*

carum, 8:231–55. A short written Beta Israel chronicle dating to the time of Menilek II refers to this Jew as "Abraham": Wolf Leslau, ed., "A Falasha Religious Dispute," *Proceedings of the American Academy for Jewish Research* 16 (1946–47): 79–80.

248. For two versions of the decrees, see Basset, "Études sur l'histoire," v. 18, p. 126; Foti, "Cronaca," p. 115. An excellent analysis is in Berry: "Solomonic Monarchy," pp. 5–6, 128–33.

249. Esteves Pereira, *Chronica Susneyos,* 1:307–8.

250. Interview with Berhan Beruk on 14 August 1975: *Azmach* Zakaryas was one name mentioned, reputedly an ancestor of this informant.

251. Interviews with Berhan Beruk on 3 July and 14 August 1975, Balay Malku and Sammallegne Takka on 3 September 1975, Webe Akala on 27 December 1975.

252. See Berry, "Solomonic Monarchy," p. 194 for the dates.

253. Merid, "Southern Ethiopia," pp. 504–7; Telles, *Travels of the Jesuits,* p. 206.

254. Leslau, ed., "A Falasha Religious Dispute," p. 80.

255. Luzzatto, *Mémoire,* p. 102.

256. Studies of the Amhara in this area include: Simon Messing, "The Highland-Plateau Amhara of Ethiopia" (Ph.D. dissertation, University of Pennsylvania, 1957); Allan Young, "Medical Beliefs and Practices of Begemder Amhara" (Ph.D. dissertation, University of Pennsylvania, 1970); Donald Levine, *Wax and Gold* (Chicago, 1965), pp. 18–54; Marcel Griaule, "Mythes, croyances et coutumes du Bégamder (Abyssinie)," *JA* 212 (1928): 19–123.

257. See above for explanation of this process.

258. Class analysis of African societies is often a useful framework. For the distinction between a "class in itself" and a "class for itself," which seems to apply in this case of seventeenth-century Ethiopia; see especially Emmanuel Terray, "Classes and Class Consciousness in the Abron Kingdom of Gyaman," in Maurice Bloch, ed., *Marxist Analyses and Social Anthropology,* (New York, 1975), pp. 85–135. For other samples, see Barry Hindess and Paul Q. Hirst, eds., *Pre-Capitalist Modes of Production* (London, 1975); Samir Amin, *Unequal Development* (New York, 1976); David Seddon, ed., *Relations of Production* (London, 1978); Claude Meillassoux, "From Reproduction to Production: A Marxist Approach to Economic Anthropology," *ES* 1 (1972): 93–105; Stanley Diamond, ed., *Toward a Marxist Anthropology* (The Hague, 1979); Donald Crummey and C. C. Stewart, eds., *Modes of Production in Africa* (Beverly Hills, 1981). For a critique of some of these approaches, see Robin Law, "Review Article: In Search of a Marxist Perspective on Pre-Colonial Tropical Africa," *JAH* 19 (1978): 441–52.

259. The Qemant occupational position is less well-defined before the seventeenth century, and the existence of Zalan and Wayto is extrapolated backward in time from accounts of them in the nineteenth century. On the Qemant, see Frederick Gamst, *The Qemant. A Pagan-Hebraic Peasantry of Ethiopia* (New York, 1969); J. Quirin, "The Beta Israel (Felasha) in Ethiopian History: Caste Formation and Culture Change," pp. 269–302. On the Wayto, see Frederick Gamst, "Wayto Ways: Change from Hunting to Peasant Life," in R. Hess, ed., *Proceedings of the Fifth International Conference on Ethiopian Studies, Session B, Chicago* (Chicago, 1979), pp. 233–38. The "Zalan" no longer exist as a group, but scattered references to them

occurred in the accounts of nineteenth-century travelers where they were seen as nomadic herders in Dambeya or Fogara near Tana: Samuel Gobat, *Journal,* pp. 469–70; J. L. Krapf, *Travels, Researches, and Missionary Labours* (2nd ed., London, 1968), p. 466; G. Lejean, "Notes d'un voyage en Abyssinie," *Le Tour du Monde,* 12 (1865): 241; 15 (1867): 363; Arnauld d'Abbadie, *Douze ans de séjour dans la Haute-Éthiopie (Abyssinie)* (Vatican, 1983), 3:92–94.

260. Ronald Reminick, "The Structure and Functions of Religious Belief among the Amhara of Ethiopia," in H. G. Marcus, ed., *Proceedings of the First United States Conference on Ethiopian Studies, 1973* (East Lansing, Mich., 1975), 25–42; Gedamu Abraha, "Wax and Gold," pp. 226–43, an important critique of Levine's *Wax and Gold.* Other analyses of the *rest* system emphasized the opportunities for advancement more than the tensions or inequalities associated with the system; see Allan Hoben, *Land Tenure;* Dan Bauer, *Household and Society in Ethiopia* (East Lansing, Mich., 1977).

Chapter 3

1. Fernand Braudel, *Capitalism and Material Life, 1400–1800* (New York, 1975), p. 373.

2. Their significance is downplayed by Frederick Gamst in "Peasantries and Elites Without Urbanism: The Civilization of Ethiopia," *CSSH* 12 (1970): 373–92. For data see Richard Pankhurst, "Three Urban Precursors of Gondar: Emfraz, Gorgora and Danqaz," in Robert L. Hess, ed., *Proceedings of the Fifth International Conference on Ethiopian Studies* (Chicago, 1979), pp. 415–29; idem., *History of Ethiopian Towns* (Wiesbaden, 1982). See also Akalou Wolde-Michael: "Some Thoughts on the Process of Urbanization in Pre-Twentieth Century Ethiopia," *EGJ* 5/2 (1967): 35–38; idem., "Urban Development in Ethiopia in Time and Space Perspective" (Ph.D. dissertation, UCLA, 1967); Sidney Waldron, "Harar: The Muslim City in Ethiopia," in Hess, ed., *Proceedings of the Fifth International Conference on Ethiopian Studies* (Chicago, 1979), pp. 239–57; idem., "Social Organization and Social Control in the Walled City of Harar, Ethiopia" (Ph.D. dissertation, Columbia University, 1974); Wolfgang Weissleder, "The Socio-Political Character of an Historical Ethiopian Capital," *Proceedings of the EAISR Conference held at the Institute, December 1963, part E* (Kampala: Makerere College, East African Institute of Social Research, 1964); Peter Garretson, "A History of Addis Ababa from its Foundation in 1886 to 1910," (Ph.D. dissertation, University of London, 1974).

3. Braudel, *Capitalism and Material Life,* p. 373. The ongoing work of Donald Crummey is beginning to bring a reassessment of the significance of towns: "Some Precursors of Addis Ababa: Towns in Christian Ethiopia in the Eighteenth and Nineteenth Centuries," in Ahmed Zekaria, et al., eds., *Proceedings of the International Symposium on the Centenary of Addis Ababa, 1986* (Addis Ababa, 1987), pp. 9–31.

4. On Aksum see Chapter 1 above and Yuri Kobishchanov, *Axum* (University Park, Penna., 1979) and Sergew Hable Sellassie, *Ancient and Medieval* (Addis Ababa, 1972). On Lalibela, see Achille Raffray, *Les églises monolithes de la ville de Lalibela (Abyssinie)* (Paris, 1882); George Gerster, *Churches in Rock,* Taddesse Tam-

rat, *Church and State,* pp. 53–64. See also LaVerle Berry, "A Manuscript on the Zagwes," *NAS* 3/3 (1981–82): 89–93.

5. Ronald Horvath, "The Wandering Capitals of Ethiopia," *JAH* 10 (1969): 205–19. See also Akalou Wolde-Michael, "The Impermanency of Royal Capitals in Ethiopia," *Yearbook of the Association of Pacific Coast Geographers* 28 (1966): 147–56.

6. Horvath, "Wandering Capitals," p. 212. For example, Zar'a Ya'eqob "remained for twelve years without leaving Dabra Berhan"; see L. Haber, ed., "The Chronicle of Emperor Zara Yaqob (1434–1468)," *EO* 5 (1961): 163.

7. See lists compiled from the chronicles by Pankhurst in "Notes for a History of Gondar," *EO* 12 (1969): 183, 184, 189–90.

8. André Caquot, ed., "L'homélie en l'honneur de l'archange Raguel (Dersana Ragu'el)," *AE* 2 (1957): 113–14.

9. Conti Rossini, *Historia Regis Sarṣa Dengel, CSCO* 3 (1907): 50, 133 (trans.) speaks of building at Guba'e (Guzara). On the architectural style of Guzara, see Alberto Pollera, *Storie, leggende e favole del paese dei negus* (Florence, 1936), p. 226; G. Annequin, "Château de Gouzara," *AE* 5 (1963): 23–24. David Mathew described it as a "fortress": *Ethiopia, The Study of a Polity, 1540–1935* (London, 1947), p. 38. A recent reconnaissance doubts that the ruins which are still visible at Guzara are those of a building by Sarsa Dengel: Francis Anfray, "Les monuments Gondariens des XVIIe et XVIIIe siècles, Une vue d'ensemble," in Taddesse Beyene, ed., *Proceedings of the Eighth International Conference of Ethiopian Studies, Addis Ababa, 1984,* 2 vols. (Addis Ababa, 1988), 1:24.

10. Perruchon, ed., "Règne de Susenyos," pp. 175 (text), 184 (trans.); Job Ludolphus, *New History,* pp. 15, 215; Pankhurst, "Three Urban Predecessors," pp. 415–29; idem., *Ethiopian Towns,* pp. 94–112.

11. Perruchon, ed., "Le règne de Fasiladas (Adam-Sagad), de 1632 a 1667," *RS* 5 (1897): 363 (text), 6 (1898): 86 (trans.); Basset, ed., "Études sur l'histoire d'Éthiopie" 17 (1881): 344 (text), 18 (1881): 287 (trans.); Pankhurst, *Ethiopian Towns,* p. 115.

12. Garima Taffara, "Gondarna negestatwa," *Tiyinte Gondar* [Amharic] ("Gondar and Its Kings," *Gondar Municipal Herald*) year 1, no. 8. [n.d.].

13. "History of the Land of Gondar," Amharic manuscript in possession of Jammara Wande, English translation by Asrat Seyoum, in possession of James Quirin, pp. 1–2. For other variations, see Pollera, *Storie, leggende,* pp. 88–90.

14. Ghiorghis Mellessa, "Gondar Yesterday and Today," *EO* 12 (1969): 165 says they were moved northeast of the city. Other traditions refer to moving them southwest of Gondar: interview with Mangestu Tayye on 28 August 1975. Mangestu Tayye was a resident of Gondar and was a nephew of the better known writer, *alaqa* Tayye Gabra Maryam from the early twentieth century.

15. Ibid. lists only four; the fifth, Gondaroch Maryam is somewhat further away from the city center. See also *Balambaras* Mangestu Tayye, "Short History of Gondar" (unpublished manuscript written in 1944 E.C. [Ethiopian Calendar]), trans. Wondimaghene Kassa, p. 13. I thank F. J. Simoons for a copy of this manuscript.

16. Interviews with Jammara Wande on 21 July 1975, Garima Taffara on 4 August 1975, Waka Zallalaw on 5 January 1976, and Yebbabe Zawde on 2 August 1975. Garima Taffara says Weini and Seini were from Tigray: *Tiyinte,* year 1, no. 8.

For the etymology from Tigrinya, see Arnauld d'Abbadie, *Douze ans de séjour dans la haute-Éthiopie,* 3 vols. (Vatican, 1980), 1:159–60.

17. Interview with Waka Zallalaw on 5 January 1976 (untaped). A similar story without the details of time and circumstances was told by Garima Taffara on 4 August 1975; d'Abbadie, *Douze ans,* 1:160.

18. Interviews with Berhan Beruk on 3 July and 14 August 1975. The informant also claimed descent from Gedewon and from Seini, said to be a "granddaughter" of Gedewon who married Zakaryas, a "grandson" of Gedewon. Other genealogical information has Zakaryas as a great-great grandson of Gedewon: Admas Chakkol, "Descendants of Gedewon" (unpublished manuscript read into a tape on 16 December 1975, in Endabaguna, Tigray).

19. Interview with Berhan Beruk on 14 August 1975.

20. Interview with Mulunah Marsha, Tafari Neguse, and Qanu Ayyalaw on 22 November 1975.

21. Interview with Kasagne Alamayahu on 31 August 1975 and Neguse Warqu on 25 November 1975. A manuscript I saw in the possession of Neguse Warqu, a Qemant informant living at Gondaroch Maryam, contained the assertion that the Qemant were the "original inhabitants of Begamder" but that later the Tigrayans came and Gondar was established.

22. J. Tubiana, "Les noms de Gondar et d'Aksum," *GLECS* 8 (1958): 26. One popular derivation is from *guang dara,* which in Qemantinya is said to mean "between two rivers," i.e., the Angarab and Qeha which flow by each side of the city; see Ghiorghis Mellessa, "Gondar Yesterday and Today," p. 166.

23. Perruchon, "d'Amda Ṣyon," 14 (1889): 293 (text), 339 (trans.).

24. Mangestu Tayye, "Short History of Gondar," p. 3.

25. See the overview of Gondar and its stone buildings which gave it more permanence: Pankhurst, *Ethiopian Towns,* pp. 115–38.

26. Gideon Sjoberg, *The Pre-Industrial City, Past and Present.* (Glencoe, Ill., 1960). For a description of different ideal types of relationships between class structure and residential patterns, see Bruce London and William G. Flanagan, "Comparative Urban Ecology: A Summary of the Field," in John Walton and Louis H. Masotti, eds., *The City in Comparative Perspective* (New York, 1976), pp. 41–66. See also D. Jemma, *Les tanneurs de marrakech* (Algiers, 1971); and Janet Abu-Lughod, "The Legitimacy of Comparisons in Comparative Urban Studies, A Theoretical Position and an Application to North African Cities," in Walton and Masotti, *The City,* pp. 17–39. As in Gondar, in Ankobar, Ethiopia, "low-caste" artisans were also "pushed to the periphery of the community": Wolfgang Weissleder, "The Socio-Political Character of an Historical Ethiopian Capital," p. 10.

27. Interview with Jammara Wande, 21 July 1975.

28. William Jones, "A Conversation with Abram, an Abyssinian, Concerning the City of Gwender and the Sources of the Nile," *Asiatik Researches* [Calcutta], 1 (1786): 383.

29. James Bruce, *Travels,* 3:380.

30. Eighty thousand: Ghiorghis Mellessa, "Gondar Yesterday and Today," p. 166; 280,000: Garima Taffara, "Gondar and Its Kings," *Tiyinte Gondar,* year 1, no. 7, [no pages].

31. Horvath, "Wandering Capitals," pp. 212–13. On Gondar's stone construction, see Otto Jager and Ivy Pearce, *Antiquities of North Ethiopia,* 2nd ed. (Stuttgart, 1974), pp. 38–60.

32. For lists of periods of royal residence in the city, see Pankhurst, "Notes for a history," pp. 177, 183, 184, 189.

33. See below for analysis of Beta Israel land grants.

34. Garima, "Gondar and Its Kings," [Amharic], unpublished manuscript (1975), p. 16; Crummey, "Precursors of Addis Ababa," p. 22.

35. Ludolphus, *New History,* p. 395 mentions the trade routes through Gondar. Fasilidas sought to expand trade through diplomatic relations with Yemen: Hasan ben Ahmed El-Haimi, *Zur Geschichte Abessiniens im 17. Jahrhundert,* ed. F. E. Peiser (Berlin, 1898); E. van Donzel, "Correspondence between Fasilidas and the Imams of Yemen," in Gideon Goldenberg, ed., *Ethiopian Studies. Proceedings of the Sixth International Conference, Tel-Aviv, 1980* (Rotterdam, 1986), pp. 91–100; idem., *A Yemenite Embassy to Ethiopia, 1647–1649* (Wiesbaden, 1986). The slave trade was significant; see Merid Wolde Aregay, "Southern Ethiopia," pp. 303–4, 543–44; Richard Caulk, "Review of Richard Pankhurst, *History of Ethiopian Towns,*" in *IJAHS* 16 (1983): 764; Mordechai Abir, "Trade and Christian-Muslim Relations in Post-Medieval Ethiopia," in Robert L. Hess, ed., *Proceedings of the Fifth International Conference on Ethiopian Studies, Chicago, 1978* (Chicago, 1979), pp. 411–14; idem., "The Ethiopian Slave Trade and its Relation to the Islamic World," in John Ralph Willis, ed., *Slaves and Slavery in Muslim Africa,* 2 vols. (London, 1985), 2:123–36; Ralph Austen, "The Islamic Red Sea Slave Trade: An Effort at Quantification," in R. L. Hess, ed., *Proceedings of the Fifth International Conference,* p. 451; Richard Pankhurst, "The Ethiopian Slave Trade in the Nineteenth and Early Twentieth Centuries: A Statistical Enquiry," *JSS* 9 (1964): 220–28; idem., *Economic History of Ethiopia, 1800–1935* (Addis Ababa, 1968), pp. 82–84.

36. Donald Crummey, "Gondarine *Rim* Land Sales: An Introductory Description and Analysis," Robert L. Hess, ed., *Proceedings of the Fifth International Conference,* pp. 470, 474. See also Daniel Ayana, "Gult and Ethiopian Social Structure," paper presented to the African Studies Association annual meeting, Chicago, 1988.

37. Peter Garretson, "History of Addis Ababa," pp. 55, 109–14.

38. See lists of these names which do not always agree, probably because the gates often acquired more than one name over the years: Pankhurst, "History of Gondar," p. 182; Garima, "Gondar and Its Kings," pp. 30–31; Ghiorghis, "Gondar Yesterday," p. 167; Mangestu Tayye, "Short History of Gondar," p. 14. On residential and other quarters, see also A. Ferret and M. Galinier, *Voyages en Abyssinie,* 3 vols. (Paris, 1847), and atlas; Guillaume Lejean, "Notes d'un voyage en Abyssinie," *Le tour du monde* 9 (1864): 69–80; 12 (1865): 221–72; 15 (1867): 353–400, and map, 12 (1865): 250; fieldwork observations. The nineteenth-century maps and observations were, of course, based on what had been created during the previous two hundred years.

39. Lejean, "Notes d'un voyage," 12 (1865): 246; Eduard Rüppell, *Reise in Abyssinien,* 2 vols. (Frankfurt, 1838–40), 2:81, 104; Gerhard Rohlfs, *Meine Mission nach Abessinien* (Leipzig, 1883), pp. 260, 265; Arnauld d'Abbadie, *Douze ans,* 1:162–

63; Coffin in Nathaniel Pearce, *The Life and Adventures of Nathaniel Pearce . . . 1810–1819,* 2 vols. (London, 1831), 1:234–35; interview with Garima Taffara on 25 August 1975. See summary of settlement areas in Pankhurst, "Notes for the History," infra, and idem., *Ethiopian Towns,* pp. 255–57.

40. Lejean, "Notes d'un voyage," 12 (1865): 246, 250 (map); Plowden, *Travels in Abyssinia* (London, 1868), p. 42.

41. Rüppell, *Reise in Abyssinien,* 2:81; Plowden, *Travels in Abyssinia,* p. 42; Arnauld d'Abbadie, *Douze ans:* 1:161–62.

42. Van Donzel, *Yemenite Embassy,* pp. 143–45; El-Haimi, *Zur Geschichte Abessiniens,* p. 35; Ignazio Guidi, ed., *Annales Iohannis I, Iyasu I, Bakafa. CSCO,* ser. alt. 5 (1903): 8, 37; idem., *Annales Iyasu II et Iyo'as, CSCO,* 2 vols., ser. alt. 6 (1910, 1912): 76; James Bruce, *Travels,* 3:198, 4:71; Coffin in Pearce, *Life and Adventures,* 1:235; Lejean, "Notes d'un voyage," 12:246; Rüppell, *Reise in Abyssinien,* 2:78, 82; Rohlfs, *Meine Mission,* p. 260; Arnauld d'Abbadie, *Douze ans:* 1:162; Dillon, in Theophile Lefebvre, *Voyage en Abyssinie,* 6 vols. (Paris, 1845), 1:164–65; Ferret and Galinier, *Voyages en Abyssinie,* 2:238. See J. S. Trimingham, *Islam in Ethiopia* (London, 1952) for information on this group in general. More research is needed on their role in Ethiopia and Gondar in particular.

43. Garima, "Gondar and Its Kings," pp. 17–18; Jammara Wande, "Lists of Offices," unpublished manuscript [n.p.], lists the *quad serri* as a group of officials concerned with Muslim artisans. On Fasiladas's embassy to Yemen, see F. Praetorius, ed., "Ein arabisches Document sur äthiopischen Geschichte," *ZDMG* 39 (1885): 403–8.

44. Coffin in Pearce, *Life and Adventures,* 1:235–36; Garima, "Gondar and Its Kings," p. 17.

45. Edmond Combes and Maurice Tamisier, *Voyage en Abyssinie, . . . 1835–1837,* 4 vols. (Paris, 1838), 3:343; Bruce, *Travels,* 3:376.

46. Interviews with Jammara Wande on 21 July, 31 July, and 26 August 1975; Yebbabe Zawde on 2 August 1975; Neguse Eshate on 6 October 1975; Gete Asrass on 9 November 1975; Webe Akala on 27 December 1975; Neguse Warqu on 25 November 1975; Walda Sellase Aggadaw on 5 August 1975; Denqayyahu Radda on 7 October 1975; Garima Taffara on 4 August 1975; Kasagne Alamayahu on 31 August 1975; Mulunah Marsha, Tafari Neguse, and Qanu Ayyalew on 22 November 1975; Adugna Gabreyya on 7 October 1975; and Denqayyahu Radda and Yelma Yalaw on 26 December 1975. See also Bruce, *Travels,* 4:275–76; Samuel Gobat, *Journal,* p. 469; Plowden in *Parliamentary Papers: Correspondence,* p. 110; Lejean, *Voyage,* p. 2; Stern, *Wanderings,* pp. 44–45; de Cosson, *Cradle of the Blue Nile,* 2:144–45; Halévy, "Travels," p. 243; Rassam, *Narrative,* 1:209; Dillon in Lefebvre, *Voyage en Abyssinie,* 1:167–68; Van Heuglin, "Bruchstucke aus einer Reise in Abyssinien," *DA* 26 (1853): 813–14. On the Qemant at Dafacha, see C. Conti Rossini, *La langue des Kemant en Abyssinie* (Vienna, 1912), p. 313. On references to the Qemant in Amharic literature, see Roger Cowley, "Preliminary Notes on the balaandem Commentaries," *JES* 9/1 (1971): 19. For further analysis of the Qemant, see Quirin, "The Beta Israel (Felasha) in Ethiopian History," pp. 269–302; Frederick Gamst, *The Qemant.*

47. Suzanne Miers and Igor Kopytoff, eds., *Slavery in Africa Historical and Anthropological Perspectives* (Madison, Wisc., 1977); Frederick Cooper, "The Prob-

lem of Slavery in African Studies," *JAH* 20 (1979): 103–25; Paul Lovejoy, ed., *The Ideology of Slavery in Africa* (Beverly Hills, 1981); idem., *Transformations in Slavery* (Cambridge, 1983); John Ralph Willis, ed., *Slaves and Slavery in Muslim Africa,* 2 vols. (London, 1985). On Ethiopian slavery, see Pankhurst, "The History of the Bareya, Shanqella and other Ethiopian Slaves from the Borderland of the Sudan," *SNR* 59 (1977): 1–43; James McCann, "'Children of the House': Slavery and its Suppression in Lasta, Northern Ethiopia, 1916–1975," in Suzanne Miers and Richard Roberts, eds., *The End of Slavery in Africa* (Madison, Wisc., 1988), pp. 332–61.

48. Interviews with Garima Taffara on 4 August and 25 August 1975 and with Jammara Wande on 26 August 1975. War captives such as Agaw, Oromo, and "Shanqilla" were both enslaved domestically and exported: Perruchon, "Le règne de Fasilidas," p. 90; Guidi, *Annales Iohannis,* pp. 17, 28–29, 69–77, 134; Manoel de Almeida, "The History of High Ethiopia or Abassia," in C. F. Beckingham and G. W. B. Huntingford, eds., *Some Records of Ethiopia, 1593–1646* (London, 1954), p. 75; Bruce, *Travels,* 2:551–58, 3:54, 91, 385; Lefebvre, *Voyage en Abyssinie,* 1:lxvii. Also on the slave trade, see Merid, "Southern Ethiopia," pp. 287–88, 303–4; LaVerle Berry, "The Solomonic Monarchy at Gondar," pp. 273–79; Abir, "The Ethiopian Slave Trade," in Willis, *Slaves and Slavery,* 2:124, 128.

49. Garima Taffara, "Gondar and Its Kings," pp. 14–18. On the "Faras Bet," see Guidi, *Annales Regum Iyasu II et Iyo'as,* p. 77. On the Wayto, see Bruce, *Travels,* 3:402; Dillon in Lefebvre, *Voyage en Abyssinie,* 1:169. It was suggested that during the reign of Iyyasu I, the light cane carried by soldiers was substituted by a whip of hippopotamus hide, probably indicating the involvement of the Wayto, who were hippopotamus hunters: J. B. Coulbeaux, *Histoire politique et religieuse,* 2:299. On the Agaw, see Bruce, *Travels,* 3:736, 4:27. See the survey in Pankhurst, "Notes for a History," pp. 209–13.

50. Interview with Gete Asrass on 11 June 1975 and Berhan Beruk on 3 July 1975.

51. See Chapter 2 above.

52. Ludolphus, *New History,* pp. 390–91. See also Almeida, *High Ethiopia,* pp. 54–55.

53. The names of weavers known individually in Gondar's history were all Muslims; interview with Garima Taffara on 2 September 1975. Artisan officers in these crafts were all Muslims; Jammara Wande, "Lists of Offices" [n.p.].

54. See Chapter 2 above. On Gondar, see Almeida, *High Ethiopia,* pp. 54–55; Balthazar Telles, *Travels of the Jesuits,* p. 38; Ludolphus, *New History,* pp. 390–91.

55. Interviews with Garima Taffara on 4 August 1975 and with Berhan Beruk on 3 July 1975.

56. Asma Giyorgis, *Asma Giyorgis and His Work: History of the Galla and the Kingdom of Sawa,* ed. Bairu Tafla (Stuttgart, 1987). See also Volker Stitz, "The Amhara Resettlement of Northern Shoa During the Eighteenth and Nineteenth Centuries," *RA* 11 (1970): 79; Donald Levine, *Wax and Gold,* pp. 33–34.

57. See Chapter 2 above.

58. Ludolphus, *New History,* pp. 73, 390–91.

59. Interviews with Berhan Beruk on 3 July 1975 and 14 August 1975, with Balay Malku and Sammallegne Takka on 3 September 1975, and with Webe Akala on 27 December 1975.

60. Telles, *Travels of the Jesuits,* p. 206.

61. Ludolphus, *New History,* pp. 73, 390–91; James Bruce, *Travels,* 2:634, 3:123, 195; Guidi, *Annales Iyasu II,* p. 98; interviews with the Beta Israel: Berhan Beruk on 3 July and 14 August 1975; Menase Zammaru and Wande Iyyasu on 13 October 1975; Gete Asrass on 3 June, 11 June, and 9 November 1975. Interviews with the Amhara: Jammara Wande on 21 July 1975, Garima Taffara on 4 August 1975. Interviews with the Qemant: Mulunah Marsha, Tafari Neguse, and Qanu Ayyalaw on 22 November 1975. Not many scholars have discussed the question of who were the main builders, but of those who have, Conti Rossini suggested the importance of the Beta Israel ("Kayla"): "I Castelli di Gondar," *BSGI,* ser. 7, 4 (1939): 165. A general summary by Coulbeaux said the workers included the "disciples" of the Portuguese and Paez, the Falasha, and some "Indians" *Histoire,* 1:12. The palace built at Saqota in Lasta as a result of the agreement between Fasiladas and the ruler of Lasta probably involved some Beta Israel workers from Gondar: Richard Pankhurst, "Wag and Lasta: An Essay in the Regional History of Ethiopia from the 14th Century to 1800," in Sven Rubenson, ed., *Proceedings of the Seventh International Conference of Ethiopian Studies, Lund, 1982* (Addis Ababa, 1984), 219.

62. Van Donzel, *Yemenite Embassy,* p. 151; El-Haimi, *Zur Geschichte Abessiniens,* pp. 38–39.

63. Pankhurst, "Notes for the History of Gondar," pp. 178, 180.

64. Conti Rossini, "I Castelli di Gondar," p. 165. Masons were said to have been brought from India; see Jeronymo Lobo, *A Short Relation of the River Nile* (London, 1791), pp. 28–29.

65. Guidi, *Annales Iohannis,* pp. 60, 89.

66. Garima Taffara, "A History of Gondar," *Tiyinte Gonder,* year 1, no. 9.

67. For *tabiban,* see discussion in Chapters 1 and 4. Interview with Jammara Wande on 21 July 1975 mentioned Taklu.

68. Interview with Berhan Beruk on 3 July 1975. In the usually cited Christian version of this tradition, the building kept falling down because Fasiladas was being punished for keeping concubines even after his marriage. God allowed this work to continue only after Fasiladas promised to build churches to appease him; interview with Jammara Wande on 21 July 1975, and see compilation by Pankhurst, "Notes for a History of Gondar," pp. 177–79.

69. See above, Chapter 2 for this reference.

70. Interviews with Berhan Beruk on 3 July and 14 August 1975; Merid, "Southern Ethiopia," p. 565.

71. Guidi, *Annales Iohannis,* pp. 19, 21–22.

72. De Maillet, 12 May 1698, in Camillo Beccari, ed., *Rerum Aethiopicarum,* 15 vols. (Rome, 1903–17), 14:32; Antonio Maria Nacchi July 1698, in ibid., 14:43.

73. D'Abbadie, "Journal," p. 462.

74. Interview with Berhan Beruk on 3 July 1975.

75. Bruce, *Travels,* 2:634.

76. Interview with Berhan Beruk on 3 July 1975.

77. Ibid.

78. At Kayla Meda (d'Abbadie, "Journal," p. 302), and at Dafacha (Stern, *Wanderings,* p. 207).

79. Interview with Jammara Wande on 21 July 1975.

80. Hoben, *Land Tenure.*

81. Taddesse Tamrat, *Church and State,* pp. 98–103; Simon Messing, "The Highland-Plateau Amhara," p. 252.

82. Crummey, "Gondarine *rim* Land," pp. 472–73; idem., "Precursors of Addis Ababa," p. 24.

83. Bruce, *Travels,* 2:633–34; Richard Pankhurst, "Greek Land-Holding in Eighteenth and Early Nineteenth Century Ethiopia," *Abba Salama* 4 (1973): 36–39.

84. The five landlords' churches were Abwara Giyorgis, Arba'ettu Ensesa, Qeha Iyyasus, Gondaroch Giyorgis, and Gondaroch Maryam. In some lists, ten other churches are said to have been built by the "natives of the place" rather than a specific Gondar king: Mangestu Tayye, "Short History of Gondar" (1944 E.C.), p. 13. Traditions on their origins were recorded in interviews with Jammara Wande on 21 July 1975, Garima Taffara on 4 August 1975, Mangestu Tayye on 28 August 1975, Neguse Warqu on 25 November 1975, Waka Zallalaw on 5 January 1976; Berhan Beruk on 20 August 1975.

85. Interviews with Gete Asrass on 11 June and 9 November 1975, Menase Zammaru and Wande Iyyasu on 13 October 1975, and Webe Akala on 27 December 1975; Guidi, *Iyasu II,* pp. 137, 209, 211.

86. Garima Taffara, "Gondar and Its Kings," p. 16. The Beta Israel potter Gondarit was said to live at Kayla Meda during Fasiladas's reign; interview with Gete Asrass on 9 November 1975.

87. Guidi, *Annales Iohannis,* pp. 8, 37; Basset, "Études sur l'histoire," pp. 291–92.

88. D'Abbadie, "Réponses des Falasha," *AI* 12 (1851): 240.

89. Interviews with Berhan Beruk on 14 August 1975, Gete Asrass on 9 November 1975, and Webe Akala on 27 December 1975.

90. Interview with Waka Zallalew on 5 January 1976. Another tradition asserted Abwara was the earliest area of Beta Israel settlement before the founding of Gondar; interview with Gete Asrass on 9 November 1975.

91. Beta Israel lived there up to the early twentieth century; see Deborah Lifchitz, "Un sacrifice chez les Falacha, juifs abyssins," *La terre et la vie* 9 (1939): 116–23. Qemant also lived there; interview with Neguse Warqu at Gondaroch Maryam on 25 November 1975.

92. Interviews with Berhan Beruk on 3 July and 14 August 1975 and with Webe Akala on 27 December 1975.

93. Interview with Balay Malku and Sammallegne Takka at Azazo on 3 September 1975.

94. A near contemporary description of the castle is in van Donzel, *Yemenite Embassy,* pp. 149–51. The seven churches were Fit Mika'el, Fit Abo, Adababay Iyyasus, Gemja-Bet-Maryam, Elfen Giyorgis, Madhane Alam, Qeddus Gabra'el; see Garima Taffara, "Gondar and Its Kings," pp. 39–40; Mangestu Tayye, "Short History of Gondar," p. 13. The chronicle mentions only two of these; Perruchon, "Fasiladas," p. 88. It is debatable whether he actually had the "Fasil's Bath," popularly assigned to him, built; see Pankhurst, "Gondar," pp. 181, 194–95; Ghiorghis, "Gondar Yesterday," p. 174. Rüppell was told by some knowledgeable elders that it was built by Iyyasu I; *Reise in Abyssinien,* 2:118. For an overview of the major

churches of the Gondar era, including a description of their paintings, see Jager and Pearce, *Antiquities,* pp. 47–60.

95. Guidi, *Annales Iohannis,* pp. 60, 172; Guidi, *Annales Iyasu II,* p. 36. Ghiorghis Mellessa, oral communication, 27 December 1975. Mangestu Tayye, "Short History of Gondar," pp. 5, 13; Garima Taffara, "Gondar and Its Kings," *Tiyinte Gondar,* year 1, no. 7; Mangestu Tayye, "Short History of Gondar," p. 13. See also Pankhurst, "Gondar," p. 183; Wilhelm Staude, "Étude sur la décoration picturale des églises Abba Antonios de Gondar et Dabra Sina de Gorgora," *AE* 3 (1959): 185–235.

96. Guidi, *Annales Iohannis,* p. 40.

97. For Abba Entonyos: interviews with Zallaqa Damoze on 28 November 1975 and with Desse Yeshaq on 8 January 1976. For Tadda: interview on 10 August 1975 with Ratta Zawde, who claimed descent from the original *rest*-holder of this land; interviews with Garima Taffara on 25 August 1975 and with Jammara Wande on 31 July 1975.

98. Ibid. A *kelad* is about 500 × 800 meters; see Ghiorghis, "Gonder Yesterday," p. 164.

99. Mahteme Sellassie Wolde Meskal, "The Land System of Ethiopia," p. 288; Mangestu Tayye, "A Short History of Gondar," p. 6; interviews with Jammara Wande on 31 July 1975 and with Garima Taffara on 4 August 1975.

100. One source suggests he gave land rights to the Beta Israel: interview with Garima Taffara on 4 August 1975. Qemant traditions view Iyyasu as settling their land disputes; interviews with Kasagne Alamayahu on 31 August 1975, with Denqayyahu Radda on 7 October 1975, and with Denqayyahu Radda and Yelma Yalaw on 26 December 1975.

101. On the church, see Guidi, *Annales Iohannis,* pp. 314, 239; Anfray, "Monuments Gondariens," p. 12. Oral traditions are uncertain about the Beta Israel settlement date there; interviews with Berhan Beruk on 3 July and 14 August 1975 and with Gete Asrass on 9 November 1975.

102. Guidi, *Annales Iyasu II,* pp. 52–54, 89–90, 95–114.

103. Interviews with Gete Asrass on 11 June and 9 November 1975, with Berhan Beruk on 14 August 1975, and with Zallaqa Damoze on 28 November 1975.

104. Bruce, *Travels,* 2:634.

105. Interview with Zallaqa Damoze on 28 November 1975. The Beta Israel may have been granted land at Dambeya by Mentewwab (interview with Berhan Beruk on 14 August 1975), or by *Dejazmach* Maru in the early nineteenth century (interview with Sandaqqe Maharan, who claimed descent from the original holder of that land, on 24 October 1975). Gallager is near the Saqqalt region.

106. Interviews with Jammara Wande on 21 July and 26 August 1975 and with Garima Taffara on 25 August 1975 (Amhara informants). For Beta Israel traditions: interview with Berhan Beruk on 3 July 1975. The *bejrond* was later called "the best or oldest workman in their towns": Pearce, *Life and Adventures,* 2:15.

107. Interviews with Berhan Beruk on 14 August, Gete Asrass on 9 November, Yeshaq Iyyasu on 15 December, Webe Akala on 27 December, and Menase Zammaru and Wande Iyyasu on 13 October 1975.

108. Guidi, *Annales Iohannis,* p. 152; G. W. B. Huntingford, ed., *The Land Charters of Northern Ethiopia,* p. 110.

109. Interview with Webe Akala on 27 December 1975.

110. See Chapter 4 below.

111. Guidi, *Annales Iohannis,* pp. 15, 18, 53–54, 61, 152; Guidi, *Annales Iyasu II,* pp. 48–49, 51, 126–27, 155, 166, 168, 173, 194, 227, 234. In response to Berry's question, I found no evidence that *agafari* was originally a Beta Israel title; Berry, "Solomonic Monarchy," p. 306, note 3.

112. Webe's ancestry is not generally discussed, since he did not act as a Beta Israel advocate: interviews with Berhan Beruk on 20 August 1975, Admas Chakkol on 16 December 1975; d'Abbadie, "Journal," p. 463; d'Abbadie, "Réponses des Falasha," p. 267; A. Ferret and M. Galinier, *Voyages en Abyssinie,* 1:424–25. See Chapter 4 below, also on Webe.

113. Interviews with Berhan Beruk on 14 August and 20 August 1975. *Qes* Berhan claimed descent from Zakaryas, who was in the line of descent from the fifteenth-century Gedewon who fought *ase* Yeshaq. See also Admas Chakkol, "Beta Israel Genealogies," unpublished manuscript, 1975, copy in possession of James Quirin.

114. Esteves Pereira, *Chronica de Susenyos,* 1:278 (text).

115. Interview with Berhan Beruk on 14 August 1975.

116. Interviews with Berhan Beruk on 14 August 1975, Gete Asrass on 9 November 1975, and Yeshaq Iyyasu on 15 December 1975.

117. Mendez, in Beccari, *Rerum Aethiopicarum,* 8:231–55.

118. Wolf Leslau, ed., "A Falasha Religious Dispute," pp. 79–80, note 16.

119. Interviews with Berhan Beruk on 14 August 1975, with Gete Asrass on 9 November 1975, with Webe Akala on 27 December 1975, with Menase Zammaru and Wande Iyyasu on 13 October 1975, and with Admas Chakkol on 16 December 1975.

120. Interview on 10 August 1975 with Ratta Zawde, who was the leader of the Beta Israel community at Tedda in 1975 and claimed descent from Ya'eqob.

121. Ibid. Also interviews with Yeheyyes Madhane and Yalaw Siyamer on 27 October 1975 and with Yeshaq Iyyasu on 15 December 1975. He was also remembered as a Beta Israel *azmach* by an Amhara informant; interview with Jammara Wande on 31 July 1975, though he put his lifetime during the reign of Iyyasu I.

122. Interviews with Berhan Beruk on 3 July, 14 August, and 20 August 1975; with Gete Asrass on 11 June and 9 November 1975; with Webe Akala on 27 December 1975; and with Enneyaw Tarraqagne on 30 December 1975. Mammo was also remembered in Amhara traditions; interview with Jammara Wande on 31 July 1975.

123. Interviews with Menase Zammaru and Wande Iyyasu on 13 October 1975, with Gete Asrass on 9 November 1975, with Webe Akala on 27 December 1975, and with Enneyaw Tarraqagne on 30 December 1975.

124. Basset, "Études sur l'histoire," pp. 308, 363; Guidi, *Annales Iohannis,* pp. 308–9; Guidi, *Annales Iyasu II,* pp. 76–77. On crown-pretendership, including Hezkeyas, see Franz Amadeus Dombrowski, "Observations on Crown-Pretendership in Seventeenth Century Russia and Ethiopia," in Sven Rubenson, ed., *Proceedings of the Seventh International Conference of Ethiopian Studies, Lund, Sweden, 1982* (Uppsala, 1984), pp. 233–241.

125. Basset, "Études sur l'histoire," pp. 287, 317, 347–48, 350; Guidi, *Annales Iohannis,* p. 315; Guidi, *Annales Iyasu II,* pp. 51, 126–27; Bruce, *Travels,* 2:611.

126. Guidi, *Annales Iohannis*, pp. 310, 336; Guidi, *Annales Iyasu II*, p. 55; Bruce, *Travels*, 2:619–20.

127. Interviews with Berhan Beruk on 14 August and 20 August 1975, with Gete Asrass on 11 June and 9 November 1975, with Webe Akala on 27 December 1975, and with Enneyaw Tarraqagne on 30 December 1975.

128. Interview with Berhan Beruk on 20 August 1975.

129. See Chapter 1 above.

130. Interview with Gete Asrass on 9 November 1975.

131. Interview with Berhan Beruk on 14 August 1975.

132. Huntingford, *Land Charters*, pp. 48, 110.

133. Interviews with Jammara Wande on 31 July 1975, with Garima Taffara on 25 August 1975, with Mangestu Tayye on 28 August 1975.

134. Interview with Jammara Wande on 31 July 1975. Another informant said the artisans paid taxes to one person but could not say what his title was; interview with Walda Sellase Aggadaw on 5 August 1975. Leaders of other artisans, such as weavers, were said to pay twelve *shamma* annually; see Garima Taffara, "Taxes or Gifts," unpublished manuscript, 1975, p. 1.

135. Interview with Tafassaku Webshat on 15 December 1975.

136. Interviews with Berhan Beruk on 3 July 1975 and 14 August 1975. *Maggābi* was a "steward" connected with a church or monastery; Huntingford, *Land Charters*, p. 107, and interviews with Jammara Wande on 31 July 1975 and Yebbabe Zawde on 2 August 1975. *Terabi* was said to be another word for carpenter.

137. Interview with Jammara Wande on 21 July 1975.

138. Guidi, *Annales Iyasu II*, p. 98. This passage also referred to an *azaj* Mammo, also working on the church, perhaps providing a substantiation of the Beta Israel traditions concerning a Mammo.

139. Interviews with Gete Asrass on 9 November 1975 and with Menase Zammaru and Wande Iyyasu on 13 October 1975.

140. For the theoretical distinction between institutional and social incorporation, see, for example, Milton Gordon, *Assimilation in American Life* (New York, 1964); Fredrik Barth, ed., *Ethnic Groups and Boundaries* (Bergen, Norway, 1969); Michael Parenti, "Ethnic Politics and the Persistence of Ethnic Identification," *APSR* 61 (1967): 717–26; Jennie-Keith Ross, "Social Borders: Definitions of Diversity," *Current Anthropology* 16 (1975): 53–72; R. A. Schermerhorn, *Comparative Ethnic Relations* (New York, 1970).

141. Interview with Garima Taffara on 2 September 1975.

142. Interview with Jammara Wande on 26 August 1975.

143. Interview with Garima Taffara on 2 September 1975.

144. Jeronymo Lobo, *Relation historique d'Abyssinie*, trans. M. le Grand (Paris, 1728), p. 65.

145. Charles Poncet, "A Voyage to Ethiopia in the Years 1698, 1699 and 1700" [London, 1709], in Sir William Foster, ed., *The Red Sea and Adjacent Countries at the Close of the Seventeenth Century* (London, 1949), p. 125. Some years later, Bruce observed the purification of "platters and pots" that had been used by Muslims and Beta Israel by immersing them during the celebration of the Epiphany in Adwa: *Travels*, 3:326.

146. Ludolphus, *New History,* pp. 390–91; Emmanuel Barradas, *Tractatus Tres Historico-Geographici,* in Beccari, *Rerum Aethiopicarum,* 4:61.

147. Bruce, *Travels,* 4:83.

148. Admas Chakkol, "Attempts Made to Exterminate the Beta Israel," (unpublished manuscript in possession of James Quirin), p. 7; Barradas mentions the *buda* in the seventeenth century: *Tractatus,* in Beccari, *Rerum Aethiopicarum,* 4:61. See also Robert Reminick, "The Evil Eye Belief among the Amhara of Ethiopia," *Ethnology* 13 (1974): 279–94; Stefan Strelcyn, "Les écrits médicaux éthiopiens," *JES* 3/1 (1965): 82–103; James Quirin, "A Preliminary Analysis of New Archival Sources," pp. 396, 405–8.

149. Wilhelm Staude, "Le mauvais œil dans la peinture Chrétienne d'Abyssinie," *JA* 225 (October–December 1934): 231, 240. On these paintings at Abba Entonyos, see also Wilhelm Staude, "Étude sur la décoration picturale," pp. 185–235.

150. See Chapter 4 for further discussion of the *buda.*

151. Donald Crummey, "Society and Ethnicity," p. 268.

152. Taddesse Tamrat, *Church and State,* pp. 89–103.

153. Interview with Jammara Wande on 21 July 1975; interview with Neguse Eshate on 6 October 1975. In general, all Amhara informants agreed on these criteria; interviews with Jammara Wande on 26 August 1975 and with Garima Taffara on 2 September 1975.

154. On *chewa,* see Alvares, *The Prester John of the Indies,* 2:412; Getatchew Haile, "Some Notes on 'A Text in Old Amharic,' of Roger Cowley," *BSOAS* 43 (1980): 580.

155. Merid Wolde Aregay, "Southern Ethiopia," chapters 4 and 6; Berry, "Solomonic Monarchy," pp. 251–63.

156. Bruce, *Travels,* 2:551–52, 3:266, 310–11; Berry, "Solomonic Monarchy," pp. 257–58.

157. Guidi, *Annales Iohannis,* pp. 19, 21–22; De Maillet in Beccari, *Rerum Aethiopicarum,* 14:32; Nacchi in Beccari, 14:43 (see note 72 above for full reference); Guidi, *Annales Iyasu II,* p. 35. See Berry, "Solomonic Monarchy," pp. 260–63 on the Oromo.

158. Almeida, "High Ethiopia," p. 75; interviews with Garima Taffara on 4 August and 25 August 1975, with Jammara Wande on 26 August 1975.

159. Guidi, *Annales Iohannis,* p. 134.

160. Several kings engaged in slave raiding, such as Fasiladas and Iyyasu I: Berry, "Solomonic Monarchy," pp. 8, 23–24; Poncet, "A Voyage," pp. 136–37.

161. Berry, "Solomonic Monarchy," pp. 178–81.

162. This interpretation is derived from the tradition that Yohannes personally engaged in craftwork such as basket-making or mat- and rug-weaving so that he would not have to tax the peasantry; interview with Garima Taffara on 4 August 1975; "History of the Land of Gondar," pp. 6–7; Mangestu Tayye, "History of Gondar," p. 5; Berry, "Solomonic Monarchy," p. 19, n. 1. Such workshops were common among Ethiopian kings before and after Yohannes, such as Zara Ya'eqob (see Chapter 2 above), Tewodros (see Chapter 4 below), and Menilek; see Harold Marcus, "The Organization of Menilek II's Palace and Imperial Hospitality (After 1896)," *RA* 11 (1970): 57–62.

163. Interviews with Jammara Wande on 31 July 1975, with Berhan Beruk on 14 August 1975, with Mangestu Tayye on 28 August 1975, with Kasagne Alamayahu on 31 August 1975, with Yebbabe Zawde on 2 August 1975, and with Garima Taffara on 25 August 1975. On household servants or slaves, see Ludolphus, *New History,* p. 213.

164. Interviews with Gete Asrass on 11 June 1975, with Berhan Beruk on 3 July and 14 August 1975, with Jammara Wande on 21 July and 31 July 1975, with Ratta Zawde on 10 August 1975, and with Zallaqe Damoze on 28 November 1975; Guidi, *Annales Iohannis,* pp. 8, 37; Bruce, *Travels,* 3:195.

165. Interview with Jammara Wande on 21 July 1975, with Yebbabe Zawde on 2 August 1975, and with Denqayyahu Radda on 7 October 1975.

166. At unknown times, Muslims were granted land at Walaka (just north of Gondar), Azazo, and Wallaj (between Walaka and Kerkerr); interviews with Jammara Wande on 21 July 1975 and Berhan Beruk on 14 August 1975. They had been in Samen, at least since the invasion by Ahmad Ibrahim "Gragn." In general, see Trimingham, *Islam in Ethiopia,* pp. 150–53. In Samen, one center was near Mount Silki where Iyyasu I established a customs post; Guidi, *Annales Iohannis,* p. 207. Several later travelers noted the existence of Muslim villages in Samen; H. C. Maydon, *Simen, Its Heights and Abysses* (London, 1926), pp. 88–89; Clive Nicol, *From the Roof of Africa* (London, 1971), p. 323. In the 1970s, Muslims were landlords over the Beta Israel at Wefdar on the edge of the Samen; interview with Kebrate Samu'el and the elders of Wefdar on 26 October 1975. Fasilidas's grant to a Muslim is documented in G. Villari, "I 'gulti' della regione de Axum," *Rassegna Economica dell'Africa Italiana* 16 (1938): 1444, cited in Richard Pankhurst, *State and Land in Ethiopian History* (Addis Ababa, 1966), p. 56.

167. Pankhurst, "Greek Land-Holding."

168. Mahteme Sellassie Wolde Meskal, "The Land System of Ethiopia," p. 288; Mangestu Tayye, "Short History of Gonder," p. 6; interviews with Jammara Wande on 31 July 1975 and Garima Taffara on 4 August 1975.

169. Interview with Kasagne Alamayahu on 31 August 1975.

170. Basset, "Études sur l'histoire," p. 312; Mangestu Tayye, "Short History of Gondar," p. 6.

171. Guidi, *Annales Iohannis,* p. 207.

172. Ludolphus, *New History,* pp. 205–6.

173. On *gult,* see above and Alvares, *Prester John,* 1:248; 93–94; 2:412, 428, 430, 464.

174. Some kings or royal family members married or had mistresses of non-Christian origin; for example, Zar'a Ya'eqob married a Hadeyya princess; see Taddesse, *Church and State,* p. 243, n. 2. Lebna Dengel's son, Ya'eqob, apparently married a Beta Israel woman; and Sarsa Dengel had a Beta Israel mistress; see Chapter 2 above.

175. Berry, "Solomonic Monarchy," pp. 257–58.

176. Iyyasu II had an Oromo wife; see Guidi, *Annales Iyasu II,* p. 8. Decrees forbidding such unions (see below) suggested they existed; see H. Weld Blundell, ed., *The Royal Chronicle of Abyssinia, 1769–1840* (Cambridge, 1922), p. 421.

177. Interview with Yebbabe Zawde on 2 August 1975. This informant spent many years in Lasta.

178. Interview with Berhan Beruk on 14 August and 20 August 1975. Mentewwab, for example, was said by this informant to be of partial Beta Israel origin.

179. Guidi, *Annales Iohannis,* p. 8 (trans); Basset, "Études sur l'histoire," pp. 291–292.

180. Berry, "Solomonic Monarchy," pp. 187–88.

181. Guidi, *Annales Iohannis,* p. 8.

182. Ibid., p. 37.

183. El-Haimi, *Zur Geschichte,* p. 35; van Donzel, *Yemenite Embassy,* pp. 143–45.

184. See above, and interviews with Gete Asrass on 11 June 1975, with Berhan Beruk on 14 August 1975, and with Webe Akala on 27 December 1975.

185. The chronicle specifically stated a desire to decrease the "disputes" among different peoples; see Guidi, *Annales Iohannis,* p. 8.

186. On the *tewahido* and *qebat* doctrines, see Berry, "Solomonic Monarchy," pp. xvii, xix, and infra; Donald Crummey, *Priests and Politicians* (Oxford, 1972), pp. 14–27; I. Guidi, "La Chiesa Abissinia," *OM* 2 (1922–23): 123–28, 186–90, 252–56.

187. Interview with Jammara Wande on 26 August 1975.

188. Ibid.

189. Ibid.

190. Guidi, *Annales Iyasu II,* p. 81.

191. Weld Blundell, *Royal Chronicle,* p. 421.

192. Donald Crummey, "Society and Ethnicity," p. 275.

193. Guidi, *Annales Iyasu II,* p. 180.

194. Ludolphus, *New History,* p. 233; Berry, "Solomonic Monarchy," p. 306, note 3.

195. Berry, "Solomonic Monarchy," p. 110.

196. Basset, "Études sur l'histoire," p. 125; Guidi, *Annales Iohannis,* p. 54.

197. Basset, "Études sur l'histoire," pp. 285–86; Berry, "Solomonic Monarchy," p. 101.

198. Ludolphus, *New History,* pp. 205–6.

199. Bruce, *Travels,* 3:252; "Die Juden in Abyssinien," *Das Ausland* 3 (1830): 192.

200. See Chapter 4 below on Webe and his ancestors.

201. Bruce, *Travels,* 3:190, 535; 4:27.

202. Volker Stitz, "Distribution and Foundation of Churches in Ethiopia," *JES* 13/1 (January 1975): 14.

203. Interview with Menase Zammaru and Wande Iyyasu on 13 October 1975.

204. Samuel Gobat, *Journal,* pp. 277–78; Joseph Halévy, "Travels in Abyssinia," p. 242; Stern, *Wanderings, passim.*

205. Interviews with Gete Asrass on 9 November 1975 and with Webe Akala on 27 December 1975.

206. Recorded by d'Abbadie, "Journal," p. 462.

207. For the Portuguese views, see Almeida, *High Ethiopia,* p. 55; Ludolphus, *New History,* p. 73. For a convincing critique of the opinions of the Portuguese, see Wolf Leslau, "Excursus 3: Did the Falashas Speak Hebrew?" in Leslau, ed., "A Falasha Religious Dispute," pp. 89–94.

208. Bruce, *Travels,* vol. 1, between pp. 400–401. See also an appendix in Bruce, *Travels* (2nd edition, Edinburgh, 1804), vol. 2, appendix 3, pp. 491–99 that includes an extensive word list compiled by Bruce.

209. Bruce, *Travels,* 3:535, 4:27.

210. Gobat, *Journal,* p. 468; d'Abbadie, "Journal," p. 464; Halévy, "Essai sur la langue agaou. Le Dialecte des Falachas (Juifs d'Abyssinie)," *ASP* 3/4 (November 1873): 156. See also Chapter 4 below.

211. Leslau, ed., "A Falasha Religious Dispute," p. 80: a Beta Israel chronicle written during the reign of Menilek II (1889–1913).

212. See Akalou Wolde Michael, "Some Thoughts on the Process of Urbanization," p. 35.

Chapter 4

1. See Chapter 1 above for these criteria.

2. Previous explanations have oversimplified the factors; J. S. Trimingham, among others, overemphasized the idea that a fixed capital prohibited kings from maintaining control through military campaigns; see his *Islam in Ethiopia,* p. 104. In reality, at least up to Iyyasu II, the kings went on annual six- to eight-month campaigns to other parts of the realms; see LaVerle Berry, "Solomonic Monarchy," pp. 177–78; Richard Pankhurst, "Notes for a History of Gondar," pp. 183–90. Mordechai Abir emphasized the destructive impact of the "Galla" (Oromo): *The Era of the Princes,* pp. xxii–xxiii and *passim.*

3. Berry, "Solomonic Monarchy," p. 371. On geography, see also Sven Rubenson, *The Survival of Ethiopian Independence* (New York, 1976), pp. 1–2.

4. Berry, "Solomonic Monarchy," pp. 349–53.

5. Ibid., pp. 333–34, 341–42, 345–46.

6. Ibid., p. 371 and *passim.*

7. Ibid., pp. 305–11. For the Order of Precedence, see Guidi, ed., *Annales Iohannis,* p. 152; G. W. B. Huntingford, ed., *The Land Charters of Northern Ethiopia* (Addis Ababa, 1965), pp. 109–10.

8. Berry, "Solomonic Monarchy," pp. lvii, 251–56; Merid Wolde Aregay, "Southern Ethiopia," Chapters 4 and 6.

9. Guidi, *Annales Iohannis,* p. 295; Berry, "Solomonic Monarchy," pp. 293–96.

10. Donald Crummey, "Three Amharic Documents of Marriage and Inheritance from the Eighteenth and Nineteenth Centuries," in Taddesse Beyene, ed., *Proceedings of the Eighth International Conference of Ethiopian Studies, Addis Ababa, 1984* (Addis Ababa, 1988), 1:315–27.

11. Ludolphus, *New History,* p. 201.

12. Guidi, *Annales Iyasu II,* pp. 44–47; Berry, "Solomonic Monarchy," p. 312.

13. Richard Pankhurst, "Fire-arms in Ethiopian History (1800–1935)," *EO* 6 (1962): 135; Richard Caulk, "Firearms and Princely Power in Ethiopia in the Nineteenth Century," *JAH* 13 (1972): 609; Abir, *Era of Princes,* pp. 50–53.

14. Donald Crummey, "Gondarine *Rim* Land Sales," pp. 469–79.

15. Crummey, "Three Amharic Documents." The sales, at least in the Gondar area, also disproportionately favored the accumulation of land by men from women who were equal in the possession but not the exercise of land use rights: Crummey, "Women and Landed Property in Gondarine Ethiopia," *IJAHS* 14 (1981): 444–65.

16. Crummey, "Family and Property Amongst the Amhara Nobility," *JAH* 24 (1983): 211.

17. Crummey, "Three Amharic Documents," p. 7; idem., "Family and Property," pp. 211–12.

18. Crummey, "Three Amharic Documents," pp. 1–3.

19. Ibid., p. 4.

20. Donald Crummey, "Society and Ethnicity," pp. 272–78.

21. Berry, "Solomonic Monarchy," pp. 324–28; Guidi, *Iyasu II,* pp. 55, 61, 69–71, 81, 87.

22. Guidi, *Iyasu II,* pp. 173–74. Perhaps his death was not natural; see Berry, "Solomonic Monarchy," pp. 328–30.

23. Zergaw Asfera, "Some Aspects of Historical Development in Amhara-Wallo (ca. 1700–1815)" (B.A. thesis, Haile Sellassie I University, 1973); Donald Crummey, "Čäčäho and the Politics of the Northern Wällo-Bägēmder Border," *JES* 13/1 (1975): 5.

24. James Bruce, *Travels,* 2:698–700; Tadesse Gebre Igziabher, "Power Struggle in Tigray During the Zamana Masafent, 1769–1855" (unpublished B.A. thesis, Haile Sellassie I University, Addis Ababa, 1971), p. 8; Crummey, "Family and Property," pp. 212–13; Richard Pankhurst, "An Eighteenth Century Ethiopian Dynastic Marriage Contract Between Empress Mentewab of Gondar and Mika'el Sehul of Tegre," *BSOAS* 42 (1979): 457–64; Mordechai Abir, "Ethiopia and the Horn of Africa," in Richard Gray, ed., *The Cambridge History of Africa,* vol. 4, from c. 1600 to c. 1790 (Cambridge, 1975), 570–71.

25. Guidi, *Iyasu II,* p. 240.

26. Ibid., pp. 249–50.

27. Bruce, *Travels,* 2:674–78; Crummey, "Society and Ethnicity," p. 273.

28. Guidi, *Iyasu II,* p. 293; idem., "La Storia di Hayla Mika'el," *RRAL,* ser. 5, 11 (1902): 19; Crummey, "Čäčäho," p. 5.

29. Bruce, *Travels,* 4:138–39; Abir, *Era of Princes,* pp. 30–43, 119–40.

30. Abir, *Era of Princes,* pp. 30–31, and *passim.*

31. Merid, "Southern Ethiopia," pp. 138–39; group interview by Donald Crummey of elders at Waldiya, August 1972, cited in Crummey, "Society and Ethnicity," p. 277, note 43.

32. H. Weld Blundell, ed., *The Royal Chronicle of Abyssinia, 1769–1840* (Cambridge, 1922), pp. 358–59.

33. Abir, *Era of Princes,* pp. 30–43. See the convenient genealogy in Crummey, "Family and Property," 219. For the rise of the dynasty, see Seyoum Wolde Yohannes, "Ras Ali and Tewodros: The Position of Islam in Central Ethiopia" (unpublished B.A. thesis, Addis Ababa: Haile Sellassie I University, 1968).

34. Abir, *Era of Princes,* 144–82; R. H. Kofi Darkwah, *Shewa, Menilek and the Ethiopian Empire, 1813–1889* (London, 1975), 1–34. Perhaps the coffee trade rather than the slave trade was the main economic factor behind Shawa's rise: Merid W. Aregay, "The Early History of Ethiopia's Coffee Trade and the Rise of Shawa," *JAH* 29 (1988): 19–25.

35. Weld Blundell, *Royal Chronicle,* p. 445.

36. Ibid., 471.

37. Berry, "Solomonic Monarchy," pp. 178–81, 191–93.

38. A. Ferret and M. Galinier, *Voyages en Abyssinie,* 2:344–45, 489–90; Combes and Tamisier, *Voyage en Abyssinie,* 1:170–71; Nathaniel Pearce, *The Life and Adventures,* 1:183–84, 207–8, 339–40; Pankhurst, *Economic History of Ethiopia,* pp. 563–66.

39. Krapf and Isenberg, *Journals,* pp. 487, 458. Rüppell said that little agriculture was practiced owing to the "anarchy" of the times: "Remarques sur l'aspect physique de l'Abyssinie," *NA* 87 (1840): 226. See also Plowden, *Correspondence,* pp. 103–6; Abir, *Era of Princes,* p. 30; Rassam, *Narrative,* 1:215–16; T. Waldmeier, *The Autobiography* (London, 1886), p. 15.

40. Samuel Gobat, *Journal,* p. 282.

41. Weld Blundell, *Chronicle,* pp. 446, 492; Carlo Conti Rossini, ed., "Nuovi documenti per la storia d'Abissinia nel secolo XIX," *RRAL,* ser. 7, 2 (1947): 373, 394–95; Rassam, *Narrative,* 1:35, 2:230–31; Henry Stern, *The Captive Missionary* (London, 1868), pp. 298–99.

42. Bruce estimated Gondar had 10,000 families: *Travels,* 3:380–81, perhaps indicating 40,000 to 60,000 people. Jones believed it was the size of Cairo at the time and that the royal forces alone amounted to 40,000: "A Conversation with Abram," p. 383. Ferret and Galinier estimated 40,000 at the peak in *Voyages,* 2:237, 239. Hermann Norden cited 50,000 at the time of Fasiladas: *Africa's Last Empire* (Philadelphia, 1930), pp. 152–53. Ethiopian estimates are unrealistically higher, such as the 80,000 of Ghiorghis Mellessa, "Gondar Yesterday and Today," p. 166; or the 280,000 cited by Garima: "Gondar and Its Kings," (Gondar, 1975), p. 5.

43. Some population estimates are 5,000 to 6,000: Heuglin, "Th. von Heuglin's Reise nach Abessinien, 1852–1853," *PGM* (1857): 468; 6,000: Henry Stern, *Wanderings,* p. 229; 6,500: Rüppell, *Reise in Abyssinien,* 2:82; 7,000: J. M. Flad, "Twelve Years in Abyssinia," *JI* 9 (1869): 218; 8,000: Antoine d'Abbadie, *L'Abyssinie et le roi Théodore,* p. 11; 10,000 to 12,000: J. L. Krapf, *Travels,* p. 460; 18,000: Ferret and Galinier, *Voyages,* 2:237, 239.

44. Antoine d'Abbadie, "Voyage en Abyssinie," *BSG,* ser. 2, 11 (1839): 210. The city was "depopulated" and "in ruins" according to Dillon in Lefebvre, *Voyage,* 1:164, and was only a "shadow" of its former self according to L. Aubert, "Fragment sur Gondar et le Négus," *BSG* 10 (1838): 145.

45. Guillaume Lejean, "Notes d'un voyage en Abyssinie," *Le Tour du Monde* 12 (1865): 246.

46. Guidi, *Iyasu II,* pp. 137, 209; Weld Blundell, *Chronicle,* p. 204.

47. Guidi, *Iyasu II,* pp. 76–77; Weld Blundell, *Chronicle,* pp. 446, 454.

48. Bruce, *Travels,* 2:622–23, 3:380, 4:112.

49. Jones, "Conversation with Abram," p. 383.

50. Coffin said the king no longer lived there; Pearce, *Life and Adventures,* 2:234. But Gobat said three rooms were still usable and the king lived in one of them; *Journal,* 40. Rüppell found the building deserted and the interior in great disrepair in *Reise,* 2:91. A. von Katte said they were in ruins in *Reise in Abyssinien in Jahre 1836* (Stuttgart, 1838), p. 147.

51. G. Lejean, *Voyage en Abyssinie, exécuté de 1862 à 1864* (Paris, 1872), p. 24; Plowden, *Travels in Abyssinia* (London, 1868), p. 42.

52. Antoine d'Abbadie, "Journal et mélanges," Bibliothèque nationale, FNA 21300, pp. 75–76; Rüppell, *Reise,* 2:90–92.

53. Plowden, *Travels,* p. 42; Lejean, *Voyage,* 24. For later developments, see Achille Raffray, *Afrique Orientale, Abyssinie* (Paris, 1876), pp. 305–6.

54. See the list compiled by Pankhurst, "History of Gonder," p. 206; Mangestu Tayye, "Short History of Gondar," p. 13; interview with Balay Marsha on 27 November 1975.

55. Pearce, *Life and Adventures,* 1:242.

56. Norden, *Africa's Last Empire,* pp. 154–94; interviews with Balay Malku and Sammallegne Takka on 3 September 1975, Sandaqqe Maharan on 24 October 1975, Yeshaq Iyyasu on 15 December 1975.

57. Bruce, *Travels,* 2:195.

58. All the following failed to mention villages to the north, though they discussed others by name such as Kayla Meda, Dafacha, and Abwara; Pearce, *Life and Adventures;* Gobat, *Journal;* d'Abbadie, "Journal"; Stern, *Wanderings.*

59. Pearce, *Life and Adventures,* 1:244.

60. Gobat, *Journal,* p. 468.

61. George Viscount Valentia, *Voyages and Travels to India, Ceylon, the Red Sea, Abyssinia, and Egypt,* 3 vols. (London, 1809), 3:67.

62. Combes and Tamisier, *Voyage,* 1:350; Arnauld d'Abbadie, *Douze ans,* p. 165; Antoine d'Abbadie, "Journal," 459; J. M. Flad, *Notes from the Journal of J. M. Flad* (London, 1860), p. 87; Krapf, *Travels,* pp. 460–61; H. Dufton, *Narrative of a Journey Through Abyssinia* (London, 1867), 94, 164–65; J. Halévy, "Travels in Abyssinia," p. 195; Halévy, "Excursion chez les Falacha," p. 292.

63. In Dambeya, the village of Gorgora Eila consisted of potters and that of Atshergee of weavers; see Stern, *Wanderings,* 265, 267. At Jenda, 20 to 25 looms were in use; see Hermann Steudner, "Herrn Dr. Steudner's Bericht über seine abessinische Reise," *ZAE* 16 (1864): 86, 90. Also on weavers in Dambeya and Saqqalt, see Theodor von Heuglin, "Reise zu Kaiser Theodoros und nach der Festung madgala, Februar bis Mai 1862," *PGM* 13 (1867): 422. On a "village of Falasha weavers" in Gojjam, see Charles T. Beke, "Abyssinia—being a continuation of Routes in that Country," *JRGS* 14 (1844): 8.

64. Stern, *Wanderings,* pp. 152–53. They were also still smelting iron at that time; see Steudner, "Reise von Adoa nach Gondar, Dezember 26, 1861–Januar 1862," *ZAE* 15 (1863): 128.

65. Ferret and Galinier, *Voyages,* 2:478–80; Halévy, "Excursion," p. 292; Combes and Tamisier, *Voyage,* 4:76; Beke, "Abyssinia," 8.

66. Rüppell, *Reise,* 2:81–82.

67. Stern, *Wanderings,* 199.

68. Coffin, in Pearce, *Life and Adventures,* 1:240. He said this was the population of the Beta Israel in Gondar, but since he only mentioned Dafacha, he was probably referring to that settlement only.

69. Stern, *Wanderings,* pp. 205, 207. Since the figures for Abwara indicate a population of 300 to 400 with sixty houses (families), a figure of forty families for Dafacha would suggest about 200 to 250 people in 1860, a decline from the 400 cited by Coffin in 1815. The figures are obviously estimates in all cases, but the general trend of a decline seems clear.

70. See note 47 above.

71. Interview with Berhan Beruk on 20 August 1975.

72. Huntingford, *Land Charters,* 67.

73. Valentia, *Voyages and Travels,* 3:67.

74. An exception was the grant an ancestor of one of my informants was said to have received from *dejazmach* Maru; interview with Sandaqqe Maharan on 24 October 1975.

75. Pearce, *Life and Adventures,* 1:244.

76. D'Abbadie, "Journal," pp. 219–20; Flad, *The Falashas (Jews) of Abyssinia* (London, 1869), p. 25.

77. Interview with Berhan Beruk on 3 July 1975.

78. Huntingford, *Land Charters,* p. 66 and *passim.*

79. See Chapter 3 above.

80. Interview with Webe Akala on 27 December 1975.

81. Interviews with Berhan Beruk on 3 July 1975, with Kebrate Samu'el and elders of Wefdar on 26 October 1975, and with Webe Akala on 27 December 1975; d'Abbadie, "Journal," p. 255.

82. Interviews with Berhan Beruk on 14 August 1975, Gete Asrass on 9 November 1975. See Chapters 2 and 3 above.

83. Discussed below.

84. Interviews with Berhan Beruk on 14 August 1975 and with Webe Akala on 27 December 1975. See also Chapter 3 above.

85. See above.

86. Interview with Berhan Beruk on 14 August 1975.

87. Ibid.

88. Interview with Webe Akala on 27 December 1975.

89. A. Z. Aescoly, "Notices sur les Falacha," p. 113 (my translation).

90. Interviews with Gete Asrass on 11 June 1975, Yeshaq Iyyasu on 15 December 1975; Stern, *Wanderings,* 203. Other *bejronds* were recalled from Tewodros's reign; interview with Yeshaq Iyyasu on 15 December 1975.

91. Interviews with Alamayyahu Iyyasu on 15 December 1975, with Yeshaq Iyyasu on 15 December 1975, with Tafassaku Webshat and elders of Endabaguna (Tigray) on 15 December 1975, with Gete Asrass on 11 June 1975, with Mammo Sagga Amlak, and with Ya'eqob Balay and Mulu Mammo on 24 June 1975; Jacques Faitlovitch, *Quer durch,* p. 187 and *passim;* S. H. Marguiles, "Per la storia del movimento pro Falascia, due documenti," *RI* 6 (1909): fac. 4–5.

92. Ferret and Galinier, *Voyages,* 1:424; Lefebvre, *Voyage,* 1:77; Arnauld d'Abbadie, *Douze ans,* 2:59. Theodor von Heuglin, "Reise nach Abessinien," p. 470. See also Abir, *Era of Princes,* p. 33.

93. Guillaume-Marie Lejean, *Theodore II, le nouvel empire d'Abyssinie* (Paris, 1867), p. 14; Guebre Sellassie, *Chronique du règne de Menelik II,* 1:197.

94. Antoine d'Abbadie: "Extrait d'une lettre de M. Antoine d'Abbadie sur les Falacha ou Juifs d'Abyssinie," *BSG,* ser. 3, 4 (1845): 45–46; idem., "Journal," p. 463; idem., "Réponses des Falasha dits juifs d'Abyssinie aux questions fait par M. Luzzatto," *AI* 12 (1851): 267; Aescoly, "Notices sur les Falachas," p. 93; Luzzatto, *Mémoire,* p. 19. Interviews with Berhan Beruk on 20 August 1975. See also Chris Prouty, *Empress Taytu and Menilek II, Ethiopia 1883–1910* (Trenton, 1986), pp. vi–vii.

The ancestor she lists as "Helos" who married a daughter of Suseneyos is remembered in Beta Israel oral traditions as "Yelos" (d'Abbadie, "Réponses," 267), or as "Erlos" (Berhan Beruk). This must have been Yolyos in the chronicle and Portuguese sources, who, along with Yamana Krestos, the King's older brother, led a rebellion against Suseneyos: Telles, *The Travels of the Jesuits,* pp. 207–9; Perruchon, "Règne de Susneyos," pp. 183–84.

95. Ferret and Galinier, *Voyages,* 1:424–25; Lefebvre, *Voyage,* 1:77.

96. D'Abbadie, "Extrait sur les Falacha," p. 45.

97. Ferret and Galinier, *Voyage,* 2:473–74 and map; C. Conti Rossini, ed., "Nuovi documenti per la storia d'Abissinia nel secolo XIX," *RRAL,* ser. 7, 2 (1947): 367–69; J. Perruchon, ed., "Notes pour l'histoire d'Ethiopie contemporaine," *RS* 7 (1899): 253–54; C. T. Lefebvre, "Aperçu général de l'Abyssinie," *BSG,* ser. 2, 14 (1840): 70–71, 73; Arnauld d'Abbadie, *Douze ans,* 1:31, 187, 2:69 and infra; Louis Reybaud, "Voyage dans l'Abyssinie méridionale: Journal inédit de M. Rochet d'Héricourt," *RDM* 27 (July–September 1841): 62; "Abyssinie: Mort de M. Reitz, consul d'Autriche," *NA* 139 (1853): 192–93.

98. Ibid.; Lefebvre, *Voyage,* 1:78–83; 292–93, 356; Ferret and Galinier, *Voyages,* 2:463; Arnauld d'Abbadie, *Douze ans,* 2:36, 55. See also Abir, *Era of Princes,* pp. 111–12.

99. Although there are some traditions that they served as soldiers for Tewodros in his rise to power; interviews with Berhan Beruk on 20 August 1975 and with Ratta Zawde on 10 August 1975. If accurate, this was an analogous case to that of Webe.

100. Thorough linguistic studies of the Agaw languages are still needed. See Antoine d'Abbadie, "Lettre à G. C. Renouard, Gondar, September 1844," *NA,* n.s. 106 (1845): 119; d'Abbadie, "Réponses des Falasha," p. 240; d'Abbadie, "Journal," p. 464; Halévy, "Travels," p. 231; J. Halévy, "Essai sur la langue agaou," p. 156; J. Tubiana, "Note sur la distribution géographique des dialectes Agaw," *Mer rouge, Afrique orientale, CAA* 5 (1959): 297–306; Robert Hetzron, "The Agaw Languages," *AL* 3/3 (June 1976): 1–45.

101. Bruce, *Travels,* 3:535.

102. Ibid., 4:27. On the borders of Samen, Amharic was becoming the main language, though in "many villages . . . the language of Falasha is spoken"; ibid., 3:190.

103. Gobat, *Journal,* p. 468.

104. D'Abbadie, "Journal," p. 464. On the transitional nature of the era linguistically, see Hermann Steudner, "Reise von Adoa," pp. 68, 128.

105. They even used Amharic to explain Ge'ez passages from the *Orit* to their children: Halévy, "Essai sur la langue agaou," p. 156. In Gojjam, Beke spoke to them [in Amharic?] and obtained a number of words of "their language" which bore a close resemblance to the Agaw language of their neighbors: Beke, "Abyssinia," p. 8.

106. Marcel Cohen, "Rapport sur une mission linguistique en Abyssinie 1910–1911," p. 70.

107. Garima Taffara, "Gondar and its Kings," unpublished manuscript in Amharic, Gondar, 1975, p. 16.

108. The same process no doubt occurred in Tigray with Tigrinya, but I have no evidence as to when this occurred.

109. Broadly speaking, the following examples are drawn from Begamder-Samen, southern Tigray and Gojjam, though *buda* was referred to throughout the country.

110. Pearce, *Life and Adventures,* 2:340–41; Gobat, *Journal,* 332; Ferret and Galinier, *Voyages,* 2:123; Mansfield Parkyns, *Life in Abyssinia* (2nd ed., London, 1868), pp. 300–313; Halévy, "Travels," pp. 194–95. For a later period, see William Winstanley, *A Visit to Abyssinia,* 2 vols. (London, 1881), 1:278–82.

111. Ferret and Galinier, *Voyages,* 2:123.

112. Gobat, *Journal,* p. 289.

113. Dufton, *Narrative,* pp. 167–68.

114. Ibid., pp. 169–70.

115. Gobat, *Journal,* p. 332.

116. Pearce, *Life and Adventures,* 1:287; Gobat, *Journal,* p. 332; Combes and Tamisier, *Voyage,* 2:39. See the ethnographic account of the stages of possession: Allan Young, "Medical Beliefs and Practices of Begemder Amhara," pp. 244–50.

117. Gobat, *Journal,* pp. 263, 331, 335; Ferret and Galinier, *Voyage,* 2:123; Parkyns, *Life,* p. 300; Stern, *Wanderings,* pp. 152–53; Dufton, *Narrative,* p. 165; Winstanley, *Visit,* 1:278–82.

118. Gobat, *Journal,* p. 263; Dimoteos Sabrijian, *Deux ans de séjour en Abyssinie* (Jerusalem, 1871), 139–40.

119. J. G. Bell, "Extrait du journal d'un voyage en Abyssinie, dans les années 1840, 1841 et 1842," *NA* 112 (1846): 153–54; Stern, *Wanderings,* 152–53; Theophilus Waldmeier, *The Autobiography,* pp. 64–66; Dimoteos, *Deux ans,* pp. 135, 139, 140. "Villages of *buda*" existed in Damot; see Lefebvre, *Voyage,* 1:149; a peak called "aouala-negus" was said to be the home of the king of the *buda* in the region of Metcha [Macha] just south of Tana; see Lejean, "Notes d'un voyage en Abyssinie," 9:80.

120. Ferret and Galinier, *Voyages,* 2:257; Gobat, *Journal,* p. 263; Krapf, *Travels,* p. 451. Blanc said the Wayto were "supposed to be in league with boudas": "From Metemma to Damot, along the Western Shores of the Tana Sea," *JRGS* 13 (1868–1869): 45. Bruce had noted the Wayto were said to be "sorcerers," but he did not use the word *buda: Travels,* 3:403.

121. Jules Borelli, *Éthiopie méridionale* (Paris, 1890); for later examples, see R. P. Azais et R. Chambard, *Cinq années de recherches archéologique en Éthiopie* (Paris, 1931), pp. 8, 27, 108, 191; Marcel Cohen, "Cérémonies et croyances abyssines," *Revue de l'histoire des religions* 66 (1912): 198. On *buda* in Gurage traditions, see William A. Shack and Habte-Maryam Marcos, *Gods and Heroes* (Oxford, 1974), p. 41.

122. Gobat, *Journal,* p. 263. Bruce asserted both the Muslims and Falasha were addicted to a belief in "sorcery" though he did not specifically mention the *buda* phenomenon in that context; see his *Travels,* 2:19. The ambiguity of the *buda* idea among the Falasha is in Michele Schoenberger, "The Falashas of Ethiopia: An Ethnographic Study" (Ph.D. dissertation, Cambridge University, 1975), pp. 244–47.

123. Flad, *Journal,* p. 43; Gobat in *JI* 4 (1838), 139.

124. Gobat, *Journal,* pp. 329, 331.

125. Ferret and Galinier, *Voyages,* 2:123.

126. Lejean, *Voyage,* 8; idem., "Notes d'un voyage en Abyssinie," 12:242.

127. Plowden, *Travels,* p. 116. See also idem., "Report," Plowden to Clarendon, 9 July 1854, in *Correspondence,* p. 100; Dufton, *Narrative,* p. 165.

128. Parkyns, *Life,* p. 300.

129. Interview with Berhan Beruk on 3 July 1975. "Galla" refers to the Yajju kingmakers at Gondar.

130. Manoel de Almeida, "The History of High Ethiopia," p. 55, note 1; Emmanuel Barradas, *Tractatus,* in Beccari, *Rerum Aethiopicarum,* 4:61.

131. Ludolphus, *New History,* pp. 390–91.

132. See Chapter 3 above.

133. Telles, *Travels of the Jesuits,* pp. 236–37.

134. Interview with Admas Chakkol on 16 December 1975.

135. Bruce, *Travels,* 2:19, 4:83.

136. Ethiopic manuscripts contain legends about Solomon and the prayer called the "Net of Solomon" in which King Solomon destroyed the "demon-blacksmiths" trying to kill him; see Jacques Mercier, *Ethiopian Magic Scrolls* (New York, 1979), pp. 19, 115, plate 38. See also S. Euringer, "Das Netz Salomons," *ZS* 6 (1928): 76–100, 178–99, 300–314; 7 (1929): 68–85. For magical prayers, see Stefan Strelcyn, "Prières magiques éthiopiennes pour délier les charmes," *RO* 18 (1955): i–lxxvi, 1–498 (on *buda,* see pp. 331–32). On the relationship of medical and magical treatments or protection from the *buda,* see Marcel Griaule, *Le livre de recettes d'un dabtara abyssin. TMIE* 12 (Paris, 1930); Tsehai Berhane Selassie, ed., "An Ethiopian Medical Text-Book Written by Gerazmač Gäbräwäld Arägahän, Dëga Damot," *JES* 9/1 (1971): 95–180; Maxime Rodinson, *Magie, médecine et possession à Gondar* (Paris, 1967); Allan Young, "Medical Beliefs and Practices of Begemder Amhara"; Marcel Griaule, "Mythes, croyances et coutumes du Bégamder (Abyssinie)," *JA* 212 (1928): 31, 68, 70, 71, 81; A. Z. Aescoly, "Les noms magiques dans les Apocryphes Chrétiens des Éthiopiens," *JA* 220 (1932): 130. See also EMML 843, 2096, 2799 as described in Getatchew and Macomber, *Catalogue,* 3:164, 6:184, 7:141.

137. Sylvain Grébaut, "Catalogue des manuscrits éthiopien (Ge'ez) de la mission Griaule," *Aethiopica* 3 (1935). Manuscript #72 in this collection, for example, was a "prayer against the *buda* and blacksmiths" (p. 83); #81 was a "prayer against the evil eye, Barya, *buda,* blacksmiths, Falasha . . ." (p. 159). See also William Hoyt Worrell, "Studien zum abessinischen Zauberwesen," *ZA* 23 (1909): 149–183; 24 (1910): 56–96; 29 (1914): 85–141; Michel Leiris, "Le culte des zars à Gondar," *Aethiopica* 2 (1934): 96–103, 125–36 (p. 126 on equating Falasha and *buda*); Stefan Strelcyn, "Prières magiques éthiopiennes," pp. 331–32.

138. Stefan Strelcyn, "Les écrits médicaux éthiopiens," *JES* 3/1 (1965): 88–97; idem., "Les nouveaux manuscrits éthiopiens de la Bibliothèque royale de Bruxelles," *JES* 11/2 (1973): 169–88.

139. Simon Messing, "The Highland-Plateau Amhara of Ethiopia," p. 677. See also general accounts of these phenomena in Mircea Eliade, *The Forge and the Crucible* (2nd ed., Chicago, 1978 [orig. ed., 1956]); Robert Eisler, *Man into Wolf* (London, 1951); Clarence Maloney, ed., *The Evil Eye* (New York, 1976), which suggests a diffusion from the "Near East" to South Asia, Europe, North and Northeast Africa, and Central America.

140. See Chapter 1 above and some of the following, which do not agree on

whether craft groups are to be called "caste" but clearly see them as somehow distinguishable: J. Vaughan, "Caste Systems in the Western Sudan"; Nehemia Levtzion, *Ancient Ghana and Mali* (London, 1973), pp. 119–20; Camara Laye, *The Dark Child* (New York, 1954); Robert Launay, "Manding 'clans' and 'castes,'" Conference on Manding Studies, School of Oriental and African Studies, London, 1972. A recent study may capture the ambiguity surrounding blacksmiths best: Patrick McNaughton, *Mande Blacksmiths*.

141. Young, "Medical Beliefs," pp. 11, 244–50; Messing, "Highland Ethiopia," 662–77.

142. Allan Hoben, *Land Tenure;* idem., "The Role of Ambilineal Descent Groups in Gojjam Amhara Social Organization" (Ph.D. dissertation, University of California, 1963); Gedamu Abraha, "Wax and Gold."

143. Ronald Reminick's sociopsychological emphasis supplements the political-economic factors that were at the basis of the *buda* belief: "The Structure and Functions of Religious Beliefs among the Amhara of Ethiopia," in Harold Marcus, ed., *Proceedings of the First United States Conference on Ethiopian Studies, 1973* (East Lansing, Mich., 1975), pp. 34–35; idem., "The Evil-Eye Belief Among the Amhara of Ethiopia," *Ethnology* 13 (1974): 279–92 [also reprinted in Maloney, *The Evil Eye,* pp. 85–101]; Simon Messing, "Health Care, Ethnic Outcasting and the Problem of Overcoming the Syndrome of Encapsulation in a Peasant Society," *Human Organization,* v. 34, no. 4 (Winter 1975), 395–97.

144. Parkyns, *Life,* p. 301. Parkyns said he had observed over a hundred cases of *buda* possession. See also d'Abbadie, "Journal," p. 439; Krapf, *Travels,* p. 240.

145. Stern, *Wanderings,* 154.

146. H. Weld Blundell, "History of King Theodore," *Journal of the African Society* 6 (1906): 26; Walda Maryam, *Chronique de Théodoros II, roi des rois d'Éthiopie (1853–1868),* trans. and ed. C. Mondon-Vidailhet (Paris, 1905), pp. 56–57.

147. Arnauld d'Abbadie, *Douze ans,* 1:377 (my translation).

148. Ibid. On the army as a path for advancement, see, for example, in Great Britain, *Parliamentary Papers,* Paper 184, p. 105.

149. Dillon, in Lefebvre, *Voyage,* 1:165.

150. Barthelemy Louis Denis de Rivoyre, *Mer rouge et Abyssinie* (Paris, 1880), p. 157.

151. Parkyns, *Life,* 2 vols. (London, 1853), 2:121. (The second edition in one volume [1868] called them hereditary, but omitted the word "caste": p. 300.) The comparison with India is from Paul Chaix, "Étude sur l'ethnographie de l'Afrique," *Mémoires de la société de géographie de Genève* 1 (1860): 27.

152. Gobat, *Journal,* p. 468.

153. Krapf, *Journals* p. 240. This statement referred specifically to the *tabiban* in Shoa. For Gondar, see Steudner, "Reise von Adoa nach Gondar," p. 129.

154. Halévy, "Travels," p. 237.

155. D'Abbadie, "Journal," p. 464; idem., "Réponses," p. 180; Gobat, *Journal,* p. 279; "Voyage de M. Rüppell en Abyssinie," *NA* 63 (1834): 101. See also Parkyns, *Life,* pp. 289–90.

156. "Reminiscences of Dr. Wolff," *JI,* n.s. 1 (December 1885): 193. Wolff had accompanied Gobat on his original visit in the 1830s.

157. See above, Chapters 1 and 2 and Shelemay, *Music, Ritual;* Ullendorff, *Bible,* pp. 115–18. The seventeenth-century Portuguese missionaries and travelers, of course, elaborated on the "Judaic" aspects of Orthodoxy: Pero Pais [Pedro Paez], *Historia da Etiopia,* 3 vols. (Porto, 1946), 2:66–73; Emmanuel Barradas, *Tractatus,* in Beccari, *Rerum Aethiopicarum,* 4:290–91; Telles, *Travels of the Jesuits,* p. 72; M. Le Grand, *A Voyage to Abyssinia by Father Jerome Lobo,* trans. Samuel Johnson (London, 1789), pp. 281–93; Jeronymo Lobo, *The Intinerario of Jeronimo Lobo,* trans. Donald Lockart (London, 1984), p. 180.

158. On the distinction between social and cultural incorporation, see Chapter 3 above and especially Edmund Leach, *Political Systems of Highland Burma* (Cambridge, Mass., 1954).

159. The best recent summary in Shelemay, *Music, Ritual,* pp. 47–57. See also Leslau, *Coutumes et croyances.*

160. *Te'ezaza Sanbat,* in Leslau, *Anthology,* pp. 19–20; Halévy, *Te'ezaza Sanbat;* Stern, *Wanderings,* p. 191.

161. D'Abbadie, "Journal," p. 460; Leslau, *Anthology;* Henry Stern, in *JI* 4 (May 1, 1864): 114; Waldmeier, *Autobiography,* p. 25.

162. Luzzatto, *Mémoire,* pp. 78–79; d'Abbadie, "Réponses," p. 237.

163. Leslau, *Anthology,* p. 20. Leslau noted fasting was allowed only if the Day of Atonement, *astasreyo,* fell on that day, but Luzzatto and d'Abbadie specifically noted that fasting was not allowed even on that day in the 1840s: Leslau, 148, note 126. Also during the fast of *ab som,* which was to be observed by the total population during the first seventeen days of the fifth lunar month, two days were added to the number of fast days to compensate for the two Saturdays during this period in which the fast was broken: Luzzatto, *Mémoire,* pp. 70–71; d'Abbadie, "Réponses," p. 236. Another day was also added to compensate for the celebration of *arfe asart* on the tenth of the month.

164. D'Abbadie, "Extrait," p. 66; idem., "Réponses," p. 185; Halévy, "Excursion," p. 292; Luzzatto, *Mémoire,* pp. 59–60; J. M. Flad, *The Falashas,* p. 52. Described also in an interview with Gete Asrass on 9 November 1975. The word *fasika* is, of course, the same word used by Christians for Easter, both derived from the Hebrew, *pesach;* see Shelemay, *Music, Ritual,* p. 51 and p. 65, note 73.

165. D'Abbadie, "Réponses," p. 185; Halévy, "Excursion," p. 291; Luzzatto, *Mémoire,* pp. 61–63; Flad, *Falashas,* p. 52. D'Abbadie, "Extrait," pp. 67–68, called this *tuvani ma'rar* because it was in the dry season. Some observers, e.g., Luzzatto, used the term "Pentecost," according to Western Jewish practice, but the Beta Israel did not use that term themselves. In the mid–twentieth century, Leslau stated the second Ma'rar was on the 12th day of Kyslev, the ninth rather than the tenth month. The Christian observance of 12th Hedar honors Saint Michael: Bernard Velat, ed., *Études sur le Me'eraf, Patrologia Orientalis* 33 (1966): 28.

166. D'Abbadie, "Réponses," p. 236; Halévy, "Excursion," p. 291; Luzzatto, *Mémoire,* pp. 70–75. Also described in an interview with Gete Asrass on 9 November 1975. D'Abbadie, "Extrait," p. 66, gives a different reason for this fast and seems to confuse it with the Fast of Tomos. He also said the first ten days of the Fast of Ab was called the Fast of Heddar, which he elsewhere put in the tenth month. The usual method of fasting by the Beta Israel—eating anything but only after sunset—is similar to the Muslims in Ethiopia.

167. D'Abbadie, "Réponses," p. 185.

168. Leslau, *Anthology,* p. xxxi, uses both terms (Ge'ez: *za barabu sanbat*) but says it was the third Saturday of Ab while all 1840s sources agree on the fourth, which is the meaning of the Ge'ez term!

169. D'Abbadie, "Réponses," pp. 236–37; Luzzatto, *Mémoire,* pp. 75–78.

170. D'Abbadie, "Réponses," pp. 235, 237; idem., "Extrait," pp. 66–67; Luzzatto, *Mémoire,* pp. 63–64; Flad, *Falashas,* p. 52. The book does not seem to be known any longer, but Flad said it was "an extract from the Law, Psalms, and the Prophets, referring to Atonement." I observed Astasreyo in the village of Sanbatge, Wagara region, in October 1975. People only fasted one day before, the priests prayed all night in the prayer house, and the next day the fast was broken with a meal. Some grains were left scattered on the stones for the birds, and the priest read passages from the *Te'ezaza Sanbat* and the *Orit*. See also the description in Leslau, *Anthology,* p. xxxiv, and Shelemay, *Music, Ritual,* pp. 47–48.

171. Luzzatto, *Mémoire,* pp. 65–66; d'Abbadie, "Réponses," p. 235; idem., "Extrait," p. 67; Flad, *Falashas,* p. 52. The nineteenth-century sources do not mention Leslau's description (*Anthology,* xxxii) that they did not make booths in the wilderness as prescribed in Leviticus 23 because they already lived in exile in the wilderness.

172. D'Abbadie, "Réponses," p. 235.

173. Leslau, *Anthology,* pp. xxxiv–xxxv, called it a Fast of Supplication but says it was the twenty-ninth (and hence last) day of the eighth rather than the ninth month. See also Kay Shelemay, "Seged: A Falasha Pilgrimage Festival," *Musica Judaica* 3 (1980–81): 43–62; idem., *Music, Ritual,* pp. 48–50; J. Abbink, "Seged Celebration in Ethiopia and Israel: Continuity and Change of a Falasha Religious Holiday," *Anthropos* 78 (1983): 789–810; interview with Gete Asrass on 9 November 1975 describes the modern *segd,* which I also observed in Ambober in November 1975. See Chapter 2 above, where this day was mentioned in the *Gadla Takla Hawaryat* as being observed by the *ayhud* in Samen.

174. One informant told d'Abbadie it was the first ten days of the fifth month ("Extrait," p. 66), but another informant said it was the first ten days of the tenth month ("Réponses," p. 237). In each case, fasts known by other names were held at that same time. See also Luzzatto, *Mémoire,* pp. 79–80. Perhaps this fast was being phased out or just forgotten, or perhaps it was held two different times in two different places.

175. D'Abbadie, "Extrait," p. 68.

176. D'Abbadie, "Réponses," p. 235; Luzzatto, *Mémoire,* p. 79.

177. D'Abbadie, "Extrait," p. 43; idem., "Réponses," pp. 181–82. Leslau did not mention 18 Yekatit, but referred to the Festival of the 18th day in the sixth moon (Lul) which commemorated the death of Abraham, Isaac, and Jacob. Perhaps the day had been moved since the 1840s from the sixth month to the sixth moon. Or perhaps, either d'Abbadie or the informant was confused about the difference between sixth moon and sixth month. In general, in the article based on his 1842 trip, d'Abbadie put several holy days in terms of months when he clearly meant moon because he did not change the days: for example, Passover on 14 Miyazeya when he meant 14 Nisan; Ma'erar on 12 Sane when he meant 12 Sivan; Astasreyo on 10 Maskaram when he meant 10 Tahasaran.

178. D'Abbadie, "Extrait," p. 66 said it was the fifth moon (Ab), but that does not fit well since this was also the first day of the Fast of Ab, and d'Abbadie also said the first ten days of that month were the Fast of Heddar, which elsewhere he put in the tenth moon: "Réponses," p. 237. Leslau says the first day of Tahasaran was the *tazkara Abraham: Anthology,* pp. xxxi–xxxii. This day is only a few days from 28 Nahase. See Yona Bogale, *Jewish Calendar* (The Jewish Agency, 1975–76), p. 3. The text of the Beta Israel book, *Gadla Abraham,* which is to be read on that day specifically says 28 Nahase (see text edited by Conti Rossini, "Nuovi appunti sui Guidei d'Abissinia," in *RRAL,* ser. 5, 29 [1922]: 230); translation was made by Leslau from that text, *Anthology,* p. 96.

179. Explained in oral traditions as the day of the moon that Noah left the Ark and received promises from God; interview with Gete Asrass on 9 November 1975.

180. D'Abbadie, "Réponses," p. 235; Leslau, *Anthology,* p. xxx. See also C. Conti Rossini, *La Langue des Kemant,* 286.

181. D'Abbadie, "Réponses," p. 236; Leslau, *Anthology,* p. xxx. For *ankua* ("five"), see Conti Rossini, *Kemant,* p. 167.

182. D'Abbadie, "Réponses," pp. 235–36. By the 1940s, none of this was recalled, and the 12th of each moon was explained as a commemoration of the Harvest Festival on the 12th of the third moon; see Leslau, *Anthology,* p. xxx.

183. D'Abbadie, "Réponses," p. 235. In his earlier article, d'Abbadie had confused this with the 10th of each moon ("Extrait," pp. 67–68), as pointed out by Luzzatto, *Mémoire,* pp. 66–67. Leslau could find no reason for this holiday but said *arfe* must be "Cushitic" in his *Anthology,* p. xxx. See Conti Rossini, where *arfa* is the word for "moon" and hence also "month," *Kemant,* p. 169.

184. D'Abbadie, "Réponses," p. 236; Luzzatto, *Mémoire,* p. 80. See also Leslau, *Anthology,* p. xxx, who lists the Fast of *maleya* on the 29th of each moon. It is not clear if this was only on the 29th or alternately on the 30th, or in other words the last day of the moon.

185. D'Abbadie, "Réponses," p. 237; idem., "Extrait," p. 65; Halévy, "Excursion," p. 291; Luzzatto, *Mémoire,* p. 80. By the 1940s only the Thursday fast was maintained and that mainly by priests and elders: Leslau, *Anthology,* p. xxxiii.

186. Gobat, *Journal,* pp. 277–78; Leslau, *Anthology.*

187. Although the missionaries viewed their eagerness only as a desire to convert: Stern, in *JI* 4 (1864): 105–6; Bronkhorst, ibid., 1 (1861): 227.

188. For Beta Israel religious practitioners, see Flad, *Falasha,* pp. 29–37, 39. Flad also referred to the use of amulets by a Falasha "sorcerer" (probably a *dabtara*), a practice similar to that of the Christians, in "Journal," *JR* 28–29 (1863): 14. For the Christians' amulets and *dabtara,* see Parkyns, *Life,* pp. 270–71.

189. D'Abbadie, "Extrait," pp. 49–50; Flad, *Falashas,* pp. 35–36; Parkyns, *Life,* p. 294. Lefebvre said Beta Israel priests could not marry, and hinted at a way they had of making sexual organs atrophy(!), but he was probably referring to monks: "Aperçu général de l'Abyssinie," pp. 137, 139. See also Leslau, *Anthology,* p. xxiii.

190. Pearce, *Life and Adventures,* 1:289; William Cornwallis Harris, *The Highlands of Aethiopia,* 2:291; Gobat, *Journal,* pp. 278–79; d'Abbadie, "Journal," p. 464; Bronkhorst, in *JR* 13 (January 1862): 4. On the *buda* belief, see above. On *zar,* see also Marcel Griaule, "De quelque règles de nourriture concernant les genies zar,"

Aethiopica 3 (1935): 125–28; Michel Leiris, "Le culte des zars à Gondar," *Aethiopica* 2 (1934): 96–103, 125–36; idem., "Un rite médico-magique Ethiopien: Le jet du *danqara*," *Aethiopica* 3 (1935): 61–74; Wolf Leslau, "An Ethiopian Argot of a People Possessed by a Spirit," *Africa* 19 (1949): 204–12 [a description of a *zar* ceremony by the Falasha]; Maxime Rodinson, *Magie, Médecine,* pp. 61–71; E. Fuller Torrey, "The Zar Cult in Ethiopia," *Proceedings of the Third International Conference of Ethiopian Studies, Addis Ababa, 1966,* 3 vols. (Addis Ababa, 1969), 3:51–59.

191. Parkyns, *Life,* pp. 251–52; Sabrijian, *Deux ans,* 2:49. In the seventeenth century, one source said women needed 24 days of purification after childbirth. See Jeronymo Lobo, *A Voyage to Abyssinia,* pp. 281–93. Another source said Orthodox Christian women could not go to Church for forty or eighty days; Barradas, *Tractatus,* in Beccari, *Rerum Aethiopicarum,* 4:290. Christian practices may have been more rigid in the seventeenth century.

192. Flad, *Falashas,* p. 27; d'Abbadie, "Extrait," p. 46; Leslau, *Anthology,* p. xvii.

193. Bruce, *Travels,* 3:340–41; Parkyns, *Life,* pp. 252–53; Flad, *Falashas,* p. 27.

194. D'Abbadie, "Extrait," p. 46; Halévy, "Excursion," p. 285; Luzzatto, *Mémoire,* pp. 114–15.

195. Luzzatto, *Mémoire,* pp. 113–15, citing Poncet, a seventeenth-century traveler. He suggested some texts of the Ethiopian Bible had substituted 7th for 8th in translation from the Greek. In the early twentieth century, in Shawa, circumcision was on the eighth day, but excision was on the seventh day: Cohen, "Cérémonies et croyances abyssines," pp. 194–95.

196. Parkyns, *Life,* p. 253; Sabrijian, *Deux ans,* 2:48.

197. D'Abbadie, "Extrait," p. 46; idem., "Réponses," p. 264; Luzzatto, *Mémoire,* p. 85.

198. Flad, *Falashas,* p. 59.

199. D'Abbadie, "Extrait," p. 53; idem., "Réponses," pp. 240, 259; Flad, *Falashas,* p. 59; Stern, *Wanderings,* pp. 187–88; Parkyns, *Life,* p. 255.

200. D'Abbadie, "Extrait," pp. 55–56; Parkyns, *Life,* pp. 263–66.

201. D'Abbadie, "Extrait," p. 54; Lefebvre, "Aperçu général," p. 279.

202. Parkyns said Christian girls were betrothed as early as age 8 or 9 and men correspondingly early, while Flad said Beta Israel girls were married between 8 and 15 and men between 16 and 20; see Parkyns, *Life,* p. 255; Flad, *Falashas,* pp. 58–59. Only Stern, *Wanderings,* p. 187, said the Falasha married a bit later than Christians: girls at age 15 to 20 and boys at age 20 to 30.

203. D'Abbadie, "Extrait," pp. 46–47, 51; Luzzatto, *Mémoire,* pp. 91–94; Flad, *Falashas,* p. 32. For Christians, it was said the Sacrament of Confession had been abolished, but the practice was still carried on somewhat; see Sabrijian, *Deux ans,* 2:50.

204. D'Abbadie, "Extrait," p. 52; Flad, *Falashas,* pp. 65–67; Parkyns, *Life,* p. 271.

205. D'Abbadie, "Extrait," pp. 46–47, 52. No documentation on these points for Christians was forthcoming.

206. Parkyns, *Life,* pp. 202–3, 277–78, 290–91, 294; Dillon in Lefebvre, *Voyage,* 1:166.

207. D'Abbadie, "Journal," p. 470; C. H. Walker, *The Abyssinian at Home*

(London, 1933), p. 33. But Walker's observations were made in the early twentieth century while a century earlier, d'Abbadie, "Journal," p. 470, had stated that the Beta Israel were different from all other Ethiopians in their negative view of tanners.

208. Luzzatto, *Mémoire,* pp. 54–59.

209. D'Abbadie, "Extrait," p. 47; idem., "Réponses," p. 264.

210. Stern, *Wanderings,* p. 189.

211. Halévy, "Travels," p. 225.

212. Flad, *Falashas,* pp. 52–54.

213. Parkyns, *Life,* p. 294.

214. Parkyns, *Life,* pp. 228–30; d'Abbadie, "Extrait," p. 68; Halévy, "Excursion," p. 283. On class differences in clothing, particularly the differences between wearing silk or cotton, see Lefebvre, "État social des Abyssins," *NA* 105 (1845): 327.

215. One source called it the hot springs of "Abou-Mahari," about four hours from the monastery of Mahaber Sellase in Qwara; A. Charles Grad, et al., "Les expeditions allemands à la recherche d'Eduard Vogel (de 1861 à 1862)," *NA* 178 (1863): 316; Dimoteos Sabrijian, *Deux ans,* p. 157. In the twentieth century, a place not far from Chelga was called "Amba Mahari": Norden, *Africa's Last Empire,* pp. 223–24 and map. For a description of *abba* Mahari, see Stern, in *JI,* n.s. 1 (1861): 133–34.

216. D'Abbadie, "Extrait," p. 49.

217. Halévy, "Travels," p. 224.

218. Many sources indicate the Christian attitude toward the Gondar *rases,* such as Ferret and Galinier, *Voyages,* 2:463.

219. Wolf Leslau, ed., "A Falasha Religious Dispute," p. 80. Forced conversions by the Yajju rases were remembered in oral traditions; interview with Gete Asrass on 11 June 1975.

220. Interview with Menase Zammaru on 15 October 1975.

221. Combes and Tamisier, *Voyage,* 1:349–50 (my translation).

222. Samuel Gobat, in *JI* 4 (1838): 139. I have not seen references to conversions to Islam elsewhere, but perhaps this topic needs further investigation.

223. Interview with Gete Asrass on 11 June 1975. See Chapter 2.

224. D'Abbadie, "Réponses," p. 235.

225. Crummey, *Priests and Politicians,* pp. 128–34 summarizes these missions. In addition, see Great Britain, *Parliamentary Papers,* pp. 224, 252, 253, 255–56, 261–63, 290–92.

226. Rassam, *Narrative,* 1:250.

227. Flad, "Twelve Years in Abyssinia," *JI* 9 (1869): 219.

228. Flad, *Journal,* p. 61. See also the chronicle edited by Conti Rossini: "Vicende dell'Etiopia, e delle missioni cattoliche ai tempi di ras Ali, deggiac Ubie e re Teodoro secondo un documento abissino," *RRAL,* ser. 5, 25 (1916): 522.

229. Stern, *Wanderings,* pp. 56–57, 113, 228; Halévy, "Travels," p. 195; Waldmeier, *Autobiography,* p. 77; Flad, "Twelve Years in Abyssinia," p. 219.

230. Stern, letter from Gafat on 23 August 1860, in *JI,* n.s. 1 (1861): 89.

231. Flad, "Journal," *JR* 28–29 (1863).

232. I owe these insights on Tewodros to Donald Crummey in a personal communication of 5 January 1978.

233. Waldmeier, *Autobiography,* pp. 70–73.

234. Waldmeier, *Autobiography,* p. 77; Staiger, "Journal," December 1862, in Church of Scotland, General Assembly, *The Home and Foreign Missionary Record of the Church of Scotland,* n.s. 2 (1863): 81. Also on Gafat, see C. H. Blumhardt, "Deutsche Missionen in Abessinien," *Das Ausland* 36 (1863): 520–21.

235. Crummey, *Priests and Politicians,* pp. 137–40.

236. Flad, *Journal,* pp. 27, 44–45, 58, 84–85; Stern, in *JI,* n.s. 3 (1863), 67–69; Flad, "Journal of Mr. J. M. Flad," *JR* 28–29 (1863): 14; Flad, "Twelve Years in Abyssinia," *JI* 9 (1869): 191, 244–45. Oral traditions suggest the missionaries had very little success during the Tewodros years: interview with Berhan Beruk on 3 July 1975. See also Crummey, *Priests and Politicians,* p. 122, note 5.

237. In Leslau, "A Falasha Religious Dispute," p. 81. The date (1845), of course, indicates the general time range, but not necessarily the precise year. Oral traditions also recall the importance of *abba* Wedaje; interviews with Berhan Beruk on 3 July 1975, with Menase Zammaru on 15 October 1975, and with Ayyallegn Adgwachaw and Kebrate Samu'el on 26 October 1975. Menase Zammaru pointed out a connection between *abba* Sabra and *abba* Wedaje.

238. D'Abbadie, "Journal," p. 461.

239. Halévy, "Travels," p. 227.

240. Stern, *Wanderings,* pp. 199, 203–4, 241–46, 248–49. Interviews with Berhan Beruk on 3 July 1975, with Menase Zammaru and Wande Iyyasu on 13 October 1975, and with Ayyallegn Adgwachaw and Kebrate Samu'el on 26 October 1975; Gobat, *Journal,* pp. 277–78; Stern, "Journal of the Exploratory Missionary Journey Recently Made to the Jews or Felashas of Abyssinia," *JI,* n.s. 1 (1861): 171–203; Halévy, "Excursion," p. 288.

241. Interview with Menase Zammaru on 15 October 1975; Leslau, "A Falasha Religious Dispute," p. 81.

242. Flad, letter from Jenda, 4 December 1861, *The Home and Foreign Missionary Records of the Church of Scotland,* n.s. 1 (1862): 127; Stephen Bronkhorst, in *JR* (January 1862): 2.

243. Flad, "Journal," in *JR* 28–29 (1863): 13. On sacrifices, see d'Abbadie, "Journal," p. 459; Flad, *Kurze Schilderung der bisher fast unbekannten abessinischen Juden* (Basel, 1869), pp. 55–57. For a twentieth-century description of a sacrificial ceremony, see Deborah Lifchitz, "Un sacrifice chez les Falacha, Juifs Abyssins," *La terre et la vie* 9 (1939): 116–23. Swearing in the name of the King had the effect of an extremely strong interdiction.

244. Flad, "Journal," in *JR* 28–29 (April–May 1863): 15. This source is the most complete contemporary record of the dispute, but the "Journal" states specifically only the month and day and not the year. Since it was published in 1863, it may be assumed to refer to 1862. This is confirmed by a statement in *JI* (1 March 1863): p. 69, referring to events up to "November last" and mentioning the baptism of the first twenty-two converts on 21 July. In addition, a journal retrospectively written by Flad specifically refers to the baptism of the twenty-two on "July 1, 1862": "Twelve Years in Abyssinia," *JI* 9 (1869): 244–45. Hence, it is clear the main dispute argued before Tewodros occurred in 1862 and not 1861 as previously stated by another otherwise excellent summary of the dispute; Crummey, *Priests and Politicians,*

pp. 130–33. But as stated above (note 242), there had been another "crisis" in the rainy season of 1861, about which there does not seem to be more information.

245. In Flad, "Journal," *JR* 28–29 (1863): 15.

246. Ibid., p. 18.

247. Ibid., p. 19. See the remembrance of these events thirty years later: Aragawi, 28 March 1892, in *JI,* n.s. 9 (February 1893): 24 and map. On Beru Webe's name, see Chapter 5 below.

248. In Leslau, "A Falasha Religious Dispute," pp. 81–82; interviews with Berhan Beruk on 3 July 1975; Webe Akala on 27 December 1975.

249. Flad, "Journal," *JR* 28–29 (April–May 1863): 19. On Beru Webe's name, see Chapter 5, note 135.

250. In Leslau, "A Falasha Religious Dispute," pp. 81–82.

251. Ibid., p. 82.

252. Halévy, "Travels," p. 247.

253. Ibid., pp. 247–48. One source said they received twenty head of cattle; interview with Gete Asrass on 11 June 1975. Another said they received seven cattle; interview with Mammo Sagga Amlak, Ya'eqob Balay, and Mulu Mammo on 24 June 1975. Other traditions exist concerning Tewodros's close relations with the Beta Israel, such as that the Beta Israel priest, *abba* Wedaje, was helping his mother before he was born and that he prophetized she would give birth to a strong man, or that Tewodros was himself of partial Beta Israel background: interviews with Berhan Beruk on 3 July and 20 August 1975.

254. Flad, "Journal," *JR* (1863): 20.

255. Staiger, "Journal," December 1862, *Home and Foreign Missionary Record of the Church of Scotland,* n.s. 2 (1863): 81.

256. See Chapter 2 above for this dispute and the references there. Leslau, "Falasha Religious Dispute," p. 82, note 28, pointed out that the use of these passages in Genesis was common historically in theological disputes of this nature.

257. The letter was taken by the missionary Bronkhorst to Jerusalem and given to Bishop Gobat but was never delivered to the intended head of the Jews in Jerusalem. The text was published with a French translation a few years later: Hermann Zotenberg, "Un document sur les Falachas," *JA,* ser. 6, 9 (1867): 265–68. An English translation made by David Appleyard is included in David Kessler, *The Falashas,* pp. 123–24 which I have cited here. Parenthetically, this Abbā Ṣaggā may be the "prophet" referred to as Abba Siraq in Flad, *The Falashas,* pp. 36–38. See also Crummey's brief reference to Abba Siraq as a "prophet": "Shaikh Zäkaryas: An Ethiopian Prophet," *JES* 10/1 (1972): 55.

258. Halévy, "Travels," p. 248.

259. The Christian belief in a Messiah named Tewodros is based on the book *Fekkare Iyyasus.* For the Beta Israel belief, see Weld Blundell, *Royal Chronicle,* appendix F, p. 516; Gobat, *Journal,* pp. 278–79; d'Abbadie, "Journal," p. 464; Sven Rubenson, *King of Kings Tewodros of Ethiopia* (Addis Ababa, 1966), pp. 49–51.

260. Halévy, "Travels," pp. 248–49; Flad, *Falashas,* pp. 37–38; interviews with Menase Zammaru on 15 October 1975, Yeshaq Iyyasu on 15 December 1975. On *abba* Mahari into the 1870s, see Chapter 5.

261. Flad, *Falashas,* p. 18.

262. Halévy, "Travels," 219. See also Halévy, "Excursion," p. 286; interviews with Gete Asrass on 11 June 1975 and with Berhan Beruk on 3 July 1975.

263. Lefebvre, "Aperçu général," p. 137; Parkyns, *Life,* p. 208. One Beta Israel view was that Christians did eat those cattle killed even by a hyena instead of properly slaughtered: interview with Gete Asrass on 11 June 1975.

264. Ulrich Braukämper, "On Food Avoidances in Southern Ethiopia: Religious Manifestations and Socio-Economic Relevance," in Sven Rubenson, ed., *Proceedings of the Seventh International Conference of Ethiopian Studies, Lund, 1982* (Uppsala, Sweden, 1984), p. 437. I tend to agree with Braukämper that both a "materialist" and an "idealist" approach are necessary to understand this phenomenon. For both sides of the debate, see Mary Douglas, *Purity and Danger* (New York, 1970); Marvin Harris, *Cows, Pigs, Wars and Witches* (New York, 1975).

265. Flad, *Journal,* p. 86; idem., *Falashas,* p. 27; d'Abbadie, "Journal," pp. 464, 467.

266. Parkyns, *Life,* pp. 331–32; Lefebvre, "Aperçu général," p. 279: a man who had a child in adultery had only to pay the mother a bushel of grain, and sometimes $2.00 per year.

267. D'Abbadie, "Journal," pp. 464, 470. The "prayer house" (*bēta ṣalot*) was the main religious building often called by the Western term "synagogue" in European sources. Beta Israel also called it *masgid,* the same word used by Muslims in Ethiopia for "mosque."

268. Flad, *Journal,* pp. 32, 86.

269. Ibid., p. 86.

270. Bruce, *Travels,* 3:315. The time reference is not clear here, but since this reference occurs in a statement that sexual intercourse during the previous twenty-four hours made one unclean, perhaps the twenty-four–hour time period also applied to touching the dead.

271. D'Abbadie, "Journal," p. 470.

272. Walker, *Abyssinian at Home,* p. 33. D'Abbadie said only the Beta Israel saw tanners as impure: "Journal," 470.

273. Walker, *Abyssinian at Home,* p. 33.

274. Parkyns, *Life in Abyssinia,* p. 282.

275. Interviews with Menase Zammaru on 15 October 1975 and with Ayyallegn Adgwachew and Kebrate Samu'el on 26 October 1975. D'Abbadie, "Journal," p. 470, also outlined procedures for Beta Israel reconversion back from Christianity.

276. Stern, *Wanderings,* p. 187.

277. Ibid.; Gobat, *Journal,* pp. 279, 468; Halévy, "Travels," pp. 217, 219.

278. Beke, "Abyssinia," p. 8. This example referred to Beta Israel in Gojjam. The same existed in the Gondar region: Steudner, "Reise von Adoa nach Gondar," p. 129 who said they also washed in the creek every evening.

279. Gobat, *Journal,* p. 468; Halévy, "Travels," p. 217.

280. Ibid.; d'Abbadie, "Extrait," p. 50.

281. D'Abbadie, "Extrait," p. 50.

282. Quotation from Bronkhorst, in *JR* 12 (January 1862): 3. Statement on occupations from: Lefebvre, "Aperçu général," p. 138.

283. Flad, *Journal,* p. 33.

284. Stern, in *JI,* n.s. 1 (1863): 134.

285. Beke, "Abyssinia," p. 8.

286. In some senses, the Beta Israel caste position was theoretically comparable to the concept of "strangers" within a dominant society. For a good analysis of some of the interpretations—and misinterpretations—of this concept delineated originally by George Simmel, see Donald Levine, "Simmel at a Distance: On the History and Systematics of the Sociology of the Stranger," in William A. Shack and Elliott P. Skinner, eds., *Strangers in African Societies* (Berkeley, 1979), pp. 21–36. Though the extent to which the Beta Israel were literally "strangers" is debatable (see Chapter 1 above), their social position and relations by the mid-nineteenth century are somewhat comparable. For various uses of the concept, see other articles in the Shack volume and also Patricia Romero Curtin, "Generations of Strangers: The Kore of Lamu," *IJAHS* 18 (1985): 455–72. For some interesting comparative comments on the relationship between "caste" and "class" in another part of Ethiopia, see Werner Lange, "Status and Function of Kafa Bards in Feudal Ethiopia," *NAS* 1 (1979–80): 85–90.

Chapter 5

1. Referring to the time from Tewodros to Yohannes; L. Fusella, trans., "Il *Dagmawi Menilek* di Afawarq Gabra Iyasus," *RSE* 27 (1961): 16. See also Richard Caulk, "Armies as Predators: Soldiers and Peasants in Ethiopia, c. 1850–1935," *IJAHS* 11 (1978): 457–93; Richard Pankhurst, "Some Factors Depressing the Standard of Living of Peasants in Traditional Ethiopia," *JES* 4/2 (1966): 45–98.

2. Martino Moreno, ed., "La cronaca di re Teodoro attribuita al dabtara 'Zaneb,'" *RSE* 2 (1942): 167, 169–71, 177; Sven Rubenson, *King of Kings Tewodros of Ethiopia* (Addis Ababa, 1966), pp. 54–55; Caulk, "Armies as Predators," pp. 463–64; Donald Crummey, "The Violence of Tewodros," *JES* 9/2 (1971): 107–25.

3. Caulk, "Armies as Predators," p. 465; idem., "Firearms and Princely Power in Ethiopia in the Nineteenth Century," *JAH* 13 (1972): 609–30; Donald Crummey, "Banditry and Resistance: Noble and Peasant in Nineteenth-Century Ethiopia," in Crummey, ed., *Banditry, Rebellion and Social Protest in Africa* (London, 1986), pp. 133–49; Great Britain, *Correspondence,* p. 106.

4. Harold Marcus, *The Life and Times of Menelik II* (London, 1975), pp. 33–35; Chris Prouty Rosenfeld, *A Chronology of Menilek II of Ethiopia* (East Lansing, Mich., 1976), pp. 43–47; Zewde Gabre-Sellassie, *Yohannes IV,* pp. 21–24, 31–33.

5. Such as the April 1872 rebellion of Walda Maryam who had also previously revolted against Takla Giyorgis; Rosenfeld, *Chronology,* pp. 45, 53; Marcus, *Menelik II,* p. 36. On other revolts, see Rosenfeld, *Chronology,* pp. 53, 55–58, 60, 62–63, 64, 69; Zewde, *Yohannes IV,* pp. 44–45.

6. Beroo to London Society, *Report* 64 (1872): 92.

7. Mission agents' letter of October 1874 in *Report* 67 (1875): 105–6.

8. Ibid., p. 106.

9. Ibid.

10. In *JI* 17 (March 1877): 66. See also Gerhard Rohlfs, *Meine Mission nach Abessinien* (Leipzig, 1883), pp. 277–78.

11. In *Report* 68 (1876): 107.

12. Rosenfeld, *Chronology*, pp. 71–74; Zewde, *Yohannes IV*, pp. 90–93.

13. Flad in *JR* (April 1878): 14; Argossy to Flad, *Report* 70 (1878): 117; *JI* 19 (June 1879): 183; letter in *Report* 72 (1880): 127; *JI* 21 (June 1881): 166; letters to Flad in May, June, July, 1883, in *JI* 24 (June 1884): 175.

14. Richard Pankhurst, "The Great Ethiopian Famine of 1888–1892: A New Assessment," *Journal of History of Medicine and Allied Sciences* 21 (1966): 95–124, 271–94.

15. Letter in *Report* 71 (1879): 122–24; Beroo, Sanbatu, Aragawi, letter in *Report* 72 (1880): 127; *JI* 19 (October 1879): 276–77; *JI* 22 (October 1882): 260. In the "north" in general, famine had begun by 1882; see Rosenfeld, *Chronology*, p. 98.

16. P. M. Holt and M. W. Daly, *A History of the Sudan* (3rd ed., Boulder, 1979), pp. 85–113; P. M. Holt, *The Mahdist State in the Sudan, 1881–1898* (Oxford, 1958), pp. 150–55. For "spiral of violence," see Richard Caulk, "Yohannes IV, the Mahdists, and the Colonial Partition of North-East Africa," *TJH* 1/2 (1971): 22–42.

17. Michael Aragawi letter, in *JI*, n.s. 5 (July 1889): 107; Rosenfeld, *Chronology*, pp. 111, 117, 122.

18. Rosenfeld, *Chronology*, pp. 124–25; Richard Caulk, "Firearms and Princely Power," p. 622.

19. Quotation from Aragawi in *JI*, n.s. 5 (July 1889): 107. The Gondar clergy appealed to Yohannes; Bairu Tafla, ed., *A Chronicle of Emperor Yohannes IV (1872–1889)* (Wiesbaden, 1977), p. 155; Rosenfeld, *Chronology*, p. 128; Zewde, *Yohannes IV*, pp. 238–45; Marcus, *Menelik II*, pp. 100–110. See also Augustus Wylde, *Modern Abyssinia* (London, 1901), p. 40; Haggai Erlich cites sources stating forty-five churches were set on fire; *Ethiopia and Eritrea During the Scramble for Africa: A Political Biography of Ras Alula, 1875–1897* (East Lansing, Mich., 1982), p. 119.

20. Rosenfeld, *Chronology*, pp. 128–30.

21. Tafla, ed., *Yohannes IV*, p. 157; Caulk, "Yohannes IV, Mahdists," p. 31; Erlich, *Ras Alula*, pp. 130–35; Rosenfeld, *Chronology*, pp. 131–32, 135–36; Zewde, *Yohannes IV*, pp. 246–49; Sahle Woldegaber, "The Background and the Consequences of the Battle of Metemma," (B.A. thesis, Haile Sellassie I University, 1968).

22. Aragawi, letter of 28 March 1892, in *JI* 9 (February 1893): 22.

23. Aragawi to Flad, 28 March 1892, in *JI*, n.s. 9 (February 1893): 20–22.

24. Rosenfeld, *Chronology*, pp. 137, 140, 143–46, 150, 155; Guebre Sellasie, *Chronique du règne de Menelik II, Roi des Rois d'Éthiopie*, 2 vols. (Paris, 1930–32), 1:291–313.

25. Flad in *JI*, n.s. (February 1891): 18; Pankhurst, "The Great Ethiopian Famine," p. 100 and infra.

26. Aragawi to Flad, 18 June 1891, in *JI*, n.s., 8 (February 1892): 20; idem., to Flad, 28 March 1892, in *JI*, n.s. 9 (February 1893): 20–22.

27. Aragawi to Flad, 18 June 1891, in *JI*, n.s. 8 (February 1892): 18; idem., in *JI*, n.s. 7 (May 1891): 65–66.

28. Aragawi to Flad, 18 June 1891, in *Report* 84 (1892): 148.

29. Aragawi to Flad, March to October 1890, in *Report* 83 (1891): 140; idem., 18 June 1891, in *JI*, n.s. 8 (February 1892): 20.

30. Letters in *JMI*, n.s. 9 (November 1893): 163–64; Flad, 11 March 1894, in *JMI*, n.s. 10 (May 1894): 66; Alaca Worke to Flad, 27 August 1894, in *JMI*, n.s. 10 (November 1894): 171.

31. W. H. Negoosie and Goshu Beleta, in *JMI* 19 (July 1903): 108.

32. Interview with Sannayt Ayyanaw on 11 June 1975.

33. "A Letter from Falashas," *Jewish Chronicle*, 13 October 1905, p. 11. The same letter appears with the Amharic text and a French translation in Jacques Faitlovitch, "Une lettre amharique des Falachas ou Juifs d'Abyssinie," *RS* 14 (1906): 92–95. During my fieldwork, I was shown many ruins of Beta Israel buildings said to have been destroyed by the Mahdists ("Dervishes").

34. And Alem Mulaw, "Bage-Mdir and Simen (1910–1930)" (B.A. thesis, Haile Sellassie I University, 1971); Jacques Faitlovitch, "The Falashas," *American Jewish Yearbook 5681* 22 (1920–21): 94.

35. Rosenfeld, *Chronology*, p. 43; Zewde, *Yohannes IV*, p. 24.

36. Gerhard Rohlfs, "Ergebnisse meiner Reise nach Abessinien; Bermerkungen zur Karte," *PGM* 28 (1882): 404; Felix Rosen, *Eine deutsche Gesandtschaft in Abessinien* (Leipzig, 1907), p. 414.

37. Stern, "Journal," *JI*, n.s. 1 (1861): 174–75; idem., *Wanderings*, p. 203.

38. *Report* 68 (1876): 108; Agashy Scheloo in *JR* (April 1878): 15; Negoosie to Flad, in *JMI* 14 (April 1898): 55.

39. Aragawi, letter from Djenda, 25 May 1901, in *JMI* 18 (January 1902): 6–7; Rosen, *Deutsche Gesandtschaft*, p. 400. One source said a "Falashabet" did remain in the 1920s: Ernst Schrenzel, *Abessinien. Land Ohne Hunger, Land Ohne Zeit* (Berlin, 1928), p. 126.

40. Raffray, *Afrique Orientale*, p. 314; Sanbatoo to Flad, in *JMI* 13 (September 1897): 131.

41. Haim Nahoum, "Mission chez les Falachas d'Abyssinie," *BAIU*, ser. 3, 33 (1908): 115; Faitlovitch, *Quer durch*, pp. 63–64.

42. Nahoum, "Mission," pp. 115–16; Faitlovitch, *Quer durch*, pp. 61–62. *Ras* Gugsa Wale was governor of Begamder, 1901–10 and 1918–30; see And Alem Mulaw, "Bage-Mdir and Simen," p. 42. One oral tradition says Beta Israel began to live at Walaka under *ras* Walda Giyorgis who was governor of Begamder, 1910–18; interview with Berhan Beruk on 20 August 1975. Barkoligne, as well as several other *bejronds*, such as Bogale, Fante, Yeshaq, and others from the time of Menilek are remembered in oral traditions as well; interviews with Gete Asrass on 11 June 1975, with Menase Zammaru and Wande Iyyasu on 13 October 1975, with Webe Akala on 27 December 1975, and with Enneyaw Tarrakagne on 30 December 1975.

43. My emphasis; Hermann Norden, *Africa's Last Empire* (Philadelphia, 1930), pp. 154, 194.

44. Agashy Scheloo, in *JR* (April 1878): 15.

45. M. Chaine, ed., "Histoire du règne de Iohannes IV, roi d'Éthiopie (1868–1889)," *RS* 21 (1913): 188.

46. Dermot R. W. Bourke, Earl of Mayo, *Sport in Abyssinia* (London, 1876), p. 219; E. A. de Cosson, *The Cradle of the Blue Nile*, 2 vols. (London, 1877), 1:114, 120, 184; Gerald Portal, *My Mission to Abyssinia* (London, 1892), pp. 185–86; idem., *An Account of the English Mission to King Johannes of Abyssinia in 1887* (Winchester, n.d. [1888]), pp. 80–81. See also Rosenfeld, *Chronology*, p. 118; Richard Pankhurst, "Towards a Theory of Ethiopian Innovation," *RA* 11 (Spring 1970): 51; idem., "Misoneism and Innovation in Ethiopian History," *EO* 7/4 (1964): 298; Chris Prouty, *Empress Taytu*, p. 144.

47. Wylde, *Modern Abyssinia,* pp. 299–300, 51–52.

48. The name of the *bejrond* at Maqale was given by an informant in Tigray; interview with Yeshaq Iyyasu on 15 December 1975. Beta Israel lived throughout Tigray in the early twentieth century, including at Aksum, though they often shifted residence with the availability of work; Faitlovitch, *Quer durch,* pp. 36–45, 152. Other *bejronds* in Tigray were said to be Beru, Sahalu, Zallaqa, and Gwangul; interviews with Yeshaq Iyyasu on 15 December 1975 and with Tafassaku Webshat and elders of Endabaguna on 15 December 1975.

49. Interviews with Mammo Sagga Amlak, Ya'eqob Balay, and Mulu Mammo on 24 June 1975; with Berhan Beruk on 3 July 1975; Ratta Zawde on 10 August 1975; with Sandaqqe Maharan on 24 October 1975; and with Ayyallegn Adgwachaw and Kebrate Samu'el on 26 October 1975.

50. Interviews with Ratta Zawde on 10 August 1975, with Sandaqqe Maharan on 24 October 1975, with Gete Asrass on 9 November 1975, and with Enneyaw Tarrakagne on 30 December 1975.

51. Interviews with Gete Asrass on 11 June and 9 November 1975; with Mammo Sagga Amlak, Ya'eqob Balay, and Mulu Mammo on 24 June 1975; with Berhan Beruk on 3 July 1975; and with Balay Malku and Sammallegne Takka on 3 September 1975.

52. Wylde, *Modern Abyssinia,* pp. 359–67 (quotation p. 363); Faitlovitch, *Quer durch,* pp. 145–46. Also on Wale, see Prouty, *Taytu, passim.*

53. Guebre Sellasse, *Chronique,* pp. 209–10; Pankhurst, "Misoneism," p. 300; idem., "The Foundation and Growth of Addis Ababa to 1935," *EO* 6 (1962): 34; idem., "Menelik and the Foundation of Addis Ababa," *JAH* 2 (1961): 105; idem., "The City Fifty Years Ago," *EO* 1/2 (March 1957): 60–66; Rosenfeld, *Chronology;* Prouty, *Taytu,* 44.

54. The other nine were named Bartoli, Bogale, Makonnen, Meshesha, Fanta, Yeshaq, Alamu, Aynalem, and Malku; interview with Gete Asrass on 11 June 1975. Genealogical evidence provided by an informant claiming to be a nephew of Desta indicates Malku and Bogale were two of these brothers; interview with Balay Malku and Sammallegne Takka on 3 September 1975.

55. Paul Soleillet, *Voyages en Ethiopie* (Rouen, 1886), p. 304, cited in Pankhurst, "Foundation and Growth of Addis Ababa," p. 34.

56. Guebre Sellassie, *Chronique,* 1:72–73; Lincoln de Castro, *Nella Terra dei Negus,* 2 vols. (Milan, 1915), 2:237, 244, and pictures, 2:177 (facing), figures 61 and 62, 2:184 (facing), figure 63; Marcel Cohen, "Rapport sur une mission linguistique en Abyssinie, 1910–1911," *NAMSL* 20/6 (1912): 35–38 and plate 1.

57. Charles Singer, "The Falashas," in *JQR* 17 (1905): 142.

58. On Addis, see Peter Garretson, "A History of Addis Ababa from Its Foundation in 1886 to 1910" (Ph.D. dissertation, University of London, 1974).

59. Rosen, *Deutsche Gesandtschaft,* pp. 278–82; J. G. Vanderheym, *Une expédition avec le Négous Menelik* (Paris, 1896), pp. 62–64, 76, 119; Harold Marcus, "The Organization of Menilek II's Palace and Imperial Hospitality (After 1896)," *RA* 11 (Spring 1970): 57–62.

60. Gleichen said Menilek's chief carpenter was an Indian, Haj Kewas, and that he was told there were only one or two carpenters in the city; Count Edward Gleichen, *With the Mission to Menilek* (London, 1898), pp. 164–66. But see Mérab

for a more complete ethnic breakdown of the population of Addis in the early twentieth century; Paul Mérab, *Impressions d'Éthiopie (L'Abyssinie sous Menelik II)*, 3 vols. (Paris, 1921–29), 2:115; Faitlovitch, *Quer durch*, p. 124; Garretson, "History of Addis Ababa."

61. Singer, "The Falashas," p. 143; Yona Bogale who lived for years in Addis recalled the name "Abwarre": personal communication 1975, and quoted in Kessler, *The Falashas*, p. 145; Mérab said 100 individual Falasha lived in Addis (*Impressions*, 2:115), while Faitlovitch said there were fifty to sixty families (*Quer durch*, p. 124); Pankhurst, "Foundation and Growth of Addis Ababa," pp. 35–36; interview with Berhan Beruk on 3 July 1975.

62. Mérab, *Impressions*, 1:112.

63. Faitlovitch, *Quer durch*, p. 136; see Chapters 1 and 2 above.

64. Wylde, *Modern Abyssinia*, 338–39; Faitlovitch, *Quer durch*, p. 150; Aragawi to Flad, 20 August 1892, in *JMI*, n.s. 9 (February 1893): 26.

65. The Gojjam Falasha received numerous missionary trips: *Report*, 69 (1877): 105; *JI* 21 (June 1881): 166; Aragawy in *Report* 74 (1882): 140; ibid., 76 (1884): 122–24; Hiob Negusie, in *JMI* 15 (November 1899): 169–71.

66. Richard Pankhurst, "Menilek and the Utilisation of Foreign Skills in Ethiopia," *JAH* 5 (1967): 29–86.

67. Erlich, *Alula*; Zewde, *Yohannes IV*. But see also Crummey, "Review of Zewde Gabre-Sellasie, *Yohannes IV of Ethiopia*," in *JAH* 17 (1976): 633–34; Caulk, "Religion and State in Nineteenth Century Ethiopia," *JES* 10/1 (1972): 23–41.

68. Gabira Madihin Kidana, "Yohannes IV, Religious Aspects of His Internal Polity" (B.A. thesis, Haile Sellassie I University, 1972), pp. 1–10.

69. Chaine, "Iohannes IV," pp. 188–89; Bairu Tafla, *Yohannes IV*, pp. 151–53.

70. See chapters above; Zewde, *Yohannes IV*, pp. 94–100; Gabira, "Yohannes IV," pp. 12, 30.

71. Rosenfeld, *Chronology*, p. 47.

72. Zewde, *Yohannes IV*, pp. 36–41.

73. Rosenfeld, *Chronology*, p. 55.

74. Rosenfeld, *Chronology*, pp. 78, 86; Zewde, *Yohannes IV*, p. 93.

75. Erlich, *Alula*, p. 23. For typical views see Waldmeier, *Autobiography*, pp. 33–34, 137; J. B. Coulbeaux, *Histoire*, 2:469.

76. Erlich, *Alula*, p. 23.

77. Caulk, "Religion and State," pp. 30–31.

78. MS Eth 259 in Institute of Ethiopian Studies: Chronicle of Takla Giyorgis and Yohannes IV, trans. Tesfayohannes, folio 26, pp. 21–22.

79. Ibid., p. 22. He ordered the forced conversion of Muslims near Ankobar: Orazio Antinori, letter in *BSGI* 17 (1880): 451.

80. Guebre Sellassie, *Chronique*, p. 156.

81. Chaine, "Iohannes IV," p. 180; Caulk, "Religion and State," pp. 25–30; Gabira, "Yohannes IV," pp. 24–27, 39–40; Waldmeier, *Autobiography*, pp. 33–34; Gabriel Simon, *Voyage en Abyssinie et chez les Gallas* (Paris, 1885), pp. 211–13.

82. Rosenfeld, *Chronology*, pp. 79, 80, 98; Chaine, "Iohannes IV," pp. 182, 183 (text), 186, 187 (text).

83. In Wolf Leslau, ed., "Religious Dispute," pp. 78 (text), 83 (trans). I have altered the transcription some.

84. Interview with Yeshaq Iyyasu on 15 December 1975 in Endabaguna, Tigray. See also interviews with Alamayyahu Iyyasu on 15 December 1975 in Endabaguna and with Webe Akala on 27 December 1975 in Gondar.

85. A Christian Ethiopian, "Woldah Haimanaot" (Walda Haymanot) obtained this information from two Beta Israel artisans in Addis Ababa, "Yetemengo" and "Afawark" and sent it to Charles Singer, "The Falashas," p. 146.

86. Flad in *JR* (November 1874): 45. See similar statements by Yohannes quoted in *JI* 14 (August 1874): 215–16; Flad in *Report* 67 (1875): 104. His desire not to have European missionaries in the country was affirmed many times: Gerhard Rohlfs, letter in *PGM* 27 (1881): 73.

87. In *JI* 20 (July 1880): 185, italics in original.

88. Flad, "Journal," in *JR* (November 1874): 41–48.

89. Aragawy letter in *Report* 75 (1883): 119.

90. Flad, "Journal," *JR* (November 1874): 45.

91. In Leslau, "Religious Dispute," pp. 78, 83–84. See also "Letter," *Jewish Chronicle,* 13 October 1905, p. 11; Faitlovitch, "Lettre," *RS* 14 (1906): 94; S. H. Marguiles, "Per La Storia del Movimento pro Falascia, due documenti," *RI* 6/4–5 (1909): 158.

92. Interview with Gete Asrass on 11 June 1975.

93. Interview with Menase Zammaru and Wande Iyyasu on 13 October 1975.

94. Menilek, letter to Mr. Clarke, cited in *JMI,* n.s. 12 (May 1896): 81 note. To Faitlovitch, he said: "Moreover, I also come from the Jews," cited in *Quer durch,* p. 126.

95. That is, mission teachers; *Report* 83 (1890): 134.

96. Alaca Workie, letter, 22 July 1895, in *Report* 88 (1896): 136. Permission to work was renewed periodically thereafter by Menilek or by *ras* Mangasha: Meheret to Flad, in *JMI* 13 (1897): 133; *Report,* 90 (1898): 113; *Report* 93 (1901): 158; Flad in *JMI* 18 (July 1902): 104; *Report* 95 (1903): 96; *JMI* 22 (May 1906): 68.

97. On Menilek's favor toward missions to the Oromo and his desire for European technological assistance, see his letter to Waldmeier quoted in "Johann Mayer's Missionreise nach Shoa in Sudabyssinien; Januar bis Juni 1872," *Globus* 23 (1873): 157–58. On his views toward the Beta Israel, see Flad, in *Report* 95 (1903): 96; *JMI* 22 (May 1906): 68; Wylde, *Modern Abyssinia,* pp. 471–72; Eric Payne, *Ethiopian Jews: The Story of a Mission* (London, 1972), pp. 70–71.

98. *Report* 77 (1885): 122.

99. Gobat, in *JI* 4 (1838): 139.

100. Crummey, *Priests,* pp. 115–34; Thomas Halstead, *Our Missions: Being a History . . . of the London Society for Promoting Christianity Amongst the Jews* (London, 1866); William Gidney, *The History of the London Society for Promoting Christianity Amongst the Jews, from 1809 to 1908* (London, 1908); Eric Payne, *Ethiopian Jews;* A. McLeish, ed., *Light and Darkness in East Africa* (London, 1927); George Stevens, *"Go, Tell My Brethren": A Short Popular History of the Church Mission to the Jews (1809–1959)* (London, 1959); J. S. Trimingham, *The Christian Church and Missions in Ethiopia* (London, 1950). See also the excellent recent account by Steven Kaplan, "The Beta Israel (Falasha) Encounter with Protestant Missionaries: 1860–1905," *Jewish Social Studies* 49 (1987), reprinted in *Truman Institute Reprints* [Hebrew University], which I read after writing this chapter.

101. Crummey, *Priests*, pp. 128, 131; David McDougall, *In Search of Israel. A Chronicle of the Jewish Missions of the Church of Scotland* (London, 1941); Church of Scotland, General Assembly, *The Home and Foreign Missionary Record of the Church of Scotland*, v. 16–17 (January 1861–March 1862), n.s. 1–6 (1862–69) [hereafter *HFMR*].

102. Stern, letter of 15 May 1860, in *JI* (November 1860): 360.

103. Stern, "The Abyssinian Church, and the Difficulties to Effect a Reform," *JI* 8 (February 1868): 32.

104. Flad, 4 December 1861, in Church of Scotland, *HFMR*, n.s. 1 (1862): 127. See similar sentiments in: *JI*, n.s. 1 (1861): 124.

105. *Report* 67 (1875): 103–5; Flad, in *JR* (November 1874): 45.

106. Stern, in *JI*, n.s. 3 (1863): 92.

107. Falasha agents letter to Flad, October 1874, in *Report* 67 (1875): 106.

108. *JI* 11 (1871): 17–19, 158; ibid., 14 (1874): 40, 175, 269; *JR* (November 1874): 41–48; *Report* 67 (1875): 103–7; *JI* 20 (1880): 292; ibid., 21 (1881): 4, 90, 166; *Report* 82 (1890): 133; *JI*, n.s. 6 (1890): 29, 46, 61, 101; *JMI* (May 1894): 65–66; ibid. (June 1894): 83–86; ibid., 17 (March 1902): 41. There was possibly another visit to the borders by Flad in 1876.

109. Michael Aragawi visited him in Europe; *JI*, n.s. 1 (1885): 111, 195; *Report* 78 (1886): 123; *JMI*, n.s. 9 (1893): 80, 126; *Report* 86 (1894): 136; Flad in *JMI* 10 (1894): 3.

110. *Report* 57 (1865): 103.

111. Flad in *JI* 6 (May 1866): 112; *Report* 58 (1866): 101–2.

112. *JI* 5 (June 1865): 171.

113. *Report* 62 (1870): 76.

114. Flad, "Journal," *JR* (May 1871): 17–20; idem., in *JI* 11 (June 1871): 158–59.

115. Beroo, letter to Flad 6 January 1870, in *JI* 10 (June 1870): 162.

116. Beroo, letter of 27 November 1872, in *Report* 65 (1873): 107–8, and in *JI* 13 (June 1873): 158.

117. *JI*, n.s. 13 (December 1873): 288–94. On these and others' studies, see also Flad, in *Report* 65 (1873): 106; Flad, letter in *JI*, n.s. 14 (February 1874): 40.

118. *Report* 68 (1876): 107.

119. Flad, in *JI*, n.s. 16 (September 1876): 231.

120. Flad, in *JR* (April 1878): 14; idem., *JI* 17 (March 1877): 65–67.

121. Falasha agents' letter of 16 January 1879, in *Report* 71 (1879): 123–25. On Gobbaw, who later changed his name, left missionary work, and became an emissary and appointee of Menilek who was known as *kantiba* Gabru, see below.

122. Argossy to Flad in *Report* 70 (1878): 117–20; Beru in *JI* 21 (September 1881): 235–37; Michael Aragawi, in *JR* (November 1882): 41–44; idem., *JR* (May 1884): 17–19; letter to Flad in *JI* 22 (1882): 260–61.

123. Flad, in *Report* 73 (1881): 160.

124. Aragawi in *JI*, n.s. 1 (April 1885): 54; idem., *Report* 77 (1885): 122.

125. Aragawi to Flad, from Abu Hara, 24 August 1892, in *JMI*, n.s. 9 (February 1893): 28.

126. Flad, letter 12 May 1893, in *JMI*, n.s. 9 (June 1893): 96.

127. In *JMI*, n.s. 9 (August 1893): 126.

128. Flad in *JMI* (June 1894): 83–85; idem., in *Report* 86 (1894): 139; *Report* 87 (1895): 133.

129. *JMI,* n.s. 11 (June 1895): 90.

130. I use Michael Aragawi's last name for convenience as that is how he is always called in the sources. The precise issue of the accusation is not clear but probably reflected Orthodox unhappiness and suspicion that converts were preaching among Christians as well as among Falasha; Meheret to Flad, in *JMI* 13 (1897): 132–33.

131. Flad in *JMI* 15 (August 1899): 114; idem., *JMI* 16 (February 1900): 30.

132. Sanbatoo to Flad, in *JMI* 13 (September 1897): 132.

133. *Report* 102 (1910): 111.

134. Beta Israel population estimates were mere guesses, albeit by people on the scene for several years. Stern said "at least 250,000" in 1861, *JI,* n.s. 1 (1861): 132, and "250,000" in 1862, *Wanderings,* p. 194. Flad estimated 200,000 in the 1860s: *The Falashas,* p. 14, and lowered it to 150,000 in his reflections years later: *Sechzig Jahre in der Mission,* p. 20. Bruce had estimated 100,000 in the 1770s: *Travels,* 1:486. The accepted figure was about 200,000: *JI,* n.s. 8 (September 1892): 146–49. Antoine d'Abbadie estimated about 80,000: *L'Abyssinie et Théodore,* p. 15.

135. There is some confusion about whether his name was Beru Webe ("Biography of Dabtara Beroo," *JMI,* n.s. 9 (October 1893): 154) or Webe Beru (Leslau, "Falasha Religious Dispute," pp. 76, 81). In the Gondar region, the custom often reversed the typical Amharic word order; see Rubenson, *Tewodros,* p. 15, note 2.

136. His age is not exactly clear in the sources. He was said to have been born during the reign of *dejazmach* Mareyye, who was kingmaker, ca. 1828–31: Abir, *Era of Princes,* pp. 34, 36; "Biography of Dabtara Beroo," *JMI* (October 1893): 154. This would put his birthdate within five years of what Flad indicated when he said Beru was "about 34" in 1870: *JI* 11 (June 1871): 158–59. Payne says he was born in 1837: *Ethiopian Jews,* p. 39.

137. "Biography," *JMI* (October 1893): 155.

138. "Four Abyssinian Missionaries," in *JMI* (April 1893): 56; Flad, in *JI,* n.s. 13 (1873): 289; Payne, *Ethiopian Jews,* pp. 68–74, says he was age 75 in 1922, making his birthdate about 1847–48. See also Rita Pankhurst, "Mikael Argawi, Ethiopia's First Protestant Missionary," *EO* 10 (1966): 215–19, who, however, says he was born a Falasha, whereas all local sources have him as an Amhara who worked among the Falasha. He was also not the "first" missionary, as Beru clearly filled that description since he had been proselytizing since the 1860s, though Beru was not trained overseas.

139. "Samani, the Young Falasha Missionary," in *JI* 22 (May 1882): 104–7; 22 (July 1882): 178–81; Flad, in *JI,* n.s. 13 (December 1873): 290.

140. Flad, in *JI,* n.s. 13 (December 1873): 290–91.

141. *JI* 12 (September 1872): 227–28.

142. Flad, in *JI,* n.s. 13 (December 1873): 289–90; Goshu Mersha, letter to Flad in *JI* 24 (September 1884): 239–40; "Four Abyssinian Missionaries," *JMI,* n.s. 9 (April 1893): 56–58.

143. See Chapter 4 above; Flad in *JR* 28–29 (1863): 19.

144. Stern in *JI* 4 (May 1864): 114.

145. W. H. Negoosie, letter from Tsherkau, 25 October 1904, in *JMI* 21 (September 1905): 131–32.

146. Hiob Negoosie, in *JMI* 17 (June 1901): 9. See also Beroo letter of 27 November 1872, in *Report* 65 (1873): 107; Aragawi in *Reports* 82 (1890): 132.

147. Beroo, letter 27 November 1872, in *Report* 65 (1873): 107. On the "goddess" called "Sanbathoo," see Waldmeier, *Autobiography,* p. 25.

148. Letter from converts, in *JI* 14 (August 1874): 217.

149. Dabtara Ain Alem, Djenda, 18 January 1904, in *JMI* 20 (July 1904): 101–2.

150. Beroo, in *JI* 10 (June 1870): 162; Flad, journal in *JI* 11 (June 1871): 158–59; Aragawi, Beroo, Sanbatoo, letter to Flad, in *JI,* n.s. 16 (February 1876): 43; Flad, in *JMI* 19 (June 1903): 82.

151. Stern, journal in *JI* 4 (May 1864): 107; letter from converts, *JI* 4 (August 1874): 217; Sanbatu et al., in *Report* 86 (1894): 137.

152. Flad, letter in *JI* 6 (May 1866): 112; Agashy in *JR* (April 1878): 15–16; Debtera Liena, to Flad in *JI* 19 (September 1879): 251; Aragawi, letter of 24 January 1904, in *Report* 97 (105): 103.

153. Letter of 20 December 1869, in *JI* 10 (1869): 91.

154. Converts' letter, *JI* 14 (August 1871): 217–18.

155. Debtera Liena to Flad in *JI* 19 (September 1879): 251.

156. *Report* 68 (1876): 104–6; *JI* 17 (March 1877): 66.

157. Aragawi to Flad, 14 March 1889, in *JI,* n.s. 5 (Juen 1889): 81, and in *Report* 81 (1889): 120–21.

158. Aragawi, 28 March 1893, in *JI* 9 (February 1893): 23. On the ***buda*** accusation in Shawa and Gojjam, see Antonio Cecchi and Giovanni Chiarini, "Lettere," *BSGI* 16 (1879): 425–26.

159. Flad, *JR* (May 1871): 18; letter to Flad October 1874, in *JI* 67 (1875): 106–7; *JI* 17 (March 1877): 66; Aragawi letter of 24 January 1904, in *JMI* 20 (June 1904): 85.

160. *JI* 17 (March 1877): 65–66; Aragawi, letter from Dabra Tabor, 6 February 1897, in *JMI* 13 (September 1897): 130.

161. No mention is made of Tigray province because the missions were not active there, even to the extent of proselytizing trips.

162. Argossy to Flad in *Report* 70 (1878): 120.

163. Flad, letter of 17 November 1880, in *JR* (February 1881): 7.

164. Flad, letter, in *JI* 6 (1866): 113.

165. See evidence in Caulk, "Religion and State," p. 28.

166. Beroo to Flad, 28 February 1890, in *JI,* n.s. 6 (May 1890): 69.

167. Aragawi to Flad, in *JMI* 16 (December 1900): 184. (He was recalling events eight years previously in this letter.)

168. "The Falashas: Interviews with J. Faitlovitch and Rabbi Dr. Margulies," *JC* 10 January 1908, p. 16; "The Falashas: Interview with M. Faitlovitch," *JC* 27 October 1905, p. 19.

169. Simon Messing, *The Story of the Falashas* (Hamden, 1982), pp. 93–99.

170. Cited ibid., p. 97.

171. Cited in Stern, *JI* 4 (May 1864): 111, 116.

172. Cited in W. H. Negoosie and Goshu Beleta in *JMI* 19 (June 1903): 108.

173. Aragawi in *JR* (November 1882): 42. This argument was still given during my 1975 fieldwork; interview with Berhan Beruk on 3 July 1975.

174. Cited by Flad, in *Report* 63 (1871): 92.

175. In Negoosie, Beleta, Meherat, from Dabra Tabor, 28 August 1899, in *JMI* 17 (March 1901): 44.

176. Waldah Haimanot, in Singer, "The Falashas," pp. 143–45.

177. In Argossy to Flad, *Report* 70 (1878): 118.

178. Letter of Beru, Aragawy, and Sanbatu, in *JI* 20 (July 1880): 183.

179. Cited in Negoosie to Flad, in *JMI* 14 (April 1898): 55.

180. Cited by Aragawi, in *JMI* 21 (July 1905): 98.

181. I have only listed names mentioned more than once. Not all traditions agree completely on the monks' locations, but there is a great deal of congruence, and sometimes they moved. On Simon and Mahari, see Chapter 4 above and also interviews with Ayyallegne Adgwachaw and Kebrate Samu'el on 26 October 1975 and with Yeshaq Iyyasu on 15 December 1975; *Report* 69 (1877): 105; ibid., 70 (1878): 118. On the later monks, mainly during the times of Yohannes and Menilek, see interviews with Gete Asrass on 11 June 1975, with Menase Zammaru and Wande Iyyasu on 13 October 1975, with Ayyallegne Adgwachaw and Kebrate Samu'el on 26 October 1975, with Yeheyyes Madhane and Yalaw Siyamer on 27 October 1975, and with Yeshaq Iyyasu on 15 December 1975.

182. For example, in Beru, Aragawy, and Sanbatu, letter, in *JI* 20 (July 1880): 184. These pressures are evident throughout the missionary records.

183. Beru to Flad, in *Report* 64 (1872): 92; Aragawy in *Report* 74 (1882): 140–41; *JI* 16 (June 1876): 167.

184. Agashy in *JR* (April 1878): 15.

185. Aragawi, in *JR* (November 1882): 42.

186. Aragawi, in *Report* 84 (1892): 150.

187. Beru, Aragawi, and Sanbatu, letter in *JI* 20 (July 1880): 184.

188. Flad, in *JR* (November 1874): 47–48.

189. See earlier references and also Beru, letter to Flad, 6 January 1870, in *Report* 62 (1870): 76–77.

190. See Chapter 4 above.

191. Flad, in *JI* 14 (November 1874): 292–93.

192. Argossy to Flad, in *Report* 70 (1878): 119–20; *Report* 69 (1877): 105.

193. Jacques Faitlovitch, *Gli ebrei d'Abissinia (Falascia)* (Acqui, 1907), pp. 10–13; "The Falashas," *JC*, 27 October 1905, p. 19; Leslau, *Anthology;* idem., *Coutumes et croyances*. Despite the decline of monasticism after World War II, priests trained by monks still kept the traditions and liturgy where they were recorded in the 1970s by Shelemay and Quirin.

194. See references in Leslau, "Religious Dispute."

195. This section only lays the historical groundwork for a more thorough analysis of this question. See also Kessler, *The Falashas;* Messing, *Story of the Falashas*.

196. Hermann Zotenberg, "Un document sur les Falachas," *JA*, ser. 6, 9 (1867): 265–68; Kessler, *The Falashas*, p. 124.

197. Chouraqui, *L'alliance israélite universelle*, p. 110.

198. Israel Hildesheimer, "Very Urgent Appeal to all my Fellow Believers," *JC* 516 (4 November 1864): 6; Kessler, *The Falashas*, p. 119. See also Israel Hildesheimer, "Nehmet euch der Falacha's an! Ein Aufruf an alle Glaubensgenossen," *Der Israelit* 5/44 (1864): 575–78; idem., "Bericht über die Entwickelung der Falascha-Angelegenheit und Beurtheilung der hierbei gemachten Vorshlage," *Der Israelit*

5/49 (1864): 641–42; David Ellenson, "'Our Brothers and our Flesh': Rabbi Esriel Hildesheimer and the Jews of Ethiopia," *Judaism* 35 (1986): 63–65.

199. Halévy, "Travels," p. 189; idem., "Lettre adressée à l'Alliance israélite universelle," *AI* 28 (1867): 1,084–86.

200. Halévy, "Travels," pp. 250–51.

201. Faitlovitch, *Quer durch,* p. 2.

202. Halévy, *Rapport au comité central de l'alliance israélite universelle concernant la mission auprès des Falachas* (Paris, 1868), p. 18; Chouraqui, *L'alliance,* p. 393.

203. Halévy, note 2 in Faitlovitch, "Une lettre amharique des Falachas ou Juifs d'Abyssinie," *RS* 14 (1906): 94–95; Faitlovitch, *Quer durch,* p. 2.

204. Faitlovitch, *Quer durch,* p. 3.

205. Faitlovitch, *Notes d'un voyage chez les Falachas (Juifs d'Abyssinie)* (Paris, 1905); "The Falashas: Interview with M. Faitlovitch," *JC* (27 October 1905), p. 19.

206. Messing, *Story of Falashas,* p. 54. See also Leslau's comments on Faitlovitch in "A Falasha Book of Jewish Festivals," *For Max Weinrich on his Seventieth Birthday* (The Hague, 1964).

207. See the recent important article on the "second generation" of culture broker, a man who did not have the advantages of foreign education but worked between 1964–65 to 1981 to change a Beta Israel community to conform to Orthodox Judaism: Jon Abbink, "An Ethiopian Jewish 'Missionary' as Culture Broker," in M. Ashkenazi and A. Weingrod, eds., *Ethiopian Jews and Israel* (New Brunswick, N.J., 1987), pp. 21–32. For the efforts of another culture broker, see Leslau, "A Falasha Book of Jewish Festivals," which describes the calendar compiled by Yona Bogale under the auspices of the Jewish Agency.

208. Faitlovitch, *Quer durch,* map, and pp. 4–5.

209. "The Falashas: Interview with M. Faitlovitch," *JC* (27 October 1905), p. 19.

210. Hiob Negoosie to Flad, in *JMI* 22 (July 1906): 107.

211. Debteras Ishanow, Asressa, Desta, Awaka, in *Report* 99 (1907): 112.

212. Kessler, *The Falashas,* 139; Payne, *Ethiopian Jews,* pp. 67–68.

213. Aragawi, in *Report* 104 (1912): 88; see also statements already quoted above that include references to money.

214. Kessler, *The Falashas,* p. 139, citing Payne, *Ethiopian Jews,* asserts no more conversions took place until 1909, but other records show a few did occur: *Report* 99 (1907): 107, 113.

215. Aragawi in *Report* 104 (1912): 88.

216. Interview with Gete Asrass on 11 June 1975.

217. On the continuation of sacrifices in the early twentieth century, especially on Passover (*fasika*), see Hiob Negoosie, in *Report* 93 (1901): 159; *Report* 94 (1902): 110–11; ibid. 99 (1907): 109–10. For more details of later practices, see Deborah Lifchitz, "Un sacrifice chez les Falacha"; Wolf Leslau, *Coutumes et croyances,* pp. 70–71.

218. Messing, *Story of Falashas,* pp. 58, 103, note 50; Faitlovitch, *Quer durch,* pp. 41–42.

219. "The Falashas: Interviews with Dr. J. Faitlovitch and Rabbi Dr. Margulies," *JC* (10 January 1908), p. 16; $25,000 was raised and spent on the Beta Israel

by the American committee in 1922–23: American Pro-Falasha Committee, *Report for the Year of July 1, 1922–June 30, 1923* (New York [1923]). See also, idem., *The Romance of the Falashas* (New York, [194–?]); Kessler, *The Falashas,* pp. 135, 143; Messing, *Story of Falashas,* p. 56.

220. Faitlovitch, *Quer durch,* pp. 11–12; "The Falashas," *JC* 10 January 1908, pp. 16–17.

221. Faitlovitch, *Quer durch,* pp. 182–88; idem., "Une Lettre amharique des Falachas ou Juifs d'Abyssinie," *RS* 14 (1906): 92–94; idem., *Falascha-Briefe* (Berlin, 1913).

222. Interview with Rabbi Nahoum: "The Mission to the Falashas," *JC* (7 August 1908), p. 14; Haim Nahoum, "Mission chez les Falachas d'Abyssinie," *BAIU,* ser. 3, 33 (1908): 100–133; Rabbi George Zepin, *The Falashas, A Report* (Cincinnati, 1912), p. 17 and *passim.*

223. Messing, *Story of Falashas,* pp. 58, 64; Kessler, *Falashas,* pp. 143–44.

224. Messing, *Story of Falashas,* p. 65; Kessler, *Falashas,* pp. 145–46 (including statement by Yona Bogale about the school); Itzhak Grinfeld, "Jews in Addis Ababa: Beginnings of the Jewish Community until the Italian Occupation," in G. Goldenberg, ed., *Ethiopian Studies. Proceedings of the Sixth International Conference, Tel-Aviv, 1980* (Rotterdam, 1986), pp. 256–57; Geoffrey Harmsworth, *Abyssinian Adventure* (London, 1935), p. 269; Richard Pankhurst, "The Foundations of Education, Printing, Newspapers, Book Production, Libraries, and Literacy in Ethiopia," *EO* 6/3 (1962): 279.

225. See letters of Faitlovitch cited in Grinfeld, "Jews in Addis Ababa," p. 254.

226. Robert Hess, "Introduction," to Henry A. Stern, *Wanderings,* p. xxx.

227. On Ethiopian Orthodox Church education, see *alaqa* Imbakom Kalewold, *Traditional Ethiopian Church Education,* trans. Menghestu Lemma (New York, 1970); Girma Amare, "Aims and Purposes of Church Education in Ethiopia," *EJE* 1 (1967): 1–17; Paulos Milkias, "Traditional Institutions and Traditional Elites: The Role of Education in the Ethiopian Body-Politic," *ASR* 19/3 (December 1976): 79–93. See Teshome G. Wagaw, *Education in Ethiopia* (Ann Arbor, 1979).

228. Further work on the two would illuminate these themes. See the biographical sketches on Taamrat by Messing, *Story of Falashas,* pp. 64–68, and on Gabru by Bairu Tafla, "Four Ethiopian Biographies: Däjjazmač Gärmamē, Däjjazmač Gäbrä-Egzi'abehēr Moroda, Däjjazmač Balča and Kantiba Gäbru Dästa," *JES* 7/2 (July 1969): 22–31.

Conclusion

1. Rudolph Windsor, *From Babylon to Timbuktu: A History of Ancient Black Races Including the Black Hebrews* (Philadelphia, 1988 [orig. 1969]); Joseph J. Williams, *Hebrewisms of West Africa* (New York, 1930), pp. 159–85. It is also true that the direction of influences between Africa and West Asia cannot always be taken for granted, but more research is needed in this area. See Hailu Habtu, "The Fallacy of the 'Triple Heritage' Thesis: A Critique," *Issue* 13 (1984): 26–29; George G. M. James, *Stolen Legacy* (New York, 1954); Yosef A. A. ben-Jochannan, *Black Man of the*

Nile and His Family (New York, 1981), pp. xxxvii–lxxii; Drusilla D. Houston, *Wonderful Ethiopians of the Ancient Cushite Empire* (Baltimore, 1985 [orig. ed., 1926]).

2. For a summary, see Donald Crummey, "State, Society and Nationality in the Recent Historiography of Ethiopia," *JAH* 31 (1990): 103–19. See also references in the bibliography, including Triulzi, Braukamper, McClellan, Donham and James, and Taddesse Tamrat on the Agaw and Gafat.

3. Esteves Pereira, *Chronica Susneyos,* 1:155–56, and see Chapter 2 above.

Glossary

abbā: title of respect especially for men in religious life.
abun: the head or bishop of the Ethiopian Church who was an Egyptian until the twentieth century.
agafari: title of governor of Samen.
Agaw: Cushitic-speaking early inhabitants of highlands.
alaqā: leader.
alaqenāt: the right to seniority, precedence, or leadership among a group of heirs or claimants.
ambā: flat-topped peak.
Amhārā: a Semitic-speaking people with dominant political role since the thirteenth century.
anāṣi: worker, carpenter, mason.
arde'et: naming ceremony among the Beta Israel.
aqēt zar: masons and king's advisors since time of Sarsa Dengel.
aṣē: honorific title to refer to the Ethiopian king.
ayhud: Jews, Jewish group.
azāj: commander.
azmāch: general.
"*Bāryā*": "slave," inhabitants of Sudanese lowlands.
bēgamder: title of governor of area immediately east of Lake Tana.
beḥtwaddad: "beloved," title of the senior ministers of Ethiopian state, fifteenth-sixteenth centuries.
bejrond: for Beta Israel, chief of the workers.
Beta Israel (*bēta esrā'ēl*): "House of Israel," one of the terms used by this group, also known as "Falasha," to refer to themselves.
budā: "evil eye," a person said to be capable of causing harm and death by looking at someone; also the spirit which causes harm.
ċhewā: originally, soldiers of the crown located along kingdom's frontiers; became lesser nobles possessing their own land and troops.
dabtarā: a learned man who often assisted priests but was not himself ordained.
dagā: the highest lands, above 2,500 meters (8,200 feet).
degwa: Ethiopian Church hymnary.
dejāzmāch: a general, specifically, the general of the king's gate.
eċhegē: the highest-ranking Ethiopian-born official in the Church.
Falāshā: a name apparently originating in the fifteenth or sixteenth century to refer to some of the *ayhud,* or Beta Israel.
fuga: occupational castes among the Gurage.

gadl: "combat," "struggle"; therefore, title of written works on lives of saints or ascetics.

"Galla": the previous, pejorative, term used to refer to the group better known as Oromo.

Gēdēwon: the name of several but not all Beta Israel leaders; perhaps even a title because it was so prominently used.

Ge'ez: or "Ethiopic," an ancient Semitic language of Ethiopia, and the principal religious and literary language of both Christians and Beta Israel.

gerāzmāch: a general, specifically, a general of the left wing.

Gudit: a tenth-century queen, sometimes said to be Jewish.

gult: tribute-collection rights over land, granted to the Church or individuals for service to the King.

jabārti: Ethiopian/Abyssinian Muslims, usually traders or artisans.

kantibā: title of governor of Dambeya and later mayor of Gondar; originally a title from Tigray province.

Kāylā: one of the names by which the Beta Israel/Falasha were also known, dating to the seventeenth century.

Kāylāshā: another term for the Beta Israel, especially in Armacheho region, combining "Kayla" and "Falasha."

Kebra Nagast: "Glory of the Kings," the book containing the founding story of the Ethiopian dynasty.

kelād: a measurement of land.

liqāwent: nobles.

makwānnent: nobility, great nobility, upper nobility.

masgid: Beta Israel prayerhouse; also Muslim mosque.

nagādrās: head of the traders; leader of large trading caravan.

Orit: the Pentateuch or, more broadly, Old Testament for Christians; the same book and same word is used by the Beta Israel.

Oromo: previously called "Galla," the largest ethnic group in contemporary Ethiopia.

qanyāzmāch: a general, specifically of the right wing.

Qemānt: a "pagan-Hebraic" people in the Gondar region.

qēs: "priest" for Ethiopian Christians; same title used by Beta Israel to designate principal religious officials.

qollā (or *qwallā*): lowlands, below 1,500 meters (5,000 feet).

qwerbān: for Beta Israel, "offering" or "sacrifice"; for Christians, the term used for Communion.

rās: "head," high-ranking political-military title.

rās-beḥtwaddad: "beloved head," or first minister.

rest: inherited land-use rights, characteristic of the land system in northern Ethiopia.

rest-gult; a land tenure in which *gult* rights become inheritable over several generations.

rim: tribute rights over land granted to churches.

segd: in the twentieth century, the principal Beta Israel holiday.

"*Shānqillā*": a name used to refer to lowland dwellers along the Sudan border who were often subject to enslavement.

shum: "chief," particularly used as title of governor of Wagara and also of Wag provinces.

ṭabib/ṭabibān/ṭayb (Ge'ez: *ṭabba,* to be wise; skilled; expert): applied to blacksmiths and potters, including Beta Israel, but with derogatory connotation.

tazkar: memorial service or remembrance for the dead, observed by both Christians and Beta Israel.

ṭēf: a principal grain foodcrop of highlands.

Te'ezāzā Sanbat: "Commandments of the Sabbath," the principal Beta Israel book after the *Orit.*

Tigrāyān: inhabitants of Tigray province who speak Tigrinya, a Semitic language related to ancient Ge'ez.

watta: refers to occupational castes among the Oromo.

waynā dagā: the midrange of highland Ethiopia, 1,500–2,500 meters (5,000–8,200 feet) that contains most of the population.

Wayto: a people dwelling near Lake Tana, who historically lived by hippopotamus-hunting.

wellāj: people of mixed Amhara-"Shanqilla" ancestry.

westˌ azāj: "inside commander," in Gondar official(s) in charge of royal household servants and slaves.

Yodit: the name (or title) often given to the principal female Beta Israel leader.

Zāgwē: the name of the Christian Agaw dynasty ruling from the highland regions of Wag and Lasta, between ca. 1137–1270.

Zalān: a nomadic, cattle-keeping people mentioned in the Begamder region in the nineteenth century.

zar: a spirit that can enter a person and cause either good or evil.

Bibliography

Oral Sources

The following people were interviewed in Begamder (now Gondar) Province and southern Tigray, 1975–76. Ages given are approximate at the time interviewed. Tape copies have been deposited in the Institute of Ethiopian Studies. All Ethiopian names are alphabetized here and elsewhere following the Ethiopian convention of using one's own (first) name.

Beta Israel (Falasha) Informants

Admas Chakkol. Age 45. Interviewed in Endagabuna, Shire District, Tigray Province, 16 December 1975. His information is derived from his own research into oral and written sources.

Alamayyahu Iyyasu (*blatta*). Age 75. Interviewed in Endagabuna, Shire (Tigray), 15 December 1975. Local history of Beta Israel in Tigray, especially since Yohannes IV (1871–89).

Ayyallegn Adgwachaw (*qes*). Age 40. Joint interview with Kebrate Samu'el at Wefdar (Wagara), 26 October 1975.

Azalach Sem'on. Age 80. Interviewed at her home in Arnajig (near Ambobar), 7 November 1975. Knowledge of Qwarenya.

Balay Malku. Age 50. Joint interview with Sammallegne Takka from Kosheshelit (Dambeya) in *ato* Belay's home in Azazo, 3 September 1975. Local history of Azazo in Gondar area.

Berhan Beruk (*qes*). Age 76. Interviewed at his home in Walaka (greater Gondar area) on 3 July 1975, 14 August 1975, and 20 August 1975. Educated by Beta Israel monks and descended from fifteenth-century Beta Israel rulers. Very cooperative and knowledgeable on all aspects of Beta Israel history, religion, and culture.

Dane'el Zawditu (*wayzaro*). Age 70. Interviewed at Ambobar, 10 June 1975. Local culture and pottery-making.

Dasse Yeshaq (*basha*). Age 69. From Abba Entonyos (greater Gondar area), interviewed at my house in Gondar, 8 January 1976. Local history, particularly of Beta Israel at Abba Entonyos.

Enneyaw Tarraqagne. Age 42. From Gondar, interviewed at my house in Gondar, 30 December 1975. Descended from prominent Wagara family and knowledgeable of Wagara Beta Israel, especially since the fifteenth century.

Gete Asrass (*abba*). Age 78. Interviewed at Ambobar, 3 June, 11 June, and 9 November 1975. Educated by Beta Israel monks in Guraba (Saqqalt); very cooperative and knowledgeable about all aspects of ancient and recent Beta Israel history, religion, and culture.

Kebrate Samu'el. Age 78. Joint interview with *qes* Ayyallegne Adgwachaw at Wefdar (Wagara) on 26 October 1975. Descended from Samen family and information about Samen and Wagara.

Mammo Sagga Amlak (qes). In his 80s. Joint interview with Mulu Mammo and Ya'eqob Balay at Bankar (Wagara), 24 June 1975. Wagara history especially since the fifteenth century.

Menase Zammaru (*qes*). In late 70s. Joint interview with *abba* Wande Iyyasu at Sanbatge (Wagara) on 13 October 1975; individual interview on 15 October 1975. Educated by monks in Samen and very knowledgeable about Samen and Wagara, especially since the fifteenth century.

Mulu Mammo. Age 42. Joint interview with his father, *qes* Mammo Sagga Amlak at Bankar (Wagara) on 24 June 1975.

Ratta Zawde. Age 81. Interviewed at his home in Tadda (greater Gondar area) on 10 August 1975. Hereditary leader of Beta Israel community at Tadda and knowledgeable about their local history.

Sammallegne Takka. Age 67. From Kosheshelit (Dambeya); joint interview with Balay Malku in Azazo (Gondar area). Local history of Azazo, Dambeya, and Gondar area, since nineteenth century.

Sannayt Ayyanaw (*wayzaro*). Age 83. Interviewed in Wuglo (near Ambobar) on 11 June 1975. Knowledge of some Qwarenya and personal history.

Sandaqqe Maharan. Age 79. Interviewed at his house in Attege (Dambeya) on 24 October 1975. Twentieth-century local history.

Tafassaku Webshat. In his 70s. Part of a group interview with the elders of Endabaguna (Shire), Tigray, on 15 December 1975. Local Tigray history.

Wande Iyyasu (*abba*). In his late 70s. Joint interview with *qes* Menase Zammaru at Sanbatge (Wagara) on 13 October 1975. Knowledge of Wagara history.

Webe Akala. Age 56. Interviewed at his house in Gondar on 27 December 1975. Descended from a Qwara family. Knowledge especially of history since the Gondar dynasty.

Ya'eqob Balay. Age 58. Joint interview with *qes* Mammo Sagga Amlak and Mulu Mammo at Bankar (Wagara) on 24 June 1975. Local history.

Yalaw Siyamer (*abba*). Age 76. Joint interview with *qes* Yeheyyes Madhane at Shembra Weha (Wagara) on 27 October 1975. Knowledge about Wagara region since fifteenth century.

Yeshaq Iyyasu (*qes*). Age 78. Interviewed at Endabaguna (Shire), Tigray on 15 December 1975. Tigray history and some general history since fifteenth century.

Yeheyyes Madhane (*qes*). Age 73. Joint interview with *abba* Yalaw Siyamer at Endabaguna on 15 December 1975. Tigray and some general history since fifteenth century.

Zallaqa Damoze. Age 64. Interview at Abba Entonyos (Gondar area) on 28 November 1975. Local Abba Entonyos history.

Amhara Informants (All in Gondar)

Balay Marsha (*mamher*). Age 59. Interviewed 27 November 1975. Associated with Qeddus Cherqos church in Gondar.

Garima Taffara (*abba*). Age 59. Interviewed 4 August, 12 August (untaped), 25 August, 30 August, 2 September 1975 in his home. Prominent local historian with published books and articles on Gondar and Ethiopia since the nineteenth century. Very knowledgeable of Gondar dynasty era.

Jammara Wande (*gerazmach*). Age 78. Interviewed in his home on 21 July, 31 July, 16 August, 26 August 1975. Descended from kings of the Gondar dynasty and knowledgeable of Gondar era from both oral traditions and written sources he had collected.

Mangestu Tayye (*balambaras*). Age 77. Interviewed at his home 28 August 1975. Descendant of *alaqa* Tayye, a prominent figure from Menilek era. Knowledgeable about Gondar history from both oral and written sources.

Neguse Eshate (*qanyazmach*). About 75. Interviewed at his home 28 August 1975.

Waka Zallalaw (*gerazmach*). Interviewed at his home on 5 January 1976 (untaped).

Walda Sellase Aggadaw (*balambaras*). Age 62. Interviewed at the home of *mamher* Yebbabe Zawde on 5 August 1975.

Yebbabe Zawde (*mamher*). Age 51. Interviewed at his home on 2 August 1975. Priest at Madhane Alam church; had spent many years in Lasta region.

Qemant Informants

Adugna Gabreyya. Age 56. Interviewed at his home in Kerkerr on 7 October 1975.

Denqayahu Radda. Age 82. Interviewed in Kerkerr on 7 October 1975, and in a joint interview with Yelma Yalaw in Kerkerr on 26 December 1975.

Gabbaw Tafarra. Age 74. Interviewed in his home in Kerkerr on 26 December 1975.

Kasagne Alamayahu (*gerazmach*). Age 66. Interviewed at the Tewodros Hotel in Gondar on 13 August and 8 October 1975. Knowledgeable in general on Qemant history and had written information as well.

Qanu Ayyalaw. Age 32. Group interview with *wambar* Mulunah Marsha and Tafari Neguse at home of Tafari Neguse in Saraba (Chelga) on 22 November 1975.

Mulunah Marsha (*wambar*). Age 42. Group interview with Qanu Ayyalaw and Tafari Neguse in Saraba (Chelga) on 22 November 1975. He is the last of a long line of *wambars,* the leader of he Qemant community in Chelga.

Neguse Warqu. Age 81. Interviewed in his home at Gondaroch Maryam (Gondar area) on 25 November 1975, and in a group interview with Teru Alamu and Wabashaw Alamu on 25 November 1975. Knowledgeable about Qemant role in Gondar especially.

Tafari Neguse. Age 49. Group interview with *wambar* Mulunah Marsha and Qanu Ayyalaw in Saraba (Chelga) on 22 November 1975. He is the son of Neguse Warqu.

Teru Alamu. In his 70s. Group interview with Neguse Warqu and Wabashaw Alamu in the home of Neguse Warqu at Gondaroch Maryam on 25 November 1975. Some knowledge of Qemant language.

Wabashaw Alamu. In his 70s. Group interview with Neguse Warqu and Teru Alamu at the home of Neguse Warqu on 25 November 1975.
Yelma Yalaw. Age 58. Joint interview with Denqayyahu Radda in Kerkerr on 26 December 1975.

Archival Sources

1. Bibliothèque Nationale, Paris

(Read on microfilm, Institute of Ethiopian Studies, Addis Ababa)
France Nouvelle Acquisition 21299. Arnauld d'Abbadie, "Récit des voyages en Éthiopie faits par Arnauld d'Abbadie."
France Nouvelle Acquisition 21300. Antoine d'Abbadie, "Journal et mélanges."
France Nouvelle Acquisition 21301. Antoine d'Abbadie, "Mélanges sur l'Éthiopie."

2. Church Missionary Society Archives, London

(Read on microfilm in Institute of Ethiopian Studies, Addis Ababa)

East Africa Mission. Especially C.A5/016 for J. L. Krapf's visit to Gondar in 1855.

3. Institute of Ethiopian Studies, Addis Ababa

IES 259 (Mondon 72). History of Takla-Giyorgis and Yohannes. English translation by Tesfayohannes Fessehaye.
IES 361. Tarika Nagast from Dabra Berhan Sellase church in Gondar. Copied by Andalam Mulaw, translated to Amharic by Garima Taffara.

4. Ethiopian Microfilm Manuscript Library

Collegeville, Minnesota, and Addis Ababa:
EMML 932. Gadla Zena Marqos, and miracles.
EMML 954, Ff. 175a–184b. Ser'ata Mangest.
EMML 1312, Ff. 34a–81b. Maheleta Sege.
EMML 1834. Gadla Takla Haymanot.
EMML 1838, Ff. 1a–50b. Gadla Giyorgis of Gasecha.
EMML 2142, Ff. 2a–29b. Gadla Abuna Habta Maryam.
EMML 2490, F. 63b. Varia about Lebna Dengel.
EMML 3987. Gadla Zena Marqos.
EMML 4741. Gadla Zena Marqos.

EMML 4922. Gadla Zena Marqos.
EMML 6678. Gadla Zena Marqos.
EMML 7334. Tarika Nagast.

Unpublished Theses and Papers

Admas Chakkol. "Attempts Made to Exterminate the Beta Israel." Unpublished essay, n.d.

———. "Beta Israel Genealogies." Unpublished essay, 1975.

Akalou Wolde-Michael. "Urban Development in Ethiopia in Time and Space Perspective." Ph.D. dissertation, University of California at Los Angeles, 1967.

Aleme Eshete. "General Examination of Ethiopian Feudalism." Paper presented at Conference on Ethiopian Feudalism, March 1976.

And Alem Mulaw. "Bage-Mdir and Simen (1910–1930)." B.A. thesis, Haile Sellassie I University, Addis Ababa, 1971.

Berry, LaVerle. "The Solomonic Monarchy at Gonder, 1630–1755: An Institutional Analysis of Kingship in the Christian Kingdom of Ethiopia." Ph.D. dissertation, Boston University, 1976.

Crummey, Donald, and Shumet Sishagne. "Land Tenure and the Social Accumulation of Wealth in Eighteenth Century Ethiopia: Evidence from the Qwesquam Land Register." Paper presented to Symposium on Land in African Agrarian Systems, Urbana, Ill., April 1988.

———. "The Lands of the Church of Dabra S'ahay Qwesqwam, Gondar." Paper presented to the Tenth International Conference of Ethiopian Studies, Paris, 1988.

Crummey, Donald, Shumet Sishagne, and Daniel Ayana. "Oral Traditions in a Literate Culture: The Case of Christian Ethiopia." Paper presented to the International Symposium on Unwritten Testimonies of the African Past," University of Warsaw, 7–8 November 1989.

Daniel Ayana. "*Gult* and Ethiopian Social Structure." Paper presented to the African Studies Association annual meeting, Chicago, 1988.

Fisseha Demoz Gebre Egzi. "A Regional Study of the Ambober-Seramle Region (A Falasha Region)." B.A. thesis, Haile Sellassie I University, Addis Ababa, 1970.

Gabira Madihin Kidana. "Yohannes IV, Religious Aspects of His Internal Policy." B.S. thesis, Haile Sellassie I University, Addis Ababa, 1972.

Garima Taffara. "Gondar and Its Kings [Gondarna Nigestatwa]." Unpublished manuscript, Gondar, 1975.

———. "Taxes or Gifts." Unpublished manuscript, Gondar, 1975.

Garretson, Peter. "A History of Addis Ababa from Its Foundation in 1886 to 1910." Ph.D. dissertation, University of London, 1974.

Gaugine, Maurice. "The Falasha Version of the Testaments of Abraham, Isaac, and Jacob." Ph.D. dissertation, University of Manchester, 1965.

"History of the Kings [Tarik Zanagast]." Amharic manuscript in possession of Jammara Wande, Gondar.

"History of the Land of Gondar [Tarik Zameder Gondar]." Amharic manuscript in possession of Jammara Wande, Gondar.

Hoben, Allan. "The Role of Ambilineal Descent Groups in Gojjam Amhara Social Organization." Ph.D. dissertation, University of California, Berkeley, 1963.

Hubbard, D. A. "The Literary Sources of the Kebra Nagast." Ph.D. dissertation, Saint Andrews University, 1956.

Kaplan, Steven. "The Monastic Holy Man and the Christianization of Ethiopia, 1270–1468." Ph.D. dissertation, Hebrew University, 1982.

Kasagne Alamayahu. "Autobiography." Unpublished essay, Gondar, 1975.

———. "The Kimant." Unpublished essay, Gondar, 1966 [E.C.].

———. "Kimant Culture." Unpublished essay, Gondar, 1975.

Krempel, Veronika. 1972. "Die soziale und wirtschaftliche Stellung der Falascha in der christlich-amharischen Gesellschaft von Nordwest Aethiopien." Ph.D. dissertation, Free University of Berlin.

"Lists of Offices." Unpublished manuscript in possession of Jammara Wande, Gondar, n.d.

Mangestu Tayye. "A Short History of Gondar." Unpublished essay, Gondar, 1944 [E.C.].

———. "List of Judges." Unpublished essay, Gondar, 1975.

Merid Wolde Aregay. "An Evaluation of the Government and Administration of Emperor Libne Dingil, 1508–1529." Paper presented to Interdisciplinary Seminar of the Faculties of Arts and Education, Haile Sellassie I University, 1966–67.

———. "Southern Ethiopia and the Christian Kingdom, 1508–1708, with Special Reference to the Galla Migrations and their Consequences." Ph.D. dissertation, University of London, 1971.

Messing, Simon. "The Highland-Plateau Amhara of Ethiopia." Ph.D. dissertation, University of Pennsylvania, 1957.

Nur Hussein A. Kadir. "Land Use Study of Ten Farmers at Adi Arkay." B.A. thesis, Haile Sellassie I University, Addis Ababa, 1972.

Quirin, James A. "The Beta Israel (Felasha) in Ethiopian History: Caste Formation and Culture Change, 1270–1868." Ph.D. dissertation, University of Minnesota, 1977.

Sahle Woldegaber. "The Background and Consequences of the Battle of Metemma." B.A. thesis, Haile Sellassie I University, Addis Ababa, 1968.

Saineano, Marius. "L'Abyssinie dans la seconde moitié du XVI siècle. Le règne de Sartsa-Dengel (Malak Sagad) (1563–1594) d'après des annales éthiopiennes inédits." Inaugural dissertation, University of Leipzig-Bucarest, 1892.

Schoenberger, Michele. "The Falashas of Ethiopia. An Ethnographic Study." Ph.D. dissertation, Cambridge University, 1975.

Seyoum Wolde Yohannes. "Ras Ali and Tewodros: The Position of Islam in Central Ethiopia." B.A. thesis, Haile Sellassie I University, Addis Ababa, 1968.

Shelemay, Kay Kaufman. "The Liturgical Music of the Falasha of Ethiopia." Ph.D. dissertation, University of Michigan, 1977.

Taddesse Tamrat. "The Sheba Legend and the Falasha: Problems of Ethiopian Historiography." Paper presented to African Studies Program, University of Illinois, February 1986.

Tadesse Gebre Igziabher. "Power Struggle in Tigray During the Zamana Mesafint, 1769–1855." B.A. thesis, Haile Sellassie I University, Addis Ababa, 1971.

Untitled Manuscript on Gondar History [Ge'ez] in possession of Neguse Warqu, Gondaroch Maryam.
Weissleder, Wolfgang. "The Political Ecology of Amhara Domination." Ph.D. dissertation, University of Chicago, 1965.
Yaecob Sulamo. "Land and Feudalism in the Abyssinian Kingdom, Gondar Period, 1650–1800." Paper presented at University of Minnesota, 1978.
Young, Allan. "Medical Beliefs and Practices of Begemder Amhara." Ph.D. dissertation, University of Pennsylvania, 1970.

Periodicals

The Church Missionary Intelligencer. A Monthly Journal of Missionary Information 1 (1850) to 15 (1864).
Church Missionary Record, Detailing the Proceedings of the Church Missionary Society 1 (1830) to 15 (1844).
The Home and Foreign Missionary Record of the Church of Scotland 16 (1861) to 17 (1862), n.s. 1 (1862) to 6 (1869).
The Jewish Chronicle [London], 1848–1966.
Jewish Intelligence and the Monthly Account of the Proceedings of the London Society for Promoting Christianity Amongst the Jews [Also called *Jewish Missionary Intelligence*], 1835–1920.
The Jewish Records of the London Society for Promoting Christianity Amongst the Jews [Often bound with *Jewish Intelligence*], 1861–84.
Reports of the London Society for Promoting Christianity Amongst the Jews, 1809–1939.
Revue d'histoire des missions 9 (1932) to 16 (1939).

Selected Published Books and Articles

This list does not include all those sources used, particularly those of a general or comparative nature, such as works on caste, class, ethnicity, gender or the state. Some such works are cited in the relevant footnotes.

Abbink, Jon. "An Ethiopian Jewish 'Missionary' as Culture Broker." In M. Ashkenazi and A. Weingrod, eds., *Ethiopian Jews and Israel,* pp. 21–32. New Brunswick, N.J., 1987.
———. "Seged Celebration in Ethiopia and Israel: Continuity and Change of a Falasha Religious Holiday." *Anthropos* 78 (1983): 789–810.
Abir, Mordechai. *Ethiopia: The Era of the Princes.* New York, 1968.
———. "Ethiopia and the Horn of Africa." In Richard Gray, ed., *The Cambridge History of Africa,* vol. 4, from c. 1600–c. 1790, pp. 537–77. Cambridge, 1975.
———. "Trade and Christian-Muslim Relations in Post-Medieval Ethiopia." In R. L. Hess, ed., *Proceedings of the Fifth International Conference on Ethiopian Studies, Session B, Chicago, 1978,* pp. 411–14. Chicago, 1979.
———. "The Ethiopian Slave Trade and Its Relation to the Islamic World." In John Ralph Willis, ed., *Slaves and Slavery in Muslim Africa* (2 vols.). Vol. 2: *The Servile Estate,* 2:123–36. London, 1985.

Abu-Salih. *The Churches and Monasteries of Egypt*. Oxford, 1895.
Addis Hiwet. *Ethiopia: From Autocracy to Revolution*. London, 1975.
Adler, Elkan, ed. *Jewish Travellers*. London, 1930.
Adler, Marcus. "The Itinerary of Benjamin of Tudela." *JQR* 16 (1904): 453–73, 715–33; 17 (1905): 123–41, 286–306, 514–30, 762–81; 18 (1906): 84–101, 664–91.
Aescoly, A. Z. "Les noms magiques dans les Apocryphes chrétiens des Éthiopiens." *JA* 220 (1932): 87–137.
———. "Falascha-Ibrim." *American Journal of Semitic Languages and Literature* 51 (1934–35): 127–30.
———. "The Falashas, A Bibliography." *Kirjath Sepher* 12 (1935): 254–65, 370–83, 498–505; 13 (1937): 250–65, 383–93, 506–12.
———, ed. *Recueil de textes Falachas*. *TMIE* 55 (1951): 1–286.
———. "Notices sur les Falacha ou Juifs d'Abyssinie, d'après le 'Journal de voyage' d'Antoine d'Abbadie." *CEA* 2 (1961): 84–147.
Akalou Wolde-Michael. "The Impermanency of Royal Capitals in Ethiopia." *Yearbook of the Association of Pacific Coast Geographers* 28 (1966): 147–56.
———. "Some Thoughts on the Process of Urbanization in Pre-Twentieth Century Ethiopia." *EGJ* 5/2 (1967): 35–38.
Al-Masudi, *Les prairies d'or*. 9 vols. Paris, 1861–77.
Al-Tabari, Muhammad ibn Jarir. *Chronique*. 4 vols. Paris, 1867.
Alvares, Francisco. *The Prester John of the Indies*. Trans. Lord Stanley of Aderley [1881], ed. C. F. Beckingham and G. W. B. Huntingford. 2 vols. Cambridge, 1961.
American Pro-Falasha Committee. *Report for the Year of July 1, 1922 to June 30, 1923*. New York, 1923.
———. *The Romance of the Falashas*. New York, n.d. [194?].
Anfray, Francis. "Aspects de l'archéologie Éthiopiennes." *JAH* 9 (1968): 345–66.
———. "Les rois d'Axoum d'après la numismatique." *JES* 6/2 (1968): 1–5.
———. "The Civilization of Aksum from the First to the Seventh Century." In G. Mokhtar, ed., *General History of Africa*. Vol. 12., *Ancient Civilization of Africa*, pp. 362–78. Paris: UNESCO, 1981.
———. "Les monuments Gondariens des XVIIe et XVIIIe siècles. Une vue d'ensemble," in Taddesse Beyene, ed., *Proceedings of the Eighth International Conference of Ethiopian Studies, Addis Ababa, 1984*, 1:9–45. Addis Ababa, 1988.
Antinori, Orazio. "Lettre." *BSGI* 16 (1879): 109–14, 361–86; 17 (1880): 118–22, 448–55.
Asma Giyorgis. *Asma Giyorgis and His Work: History of the Galla and the Kingdom of Sawa*, ed. Bairu Tafla. Stuttgart, 1987.
Aubert, L. "Fragment sur Gondar et le Négus." *BSG* 10 (1838): 145–57.
Austen, Ralph. "The Islamic Red Sea Trade: An Effort at Quantification." In R. L. Hess, ed., *Proceedings of the Fifth International Conference on Ethiopian Studies, Session B, Chicago, 1978*, pp. 443–67. Chicago, 1979.
Aymro Wondmagegnehu and Joachim Motovu, eds. *The Ethiopian Orthodox Church*. Addis Ababa, 1970.
Bahrey. "History of the Galla." In C. F. Beckingham and G. W. B. Huntingford, eds., *Some Records of Ethiopia, 1593–1646*, pp. 111–29. London: Hakluyt Society, 1954.
Bairu Tafla. "Four Ethiopian Biographies: Däjjazmač Gärmamē, Däjjazmač Gäbrä-

Egzi'abhēr Moroda, Däjjazmač Balča and Kantiba Gäbru Dästa." *JES* 7/2 (1969): 1–31.
———, ed. *A Chronicle of Emperor Yohannes IV (1872–1889)*. Wiesbaden: Franz Steiner, 1977.
Bartnicki, Andrzej, and Joanna Mantel-Niecko. "The Role and Significance of the Religious Conflicts and People's Movements in the Political Life of Ethiopia in the Seventeenth and Eighteenth Centuries." *RSE* 24 (1969–70): 5–39.
Basset, René, ed. "Études sur l'histoire d'Éthiopie." *JA*, ser. 7, 17 (1881): 315–434; 18 (1881): 93–183, 285–389.
———. "Deux lettres éthiopiennes du XVIe siècle." *GSAI* 3 (1889): 59–79.
———. "La vision de Saint Iared." In René Basset, ed., *Contes populaires d'Afrique*, pp. 124–26. Paris, n.d. [1903].
Bauer, Dan. *Household and Society in Ethiopia*. East Lansing, Mich., 1977.
Beccari, C., ed. *Rerum Aethiopicarum, Scriptores Occidentales inediti a saeculo XVI ad XIX*. 15 vols. Rome, 1903–17.
Beguinot, Francesco. *La cronoca abbreviata d'Abissinia*. Rome, 1901.
Beke, Charles. "Route from Ankobar to Dima." *JRGS* 12 (1842): 245–58.
———. "Abyssinia—Being a Continuation of Routes in that Country." *JRGS* 14 (1844): 1–76.
Bell, John. "Extrait du Journal d'un voyage en Abyssinie." *NA* 112 (1846): 136–71.
Bender, M. L. *The Non-Semitic Languages of Ethiopia*. East Lansing, Mich., 1976.
———. "The Origin of Amharic." *Journal of the Institute of Language Studies* 1 (1983): 41–52.
Ben-Dor, Shashana. "The Sigd of Beta Israel: Testimony of a Community in Transition." In Michael Ashkenazi and Alex Weingrod, eds., *Ethiopian Jews and Israel*, pp. 140–59. New Brunswick, N.J., 1985.
Bentwich, Norman. *My 77 Years*. Philadelphia, 1961.
———. "Are the Falashas Jews?" *JC* (6 January 1967): 6.
Bermudez, D. Joao. "Short Account of the Embassy which the Patriarch D. Joao Bermudez brought from the Emperor of Ethiopia" [1565]. In R. S. Whiteway, ed., *The Portuguese Expedition to Abyssinia in 1541–1543*. London, 1902.
Berreman, Gerald. "Caste: The Concept of Caste." *IESS* 2 (1968): 333–39.
Berry, LaVerle. "Factions and Coalitions during the Gonder Period, 1630–1755." In R. L. Hess, ed., *Proceedings of the Fifth International Conference on Ethiopian Studies, Session B, Chicago, 1978*, pp. 431–44. Chicago, 1979.
Beylot, Robert. "Le millénarisme, article de foi dans l'église éthiopienne, au XVe siècle." *RSE* 25 (1971–72): 31–43.
Bezold, Carl. *Kebra Nagast: Die Herrlichkeit der Konige*. Munich, 1909.
Blanc, Henry. *A Narrative of Captivity in Abyssinia*. London, 1868.
———. "From Metemma to Damot, along the Western Shores of the Tana Sea." *PRGS* 13 (1868–69): 39–51.
Blumhardt, C. H. "Deutsche Missionen in Abessinien." *DA* 36 (1863): 520–21.
Borelli, Jules. *Ethiopie méridionale, journal de mon voyage*. Paris, 1890.
Braukämper, Ulrich. "The Correlation of Oral Traditions and Historical Records in Southern Ethiopia: A Case Study of the Hadiya/Sidamo Past." *JES* 11/2 (1973): 29–50.
———. *Geschichte der Hadiya Sud-Athiopiens*. Wiesbaden, 1980.

———. "On Food Avoidances in Southern Ethiopia: Religious Manifestations and Socio-Economic Relevance." In Sven Rubenson, ed., *Proceedings of the Seventh International Conference of Ethiopian Studies, Lund, 1982,* pp. 429–45. Uppsala, Sweden, 1984.

Bruce, James. *Travels to Discover the Source of the Nile.* 5 vols. Edinburgh, 1790.

Budge, E. A. W. *The Life and Mysteries of Takla Haymanot.* London, 1906.

———. *The Queen of Sheba and Her Only Son Menyelek . . . A Complete Translation of the Kebra Nagast.* London, 1922.

———. *The Book of the Saints of the Ethiopian Church.* 3 vols. Cambridge, 1928.

———. *A History of Ethiopia, Nubia and Abyssinia.* 2 vols. London, 1928.

———. *One Hundred and Ten Miracles of Our Lady Mary.* London, 1933.

Buxton, D. R. *The Abyssinians.* New York, 1970.

Caquot, André. "L'homélie en l'honneur de l'archange Raguel (Dersāna Rāgu'ēl)." *AE* 2 (1957): 91–122.

———. "Histoire amharique de Grāñ et des Gallas." *AE* 2 (1957): 123–43.

———. "Les chroniques abrégées d'Éthiopie." *AE* 2 (1957): 187–92.

———. "Les actes d'Ezrā de Gunda-Gundē." *AE* 4 (1961): 69–121.

Caraman, Philip. *The Lost Empire. The Story of the Jesuits in Ethiopia, 1555–1634.* London, 1985.

Carmoly, Eliakim. *Itinéraires de la Terre Sainte des XIVe, XVe, XVIe, et XVIIe siècle.* Brussels, 1847.

Caulk, Richard. "Yohannes IV, the Mahdists, and the Colonial Partition of North-East Africa." *TJH* 1/2 (1971): 22–42.

———. "Religion and State in Nineteenth Century Ethiopia." *JES* 10/1 (1972): 23–41.

———. "Firearms and Princely Power in Ethiopia in the Nineteenth Century." *JAH* 13 (1972): 609–30.

———. "Armies as Predators: Soldiers and Peasants in Ethiopia, c. 1850–1935." *IJAHS* 11 (1978): 457–93.

Cecchi, Antonia, and Giovanni Chiarini. "Lettere." *BSGI* 16 (1879): 410–31.

Cerulli, Enrico. "The Folk-Literature of the Galla of Southern Abyssinia." In E. A. Hooton and Patricia Bates, eds., *Harvard African Studies, Varia Africana,* vol. 3, Appendix: "The Watta: A Low Caste of Hunters," pp. 200–214. Cambridge, Mass., 1922.

———. *Etiopi in Palestina.* 2 vols. Rome, 1943.

———. *Storia della letteratura etiopica.* Milan, 1956.

———. *Scritti teologici etiopici dei secoli XVI–XVII, Studi e Testi* 198 (1958).

———. "Gli Atti di Zena Marqos." *Studi e Testi* 219 (1962): 191–212.

Chaine, Marius, ed. "Le livre du coq (*Matzhafa Dorho*)." *RS* 13 (1905): 276–81.

———. "Histoire du règne de Iohannes IV, roi d'Éthiopie (1868–1889)." *RS* 21 (1913): 178–91.

Chaix, Paul. "Étude sur l'ethnographie de l'Afrique." *Mémoires de la société de géographie de Genève* 1 (1860): 20–42.

———. "Voyages du P. Jerome Lobo et des Jésuites en Abyssinie." *Le Globe* 27 (1888): 35–47.

Charles, R. H., ed. *The Book of Enoch.* Oxford, 1893.

———, ed. *The Book of Jubilees*. London, 1917.
Cheesman, R. E. *Lake Tana and the Blue Nile*. London, 1936 (repr. 1968).
Chihab Ed-Din Ahmed ben 'Abd el-Qader (Arab Faqih). *Histoire de la conquête de l'Abyssinie (XVI siècle)*, ed. René Basset. Paris, 1897–1901.
Chittick, Neville. "Excavations at Aksum, 1973–74: A Preliminary Report." *Azania* 9 (1974): 159–205.
Chouraqui, André. *L'Alliance israéilite universelle (1860–1960)*. Paris, 1965.
Cohen, Marcel. "Rapport sur une mission linguistique en Abyssinie 1910–1911." *NAMSL*, n.s., 20 (1912): 1–80.
———. "Cérémonies et croyances abyssines." *Revue d l'histoire des religions* 66/2 (1912): 183–200.
Colin, Gérard, ed. *Vie de Georges da Saglā*. *CSCO* 81 (1987) [text] 82 (1987) [trans.].
Combes, Edmond, and Maurice Tamisier. *Voyage en Abyssinie*. 4 vols. Paris, 1838.
Conti Rossini, Carlo. "Due squarci inediti di cronica etiopica." *RRAL*, ser. 5, 2 (1893): 804–18.
———. *Il 'Gadla Takla Haymanot,' secondo la redazione Waldebbana*. In *MRAL*, ser. 5, 2/1 (1894): 97–143.
———. "Storia di Libna Dingil, Re d'Etiopia." *RRAL*, ser. 5, 3 (1894): 617–40.
———. "Note per la storia letteraria Abissina." *RRAL*, ser. 5, 8 (1899): 197–220.
———. "Lettre." *RS* 10 (1902): 373–77.
———. "Notes et mélanges." *RS* 11 (1903): 325–30.
———. *Acta Yared et Pantalewon*. *CSCO*, ser. alt., 17 (1904): 1–60.
———. "I loggo e la legge dei Loggo Sarda." *GSAI* 17 (1904): 1–63.
———. *Acta S. Basalota Mika'el et S. Anorewos*. *CSCO* 20 (1905).
———. *Historia Regis Sarṣa Dengel (Malak Sagad)*. *CSCO* 3 (1907).
———. "Il convento di Tsana in Abissinia e le sue Laudi alla Vergine." *RRAL*, ser. 5, 29 (1910): 581–621.
———. "Les listes des rois d'Aksoum." *JA*, ser. 10, 14 (1910): 263–320.
———. "Studi su popolazioni dell'Etiopia." *RSO* 3 (1910): 894–900; 4 (1911): 599–651; 6 (1913): 365–425.
———. *La langue des Kemant en Abyssinie*. Vienna, 1912.
———. "Piccoli studi ethiopici." *ZA* 27 (1912): 358–78.
———. "Vicende dell'Etiopia, e delle missioni cattoliche ai tempi di ras Ali, deggiac Ubie e re Teodoro secondo, un documento abissino." *RRAL*, ser. 5, 25 (1916): 425–550.
———. "La cronaca reale abissina dall'anno 1800 all'anno 1840." *RRAL*, ser. 5, 25 (1916): 779–923.
———. *Principi di diritto consuetudinario dell'Eritrea*. Rome, 1916.
———. "L'autobiografia di Pawlos monaco Abissino del secolo XVI." *RRAL*, ser. 5, 27 (1918): 279–96.
———. "Appunti di storia e letteratura Falascia." *RSO*, 8 (1919–20): 563–610.
———. "Expéditions et possessions des Habashāt en Arabie." *JA* 18 (1921): 5–36.
———. "Nuovi appunti sui Guidei d'Abissinia." *RRAL*, ser. 5, 29 (1922): 221–40.
———. "Leggende geografiche giudaich del IX secolo (*Il Sefer Eldad*)." *BSGI*, ser. 6, 2 (1925): 160–90.
———. *Storia d'Etiopia*. Bergamo, 1928.

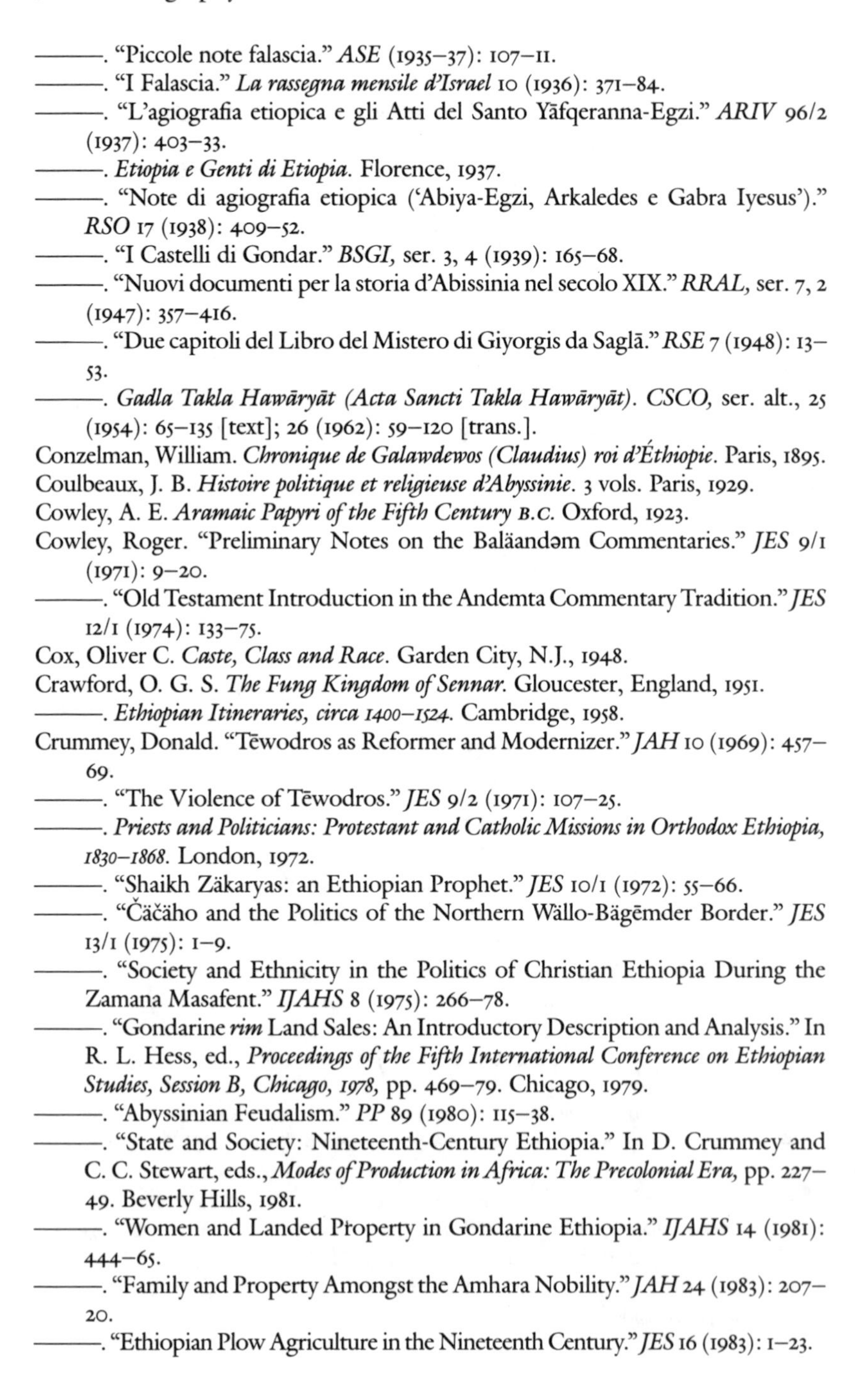

———. "Piccole note falascia." *ASE* (1935–37): 107–11.
———. "I Falascia." *La rassegna mensile d'Israel* 10 (1936): 371–84.
———. "L'agiografia etiopica e gli Atti del Santo Yāfqeranna-Egzi." *ARIV* 96/2 (1937): 403–33.
———. *Etiopia e Genti di Etiopia.* Florence, 1937.
———. "Note di agiografia etiopica ('Abiya-Egzi, Arkaledes e Gabra Iyesus')." *RSO* 17 (1938): 409–52.
———. "I Castelli di Gondar." *BSGI,* ser. 3, 4 (1939): 165–68.
———. "Nuovi documenti per la storia d'Abissinia nel secolo XIX." *RRAL,* ser. 7, 2 (1947): 357–416.
———. "Due capitoli del Libro del Mistero di Giyorgis da Saglā." *RSE* 7 (1948): 13–53.
———. *Gadla Takla Hawāryāt (Acta Sancti Takla Hawāryāt). CSCO,* ser. alt., 25 (1954): 65–135 [text]; 26 (1962): 59–120 [trans.].
Conzelman, William. *Chronique de Galawdewos (Claudius) roi d'Éthiopie.* Paris, 1895.
Coulbeaux, J. B. *Histoire politique et religieuse d'Abyssinie.* 3 vols. Paris, 1929.
Cowley, A. E. *Aramaic Papyri of the Fifth Century B.C.* Oxford, 1923.
Cowley, Roger. "Preliminary Notes on the Baläandəm Commentaries." *JES* 9/1 (1971): 9–20.
———. "Old Testament Introduction in the Andemta Commentary Tradition." *JES* 12/1 (1974): 133–75.
Cox, Oliver C. *Caste, Class and Race.* Garden City, N.J., 1948.
Crawford, O. G. S. *The Fung Kingdom of Sennar.* Gloucester, England, 1951.
———. *Ethiopian Itineraries, circa 1400–1524.* Cambridge, 1958.
Crummey, Donald. "Tēwodros as Reformer and Modernizer." *JAH* 10 (1969): 457–69.
———. "The Violence of Tēwodros." *JES* 9/2 (1971): 107–25.
———. *Priests and Politicians: Protestant and Catholic Missions in Orthodox Ethiopia, 1830–1868.* London, 1972.
———. "Shaikh Zäkaryas: an Ethiopian Prophet." *JES* 10/1 (1972): 55–66.
———. "Čäčäho and the Politics of the Northern Wällo-Bägēmder Border." *JES* 13/1 (1975): 1–9.
———. "Society and Ethnicity in the Politics of Christian Ethiopia During the Zamana Masafent." *IJAHS* 8 (1975): 266–78.
———. "Gondarine *rim* Land Sales: An Introductory Description and Analysis." In R. L. Hess, ed., *Proceedings of the Fifth International Conference on Ethiopian Studies, Session B, Chicago, 1978,* pp. 469–79. Chicago, 1979.
———. "Abyssinian Feudalism." *PP* 89 (1980): 115–38.
———. "State and Society: Nineteenth-Century Ethiopia." In D. Crummey and C. C. Stewart, eds., *Modes of Production in Africa: The Precolonial Era,* pp. 227–49. Beverly Hills, 1981.
———. "Women and Landed Property in Gondarine Ethiopia." *IJAHS* 14 (1981): 444–65.
———. "Family and Property Amongst the Amhara Nobility." *JAH* 24 (1983): 207–20.
———. "Ethiopian Plow Agriculture in the Nineteenth Century." *JES* 16 (1983): 1–23.

———. "Banditry and Resistance: Noble and Peasant in Nineteenth-Century Ethiopia." In Donald Crummey, ed., *Banditry, Rebellion and Social Protest in Africa*, pp. 133–49. London, 1986.

———. "Some Precursors of Addis Ababa: Towns in Christian Ethiopia in the Eighteenth and Nineteenth Centuries." In Ahmed Zekaria et al., eds., *Proceedings of the International Symposium on the Centenary of Addis Ababa, November 24–25, 1986*, pp. 9–31. Addis Ababa, 1987.

———. "Three Amharic Documents of Marriage and Inheritance from the Eighteenth and Nineteenth Centuries." In Taddese Beyene, ed., *Proceedings of the Eighth International Conference of Ethiopian Studies, Addis Ababa, 1984*. 2 vols., 1:315–27. Addis Ababa/Frankfort am Main, 1988.

———. "Society, State and Nationality in the Recent Historiography of Ethiopia." *JAH* 31 (1990): 103–19.

d'Abbadie, Antoine. "Extrait d'une lettre de M. d'Abbadie à M. Jomard." *BSG* 11 (1839): 112–14.

———. "Lettre à M. Garcin de Tassy." *JA*, ser. 3, 7 (1839): 364–66.

———. "Lettre à M. Jomard." *JA*, ser. 3, 7 (1839): 367–69.

———. "Sur les sources les plus intéressantes à consulter par les voyageurs." *BSG* 11 (1839): 338–40.

———. "Voyage en Abyssinie." *BSG* 11 (1839): 200–217.

———. "À. M. Jomard." *BSG* 14 (1840): 57–61.

———. "Géographie positive de l'Abyssinie." *BSG* 14 (1840): 239–56.

———. "Lettre à M. J. Mohl sur la langue hamtonga." *JA*, ser. 3, 11 (1841): 388–96.

———. "Lettres à M. J. Mohl." *JA*, ser. 4, 2 (1843): 102–18.

———. "Abyssinie, les Falacha ou juifs Ethiopiens." *Revue de l'Orient* 7 (1845): 222–35.

———. "Die Falascha oder Judennachkommen in Abyssinien." *DA* 18 (1845): 876.

———. "Extrait d'une lettre de M. Antoine d'Abbadie sur les Falacha ou juifs d'Abyssinie." *BSG*, ser. 3, 4 (1845): 43–57, 65–74.

———. "Lettres écrites d'Abyssinie." *NA*, n.s., 106 (1845): 107–22.

———. "Réponses des Falasha dits juifs d'Abyssinie." *AI* 12 (1851): 179–85, 234–40, 259–69.

———. *L'Abyssinie et le roi Théodore*. Paris, 1868.

———. *Les causes actuelles de l'esclavage en Éthiopie*. Louvain, 1877.

———. "Annexe No. 2, nouvelles et mélanges." *JA*, ser. 7, 19 (1882): 248–52.

———. *Géographie de l'Éthiopie*. Paris, 1890.

d'Abbadie, Arnauld. *Douze ans de séjour dans la Haute-Éthiopie (Abyssinie)*. 3 vols. Vol. 1: Paris, 1868 [new ed.: Vatican, 1980]. Vol. 2: Vatican, 1980. Vol. 3: Vatican, 1983.

Dacher, Michele. "Les Falasha, juifs noirs d'Éthiopie." *Nouveau cahiers: Revue d'études et de libres débats* 18 (1969): 43–52.

Danielou, Jean. *The Theology of Jewish Christianity*. Chicago, 1964.

Daoud, M. *The Liturgy of the Ethiopian Church*. Addis Ababa, 1954.

Darkwah, R. H. Kofi. *Shewa, Menilek and the Ethiopian Empire, 1813–1889*. London, 1975.

De Almeida, Manoel. "The History of High Ethiopia or Abassia." In C. F. Beckingham and G. W. B. Huntingford, eds., *Some Records of Ethiopia, 1593–1646*. London, 1954.

De Castanhoso, Miguel. *The Portuguese Expedition to Abyssinia, 1841–1843*, trans. R. S. Whiteway. London, 1902.

De Castro, Lincoln. *Nella Terra dei Negus*. 2 vols. Milan, 1915.

De Contenson, Henri. "Les principales étapes de l'Éthiopie antique." *CEA* 5 (1961): 12–23.

———. "Pre-Aksumite Culture." In G. Mokhtar, ed., *General History of Africa, vol. 2: Ancient Civilizations of Africa*, pp. 341–59. Paris, 1981.

De Cosson, E. A. *The Cradle of the Blue Nile*. 2 vols. London, 1877.

Denis de Rivoyre, B. L. *Mer Rouge et Abyssinie*. Paris, 1880.

Devens, Monica. "Remarks on a Falasha Liturgical Text for the Sanbata Sanbat." In Sven Rubenson, ed., *Proceedings of the Seventh International Conference of Ethiopian Studies, Lund, 1982*, pp. 121–23. Uppsala, Sweden, 1984.

Dillmann, August. "Zur Geschichte des abyssinischen Reichs." *ZDMG* 7 (1853): 338–64.

———. "Die Kriegsthaten des Königs Amda-Ṣion gegen die Muslim." In *Sitzungsberichte der Koniglich Preussischen Akademie der Wissenschaften zu Berlin* 43 (1884): 1,007–38.

Dombrowski, Franz. *Tānāsee 106: Eine Chronik der Herrscher Aethiopiens*. Wiesbaden, 1983.

———. "Observations on Crown Pretendership in 17th Century Russia and Ethiopia." In S. Rubenson, ed., *Proceedings of the Seventh International Conference of Ethiopian Studies, Lund, 1982*, pp. 233–41. Uppsala, Sweden, 1984.

Donham, Donald, and Wendy James. *The Southern Marches of Imperial Ethiopia*. Cambridge, 1986.

Doresse, Jean. *L'empire du Prêtre-Jean*. 2 vols. Paris, 1957.

———. "Survivances d'écrits gnostiques dans la littérature Gueze." In *Proceedings of the Third International Conference on Ethiopian Studies, Addis Ababa, 1966*. 3 vols., 2:213–16. Addis Ababa, 1970.

Dufton, Henry. *Narrative of a Journey Through Abyssinia in 1862–3*. Westport, Conn., 1970 [orig. ed. London, 1867].

Dumont, Louis. *Homo Hierarchus, An Essay on the Caste System*. Chicago, 1970.

Ehret, Christopher. "On the Antiquity of Agriculture in Ethiopia." *JAH* 20 (1979): 161–77.

———. "Cushitic Prehistory." In M. Lionel Bender, ed., *The Non-Semitic Languages of Ethiopia*, pp. 85–96. East Lansing, Mich., 1976.

Eisler, Robert. *Man Into Wolf*. London, 1951.

El-Haimi, Hasan ben Ahmed. *Zur Geschichte Abessiniens im 17. Jahrhundert*, ed., F. E. Peiser. Berlin, 1898.

Eliade, Mircea. *The Forge and the Crucible*. 2nd ed. Chicago, 1978.

Ellenson, David. "'Our Brothers and our Flesh': Rabbi Esriel Hildesheimer and the Jews of Ethiopia." *Judaism* 35 (1986): 63–65.

Ellero, Giovanni, "Il Uolcait." *RSE* 7 (1948): 89–112.

Ephraim Isaac. *The Ethiopian Church*. Boston, 1967.

———. "Social Structure of the Ethiopian Church." *EO* 14/4 (1971): 240–88.

———. "An Obscure Component in Ethiopian Church History." *Le Muséon* 85 (1972): 225–58.

———. *A New Text-Critical Introduction to Maṣḥafa Berhan*. Leiden, 1973.

Ephraim Isaac, and Cain Felder, "Reflections on the Origins of the Ethiopian Civilization," in Taddesse Beyene, ed., *Proceedings of the Eighth International Conference of Ethiopian Studies, Addis Ababa, 1984*. 2 vols., 1:71–83. Addis Ababa, 1988.

Erlich, Haggai. *Ethiopia and Eritrea During the Scramble for Africa*. East Lansing, Mich., 1982.

Esteves Pereira, F. M., ed. *Historia de Minas (Ademas Sagad), Rei de Ethiopia*. Lisbon, 1888.

———. *Chronica de Susenyos, Rei de Ethiopia*. 2 vols. Lisbon, 1892–1900.

Euringer, Sebastian. "Das Netz Solomons." *ZS* 6 (1928): 76–100, 178–99, 300–14; 7 (1929): 68–85.

Faitlovitch, Jacques. *Notes d'un voyage chez les Falachas (juifs d'Abyssinie*. Paris, 1905.

———. "Une lettre amharique des Falachas ou juifs d'Abyssinie." *RS* 14 (1906): 92–95.

———. *Mota Musē (La mort de Moïse)*. Paris, 1906.

———. *Les Falachas d'après les explorateurs: Notes apologétiques*. Florence, 1907 [Reprint from *RI*, v. 4].

———. *Gli ebrei d'Abissinia (Falascia)*. Pro-Falasha Committee, 1907.

———. *Proverbes abyssins. Paris, 1907.*

———. *Quer durch Abessinien*. Berlin, 1910.

———. *Falascha-Briefe*. Berlin, 1913.

———. "The Black Jews of Abyssinia." *American Hebrew* 97/16 (20 August 1915): 382–83.

———. "The Falashas." *The American Jewish Year Book 5681* 22 (1920–21): 80–100.

"The Falashas." [Interview with J. Faitlovitch] *JC* (27 October 1905): 19.

"The Falashas: Interviews with Dr. J. Faitlovitch and Rabbi Dr. Margulies." *JC* (10 January 1908): 16–17.

Ferret, A., and M. Galinier. *Voyages en Abyssinie*. 3 vols. Paris, 1847.

Ferry, Robert. "Quelques hypothèses sur les origines des conquêtes musulmanes en Abyssinie au XVI siècle." *CEA* 2 (1961): 24–36.

Flad, J. M. *Notes from the Journal of J. M. Flad*, ed. W. Douglas Veitch. London, 1860.

———. *A Short Description of the Falashas and Kamants in Abyssinia*. Basle, 1866.

———. *The Falashas (Jews) of Abyssinia*. London, 1869.

———. *Kurze Schilderung der bisher fast unbekannten abessinischen Juden (Falascha)*. Basle, 1869.

———. *Zwolf Jahre en Abessinien*. Basel, 1869.

———. *Sechzig Jahre in der Mission unter den Falaschas in Abessinien*. Giessen, 1922.

Fleming, Harold. "Sociology, Ethnology, and History in Ethiopia." *IJAHS* 9 (1976): 248–78.

Foti, C. "La cronaca abbreviata dei Re d'Abissinia in un manoscritto di Dabra Berhan di Gondar." *RSE* 1 (1941): 87–123.

Freehof, Solomon. "Marriage with Falashas." In Solomon Freehof, ed., *A Treasury of Responsa*, pp. 122–27. Philadelphia, 1963.

Fusella, Luigi. "La cronaca dell'imperatore Teodora II di Etiopia in un manoscritto amarico." *Annali dell'Istituto Universitario Orientale di Napoli*, n.s., 6 (1954–56): 61–121.

———. "Il Dāgmāwi Menilek di Afawarq Gabra Iyasus." *RSE* 17 (1961): 11–44.

Gamst, Frederick. *The Qemant. A Pagan-Hebraic Peasantry of Ethiopia*. New York, 1969.

———. "Peasantries and Elites without Urbanism: The Civilization of Ethiopia." *CSSH* 12 (1970): 373–92.

Garima Taffara, "Gondar and its History [*Gondarna Tarikwa*] [Amharic]." *Gondar Municipal Herald* [*Tiyinte Gonder*], year 1, no. 11 [n.d.].

———. "Gondar and its Kings" [*Gondarna Negestatwa*]." [Amharic] *Gondar Municipal Herald* [*Tiyinte Gonder*], year 1, nos. 5–10.

Gebre-Wold-Ingida Worq. "Ethiopia's Traditional System of Land Tenure and Taxation. *EO* 5 (1962): 302–39.

Gedamu Abraha, "Wax and Gold." *EO* 11 (1968): 226–43.

Gerster, George. *Churches in Rock*. London, 1970.

Getatchew Haile, "The Homily in Honour of Saint Frumentius, Bishop of Axum (EMML 1763 ff. 84ᵛ–86ʳ)." *AB* 97 (1979): 309–18.

———. "A Note on Writing History from Forgotten Documents." *NAS* 2/1 (1980): 73–77.

———. "Some Notes on 'A Text in Old Amharic,' of Roger Cowley." *BSOAS* 43 (1980): 578–80.

———. "A Preliminary Investigation of the 'Ṭomara Təsbə't' of Emperor Zär'a Yaʿəqob of Ethiopia." *BSOAS* 43 (1980): 207–34.

———. "From Strict Observance to Royal Endowment: The Case of the Monastery of Däbrä Halle Luya, EMML 6343, ff. 117–18." *Le Muséon* 93 (1980): 163–72.

———. "An Anonymous Homily in Honor of King Əllä Asbäha of Axum, EMML 1763, ff. 34v–35v." *NAS* 3/2 (1981): 25–37.

———. "Fəkkare Haymanot or the Faith of *Abba Giyorgis Säglawi*." *Le Muséon* 94 (1981): 235–58.

———. "The Letter of Archbishops Mika'el and Gäbrə'el Concerning the Observance of Saturday." *JSS* 26 (1981): 73–78.

———. "From the Markets of Damot to that of Bärara: A Note on Slavery in Medieval Ethiopia." *Paideuma* 27 (1981): 173–80.

———. "A New Ethiopic Version of the Acts of St. Mark." *AB* 99 (1981): 117–34.

———. "Religious Controversies and the Growth of Ethiopic Literature in the Fourteenth and Fifteenth Centuries." *OC* 65 (1981): 102–36.

———. "A Study of the Issues Raised in Two Homilies of Emperor Zär'a Yaʿəqob of Ethiopia." *ZDMG* 131 (1981): 85–113.

———. "The Homily of *Aṣe* Zär'a Yaʿəqob of Ethiopia in Honour of Saturday," *OLP* 13 (1982): 185–231.

———. "Inside the Royal Confinement." *NAS* 4/1 (1982): 19–25.

———. "A New Look at Some Dates of Early Ethiopian History." *Le Muséon* 95 (1982): 311–22.

———. "On the Writings of *Abba* Giyorgis Säglawi from Two Unedited Miracles of Mary." *OCP* 48 (1982): 65–91.

———. "Power Struggle in the Medieval Court of Ethiopia: The Case of Bätärgēla-Maryam." *JES* 15 (1982): 37–55.

———. "The Monastic Genealogy of the Line of Täklä Haymanot of Shoa." *RSE* 29 (1982–83): 7–38.

———. "The Cause of the Ǝsṭifanosites: A Fundamentalist Sect in the Church of Ethiopia." *Paideuma* 29 (1983): 93–119.

———. *The Different Collection of Nags Hymns in Ethiopic Literature and their Contributions*. Erlangen, Germany, 1983.

———. "The Life of Abuna Yosṭinos." *AB* 103 (1983): 311–25.

———. "On the Identity of Silondis and the Composition of the Anaphora of Mary Ascribed to Hərəyaqos of Bəhənsa." *OCP* 49 (1983): 366–89.

———. "Review of Yaqob Beyene, *L'unzione di Cristo nella teologia Etiopica [OCA, 215(1981)]*." *Annali dell'Istituto Universitario Orientale* 44 (1984): 689–95.

———. "A Christ for the Gentiles: The Case of Za-Krəstos of Ethiopia." *JRA* 15 (1985): 86–95.

———. "The Homily of Luləyanos, Bishop of Axum, on the Holy Fathers." *AB* 103 (1985): 385–91.

———. "The End of a Deserter of the Established Church of Ethiopia." In G. Goldenberg, ed., *Ethiopian Studies. Proceedings of the Sixth International Conference, Tel-Aviv, 1980*, pp. 193–203. Boston, 1986.

———. "Ethiopian Church." In Mircea Eliade, ed., *Encyclopedia of Religion* 5: 173–77. New York, 1987.

———. "Review of David Kessler, *The Falashas*." *JRA* 17 (1987): 187–88.

———. "The Forty-Nine Hour Sabbath of the Ethiopian Church." *JSS* 33 (1988): 233–54.

———. "Empress Taytu and the Ethiopian Property in Jerusalem." *Paideuma* 35 (1989): 67–81.

———. "On the Identity of Gorgoryos and the Provenance of His Apocalypse." Forthcoming, 1991.

Getatchew Haile and William Macomber. *A Catalogue of Ethiopian Manuscripts Microfilmed for the Ethiopian Manuscript Microfilm Library, Addis Ababa, and for the Hill Monastic Manuscript Library, Collegeville*. 9 vols. [Vols. 1 to 3 edited by Macomber only; vol. 4 by Getatchew only; others are jointly edited.] Collegeville, Minn., 1975–.

Ghiorghis Mellessa. "Gondar Yesterday and Today." *EO* 12 (1969): 164–76.

Gidney, William. *The History of the London Society for Promoting Christianity Amongst the Jews, from 1809 to 1908*. London, 1908.

Gigar Tesfaye. "Reconnaissance de trois églises antérieures à 1314." *JES* 12/2 (1974): 57–75.

Girma Amare. "Aims and Purposes of Church Education in Ethiopia." *EJE* 1 (1967): 1–11.

Girma Beshah and Merid Wolde Aregay. *The Question of the Union of the Churches in Luso-Ethiopian Relations (1500–1632)*. Lisbon, 1964.

Gleichen, Edward. *With the Mission to Menelik, 1897*. London, 1898.

Gobat, Samuel. *Journal of Three Years' Residence in Abyssinia*. New York, 1850 (orig. ed. 1834).

Goitein, E. David. "Note on Eldad the Danite." *JQR* 17 (1926–27): 483.

Goitein, Solomon. *Jews and Arabs*. New York, 1955.
Grad, Charles. "Résultats scientifiques de la mission allemande au soudan orientale à la recherche de Vogel (1861–1862)." *BSG* 9 (1865): 5–34.
Grad, Charles, and S. E. Achille Dinomé. "Les expéditions allemande à la recherche d'Eduard Vogel [de 1861 à 1862]." *NA* 178 (1863): 51–83, 158–94, 273–326; 184 (1864): 197–243.
Great Britain. *Parliamentary Papers (P.P.). Correspondence Respecting Abyssinia, 1846–1868*. London, 1868.
Grébaut, Sylvain. "Inventaire sommaire des manuscrits éthiopiens (Ge'ez) de la mission Griaule." *Aethiopica* 1 (1933): 23–35; 2 (1934): 16–22, 50–54, 65–69, 110–14; 3 (1935): 27–32.
———. "Catalogue des manuscrits éthiopiens (Ge'ez) de la mission Griaule." *Aethiopica* 3 (1935): 82–84, 154–61.
Griaule, Marcel. "Mythes, croyances et coutumes du Bégamder (Abyssinie)." *JA* 212 (1928): 19–123.
———. *Le livre de recettes d'un dabtara abyssin*. *TMIE* 12 (1930).
———. "Règles de l'église (documents éthiopiens)." *JA* 221 (1932): 1–42.
———. "De quelques règles de nourriture concernant les génies zar." *Aethiopica* 3 (1935): 125–28.
Grinfeld, Itzhak. "Jews in Addis Ababa: Beginnings of the Jewish Community until the Italian Occupation." In G. Goldenberg, ed., *Ethiopian Studies: Proceedings of the Sixth International Conference, Tel-Aviv, 1980*, pp. 251–59. Rotterdam, 1986.
Grottanelli, Vinigi. *Missione di Studio al Lago Tana*. Vol. 2 of *Ricerche Geografiche ed Economiche sulle Popolazioni*. Rome, 1939.
Gruber, Ruth. *Rescue. The Exodus of the Ethiopian Jews*. New York, 1987.
Guebre Sellassie. *Chronique du règne de Menelik II*, ed. Maurice de Coppet. 2 vols. Paris, 1930–31.
Guidi, Ignazio. "Le canzoni Ge'ez-Amarina in onore di re abissini." *RRAL*, ser. 4, 5 (1889): 53–66.
———. "Due notizie storiche sull'Abissinia." *GSAI* 3 (1889): 176–79.
———. "Di due frammenti relativi alla storia di Abissinia." *RRAL*, ser. 5, 2 (1893): 579–605.
———. "Historia Gentis Galla." *CSCO* 3 (1907): 195–208.
———. "La Chiesa Abissinia." *OM* 2 (1922–23): 123–28, 186–90, 252–56.
———. *Storia della letteratura Ethiopica*. Rome, 1932.
———, ed. *Annales Iohannis I, Iyasu I, Bakafa*. *CSCO*, 2 vols., ser. alt., 5 (1903).
———, ed. *Annales Regum Iyasu II et Iyo'as*. *CSCO*, 2 vols., ser. alt., 6 (1910–12).
———. "Contributi alla storia letteraria di Abissinia: Il 'Ser'ata Mangest.'" *RRAL*, ser. 5, 31 (1922): 65–95.
———. *Vocabolario Amarico-Italiano*. Rome, 1953.
Haber, L. "The Chronicle of Emperor Zara Yaqob (1434–1868)." *EO* 5 (1961): 152–69.
———. "The Chronicle of Ba'eda Mariam." *EO* 6 (1962): 63, 70–80.
Haberland, Eike. "Zum Problem der Jäger und besonderen Kasten in Nordost- und Ostafrika." *Paideuma* 8 (1962): 136–55.
———. "The Influence of the Christian Ethiopian Empire on Southern Ethiopia." *JSS* 9 (1964): 235–38.

———. "Special Castes in Ethiopia." In R. L. Hess, ed., *Proceedings of the Fifth International Conference on Ethiopian Studies, Session B, Chicago, 1978,* pp. 129–32. Chicago, 1979.

———. "Caste and Hierarchy among the Dizi (Southwest Ethiopia)." In Sven Rubenson, ed., *Proceedings of the Seventh International Conference of Ethiopian Studies, Lund, 1982,* pp. 447–50. Uppsala, Sweden, 1984.

Halévy, Joseph. "Lettre adressée à l'Alliance israélite universelle." *AI* 28 (1867): 1,084–86.

———. "Recherches sur la langue de la rédaction primitive du livre d'Enoch." *JA,* ser. 6, 9 (1867): 352–95.

———. "Lettres d'Abyssinie II." *AI* 29 (1868): 173–76.

———. *Rapport au comité central de l'Alliance israélite universelle concernant la mission auprès des Falachas.* Paris, 1868.

———. "Excursion chez les Falacha en Abyssinie." *BSG,* ser. 5, 17 (1869): 270–94.

———. "Rapport sur une mission archéologique dans le Yemen." *JA,* ser. 6, 19 (1872): 5–98.

———. "Essai sur la langue agaou. Le dialecte des Falachas (juifs d'Abyssinie)." *ASP* 3/4 (1873): 151–88.

———. *Mélanges d'épigraphe et d'archéologie sémitiques.* Paris, 1874.

———. *Prières des Falasha.* Paris, 1877.

———. "Travels in Abyssinia." In A. L. Lowy, ed., *Miscellany of Hebrew Literature,* ser. 2, vol. 2, pp. 175–256. London, 1877.

———. "Examen critique des sources relatives à la persécution des chrétiens de Nedjran par le roi juif des Himyarites." *REJ* 18 (1889): 16–42, 161–78.

———. "Remarque sur un point contesté touchant la persécution de Nedjran." *REJ* 21 (1890): 73–77.

———. "Appendice." *REJ* 21 (1890): 77–79.

———. "L'alliance des Sabéens et des Abyssiniens contre les Himyarites." *RS* 4 (1896): 64–86.

———. "Divers." *RS* 4 (1896): 187–88.

———. "Review of Ignazio Guidi, 'Il Gadla Aragawi,' and C. Conti Rossini, *Appunti ed osservazioni sui re Zague.*" *RS* 4 (1896): 92–95.

———. *Te'ezaza Sanbat (Commandements du Sabbat).* Paris, 1902.

———. "Le guerre de Sarsa-Dengel contre les Falashas." *RS* 14 (1906): 392–427; 15 (1907): 119–63, 263–87.

———. "Inscription araméenne d'Éléphantine." *RS* 16 (1908): 95–99, 224–40.

———. "Nouvelles prières des Falachas." *RS* 19 (1911): 96–104, 215–18, 344–64.

Hallpike, Christopher. "The Status of Craftsmen among the Konso of South-West Ethiopia." *Africa* 38 (1968): 258–69.

Halls, John. *The Life and Correspondence of Henry Salt.* 2 vols. 2nd ed., London, 1834.

Halstead, Thomas. *Our Missions: Being a History of the Principal Missionary Transactions of the London Society for Promoting Christianity Amongst the Jews.* London, 1866.

Hammerschmidt, Ernst. *Stellung und Bedeutung des Sabbats in Aethiopien.* Stuttgart, 1963.

———. "Jewish Elements in the Cult of the Ethiopian Church." *JES* 3/2 (1965): 1–12.

Harmsworth, Geoffrey. *Abyssinian Adventure*. London, 1935.
Harris, Joseph, ed. *Pillars in Ethiopian History. The William Leo Hansberry African History Notebook*, vol. 1. Washington, 1974.
Harris, William Corwallis. *The Highlands of Ethiopia*. 3 vols. 2nd ed. London, 1844.
Hecht, Elisabeth-Dorothea. "The Kebra Nagast, Oedipus and Menilek: A Comparison of Two Myths." In R. L. Hess, ed., *Proceedings of the Fifth International Conference on Ethiopian Studies, Session B, Chicago, 1978*, pp. 329–41. Chicago, 1979.
Heldman, Marilyn. "Jewish Christianity and Medieval Ethiopian Illumination." *Manuscripta* (March 1976): 13–14.
Henze, Paul. "Patterns of Cultural Survival on the Islands in Ethiopia's Highland Lakes." *EO* 16 (1973): 89–96.
———. *Ethiopian Journeys*. London, 1977.
Hess, Robert. "The Itinerary of Benjamin of Tudela: A Twelfth-Century Jewish Description of North-East Africa." *JAH* 6 (1965): 15–24.
———. "An Outline of Falasha History." In *Proceedings of the Third International Conference on Ethiopian Studies, Addis Ababa, 1966*. 3 vols., 1:99–112. Addis Ababa, 1970.
———. "Towards a History of the Falasha." In D. F. McCall et al., eds., *Eastern African History. Boston University Papers on Africa*, pp. 107–32. New York, 1969.
Hess, Robert, and Dalvan Colger. *A Bibliography of Primary Sources for Nineteenth-Century Tropical Africa*. Stanford, 1972.
Hetzron, Robert. "The Agaw Languages." *AL* 3/3 (1976): 1–45.
Hildesheimer, Israel. "Bericht über die Entwickelung der Falascha-Angelegenheit und Beurtheilung der hierbei gemachten Vorschlage." *Der Israelit* 5/49 (1864): 641–42.
———. "Nehmet euch der Falascha's an! Ein Aufruf an alle Glaubensgenossen." *Der Israelit* 5/44 (1864): 575–78.
———. "Very Urgent Appeal to all my Fellow Believers." *JC* (4 November 1864): 6.
Hoben, Allan. "Social Stratification in Traditional Amhara Society." In A. Tuden and L. Plotnicov, eds., *Social Stratification in Africa*, pp. 187–224. New York, 1970.
———. *Land Tenure among the Amhara of Ethiopia: The Dynamics of Cognatic Descent*. Chicago, 1973.
Hodge, Carleton. "Lisramic (Afroasiatic): An Overview." In M. Lionel Bender, ed., *The Non-Semitic Languages of Ethiopia*, pp. 43–65. East Lansing, Mich., 1976.
Holt, P. M. *The Mahdist State in the Sudan, 1881–1898*. Oxford, 1958.
Horvath, Ronald. "Towns in Ethiopia." *Erdkunde* 22 (1968): 42–51.
———. "The Wandering Capitals of Ethiopia." *JAH* 10 (1969): 205–19.
Hotten, John. *Abyssinia and Its People*. London, 1868.
Hudson, Grover. "Language Classification and the Semitic Prehistory of Ethiopia." *Folio Orientalia* 18 (1977): 119–66.
Huntingford, G. W. B. *The Galla of Ethiopia*. London, 1955.
———. *The Glorious Victories of Amda Ṣeyon King of Ethiopia*. Oxford, 1965.
———. *The Land Charters of Northern Ethiopia*. Addis Ababa, 1965.
———. "The Lives of Saint Takla Hāymānot." *JES* 4/2 (1966): 35–40.

———. "'The Wealth of Kings,' and the End of the Zāguē Dynasty." *BSOAS* 28 (1965): 1–23.

Hyatt, Harry M. *The Church of Abyssinia*. London, 1928.

Ibn Khaldun. *Histoire des Berbères*. 3 vols. Paris, 1927.

Ibn Hauqal. *Configuration de la Terre*. 2 vols. Paris, 1964.

Imbakom Kalewold. *Traditional Ethiopian Church Education*. New York, 1970.

Jager, Otto, and Ivy Pearce. *Antiquities of North Ethiopia*. London, 1974.

"Johann Mayer's Missionreise nach Shoa in Sudabyssinien, Januar bis Juni 1872." *Globus* 23 (1873): 157–58.

Johnston, Charles. *Travels in Southern Abyssinia*. 2 vols. London, 1844.

Jones, William. "A Conversation with Abram, an Abyssinian, Concerning the City of Gwender and the Sources of the Nile." *Asiatic Researches* 1 (1786): 383–88.

"Die Juden in Abyssinien." *DA* 3 (1830): 191–92.

Kammerer, Albert. *Essai sur l'histoire antique d'Abyssinie*. Paris, 1926.

Kamil, Murad. "An Ethiopic Inscription found at Mareb." *JSS* 9 (1964): 56–57.

Kaplan, Steven. "Hagiographies and the History of Medieval Ethiopia." *HA* 8 (1981): 107–23.

———. *The Monastic Holy Man and the Christianization of Early Solomonic Ethiopia*. Wiesbaden, 1984.

———. "The Falasha and the Stephanite: An Episode from the *Gadla Gabra Masih*." *BSOAS* 28 (1985): 278–82.

———. "A Brief History of the Beta Israel." In *The Jews of Ethiopia. A People in Transition*, pp. 11–29. Tel-Aviv and New York, 1986.

———. "Court and Periphery in Ethiopian Christianity." *Asian and African Studies* 20 (1986): 141–52.

———. "The Ethiopian Cult of Saints. A Preliminary Investigation." *Paideuma* 32 (1986): 1–13.

———. "Iyasus-Mo'a and Takla Haymanot: A Note on a Hagiographic Controversy." *JSS* 31 (1986): 47–56.

———. "The Beta Israel (Falasha) Encounter with Protestant Missionaries: 1860–1905." *Jewish Social Studies* 49 (1987): 27–42.

———. "The Beta Israel (Falasha) in the Ethiopian Context." In Michael Ashkenazi and Alex Weingrod, eds., *Ethiopian Jews and Israel*, pp. 9–20. New Brunswick, N.J., 1987.

———. "The Origins of the Beta Israel: Five Methodological Cautions." *Pe'amim* 33 (1987).

———. "Te'ezaza Sanbat: A Beta Israel Work Reconsidered." *Studies in the History of Religions* 1 (1987): 107–24 [reprinted in *Truman Institute Reprints*].

———. "Some Hebrew Sources on the Beta Israel (Falasha)." In Taddesse Beyene, ed., *Proceedings of the Eighth International Conference of Ethiopian Studies, Addis Ababa, 1984*, 1:199–208. Addis Ababa, 1988.

Kaplan, Steven, and Shoshana Ben-Dor. *Ethiopian Jewry. An Annotated Bibliography*. Jerusalem, 1988.

Kessler, David. *The Falashas. The Forgotten Jews of Ethiopia*. New York, 1982.

Kessler, David, and Tudor Parfitt. *The Falashas: The Jews of Ethiopia*. London, 1985.

Kinefe-Rigb Zelleke. "Bibliography of the Ethiopic Hagiographical Traditions." *JES* 13/2 (1975): 57–102.

Knibb, M. A., ed. *The Ethiopic Book of Enoch*. 2 vols. Oxford, 1978.

Kobishchanov, Yuri. *Axum*. University Park, Penna., 1979 [orig. ed. 1966].

———. "Aksum: Political System, Economics and Culture, First to Fourth Century." In G. Mokhtar, ed., *General History of Africa,* vol. 2: *Ancient Civilization of Africa,* pp. 381–99. Paris, 1981.

Kolmodin, Johannes. "Traditions de Tsazzega et Hazzega." *Archives d'études orientales*. Vol. 5, nos. 1, 2, 3 [Uppsala] (1912–14).

Krapf, J. L. *Travels, Researches and Missionary Labours*. 2nd ed. London, 1968 [orig. ed., 1860].

———. "Extracts from a Journal, Ankobar, 1839." *JRGS* 10 (1841): 469–88.

Krapf, J. L., and K. W. Isenberg. *Journals*. London, 1843.

Krempel, Vera. "Eine Berufskaste in Nordwest-Athiopien—die Kayla (Falascha)." *Sociologus,* n.s., 24 (1974): 37–55.

Kropp, Manfred. *Die Geschichte des Lebna-Dengel, Claudius und Minās*. *CSCO* 83 (1988) [text], 84 (1988) [trans.].

Kur, Stanilas. *Actes de Iyasus Mo'a*. *CSCO* 49 (1965), 50 (1965).

———. *Actes de Marḥa Krestos*. *CSCO* 62 (1972), 63 (1972).

Lange, Werner. "Status and Function of Kafa Bards in Feudal Ethiopia." *NAS* 1/3 (1979–80): 85–90.

Leach, Edmund. *Aspects of Caste in South India, Ceylon and North-West Pakistan*. London, 1960.

Lefebvre, C. T. "Aperçu général de l'Abyssinie." *BSG,* ser. 2, 14 (1840): 65–77, 129–46, 268–83.

———. "Notice de M. Lefevre [*sic*] sur son second voyage en Abyssinie." *BSG,* ser. 2, 13 (1840): 365–75.

———. 1845. "État social des Abyssins." *NA* 105 (1845): 307–34.

———. *Voyage en Abyssinie*. 6 vols. Paris, 1845–51.

Leiris, Michel. "Le culte des zars à Gondar." *Aethiopica* 2 (1934): 96–103, 125–36.

———. "Un rite médico-magique Ethiopien: Le jet du danqara." *Aethiopica* 3 (1935): 61–74.

Lejean, Guillaume. "Rapport addressé à son excellence M. le Ministere des Affaires Etrangères." *BSG* 3 (1862): 205–21.

———. "Extrait d'une lettre à M. Jomard." *BSG* 4 (1862): 61–62.

———. "Extraits des lettres à M. Ernest Desjardins." *BSG* 6 (1863): 72–76.

———. "Notes d'un voyage en Abyssinie." *Le Tour du Monde* 9 (1864): 69–80; 12 (1865): 221–72; 15 (1867): 353–400.

———. *Théodore II, Le nouvel empire d'Abyssinie*. Paris, 1867.

———. "L'Abyssinie en 1868: L'expédition anglaise et Théodore II." *RDM* 74 (1868): 187–216.

———. *Voyage en Abyssinie*. Paris, 1872.

le Roux, Hughes. *Magda Queen of Sheba*. New York, 1907.

Leslau, Wolf. "The Influence of Cushitic on the Semitic Languages of Ethiopia: A Problem of Sub-Stratum." *Word* 1 (1945): 59–82.

———, ed. "A Falasha Religious Dispute." *Proceedings of the American Academy for Jewish Research* 16 (1947): 71–95.

———. "The Black Jews of Ethiopia: An Expedition to the Falashas." *Commentary* 7 (1949): 216–24.
———. "An Ethiopian Argot of a People Possessed by a Spirit." *Africa* 19 (1949): 204–12.
———. *Falasha Anthology.* New Haven, Conn., 1951.
———. *Coutumes et croyances des Falachas. TMIE* 61 (1957).
———. "A Supplementary Falasha Bibliography." *Studies in Bibliography and Folklore* 3/1 (1957): 9–27.
———. "To the Defense of the Falashas." *Judaism* 6/2 (1957): 142–47.
———. "A Falasha Book of Jewish Festivals." In *For Max Weinrich on His Seventieth Birthday,* pp. 183–91. London, 1964.
———. *Hebrew Cognates in Amharic.* Wiesbaden, 1969.
———. "Ethiopia and South Arabia." In T. Sebeok, *Current Trends in Linguistics,* vol. 6: *Linguistics in Southwest Asia and North Africa,* pp. 467–527. The Hague, 1970.
———. "Taamrat Emmanuel's Notes of Falasha Monks and Holy Places." In *Salo Wittmayer Barron Jubilee Volume, American Academy for Jewish Research* [Jerusalem] (1975): 623–37.
"A Letter from Falashas." *JC* (13 October 1905): 11.
Levine, Donald. "On the History and Culture of Manz." *JSS* 9 (1964): 204–11.
———. *Wax and Gold.* Chicago, 1965 and 1972.
———. *Greater Ethiopia: The Evolution of a Multiethnic Society.* Chicago, 1974.
———. "Menilek and Oedipus: Further Observations on the Ethiopian National Epic." In Harold G. Marcus, ed., *Proceedings of the First United States Conference on Ethiopian Studies, 1973,* pp. 11–23. East Lansing, Mich., 1975.
Lewis, Herbert. "Historical Problems in Ethiopia and the Horn of Africa." *Annals of the New York Academy of Sciences* 96 (1962): 504–11.
———. *A Galla Monarchy.* Madison, Wisc., 1965.
———. "The Origins of the Galla and Somali." *JAH* 7 (1966): 27–46.
———. *After the Eagles Landed: The Yemenites of Israel.* Boulder, Colo., 1989.
Lifchitz, Deborah. "Un sacrifice chez les Falacha, juifs abyssins." *La Terre et la vie* 9 (1939): 116–23.
———. *Textes éthiopiens magico-religieux. TMIE* 38 (1940).
Littmann, Enno. *The Legend of the Queen of Sheba in the Tradition of Axum.* Vol. 1 of *Bibliotheca Abessinica,* 4 vols. Leiden, 1904–1911.
———. *Publication of the Princeton Expedition to Abyssinia, 1910–1915.* 4 vols. Leiden, 1910–15.
Littmann, Enno et al. *Deutsche Aksum-Expedition.* 4 vols. 1913.
Lobo, Jeronymo. *A Short Relation of the River Nile.* London, 1669 and 1791.
———. *Relation historique d'Abyssinie.* Trans. M. Le Grand. Paris, 1728.
———. *A Voyage to Abyssinia by Father Jerome Lobo.* Ed. M. Le Grand, trans. Samuel Johnson. London, 1789.
———. *The Itinerario of Jeronimo Lobo.* Trans. Donald Lockart. London, 1984.
Lozzo, Lino. "La Confessione di Claudio Re d'Etiopia." *RSE* 5 (1946): 67–78.
Ludolphus, Job. *A New History of Ethiopia.* London, 1682.
Luzzatto, P. *Mémoire sur les juifs d'Abyssinie ou Falashas.* Paris: Extrait des Archives Israelites, 1852–53.

Mahteme Sellassie Wolde Maskal. "The Land System of Ethiopia." *EO* 1 (1957): 283–301.

Maloney, Clarence. *The Evil Eye*. New York, 1976.

Mangestu Tayye, "Yetarik Tiks" ["Quotations from History"]. *Tiyinte Gonder* [*Gondar Municipal Herald*], year 2, 12 (n.d.).

Marcus, Harold. "Menelik II." In N. R. Bennett, ed., *Leadership in Eastern Africa*, pp. 1–62. Boston, 1968.

———. "The Organization of Menilek II's Palace and Imperial Hospitality." *Rural Africana* 11 (1970): 57–62.

———. *The Modern History of Ethiopia*. Stanford, Calif., 1972.

———. *The Life and Times of Menelik II*. London, 1975.

Marcus, Louis. "Notice sur l'époque de l'établissement des juifs dans l'Abyssinie." *JA* 3 (1829): 409–31; 4 (1829): 51–73.

Marguiles, S. H. "Per la storia del movimento pro Falascia, due documenti." *RI* 6 (1909): 152–59.

Markham, Clements. "The Portuguese Expeditions to Abyssinia in the Fifteenth, Sixteenth, and Seventeenth Centuries." *JRGS* 38 (1868): 1–12.

———. *A History of the Abyssinian Expedition*. London, 1869.

Marriott, McKim. "Interactional and Attributional theories of Caste Ranking." *Man in India* 39 (1959): 92–107.

Marx, Karl. *Pre-Capitalist Economic Formations*, ed. E. J. Hobsbawm. New York, 1964.

Mathew, David. *Ethiopia. The Study of a Polity, 1540–1935*. London, 1947.

Mayo, Earl of. *Sport in Abyssinia*. London, 1876.

McCann, James. "The Ethiopian Chronicles: An African Documentary Tradition." *NAS* 1/2 (1979): 47–61.

———. "Children of the House: Slavery and Its Suppression in Lasta, Northwestern Ethiopia, 1916–1975." In Suzanne Miers and Richard Roberts, eds., *The End of Slavery in Africa*. Madison, Wisc., 1986.

———. *From Poverty to Famine in Northeast Ethiopia: A Rural History, 1900–1935*. Philadelphia, 1987.

McClellan, Charles. *State Transformation and National Integration: Gedeo and the Ethiopian Empire, 1895–1935*. East Lansing, Mich., 1988.

McCrindle, J. *The Christian Topography of Cosmas*. London, 1897.

McDougal, David. *In Search of Israel*. London, 1941.

McLeish, A. *Light and Darkness in East Africa*. London, n.d. [1927].

McNaughton, Patrick. *The Mande Blacksmiths*. Bloomington, Ind., 1988.

Meillassoux, Claude. "Are There Castes in India?" *ES* 9 (1973): 89–111.

Mérab, P. *Impressions d'Éthiopie*. 3 vols. Paris, 1921–27.

Mercer, Samuel A. B. "The Falashas." *Aethiops* 3 (1930): 49–51.

———. "A New and Unrecorded Collection of Ethiopic Manuscripts in the Possession of Dr. Jacques Faitlovitch." *Aethiopica* 3 (1935): 171.

———. *The Ethiopic Liturgy*. New York, 1970 [orig. ed. 1915].

Mercier, Jacques. "Les peintures des rouleaux protecteurs Ethiopiens." *JES* 12/2 (1974): 107–46.

———. *Ethiopian Magic Scrolls*. New York, 1979.

Merid Wolde Aregay. "Political Geography of Ethiopia at the Beginning of the Sixteenth Century." *IV Congresso Internazionale di Studi Etiopici, 1972*. Rome, 1974.

———. "The Early History of Ethiopia's Coffee Trade and the Rise of Shawa." *JAH* 29 (1988): 19–25.

Mesfin Wolde-Mariam. *An Atlas of Ethiopia*. Addis Ababa, 1970.

Messing, Simon. "Journey to the Falashas." *Commentary* 22 (1956): 28–40.

———. "Non-Maximizing Marketing Patterns in a Provincial Abyssinian Town and the Traditional Division of Labor." *VI Congres International des Sciences anthropologiques et ethnologiques, Paris, 1960*. 2 vols., 1:585–90. Paris, 1963.

———. "Health Care, Ethnic Outcasting and the Problem of Overcoming the Syndrome of Encapsulation in a Peasant Society." *Human Organization* 34 (1975): 395–97.

———. *The Story of the Falashas*. Hamden, Conn., 1982.

Milkias, Paulos. "Traditional Institutions and Traditional Elites: The Role of Education in the Ethiopian Body-Politic." *ASR* 19/3 (1976): 79–93.

"The Mission to the Falashas." *JC* (7 August 1908): 14.

Mohammed Hassen. *The Oromo of Ethiopia: A History,* 1570–1860. Cambridge, 1990.

Mondon-Vidailhet. "Une tradition éthiopienne." *RS* 12 (1904): 259–68.

Moreno, Martino. "La cronaca di re Teodoro attribuita al dabtara 'Zaneb,'" *RSE* 2 (1942): 143–80.

"Mouvement géographique." *Revue de géographie* 11 (1882): 270–73.

Murchison, Rodney Impey. "Address to the Royal Geographical Society of London." *JRGS* 14 (1844): xlv–cxxviii.

Nahoum, Haim. "Mission chez les Falachas d'Abyssinie." *BAIU,* ser. 3, 33 (1908): 100–137.

Neubauer, A. "Where are the Ten Tribes?" *JQR* 1 (1889): 14–28, 95–114, 185–201, 408–23.

Neugebauer, Otto. *Ethiopic Astronomy and Computus*. Vienna, 1979.

Norberg, V. H. *Swedes in Haile Selassie's Ethiopia, 1924–52*. Uppsala, Sweden, 1977.

Norden, Hermann. *Africa's Last Empire*. Philadelphia, 1930.

———. "The Black Jews of Abyssinia." *Travel* 59 (1930): 25–29, 57–58.

Oddy, D. J., and J. D. Baker. "Some Aspects of the Socio-Economic Structure of Two Towns in the Semen Region of Ethiopia." *JES* 11 (1973): 161–78.

Pankhurst, Richard. "The City Fifty Years Ago." *EO* 1 (1957): 60–66.

———. "Status Division of Labour and Employment in Nineteenth and Early Twentieth Century Ethiopia." *Ethnological Society Bulletin* [Addis Ababa] 2/1 (1961): 7–57.

———. *An Introduction to the Economic History of Ethiopia, from Early Times to 1800*. London, 1961.

———. "Menelik and the Foundation of Addis Ababa." *JAH* 2 (1961): 103–17.

———. "Fire-Arms in Ethiopian History (1800–1935)." *EO* 6 (1962): 135–80.

———. "The Foundations of Education, Printing, Newspapers, Book Production, Libraries and Literacy in Ethiopia." *EO* 6 (1962): 241–90.

———. "Foundation and Growth of Addis Ababa to 1935." *EO* 6 (1962): 33–61.

———. "Misoneism and Innovation in Ethiopian History." *EO* 7 (1964): 287–320.

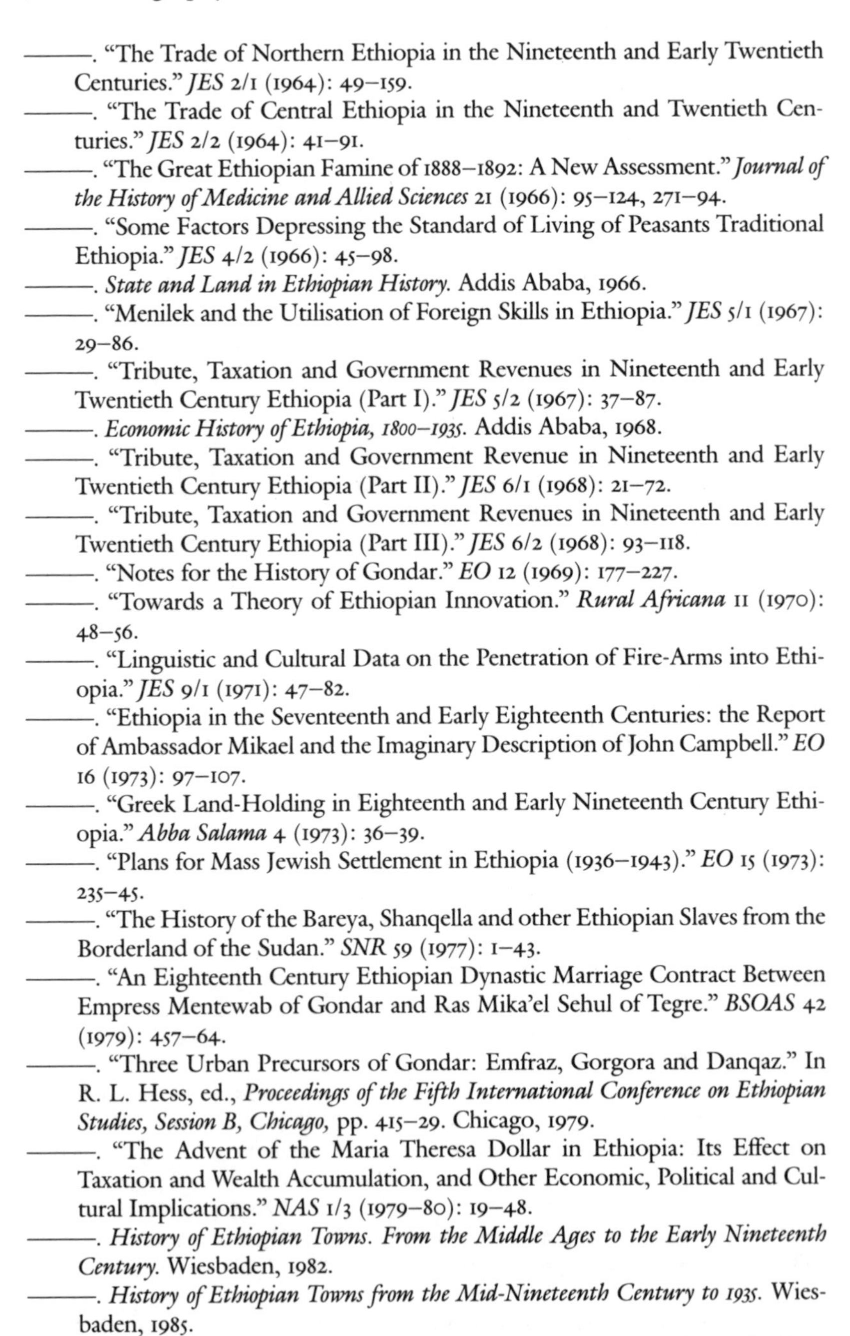

———. "The Trade of Northern Ethiopia in the Nineteenth and Early Twentieth Centuries." *JES* 2/1 (1964): 49–159.
———. "The Trade of Central Ethiopia in the Nineteenth and Twentieth Centuries." *JES* 2/2 (1964): 41–91.
———. "The Great Ethiopian Famine of 1888–1892: A New Assessment." *Journal of the History of Medicine and Allied Sciences* 21 (1966): 95–124, 271–94.
———. "Some Factors Depressing the Standard of Living of Peasants Traditional Ethiopia." *JES* 4/2 (1966): 45–98.
———. *State and Land in Ethiopian History*. Addis Ababa, 1966.
———. "Menilek and the Utilisation of Foreign Skills in Ethiopia." *JES* 5/1 (1967): 29–86.
———. "Tribute, Taxation and Government Revenues in Nineteenth and Early Twentieth Century Ethiopia (Part I)." *JES* 5/2 (1967): 37–87.
———. *Economic History of Ethiopia, 1800–1935*. Addis Ababa, 1968.
———. "Tribute, Taxation and Government Revenue in Nineteenth and Early Twentieth Century Ethiopia (Part II)." *JES* 6/1 (1968): 21–72.
———. "Tribute, Taxation and Government Revenues in Nineteenth and Early Twentieth Century Ethiopia (Part III)." *JES* 6/2 (1968): 93–118.
———. "Notes for the History of Gondar." *EO* 12 (1969): 177–227.
———. "Towards a Theory of Ethiopian Innovation." *Rural Africana* 11 (1970): 48–56.
———. "Linguistic and Cultural Data on the Penetration of Fire-Arms into Ethiopia." *JES* 9/1 (1971): 47–82.
———. "Ethiopia in the Seventeenth and Early Eighteenth Centuries: the Report of Ambassador Mikael and the Imaginary Description of John Campbell." *EO* 16 (1973): 97–107.
———. "Greek Land-Holding in Eighteenth and Early Nineteenth Century Ethiopia." *Abba Salama* 4 (1973): 36–39.
———. "Plans for Mass Jewish Settlement in Ethiopia (1936–1943)." *EO* 15 (1973): 235–45.
———. "The History of the Bareya, Shanqella and other Ethiopian Slaves from the Borderland of the Sudan." *SNR* 59 (1977): 1–43.
———. "An Eighteenth Century Ethiopian Dynastic Marriage Contract Between Empress Mentewab of Gondar and Ras Mika'el Sehul of Tegre." *BSOAS* 42 (1979): 457–64.
———. "Three Urban Precursors of Gondar: Emfraz, Gorgora and Danqaz." In R. L. Hess, ed., *Proceedings of the Fifth International Conference on Ethiopian Studies, Session B, Chicago*, pp. 415–29. Chicago, 1979.
———. "The Advent of the Maria Theresa Dollar in Ethiopia: Its Effect on Taxation and Wealth Accumulation, and Other Economic, Political and Cultural Implications." *NAS* 1/3 (1979–80): 19–48.
———. *History of Ethiopian Towns. From the Middle Ages to the Early Nineteenth Century*. Wiesbaden, 1982.
———. *History of Ethiopian Towns from the Mid-Nineteenth Century to 1935*. Wiesbaden, 1985.
Pankhurst, Rita. "Mikael Argawi, Ethiopia's First Protestant Missionary." *EO* 10 (1966): 215–19.

Parfitt, Tudor. *Operation Moses*. New York, 1985.
Parkyns, Mansfield. *Life in Abyssinia*. 2nd ed. London, 1868.
Payne, Eric. *Ethiopian Jews: The Story of a Mission*. London, 1972.
Pearce, Ivy. "The Rock-Hewn Churches of Goreme, Turkey, and the Cave and Rock-Hewn Churches of Tigre, Ethiopia." *EO* 12 (1970): 57–78.
Pearce, Nathaniel. *The Life and Adventures*. 2 vols. London, 1831.
Perruchon, Jules. "Histoire des guerres d'Amda Ṣyon." *JA*, ser. 8, 14 (1889): 271–363, 381–493.
———. *Vie de Lalibala, roi d'Éthiopie*. Paris, 1892.
———. *Les chroniques de Zar'a Yâ'eqôb et de Ba'eda Mâryâm, rois d'Éthiopie de 1434 à 1478*. Paris, 1893.
———. "Lettre addressée par le roi d'Éthiopie au roi, Georges de Nubie sous le patriarcat de Philothée (981–1002 ou 1003)." *RS* 1 (1893): 71–76, 359–72.
———. "Récit d'une ambassade envoyée au roi d'Éthiopie Sayfa-Ar'ad par le patriarche d'Alexandrie sur l'ordre du sultan d'Égypte." *RS* 1 (1893): 177–82.
———. "Le règne de Lebna Dengel." *RS* 1 (1893): 274–86.
———. "Histoire d'Eskender, d'Amda Seyon II et de Na'od." *JA* ser. 9, 3 (1894): 319–66.
———. "Le règne de Galawdewos (Claudius) ou Asnaf-Sagad." *RS* 2 (1894): 155–66, 263–70.
———. "Vie de Cosmas, patriarche d'Alexandrie de 923 à 934." *RS* 2 (1894): 78–93.
———. "Règne de Minas ou Admâs-Sagad (1559–1563)." *RS* 4 (1896): 87–90.
———. "Règne de Sarṣa-Dengel ou Malak-Sagad I (1563–1597)." *RS* 4 (1896): 177–85, 273–78.
———. "Règne de Yaqob et Za-Dengel (1597–1607)." *RS* 4 (1896): 355–63.
———. "Le pays de Zâguê." *RS* 5 (1897): 275–84.
———. "Le règne de Fasiladas (Adam-Sagad), de 1632 à 1667." *RS* 5 (1897): 360–72; 6 (1898): 84–92.
———. "Règne de Susneyos ou Seltan-Sagad (1607–1632)." *RS* 5 (1897): 75–80, 173–89.
———. "Extrait de la vie d'Abba Jean, 74e patriarche d'Alexandrie, relatif à Abyssinie." *RS* 6 (1898): 267–71, 365–72; 7 (1899): 76–85.
———. "Legendes relatives à Dawit III (Lebna Dengel), roi d'Éthiopie." *RS* 6 (1898): 157–71.
———. "Notes pour l'histoire d'Éthiopie contemporaine." *RS* 7 (1899): 251–59.
———. "Le règne de Yohannes, 1667 à 1682." *RS* 7 (1899): 166–76.
———. "Le règne de Iyasu I, roi d'Éthiopie, 1682 à 1706." *RS* 9 (1901): 71–78, 161–67, 258–62.
Petridès, S. P. "The Empire of Ethiopia in the XVth and XVIth Centuries." *EGJ* 2/2 (1964): 15–27.
Plant, Ruth. *Architecture of the Tigre, Ethiopia*. Worcester, Mass., 1985.
Plowden, Walter. *Travels in Abyssinia and the Galla Country*. London, 1868.
Pollera, Alberto. *Storie, leggende e favole del paese des negus*. Florence, 1936.
Polo, Marco. *The Travels*. Trans. R. Latham. Harmondsworth, 1958.
Polotsky, H. J. "Aramaic, Syriac, and Ge'ez." *JSS* 9 (1964): 1–10.
Poncet, Charles Jacques. *A Voyage to Ethiopia in the Years 1698, 1699, and 1700* [London, 1709]. In William Foster, ed., *The Red Sea and Adjacent Countries at the Close of the Seventeenth Century*, pp. 92–165. London, 1949.

Portal, Gerald. *An Account of the English Mission to King Johannis of Abyssinia in 1887.* Winchester, n.d. [1888?].
———. *My Mission to Abyssinia.* London, 1892.
Porten, B. *Archives from Elephantine.* Berkeley, 1968.
Praetorius, F. "Ein arabisches Document zur äthiopischen Geschichte." *ZDMG* 39 (1885): 403–8.
Prouty, Chris. *Empress Taytu and Menilek II.* Trenton, N.J., 1986.
Quirin, James. "The Beta Israel (Felasha) and the Process of Occupational Caste Formation, 1270–1868." In R. L. Hess, *Proceedings of the Fifth International Conference on Ethiopian Studies, Session B, 1978,* pp. 133–43. Chicago, 1979.
———. "The Process of Caste Formation in Ethiopia: A Study of the Beta Israel (Felasha), 1270–1868." *IJAHS* 12 (1979): 235–58.
———. "A Preliminary Analysis of New Archival Sources on Daily Life in Historical Highland Ethiopia." In Sven Rubenson, ed., *Proceedings of the Seventh International Conference of Ethiopian Studies, Lund, 1982,* pp. 393–410. Uppsala, Sweden, 1984.
———. "The *'Ayhud* and Bēta 'Esrā'ēl-Falāshā in Fifteenth-Century Ethiopia: Oral and Written Traditions." *NAS* 10 (1988): 89–104.
———. "Jews in Fourteenth-Century Ethiopia: Data from the *Gadla Zēnā Mārqos.*" Forthcoming.
———. "Oral Traditions as Historical Sources in Ethiopia: The Case of the Beta Israel (Falasha)." *HA* (forthcoming, 1993).
———. "Ethnicity, Caste, Class and State in Ethiopian History: The Case of the Beta Israel (Falasha)." In Crawford Young, ed. Madison, Wisc. Forthcoming.
———. "Ethnicity, Caste and Class in Historical Northwest Ethiopia: A Comparison of the Beta Israel (Falasha) and Qemant, 1300–1900." Forthcoming.
Raffray, Achille. *Afrique orientale: Abyssinie* Paris, 1876.
Rajak, Tessa. "Moses in Ethiopia." *JJS* 29/2 (1978): 111–22.
Rapoport, Louis. *The Lost Jews.* New York, 1980.
———. *Redemption Song.* New York, 1986.
Rassam, Hormuzd. "Extracts of a Letter of Mr. Rassam to Colonel Playfair." *PRGS* 10 (1865–66): 295–300.
———. *Narrative of the British Mission to Theodore, King of Abyssinia,* 2 vols. London, 1869.
Rathjens, Carl. *Die Juden in Abessinien.* Hamburg, 1921.
Reminick, Ronald. "The Structure and Functions of Religious Belief among the Amhara of Ethiopia." In H. G. Marcus, ed., *Proceedings of the First United States Conference on Ethiopian Studies, 1973,* pp. 25–42. East Lansing, Mich., 1975.
———. "The Evil-Eye Belief among the Amhara of Ethiopia." *Ethnology* 13 (1974): 279–92.
Rey, Charles F. *Unconquered Abyssinia as it is Today.* London, 1923.
———. *In the Country of the Blue Nile.* London, 1927.
———. *The Real Abyssinia.* New York, 1969 [orig. 1935].
———. *The Romance of the Portuguese in Abyssinia.* New York, 1969 [orig. 1929].
Reybaud, Louis. "Voyage dans l'Abyssinie méridionale: Journal inédit de M. Rochet d'Héricourt." *RDM* 27 (July–September 1841): 59–93.

Ricci, Lanfranco, "Edipo e Storia." *Paideuma* 24 (1978): 169–77.
———. "Review of Wolf Leslau, *Falasha Anthology* (New Haven, Conn., 1952)." *RSO* 29 (1954): 265–76.
Rochet d'Héricourt, Charles. *Voyage sur la côte orientale de la mer rouge*. Paris, 1841.
———. "Les moeurs religieuses dans le royaume de Choa." *BSG*, ser. 3, 4 (1845): 317–29.
———. *Second voyage sur les deux rives de la mer rouge*. Paris, 1846.
Rodinson, Maxime. "Review of Edward Ullendorff, *The Ethiopians*." *BO* 21 (1964): 238–45.
———. "Sur la question des 'influences juives' en Ethiopie." *JSS* 9 (1964): 11–19.
———. *Magie, médicine et possession à Gondar*. Paris, 1967.
———. "Sur une nouvelle inscription du règne de Dhou Nowâs." *BO* 26 (1969): 26–34.
Rohlfs, Gerhard. "Letter." *PGM* 27 (1881): 73.
———. "Ergebnisse meiner Reise nach Abessinien; Bemerkungen zur Karte." *PGM* 28 (1882): 401–5.
———. *Meine Mission nach Abessinien*. Leipzig, 1883.
Rosen, Chaim. "Core Symbols of Ethiopian Identity and Their Role in Understanding the Beta Israel Today." In Michael Ashkenazi and Alex Weingrod, eds., *Ethiopian Jews and Israel*, pp. 55–62. New Brunswick, N.J., 1987.
Rosen, Felix. *Eine deutsche Gesandtschaft in Abessinien*. Leipzig, 1907.
Rosenfeld, Chris Prouty. *A Chronology of Menilek II of Ethiopia*. East Lansing, Mich., 1976.
Rosenthal, Franz. "A Fourteenth-Century Report on Ethiopia." In S. Segert and A. J. E. Bodrogligeti, eds., *Ethiopian Studies Dedicated to Wolf Leslau*, pp. 495–503. Wiesbaden, 1983.
Rubenson, Sven. "The Lion of the Tribe of Judah: Christian Symbol and/or Imperial Title." *JES* 3/2 (1965): 75–85.
———. *King of Kings: Tewodros of Ethiopia*. Addis Ababa, 1966.
———. *The Survival of Ethiopian Independence*. New York, 1976.
Rüppell, Eduard, "Voyage de M. Rüppell en Abyssinie." *NA* 63 (1834): 91–102.
———. *Reise in Abyssinien*. 2 vols. Frankfort am Main, 1838–40.
———. "Remarques sur l'aspect physique de l'Abyssinie." *NA* 87 (1840): 209–26.
———. "Bulletin: Analyses Critique: *Reise in Abyssinien* (Voyage in Abyssinie)." *NA* 88 (1840): 87–109, 176–227, 292–340; 89 (1841): 190–242.
Russel, Stanilas. *Une mission en Abyssinie*. Paris, 1884.
Sabrijian, Dimoteos. *Deux ans de séjour en Abyssinie*. 2 vols. Jerusalem, 1871.
Safran, Claire. *Secret Exodus*. New York, 1987.
Salt, Henry. *A Voyage to Abyssinia*. London, 1814.
Schloessinger, Max. *The Ritual of Eldad ha-Dani Reconstructed*. Leipzig, 1908.
Schmerler, Henrietta. "Falashas." *The Universal Jewish Encyclopedia*, 4:234–36. New York, 1969.
Schneider, R. "Notes Éthiopiennes." *JES* 16 (1983): 105–14.
Schoff, Wilfred. *The Periplus of the Erythraean Sea*. London, 1912.
Schrenzel, Ernst S. *Abessinien. Land Ohne Hunger, Land Ohne Zeit*. Berlin, 1928.
Schwarzbaum, Haim. "Jewish and Moslem Cources of a Falasha Creation Myth."

In Raphael Patai, et al., eds., *Studies in Biblical and Jewish Folklore. American Folk-Lore Society. Memoirs,* vol. 51, pp. 39–56. Bloomington, Ind., 1960.

Semi, E. T. *Allo Specchio dei Falascia*. Florence, 1987.

Sergew Hable Sellassie. "New Historical Elements in the 'Gedle Aftse.'" *JSS* 9 (1964): 200–203.

———. *The Church of Ethiopia: A Panorama of History and Spiritual Life*. Addis Ababa, 1970.

———. "A History of Aksum: The Successors of Caleb." *RA* 11 (1970): 30–36.

———. "Die Aethiopishe Kirche im 4. bis 6. Jahrhundert." *Abba Salama* 2 (1971): 43–75.

———. *Ancient and Medieval Ethiopian History to 1270*. Addis Ababa, 1972.

———. "The Problem of Gudit." *JES* 10/1 (1972): 113–24.

———. "Giorgis Zegasitcha: Teacher and Author." *EJE* 8/1 (1975): 15–32.

Shack, William. "Notes on Occupational Castes among the Gurage of South-West Ethiopia." *Man* 54 (1964): 50–52.

———. *The Gurage*. New York, 1966.

———. *The Central Ethiopians: Amhara, Tigrina and Related Peoples*. London, 1974.

Shack, William, and Habte-Mariam Marcos. *Gods and Heroes*. Oxford, 1974.

Shack, William, and Elliot Skinner, ed. *Strangers in African Society*. Berkeley, 1979.

Shahîd, Irfan. "The *Kebra Nagast* in the Light of Recent Research." *Le Muséon* 89 (1976): 133–78.

Shelemay, Kay Kaufman. "'Historical Ethnomusicology': Reconstructing Falasha Liturgical History." *Ethnomusicology* 24 (1980): 233–58.

———. "Seged: A Falasha Pilgrimage Festival." *Musica Judaica* 3 (1981): 43–62.

———. "Music and Text of the Falasha Sabbath." *Orbis Musicae, Studies in the Arts* [Tel-Aviv] 8 (1982–83): 3–22.

———. "The Music of the Lalibeloč: Musical Mendicants in Ethiopia." *Journal of African Studies* 9/3 (1982): 128–38.

———. "Zēmā: A Concept of Sacred Music in Ethiopia." *The World of Music* 3 (1982): 52–64.

———. "Jewish Liturgical Forms in the Falasha Liturgy? A Comparative Study." *Yuval* [Jerusalem] 5 (1986): 372–404.

———. *Music, Ritual and Falasha History*. East Lansing, Mich., 1986.

Simon, Gabriel. *L'Éthiopie, ses moeurs, ses traditions, le Négouss Iohannès, les églises monolithes de Lalibéla*. Paris, 1885.

Simoons, Frederick. *Northwest Ethiopia, Peoples and Economy*. Madison, Wisc., 1960.

———. "Some Questions on the Economic Prehistory of Ethiopia." *JAH* 6 (1965): 1–13.

Singer, Charles. "The Falashas." *JQR* 17 (1905): 142–47.

Sjoberg, Gideon. *The Preindustrial City*. Glencoe, Ill., 1960.

Slousch, N. "Les Falacha (tribu d'Abyssinie)." *Revue du Monde Musulman* 8 (1909): 228–35.

Soen, D. "The Falashas: The Black Jews of Ethiopia." *Bulletin of the International Committee on Urgent Anthropological and Ethnological Research* 10 (1968): 67–74.

Solomon Deressa and Gedamu Abraha. "Non Sequitur, An Historical Experiment." *Addis Reporter* 1/27 (4 July 1969): 14–18; 1/28 (11 July 1968): 13–16.

Spencer, Diana. "Trip to Wag and Northern Wällo." *JES* 5/1 (1967): 95–108.
———. "Travels in Gojjam: Saint Luke Icons and Brancaleon Rediscovered." *JES* 12/2 (1974): 201–20.
Spencer, Meredith. "Structural Analysis and the Queen of Sheba." In R. Hess, ed., *Proceedings of the Fifth International Conference on Ethiopian Studies, Session B, Chicago, 1978,* pp. 343–58. Chicago, 1979.
Staude, Wilhelm. "Le mauvais œil dans la peinture Chrétienne d'Abyssinie." *JA* 225 (October–December 1934): 231–57.
———. "Étude sur la décoration picturale des églises Abba Antonios de Gondar et Dabra Sinā de Gorgora." *AE* 3 (1959): 185–235.
Stern, Henry. *Wanderings Among the Falashas in Abyssinia.* 2nd ed. London, 1968 [orig. 1862].
———. *The Captive Missionary.* London, 1868.
Steudner, H. "Reise von Adoa nach Gondar, Dezember 26, 1861–Januar 1862." *ZAE* 15 (1863): 43–141.
———. "Herrn Dr. Steudner's Bericht über seine abessinische Reise." *ZAE* 16 (1864): 83–117.
Stevens, George Henry. *"Go, Tell my Brethren": A Short Popular History the Church Mission to Jews (1809–1959).* London, 1959.
Stitz, Volker. "The Amhara Resettlement of Northern Shoa During the 18th and 19th Centuries." *RA* 11 (1970): 70–81.
———. *Studien zur Kulturgeographie Zentraläthiopiens.* Bonn, 1974.
———. "Distribution and Foundation of Churches in Ethiopia." *JES* 13/1 (1975): 11–36.
Stock, E. *The History of the Church Missionary Society.* 4 vols. London, 1899–1916.
Strelcyn, Stefan. "Sur une prière 'falacha' publiée par C. Conti Rossini dans les 'Appunti di storia e letteratura falascia." *RSE* 8 (1949): 63–82.
———. "La littérature falacha: état de la question." *Studi e materiali di stori dell religioni* 26 (1955): 106–13.
———. "Prières magiques éthiopiennes pour délier les charmes." *RO* 18 (1955): 1–498.
———. "Les écrits médicaux éthiopiens." *JES* 3/1 (1965): 82–103.
———. "Les nouveaux manuscrits éthiopiens de la Bibliothèque Royal de Bruxelles." *JES* 11/2 (1973): 169–88.
Summer, Claude. "The Ethiopic Liturgy: An Analysis." *JES* 1/1 (1963): 40–46.
Taddesse Tamrat. "Some Notes on the Fifteenth Century Stephanite 'Heresy' in the Ethiopian Church." *RSE* 22 (1966): 103–15.
———. "The Abbots of Dabra-Hayq, 1248–1535." *JES* 8/1 (1970): 87–117.
———. "Hagiographies and the Reconstruction of Medieval Ethiopian History." *RA* 11 (1970): 12–20.
———. *Church and State in Ethiopia, 1270–1527.* Oxford, 1972.
———. "A Short Note on the Traditions of Pagan Resistance to the Ethiopian Church (14th and 15th Centuries)." *JES* 10/1 (1972): 137–50.
———. "Problems of Royal Succession in Fifteenth Century Ethiopia: Presentation of Documents." *IV Congresso Internazionale di Studi Etiopici,* pp. 501–35. Rome, 1974.

———. "The Horn of Africa: The Solomonids in Ethiopia and the States of the Horn of Africa." In *General History of Africa,* vol. 4: D. T. Niane, ed., *Africa from the Twelfth to the Sixteenth Century,* pp. 423–54. Paris, 1984.

———. "Ethnic Interaction and Integration in Ethiopian History: The case of the Gafat." *JES* 21 (1988): 121–54.

———. "Processes of Ethnic Interaction and Integration in Ethiopia History: The Case of the Agaw." *JAH* 29 (1988): 5–18.

Taye Reta. "Gojjam Governorate General." *EGJ* 1/1 (1963): 23–30.

Tedeschi, Salvatore. "Poncet et son voyage en Éthiopie." *JES* 4/2 (1966): 99–126.

Tekle Tsadik Mekouria, "Christian Aksum." In G. Mokhtar, ed., *General History of Africa,* vol. 2: *Ancient Civilizations of Africa,* pp. 401–22. Paris, 1981.

Tel Hashomer Government Hospital. "A Survey of Some Genetical Character in Ethiopian Tribes." *American Journal of Physical Anthropology,* n.s 20 (1962): 167–208B.

Telles, Balthazar. *The Travels of the Jesuits in Ethiopia.* London, 171? [original 1660].

Terray, Emmanuel. "Classes and Class Consciousness in the Abron Kingdom of Gyaman." In Maurice Bloch, ed., *Marxist Analyses and Social Anthropology,* pp. 85–135. New York, 1975.

Teshome G. Wagaw. *Education in Ethiopia.* Ann Arbor, 1979.

———. "Ethiopia, Israel and the Resettlement of the Falashas." *Newsletter. Center for Afroamerican and African Studies.* [Ann Arbor, Mich.], 2/2 (1988): 1–11.

Todd, Dave. "Problems of Comparative Ecstasy." *NAS* 1/3 (1979–80): 49–57.

Torrey, E. F. "The Zar Cult in Ethiopia." *Proceedings of the Third International Conference of Ethiopian Studies, Addis Ababa, 1966,* 3 vols. 3:51–59. Addis Ababa, 1970.

Trimingham, J. S. *The Christian Church and Missions in Ethiopia.* London, 1950.

———. *Islam in Ethiopia.* New York, 1952.

Triulzi, Alessandro. *Salt, Gold and Legitimacy. Prelude to the History of a No-man's Land. Beta Shangul, Wallagga, Ethiopia (ca. 1800–1898).* Naples, 1981.

Tsehai Berhane Selassie, "An Ethiopian Medical Text-Book Written by Gerazmač Gäbräwäld Arägahän, Däga Damot." *JES* 9/1 (1971): 95–180.

Tubiana, Joseph. "Une culte des génies agrestes en Éthiopie." *RSE* 13 (1954): 76–86.

———. "Les noms de Gondar et d'Aksum." *GLECS* 8 (1958): 25–26.

———. "Note sur la distribution géographique des dialectes Agaw." *Mer rouge, Afrique orientale. CAA* [Paris] 5 (1959): 297–306.

Turaiev, B. *Acta S. Aronis et S. Philippi. CSCO* 20 (1905): 111–261 [text], 99–234 [trans.].

Ullendorff, Edward. "Review of Wolf Leslau, *Falasha Anthology* (New Haven, 1951)." *BSOAS* 15 (1953): 174–77.

———. *The Semitic Languages of Ethiopia.* London, 1955.

———. "The Hebraic-Judaic Elements in Abyssinian (Monophysite) Christianity." *JSS* 1 (1956): 216–56.

———. "The 'Death of Moses' in the Literature of the Falashas." *BSOAS* 24 (1961): 419–43.

———. *The Ethiopians.* 2nd ed. London, 1965.

———. "The Glorious Victories of 'Amda Seyon, King of Ethiopia.'" *BSOAS* 29 (1966): 600–611.

———. "Origin of the Falashas." *JC* (11 March 1966).
———. *Ethiopia and the Bible*. London, 1968.
———. "Comparative Semitics." In Thomas Sebeok, ed., *Current Trends in Linguistics*, vol. 6: *Linguistics in South West Asia and North Africa*, pp. 261–73. The Hague, 1970.
———. "An Aramaic 'Vorlage' of the Ethiopic Text of Enoch?" In E. Ullendorff, ed., *Is Biblical Hebrew a Language? Studies in Semitic Languages and Civilizations*, pp. 172–81. Wiesbaden, 1977.
Umārah ibn Ali. *Yaman. Its Early Mediaeval History*. London, 1892.
Valentia, G. *Voyages and Travels to India, Ceylon, the Red Sea, Abyssinia and Egypt*. London, 1809.
Vanderheym, J. G. *Une expédition avec le Négous Ménélik*. Paris, 1896.
Van Donzel, Emeri Johannes. *A Yemenite Embassy to Ethiopia, 1647–1649*. Wiesbaden, 1986.
Vansina, Jan. *Oral Tradition*. Chicago, 1965.
———. "The Use of Oral Tradition in African Culture History." In Creighton Gabel and Norman Bennett, eds., *Reconstructing African Culture History*, pp. 55–82. Boston, 1967.
———. "Anthropologists and the Third Dimension." *Africa* 39 (1969): 62–67.
———. *Oral Tradition as History*. Madison, Wisc., 1985.
Varenbergh, Joseph. "Studien zur abessinischen Reichsordnung (Ser'ata Mangešt)." *ZA* 30 (1915–16): 1–45.
Vincent, A. *La religion des judéo-araméens d'Éléphantine*. Paris, 1937.
Viterbo, C. A. "Nuovi manoscritti Falascia." *ASE* (1935–37): 113–23.
Vivian, Herbert. *Abyssinia*. London, 1901.
Von Heuglin, Theodor. "Bruchstücke aus einer Reise in Abyssinien." *DA* 26 (1853): 813–14.
———. "Th. von Heuglin's Reise nach Abessinien, 1852–1853." *PGM* (1857): 464–74.
———. *Reisen in Nord-Ost Afrika*. Gotha, 1857.
———. "Reise der Herren Th. v. Heuglin, Dr. Steudner und H. Schubert von Adoa nach Gonder in Abessinien." *PGM* 8 (1862): 241–44.
———. "Reise zu Kaiser Theodoros und nach der Festung Magdala, Februar bis Mai 1862." *PGM* 13 (1867): 421–32.
Von Katte, A. *Reise en Abyssinien in Jahre 1836*. Stuttgart, 1838.
Von Sicard, Harald. "The Derivation of the Name Mashona." *African Studies* 9 (1950): 138–43.
Wajnberg, I. "Das Leben des hl. Jafqerena 'Egzi.'" *OCA* 106 (1936): 3–12.
Walda Maryam, *Chronique de Théodoros II*, ed. C. Mondon-Vidailhet. Paris, 1905.
Waldmeier, Theophilus. *The Autobiography*. London, 1886.
———. *Erlebnisse in Abessinien*. Basel, 1869.
Waldron, Sidney. "Harrar: The Muslim City of Ethiopia." In R. L. Hess, *Proceedings of the Fifth International Conference on Ethiopian Studies, Session B, Chicago, 1978*, pp. 239–55. Chicago, 1979.
Walker, C. H. *The Abyssinian at Home*. London, 1933.
Weissleder, Wolfgang. "The Socio-Political Character of an Historical Ethiopian

Capital." *Proceedings of the East African Institute of Social Research Conference, 1963*. Kampala, Uganda, 1964.
Weld Blundell, H. "History of King Theodore." *Journal of the African Society* 6 (1906): 12–42.
———. *The Royal Chronicle of Abyssinia, 1769–1840*. Cambridge, 1922.
Wellby, Montagu. *Twixt Sirdar and Menelik*. New York, 1901.
Wilkins, Henry St. Clair. *Reconnoitring in Abyssinia*. London, 1870.
Winstanley, William. *A Visit to Abyssinia*, 2 vols. London, 1881.
Witakowski, Witold. "The Origins of the Jewish Colony at Elephantine." *Orientalia Suecana* [Uppsala], 27–28 (1978–79): 34–41.
Worrell, William Hoyt. "Studien zum abessinischen Zauberwesen." *ZA* 23 (1909): 149–83; 24 (1910): 56–96; 29 (1914): 85–141.
Wurmbrand, Max. "Fragments d'anciens écrits juifs dans la littérature Falacha." *JA* 242 (1954): 83–100.
———. "Remarks on the Text of the Falasha, 'Death of Moses.'" *BSOAS* 25 (1962): 431–37.
———. "Le '*Dersana Sanbat*' une homélie éthiopienne attribuée à Jacques de Saroug." *L'Orient Syrien* 8 (1963): 343–94.
Wylde, Augustus B. *Modern Abyssinia*. London, 1900.
Yona Bogale. *Jewish Calendar 5736 (1975–76)*. The Jewish Agency.
Young, Allan. "Magic as a 'Quasi-Profession': The Organization of Magic and Magical Healing Among Amhara." *Ethnology* 14 (1975): 245–65.
Zaborski, Andrzej. "Cushitic Overview." In M. L. Bender, *The Non-Semitic Languages of Ethiopia*, pp. 67–84. East Lansing, Mich., 1976.
Zar'a Ya'eqob. *Mashafa Berhan*, ed. C. Conti Rossini and L. Ricci. In *CSCO* 47–48 (1964); 51–52 (1965).
———. *Mashafa Milad*, ed. Kurt Wendt. In *CSCO* 41–42 (1962): 43–44 (1963).
Zepin, Rabbi George. *The Falashas. A Report Concerning the Advisability of Establishing a School for Hebrew among the Falashas of Abyssinia*. Cincinnati, 1912.
Zewde Gabre-Sellassie. *Yohannes IV of Ethiopia: A Political Biography*. Oxford, 1975.
Zotenberg, Hermann. "Un document sur les Falachas." *JA*, ser. 6, 9 (1867): 265–68.

Index

University of Pennsylvania Press
THE ETHNOHISTORY SERIES
Lee V. Cassanelli, Juan A. Villamarin, and Judith E. Villamarin, Editors

Christopher Boehm. *Blood Revenge: The Enactment and Management of Conflict in Montenegro and Other Tribal Societies.* 1987

Lee V. Cassanelli. *The Shaping of Somali Society: Reconstructing the History of a Pastoral People, 1600–1900.* 1982

Robert M. Hill II and John Monaghan. *Continuities in Highland Maya Social Organization: Ethnohistory in Sacapulas, Guatemala.* 1987

James McCann. *From Poverty to Famine in Northeast Ethiopia: A Rural History, 1900–1935.* 1987

Derek Nurse and Thomas Spear. *The Swahili: Reconstructing the History and Language of an African Society, 800–1500.* 1985

James Quirin. *The Evolution of the Ethiopian Jews: A History of the Beta Israel (Falasha) to 1920.* 1992

Norman B. Schwartz. *Forest Society: A Social History of Petén, Guatemala.* 1990

Lawrence J. Taylor. *Dutchmen on the Bay: The Ethnohistory of a Contractual Community.* 1983

This book has been set in Linotron Galliard. Galliard was designed for Mergenthaler in 1978 by Matthew Carter. Galliard retains many of the features of a sixteenth century typeface cut by Robert Granjon but has some modifications that give it a more contemporary look.

Printed on acid-free paper.